W9-DFK-846

The American Jesuits

Raymond A. Schroth, S.J.

The American Jesuits

A History

New York University Press • *New York and London*

NEW YORK UNIVERSITY PRESS
New York and London
www.nyupress.org

Library of Congress Cataloging-in-Publication Data
Schroth, Raymond A.
The American Jesuits : a history / Raymond A. Schroth.
p.   cm.
Includes bibliographical references and index.
ISBN-13: 978-0-8147-4025-5 (cloth : alk. paper)
ISBN-10: 0-8147-4025-1 (cloth : alk. paper)
1. Jesuits—United States—History.   I. Title.
BX3708.S37 2007
271'.53073—dc22   2007016965

New York University Press books are printed on acid-free paper,
and their binding materials are chosen for strength and durability.

Manufactured in the United States of America

10 9 8 7 6 5 4 3 2 1

Dedication

John F. X. Burton, S.J.
1921–1997

Thurston N. Davis, S.J.
1913–1986

Joseph R. Frese, S.J.
1914–2002

David S. Toolan, S.J.
1935–2002

Contents

Acknowledgments   ix

Preface   xi

I   In the Beginning

Prologue   3

1   The World Scene   15

2   The Maryland Tradition   21

3   The Pioneers   28

II   Suppression and Return

4   Death and Resurrection   49

5   The New America   58

6   A Nation and Faith Divided   77

7   Schoolmasters and Preachers   86

8   The Turning Point   102

III   Engaging the World

9   The Social Question   115

10   At War   131

11   The Cold War   146

12   The Golden Age   170

IV   The Modern Society Emerges

13   Freedom from Fear   199

14 The Arrupe Era   217
15 Into the 21st Century   259

    Notes and Sources   285
    Bibliography   297
    Index   307
    About the Author   313

Acknowledgments

I thank the Society of Jesus for teaching me when I was young and giving me meaningful work now when I am older, the New York Province for the time and the means to get away and write, and the Saint Peter's College Jesuit community for being my home. I had special help at the beginning from Jesuits and scholars John Padberg, S.J., Jack O'Callaghan, S.J., Joseph Novak, S.J., Gerald McKevitt, S.J., and R. Emmett Curran, who helped me line up the proper themes, sent me books and articles, and, in Emmett's case, meticulously read much of the manuscript. The Jesuit community libraries at Fordham, Fairfield, and Loyola New Orleans and the Woodstock Library at Georgetown lent me books. The Saint Peter's College reference staff, and the archivists of the New York Province, Boston College, and the New England Province were generous with their help.

Inevitably a name has been lost, but the following men and women helped me in countless ways. They sent me books, articles, dissertations, and original manuscripts. They provided statistics, made suggestions, read and critiqued chapters, and, in some cases, read the whole manuscript. They gave me hospitality at their villas or a desk to work on, or prayers, advice, and the emotional support of friendship. They are Charles Allen, S.J., Bruce Bavinger, S.J., Jason Berry, Henry Bertels, S.J., Jean Yearwood Brown, William Byron, S.J., Charles E. Curran, Tom Curran, Robert Emmett Curran, Charlie Currie, S.J., Thomas Clarke, S.J., Jerome Coll, S.J., Peter Conroy, S.J., Richard Costello, S.J., Daniel A. Degnan, S.J., Richard Dimler, S.J., Jim Dockery, Kevin Doyle, Ed Durkin, S.J., Jim Dwyer, Harvey Egan, S.J., Kerry Falloon, Al Fiorino, S.J., Mary Ellen Gallagher, Thomas Gaunt, S.J., Anne Gearity, Phillip Gleason, Ed Glynn, S.J., Mark Graceffo, James Grummer, S.J., Roger Haight, S.J., the John Holl family, Brian Hopkins, Pauline Heaney, Simon Hendry, S.J. Leon Hooper, S.J., David Horn, Alice Howe, George Hunt, S.J., Thomas Jablonsky, Michael and Kathy Jeary, George Kearney, Bob Keck, S.J. Preston Kendall, Thomas Kenny,

James Kuntz, S.J., Anthony Kuzniewski, S.J., Frank Landwermeyer, S.J., Richard McBrien, Ilona MacNamara, William McFadden, S.J., Neil P. McLaughlin, S.J., Patrick McNamara, Ralph Metts, S.J. Charles R. Morris, Dan Morrissey, Fred O'Brien, S.J., Neil O'Connell, O.F.M., John O'Gorman, Bill Rehg, S.J., Ross Romero, S.J., Philip C. Rule, S.J., Marie Schimelfening, Peter Schineller, S.J., Ellen Skerrett, Wilburn Stancil, John Standenmaier, S.J., Michael F. Steltenkamp, S.J. Jeff Theilman, George Twigg-Porter, S.J., William J. Walsh, S.J., Robert Wild, S.J., Mike Wilson, and John Wrynn, S.J. A special thanks to my own family in Trenton, New Jersey, for their love and support, and to the staffs of Jogues Retreat, Cornwall on Hudson, and Sea Bright, Chelsea Villa, and Cohasset, where I could punctuate my labor with good fellowship, bike rides, and swims.

Preface

This book began when my father the journalist and my mother the teacher decided that I should go not to Trenton's Catholic high school but should commute to Philadelphia to Saint Joseph's Prep.

There I met the first of the men to whom I dedicate this book.

Jack Burton, then a scholastic, challenged me to participate in a speech contest and made me yearbook editor. In short, he represents all those Jesuit teachers who think they see a spark in a student and try to turn that spark into a flame. Like many of the Jesuits, he wrote letters to his former students for years. When he got in trouble in Philadelphia in the late 1960s for adapting the liturgy to a team's locker room I wrote it up for *America* magazine.

At Fordham, Joe Frese was the priest on my floor in Dealy Hall in 1951. There I served his Mass every morning for four years in a little hole-in-the-wall chapel, except for my junior year in Paris. A Harvard history PhD, he took me to dinner at the Harvard Club and taught me how to order wine. Joe advised me to write my doctoral thesis on the *Brooklyn Eagle*, knowing my Uncle Frank once owned it, and this became my first published book. Finally he concelebrated my first Mass and preached at my final vows in 1976.

Our Fordham dean was Thurston Noble Davis, who became *America* editor when Robert Hartnett stepped down during the McCarthy controversy and who printed my article about trying to lead a Christian life in the U.S. Army when I was an artillery officer in Germany. When I came home and joined the Society he made me a summer editor and gave me a socio-literary column which ran for several years.

Dave Toolan, my loyal friend during my philosophy days at Shrub Oak and theology at Woodstock, succeeded me at *Commonweal* magazine as associate editor and book editor and later joined the *America* staff, where, though tormented by cancer, he traveled to hotspots and wrote eloquent articles and books about politics, science, and religion.

In the early months of my writing, for inspiration I toured the southern Maryland parishes with a Loyola New Orleans student friend, John O'Gorman. Then I drove from our villa at Cornwall on Hudson to the Jesuit graveyard at Auriesville, New York, the same spot where Isaac Jogues and Rene Goupil were killed. There I walked through the hundreds of gravestones and prayed briefly at those of the Jesuit historians on whose books I rely and gave thanks to Joe, Thurston, Dave and others for bringing me to this moment. Jack was buried in Colorado, where he worked during his last years.

There is no way I could do justice to the whole American Society in the space allotted. A full Jesuit history should have more on the high schools, on sports, on the brothers, on lay collaborators, on the parishes, retreat houses, and missions. I have centered on a few themes: the impact of the person of St. Ignatius and the Spiritual Exercises as the source of Jesuit and lay spiritual energy; the narrative of the "three societies"—pre-suppression, post-suppression, and the new Society that struggled out of the 1960s reforms; the effort, over three centuries, of the foreign Jesuit missionaries who came to America to deal with both the Western and urban frontiers; the educational reformers who forced the Society to face its shortcomings and then surge forward into academic leadership; the heroism of missionaries, and the social and theological pioneers who endured frustration and sometimes abandonment when they deserved support.

And there is a dark side: the divisions within the Society, the end-runs to Rome and rash judgments, sometimes by superiors, which undermine the Society's goals and hurt fellow Jesuits. But, as my tertianship spiritual director reminded me, Ignatius foresaw this. In the Constitutions [101–44, 102–45] he proposed to ask those entering the Society if, in imitation of Our Lord, they "would wish to suffer injuries, false accusation, and affronts, and to be held and esteemed as fools (but without their giving occasion for this)." Ignatius was speaking about abuse from both outside and *within* the Society.

This is simply an acknowledgment that we are all sinners, who live not in a heavenly banquet hall but in the Bronx or in Kansas City or Worcester with sinners like ourselves.

I ended my research with a visit to Rome, where I briefly met Fr. General Peter-Hans Kolvenbach and visited the little apartment at the church of the Gesu where Ignatius worked, lived, and died; and the altars where he and Fr. Pedro Arrupe are buried. At the archives I held in my hands documents from 1540 which Ignatius and the very first Jesuits held in their hands as they picked up their pens.

PART I

In the Beginning

Prologue

The First Sight

The Society of Jesus' first adventure in North America neither began nor ended well.

It is September 14, 1566, the Feast of the Exaltation of the Holy Cross, and a large Spanish ship, with a Flemish crew, a contingent of Spanish soldiers, and three Jesuit missionaries aboard, having been blown out to sea twice by hurricanes and storms, sits tranquilly offshore by the northern coast of Florida, right near the future Georgia border, waiting for the proper moment to send an exploratory team to the beach in their one remaining boat.

They are lost. And they are almost out of water. They separated from their main fleet a month before and have been wandering up and down the Florida coast in search of the port of Saint Helena. There they will deliver the Jesuits to the service of Don Pedro Menendez de Aviles, whom Phillip II of Spain had appointed to destroy the French Huguenot colony on the St. John's River, from which the French would raid the Spanish ships laden with treasure from Mexico as they passed north of Cuba on their way home. Governor Menendez, with a reputation for cruelty, ruthlessly wiped the Huguenots out in 1565 and established the city of St. Augustine. But to pacify the Indians he needed a different kind of force. He implored the general of the Society of Jesus to send help, for, he wrote, "My ultimate object and desire is to procure that Florida be settled in perpetuity so that the Holy Gospel be extended and planted in these provinces." These three men were to plant the faith in this new colonial garden.

These young men were part of a dynamic religious missionary movement that within a few years of its founding had already reached India, Japan, and what is now South America. In 1549, while across the world in Japan Francis Xavier was preparing to spread the faith to China, a party of six Jesuits had sailed into the beautiful harbor of

3

Salvador de Bahia, Brazil. Men of various talents, they established a missionary method, a development strategy that would be the model for similar efforts throughout both South and North America: make the colony a bastion of civilized culture; establish schools for both the colonists' children and the natives; teach them to write, to speak, to sing, and to pray. Then branch out through the jungles or to the frontier to native villages to teach and to baptize.

Pedro Martinez, 35 years old, a Jesuit since 1553 and ordained in 1558, the religious superior of the band of three, stands on the deck overlooking the Florida coast, his eyes on the palm trees and the sand of this strange new land. For years he has pleaded with the Jesuit authorities to send him to the missions. Again and again he expressed his willingness—indeed his desire—to die for the faith. This is the greatest day of his life.

The Pilgrim's Journey

The chain of events that brought Martinez to this spot began at the battle of Pamplona on May 20, 1521. There, in a skirmish between the troops of King Francis I of France and Charles V of Hapsburg, King of Spain and Holy Roman Emperor, a cannon ball smashed the right leg of a thirty-year-old Basque knight named Inigo Lopez de Loyola, who had, with foolhardy bravery, led a hopeless defense.

His head turned by dreams of military glory, young Inigo had led the life of an occasional brawler, gambler, and libertine; but now those dreams were as shattered as the bones in his leg. His recuperation was long and painful, as the doctors were required to break his leg again, in a failed attempt to restore it to a shape that would still look good in a gentleman's tight stocking. For who would follow a leader with a limp?

We know Ignatius and his life through six sources: the *Spiritual Exercises*, based on notes he began in 1522; a collection of almost 7,000 letters; his Deliberations on Poverty and his Spiritual Diary from 1544 to 1545; the *Constitutions of the Society of Jesus*, composed in stages with the help of his secretary, Juan Polanco; and his brief autobiography on his early years dictated during his last year. Finally, there are the recollections of his colleagues who had gathered after his death.

Perhaps the word which best captures Ignatius Loyola is pilgrim

—a term he applied to himself and which biographers agree catches his spirit. He was a traveler and seeker, a man in process, constantly analyzing his experiences and incorporating them into a unique vision that would touch the lives of millions and influence world history over the next 470 years.

As he meticulously, scrupulously, moved through the steps of his personal conversion, without realizing it he was preparing to confront a Europe, a world, and a church that desperately needed what he would offer. Inigo, the name he kept until he felt the time had come to change, recuperated in the ancestral castle where he was born in 1491, in beautiful Guipuzcoa, his mountainous Basque country homeland in northern Spain. Deprived of the popular novels on chivalry he used to read, he read spiritual books like *The Golden Legend*, a popular collection of tales about the saints, and a scholarly life of Jesus by the Carthusian Ludolph of Saxony. The latter both summarized the Gospels and offered a theological interpretation of salvation history, God's plan in which the Incarnation of the Word in Jesus rescues mankind from the consequences of Adam's sin.

As he read, Ignatius took notes that measured his emotional reactions to scenes in the life of Christ. He began to pray over what he was learning, to transform worldly ambitions of chivalry into a desire to serve a spiritual Lord. In February 1522 he slipped away from his castle, leaving his whole past behind, and went to the Benedictine monastery of Montserrat near Barcelona. There he confessed the sins of his whole life, discarded his fine clothes, put on a pilgrim's tunic, and, imitating the vigil of knighthood, spent the night in prayer before the altar of the legendary "Black Virgin" statue—named for the color of its wood—of Our Lady.

For the next eleven months he moved to nearby Manresa, where, living in a Dominican priory and retiring often to the solitude of a cave, he put himself through a series of experiments, penances, and prayers that raised his spiritual consciousness to a level of mysticism which eventually gave birth to the Spiritual Exercises, a systematic method of prayer and self-examination based largely on scenes from the life of Jesus—the instrument of personal transformation with which he would train his new "army."

He worked in hospitals with the poor, begged for his food, taught catechism to children, and struck up conversations wherever he went. These were the years in which Martin Luther's rebellion led to his excommunication in 1521; when Henry VIII was about to declare himself head of the Church of England; when a large percentage of bishops neglected their dioceses; when many priests didn't even know the words for the consecration at mass, worked as day laborers, and didn't know how to preach; when fewer than 5 percent of adults were as well educated as a seven-year-old today. Under these circumstances, a charming young man in a poor man's clothes but with an aristocrat's manner, who had read books and mastered some spiritual secrets, was an obvious attraction—including to well-bred women drawn by his piety and conversation. If it was an age of scandals, it was also an age of reform.

Ignatius's mysticism emerged from struggles with scruples that drove him to temptations to suicide, to profound illuminations—more intellectual experiences than images—including his understanding of the Trinity under the form of the harmony of three musical keys. He "saw" how God brought forth light at the creation and how Jesus was present in the Blessed Sacrament. Finally, on the banks of the Cardoner River, he formed an integrating picture of the purpose of his life: he would seek companions and labor for the good of others.

So Inigo set out to Jerusalem where, in the custom of pilgrims, he retraced the footsteps of Christ. Then, at the age of 33, he moved first to Barcelona, and then to Alcala and Salamanca, to learn Latin and philosophy, to teach Christian doctrine to the large crowds he and his friends attracted, and to administer the early stages of the Exercises he had evolved in his notebooks at Manresa. But as was inevitable in the religious climate of 16th-century Spain, Inigo and his followers attracted the attention of the Inquisition.

After all, he and his friends dressed alike, associated themselves with the poor, and, contrary to common practice, received communion every week. Were they members of the movement called "enlightened ones," pseudo mystics who would undermine traditional piety? In Alcala, Inigo was hauled in and slapped into prison for 42 days, until he was found innocent; but the Inquisition ordered him to dress like other students and not speak in public until he had studied religion for four more years. In Salamanca he was arrested again within two weeks. Here the judges examined his manuscript of the *Exercises* and allowed him to teach again, but not to talk about the distinction between venial and mortal sin until he had completed more study.

Inigo reacted with typical decisiveness. At the age of 37 he made the trek to Paris and, surrounded by younger men, some of whom would become the first Jesuits, began studies that led to his Master of Arts degree in 1535. He improved his Latin, cut down on his ministries in order to emphasize his studies, which included lectures on Thomas Aquinas with the Dominicans and Aristotle's physics, metaphysics, and ethics; but he still pursued those religious conversations which were the glue that began to fasten this extraordinary group of young men to one another.

Significantly, it is also in his first year of serious studies that Ignatius changed his first name from Inigo to Ignacio or Ignatius—a decision which usually means that the person has come to see himself as somehow a new person and wants his public to see him in this same new light. The vision by the Cardoner River to serve the church was slowly taking concrete form in a group of students who now called themselves "friends in the Lord."

Two were Ignatius's roommates—Pierre Favre from Savoy, studying for the priesthood, and the gallant fellow-Basque, Francis Xavier. In 1533 two young Spaniards, Diego Lainez and Alfonso Salmeron, joined the group. Lainez, whose great-grandfather has converted from Judaism, would eventually succeed Ignatius as the second general of the Society of Jesus and Salmeron would write a voluminous commentary on the New Testament. The following year, Nicolas de Bobadilla and Simao Rodrigues, both of whom would become the source of controversy within the Society 20 years later, made the friends in the Lord a band of seven. Most important, by the summer of 1534 all six had made the Spiritual Exercises—that is, led over thirty days step-by-step through its designated meditations and prayers—which by now had assumed close to their final form, with the Latin text about to be published as a manual, under Ignatius's personal direction.

How to Find God's Will

What does it mean to find God's will? One of the differences between Jesuits and other religious orders and movements is the way in which the members come to know and identify with their founder. New Jesuits in their first year will certainly read one or more of the Ignatian biographies; but above all, through the Exercises, they will repeat the most formative experience of their founder's life, and, through God's grace, thus undergo a transformation or conversion similar to his. Though they comprise a book, the Exercises are not to be read but done—just as a marathon runner will stretch, do push-ups, and run 40 miles every week in preparation for the big race. And the director, the person who presents the material to the "exercitant" or "retreatant" (the one making the Exercises), though he is similar to a coach, is less a teacher than a guide. The assumption is that if the retreatant will truly open his or her soul to grace, the Spirit will enter in and take over; the director's role will be to help one hear what the Spirit is trying to say.

Indeed, perhaps the most extraordinary aspect of Ignatius's spirituality is his confidence that the Spirit does work directly in our lives and that, if we are free from "disordered attachments," we will be able to read the Spirit's movements by monitoring our feelings. Ignatius gives us a remarkable, even bizarre, example in his *Autobiography.*

In February 1522, before his conversion was complete, Inigo met a Moor, like him riding on a mule. As they rode along together discussing religion, the Moor agreed that the Virgin Mary had conceived Jesus without a man, but could not believe she could still, giving birth, remain a virgin. Inigo tried to convince him, but failed, and the Moor rode on ahead. Very upset, Inigo feared he had failed to protect Our Lady's honor; he decided to pursue the Moor and to stab him with his dagger. But as he approached the fork in the road that led to the town where the Moor was staying, Inigo had second thoughts. He would let the Lord decide—and the mule would be His instrument. At the turn, Inigo let the rains go slack and gave the mule his head. The mule passed up the road to the village and continued on the highway.

The day-to-day steps of the Spiritual Exercises, which in their pure form take 30 days, divided into four "weeks," replicate the steps of Inigo's conversion to Ignatius, from the shattered leg to the Paris degree, from the brash cavalier devoted to his own glory to a humble pilgrim whose motto would be "Ad Majorem Dei Gloriam," for the greater glory of God. The "weeks," which vary in length depending on the degree of progress, begin with a Principle and Foundation, according to which we are to use all of God's creation "insofar as" each object or person contributes to our salvation, followed by a detailed consideration of our sins, not in the morbid sense but in the context of God's love and Christ's sacrifice.

The second week dwells on Jesus' public life, which we view cinematically in our imagination: we see him cure the lame and the blind and hear his words in the Sermon on the Mount. The third focuses on the Passion, and the fourth, the shortest, on the Resurrection and Ascension. Throughout there are dramatic meditations designed to distinguish between valid and invalid "spirits," or emotions that move us toward wise or unwise decisions, to render us indifferent to wealth and power, to seek suffering and humiliation if that will serve the needs of the apostolate, to help us "think with the Church," and to follow Christ more zealously than we would any earthly prince or politician.

In the process of "finding God's will," we do not presume that the more dramatically "religious" decision is the one God calls us to make. A young man might just as well finish his retreat determined to marry the girl next door and get a degree in accounting, or a young Jesuit may decide to leave the Society and become a journalist rather than volunteer for the missions.

The final meditation, to "obtain the love of God," is the heart of Ignatian spirituality. It catapults the retreatant back into the world, as if with "magic" spiritual glasses that enable him or her to view not merely the surface of things but the inevitable and universal presence of God constantly at work in His creation. Like Ignatius, the typical Jesuit will enjoy the countryside but love the cities, because here, in the thousands and millions teeming into the streets—poor and rich, young and old of every nation and color—God's love is trying to break through, but needs help.

The Company Is Formed

On August 15, 1534, the feast of the Assumption of Mary, at a mass said by Pierre Favre, the seven united in a vow to become priests, to live lives of poverty, to go to Jerusalem, and to then offer themselves to the pope in Rome for whatever work would best serve the church. On June 24, 1537, the other six were ordained in Venice. They began to refer to themselves as the "Company of Jesus," not as a military metaphor, but more to resemble the religious confraternities or brotherhoods of the time, and, of course, to present themselves literally as companions, not just of one another but of Jesus Christ himself who lived and worked through them.

The political climate canceled their trip to Palestine, so, after dispersing for a while to university towns with the hope of attracting more followers, they regrouped in Rome. On the outskirts, in a little chapel at La Storta, Ignatius was graced with another vision, in which Jesus, carrying his cross, asks Ignatius to serve Him, and the Father promises to "be propitious" to him in Rome. This experience confirmed Ignatius in their decision, in spite of criticisms, to name their company for Jesus. Their critics had followed them from Alcala to Paris and to Rome, objecting to the name, suggesting they might still be "Illuminati" or Lutherans in disguise, and, protesting their daily order that did not include the Divine Office, the Psalms, and breviary, sung eight times a day in choir, as in all the traditional religious orders.

But the elimination of choir caught the essence of this new concept of the religious order. They meditated, said Mass, examined their consciences, and read their breviaries every day; but they were too busy finding God on the streets to spend another four or five hours a day in church. Furthermore, they were not monks, who took vows of stability that might implant them in one place for the rest of their lives. Their rule was to "travel to various places," one reinforced by a special fourth vow to the pope to go wherever he might send them.

In spite of all the questions raised and because the companions had made a strongly favorable impression by directing retreats based on the Exercises in Rome and had doubled their numbers to more than 20, after a year of deliberations, on September 27, 1540, Pope Paul III, in the bull *Regimini militantis Ecclesiae*, confirmed the establishment of the Society of Jesus.

Ignatius's pilgrim years were over. Elected as general for life, until his death in 1556 he governed from his office in Rome what became a worldwide educational and missionary organization during his lifetime.

What about Women?

It was during this time that a whole other aspect of his personality came to the fore—his administrative genius. Their Constitutions, the laws which would govern the election of Ignatius's successor and the entire structure of the Society for years to come, took their final form, and the *Ratio Studiorum*, the practical compendium of teaching rules that came to embody the Jesuit philosophy of education, took its early form. He governed from a tiny desk in a small upstairs apartment in Rome's Church of the Gesu, writing thousands of letters to Jesuits and other men and women all over the world. A major concern was to establish norms for membership in the Society, since his administrative headaches made him wish he had been more selective in accepting recruits. According to a survey in the 1560s, the early Jesuits joined first to save their own souls and were attracted by the community affection of Jesuits they met. In time the main motive became to "help souls," even at the cost of their own lives.

The stories of two groups who sought membership have contemporary relevance: Jews and women. In 16th-century Spain there was a common prejudice that Jewish and Muslim converts to Christianity, known as "new Christians," and their descendants were somehow inferior because of their "tainted blood," and were therefore banned from church offices and religious orders. Ignatius, however, refused to go along with this notion. He expressed the wish that he could have Jewish blood so as to share in the lineage of Jesus and Mary; some of the most distinguished early Jesuits had descended from Jews. After his death, however, the Society, to its disgrace, in 1593 banned all those of "Hebrew and Saracen stock," and did not lift the ban till 1947.

Unlike the 20th-century American Jesuits, most of whom, prior to the 1960s, entered right after high school and spent their 20s with few opportunities to socialize with women, Ignatius knew many women as a courtier in his early life and worked closely with women on church projects, particularly in the Saint Martha Houses in Rome that he had founded, dedicated to the care and rehabilitation of prostitutes. At that time, women had very limited career opportunities: marriage, the convent, or prostitution. Laypersons who wanted to serve the church formed confraternities, religious associations guided by rules to perform good works: bury the executed, feed the poor, care for orphans, or promote special religious devotions. But following the Council of Trent, the church tended to channel women who wished to be active into religious orders, where the traditions of the cloister limited their activism.

In 1542, Isabel Roser, a wealthy Barcelona noblewoman whose husband had died in 1541, set out for Rome with two women companions, determined to work under obedience with Ignatius. He put her in charge of a Martha House, which she referred to as a convent and where she kept her servants and possessions. Her petition to Pope Paul III to be "admitted to the least Society of Jesus" was granted, and in 1545 she and two woman friends took a version of the vows of poverty, chastity, and obedience. They were Jesuits in the sense that they were vowed to obey Ignatius; but they lacked, for social and cultural reasons, the one quality Ignatius most required, what he called the "foot in the air" quality, the ability to "run freely from one place to another." Lisa Fullam, in her essay in *Studies in the Spirituality of Jesuits* (November 1999) concludes that they in fact were the core of an essentially monastic second order under obedience to the Society.

Within a year, Ignatius saw the experiment had failed and asked the pope to release them from their vows. They didn't go quietly. Roser demanded the return of all the money she had given the Society; Ignatius responded with a bill for the 150 ducats she owed them. Eventually they were reconciled and resumed their correspondence. Roser joined a Franciscan convent, where she died in 1554.

The story of Juana of Spain, the second daughter of Emperor Charles of Spain, married in 1552 to the heir to the throne of Portugal, is different. When her husband died in 1554 she asked to enter the Jesuits. She was nineteen. Problem: admit her and the Society angers the emperor; deny her and the Society angers the regent of Spain, who is Juana, appointed to that post by her father the emperor in 1554. After much discussion, the fathers decided that she should be admitted— but secretly. Hugo Rahner, editor of a monumental volume, *Saint Ignatius Loyola: Letters to Women,* concludes that Ignatius "took the princess's vocation seriously" and also measured her spiritual progress. Today an observer might say she was a secret agent, a woman with great political influence in Spain who was also a member of the Society of Jesus and promoting its agenda. She died at age thirty-eight, still a member of the Society of Jesus, "the only woman known to have lived and died a Jesuit." Professor Fullam concludes, "Most basically, the Jesuits decided that being a woman was not an absolute bar to membership in the Society." The implications of this will return in the 20th century when the Society of Jesus will once again ask where do they stand with women.

Meanwhile, men who started with teaching children catechism, establishing shelters for prostitutes, working in hospitals, preaching and hearing confessions, soon found themselves as theologians at the Council of Trent; administering a school system throughout Europe,

Asia, and the New World. They found themselves, like Xavier, dying on the little island of Sanchen waiting for a boat to China, or like Pedro Martinez, gazing anxiously at the Florida coast.

The First to Die

A historian would like to imagine a personal meeting between Ignatius Loyola and Pedro Martinez, but Ignatius spent most of his final years governing the Society from Rome and died there three years after Martinez entered. At the University of Valencia, Pedro was known for his quick wit, his mastery of Latin, his good grades in philosophy, but above all for his skill as a swordsman. As one of his friends wrote, "There was rarely a challenge or a duel in the city in which he was not principal, second or promoter."

He also seemed to despise the local Jesuits to whom his university friends were attracted, until one day, when he accompanied his friends to the Jesuit house in order to make fun of them, he was so impressed by their religious demeanor that he abruptly asked if he might join. The superior, Jerome Nadal, put him off for several months; but within a short time he was not only a minister of the novitiate, a college teacher, and a successful preacher, but on his way to Oran with 12,000 troops as a chaplain in the campaign against the Moors.

He visited the sick and wounded, mastered the business management of religious communities, and was also a master cook. Afraid he was accepting too many administrative jobs without enough theological background, he studied more theology at Salamanca, then became rector at Valladolid, all the while pleading that because he could toil, bear hunger and thirst, sleep on the ground, speak Latin and read Hebrew, and, except for a week in Oran, had never been sick, he belonged in the missions.

The summer of their voyage, Pedro, with his companions, Father Juan Rogel and Brother Francisco Villareal, prepared not just themselves but also the crews of the ships of the fleet for the expedition by preaching, hearing confessions, and exacting pledges from the sailors not to curse or use obscene language. Pedro taught himself to speak Flemish and the Flemish sailors to sing the catechism daily at noon. According to Rogel, the long voyage took on the atmosphere of a pilgrimage.

This September day, six Flemish sailors and two soldiers lower the boat into the water and board; then, in a panic, knowing the reputation of the barbarous Indian tribes that may await them, they refuse to go ashore unless Father Martinez goes with them.

At this, as if accepting a challenge to a duel, Martinez springs into the boat and they row ashore.

Then the ship is again blown out to sea. The reconnaissance party waits twelve days for it to return. They patrol the shore, first on foot, then by boat, looking for the fort. They are starving, but Martinez keeps their spirits up by holding his cross high and leading them in prayer. They follow a river inland and encounter small villages of friendly Indians who feed them. But on October 6, with one band of Indians, the mood changes. Thirty Indians surround the boat.

Flores, a Spanish soldier, calls a warning: "These Indians mean trouble. Let us make off in the boat." But Martinez hesitates; he will not desert the sailors who are some distance away. They call to the sailors.

Flores reaches for his sword. The Indians grab Martinez and five others from behind and drag them into the river and shove them under. They drag Martinez out, half strangled, and as he raises his hands, club him to death.

Flores and three others, wounded with arrows, escape in the boat to tell the story.

For a number of reasons, the Jesuit mission in Florida did not succeed. In 1570 seven Jesuits moved their missionary effort north to the Chesapeake Bay, but within a few months the Indians turned against them and slew them all. In defeat again they withdrew to Havana, to the southwest, to Mexico and the Pacific coast, to labor where official Spanish presence offered some protection. Another generation would succeed where they first had failed. But neither Jesus Christ nor Ignatius Loyola had ever promised their followers success. They had offered their apostles only an opportunity for God's glory, not their own. In 1634 a new colony that included Jesuits would settle in Maryland; in the 1640s French Jesuits would pour down from Canada; and in the 1680s an Italian Jesuit with Spanish backing would open Arizona and Southern California. Meanwhile the first Jesuit blood had been spilled in what would become, within a little more than 200 years, the United States of America.

I

The World Scene

From the Beginning: Church versus State?

One Jesuit historian suggests that the decades following the coming of the Jesuits to Mexico "were the most glorious" of the Society's history. He then enlarges the scope of his judgment to encompass the leadership of the fifth and sixth generals of the order—Claudius Aquaviva (1582–1615) and Mutius Vitellechi, who ruled until 1645. This may be, he writes, the Society's "golden age."

Tragically—or providentially, depending on one's point of view—the age began in bloodshed and ended in a multitude of baptisms. Jesuits inspired by their brothers' martyrdoms rushed to replace them in the front lines—sometimes fulfilling the 3rd-century prophecy of Tertullian that the blood of martyrs is the seed of Christians. And sometimes it is not.

In July 1570 a group of 70 Portuguese Jesuits sailing on several ships to the mission in Peru was attacked by French Calvinist pirates. On one galleon, all 40 Jesuits onboard, led by Ignatius Azevedo, were slashed, stabbed, and thrown into the sea.

But between 1573 and 1579 the number of Jesuits in Japan rose from eight to 29; and between 1581 and 1595 Jesuits reached out from Mexico to the Philippines, where they established a series of missions and two colleges. In 1588 they entered Paraguay and built the famous *reductions,* planned native agricultural communities, some with populations as large as 10,000, centered around the church, where crafts, industry, and the arts thrived—until the Jesuits were expelled in 1767.

Since the mid-20th century, Catholic theology has not assumed that the souls of the unbaptized will never see God. Even in the 1940s Catholic schoolchildren learned about "baptism of desire," which meant that pagans of goodwill who never heard the gospels actually "desired" baptism, and thus were redeemed by their charitable lives. A few years later, on a more sophisticated level, German Jesuit theologian Karl Rahner developed the term "anonymous Christian," one who is open to ultimate reality, to God's grace and love, though he or she may lack the background or vocabulary to make this relationship to God explicit. But in the Age of Exploration, when navies, armies, merchants, and missionaries of the world powers were mutually dependant and often worked as one, the baptism count was the statistical measure of success. Jesuit missionaries were inspired by the meditation in the Spiritual Exercises on the Two Standards, the image of Christ, the "supreme commander" who sends his disciples to the whole world to rescue "people of every state and condition" from the "standard of Satan." To them Satan was a living, personal force, to be confronted in the jungles of Peru or in the Iroquois villages of North America.

In 1583, Rudolph, the nephew of General Aquaviva, and four companions were martyred on an island off India; but within five years 3,800 island natives were baptized. By 1589, 36 years after Xavier's death, 11,500 Japanese were at least technically Christian.

General Aquaviva's challenge was to efficiently govern what grew over 24 years from a group of friends to 13,000 men, 372 schools, and 123 residences in 32 provinces, many of whom were working in villages all over the world to adapt the expression of the Catholic faith to cultures as exotic as India and China and other foreign missions.

To an extraordinary degree, as the colleges multiplied, the arts and sciences thrived. But with growth came trouble, and some of the trouble was home grown. The Society's history is not one of uninterrupted harmony. Ignatius's policy had been to deliberately appoint a Spaniard as a superior in Paris or put a Frenchman in charge of the Roman College. But the larger the Society became, the more its members were inclined to identify with their national, political, theological, or even spirituality subgroups; and in a strategy that has continued into the 21st century, the traditional Jesuit allegiance to the papacy has cut both ways.

Jesuit factions have used their access to the papal court to undermine fellow Jesuits. During Aquaviva's rule, Spanish Jesuits conspired with Rome to restructure the Society so as to limit the general's powers. The gap between those who wanted a more contemplative order, emphasizing long prayers and penances over apostolic activity, and those committed to Ignatius's priorities grew. Aquaviva stressed the middle ground: moderation in penances, freedom to give more time to prayer, and pious reading after finishing one's work.

Among special initiatives, Aquaviva had a committee complete the 15-year project of compiling the *Ratio Studiorum*, a detailed plan of studies setting the curriculum and teaching methods for the schools. Lest Jesuit intellectual training blunt one's pastoral touch, bands of two or three Jesuits, based in the colleges and residences, spread throughout Europe to preach to the neglected countrysides.

The Society's major contribution to philosophy during these years was through the work of the gentle Spaniard, Francisco Suarez (1548– 1617), who, specializing in issues of law, both helped to reanimate scholastic philosophy and developed a Thomistic school of thought, that is, an approach based on St. Thomas's original texts but which would rival traditional Thomism. Although Suarez's *Defensio Fidei* (1613) was directed against Anglican theologians and the oath of supremacy demanded by England's James I, his legal philosophy would help set the stage for the democratic ideas that would eventually flower in the New World: the people themselves are the source of political authority; each person has natural rights to life, liberty, and property; the Spanish colonizers have no right to invade, conquer, and enslave the natives of the newly discovered Indies in order to convert them to Christianity.

In France the Society endured a political crisis that moved through several stages. In 1580, when Jesuit allegiance was split between the Valois king, Henry III, and Henry the Duke de Guise, head of the Holy League, Aquaviva ordered French Jesuits to stay out of politics, to not even talk about it among themselves. When both Henry III and Guise were murdered, in 1593–1594, the Society split on whether or not to take the oath of allegiance to the Calvinist king, Henry IV of Navarre. Then when a deranged law student who had attended philosophy lectures at the Jesuit College of Clermont tried to assassinate the king, the Jesuits, accused of teaching regicide, were expelled from Paris until they personally reconciled with the king in 1603. When Henry was finally assassinated in 1610, the Society's enemies again tried to hold them responsible.

The basic issue, one which would dog Catholicism and Jesuits in 19th-century America, was the tug of loyalties between the state and church. Can one be a loyal French or American citizen and a faithful

Catholic at the same time? During the 16th century, several popes and Jesuit scholars like Robert Cardinal Bellarmine taught that the pope's authority superseded the monarch's in certain circumstances, including temporal affairs. The theological-political position that restricted papal powers, over either temporal leaders or local bishops, and with which most French clergy identified, was called Gallicanism. The rival school, which emphasized papal power as a defense against political liberalism and modern trends and which included most Jesuits, was called in the 19th century Ultramontanism (meaning that it came from the other side of the Alps). But in the context of 1613 this kind of thinking was evidence that the Jesuits were enemies of the state—in France to be banished, in England to be hanged.

In England under Queen Elizabeth I the Society was outlawed, so it trained its English recruits in France and returned them to minister secretly to British Catholics, usually members of the upper class who had chapels in their homes and would hide the Jesuits in "priest holes," secret compartments, if the estates were raided. Under Elizabeth, 11 Jesuits were martyred, including the brilliant pamphleteer and orator Edmund Campion, who was tortured, hanged, drawn and quartered in 1581, and the poet Robert Southwell. Some Catholics, however, did not welcome the Jesuits' zeal and remained loyal to the throne.

How Far Does One Go to Adapt?

On the other side of the world—in India, Japan, and China—missionary Jesuits like Robert de Nobili, Alexander Valignano, and the mathematician Matteo Ricci experimented boldly with a strategy radical in its day. Today we call it inculturation; in the 16th and 17th centuries it meant to break out of European cultural and social patterns and enter the language and culture of the place. They struggled for a vocabulary to express complex, historically conditioned elements of Christian theology like the Trinity, Incarnation, Redemption, and the afterlife in local languages that had no words for those ideas, and occasionally adapted their dress and worship to where they lived. But this melding of cultures inevitably raised both theological and ethical questions, some of which lingered and festered for centuries.

In India, Roberto de Nobili, an Italian nobleman, saw himself as an Indian *sannyasi,* or holy man, and moved about among the Brahmins and other social elites. But who would evangelize the "untouchables," the poor? De Nobili's response was to train cadres of Jesuits to play the roles of Hindu ascetics, wearing yellow tunics and gold earrings, to evangelize the various stratified levels of society without attempting to integrate the classes separated by local custom. Thus teaching the principle of universal Christian love was postponed.

In Angola in 1583, the Portuguese Jesuits identified too closely with the Portuguese troops, celebrating their victory when the army put down a native rebellion and carrying to the governor a load of thirty boxes filled with the noses cut from dead black rebels. The Jesuits received slaves as gifts, kept them as servants, and sold them, until Aquaviva ordered a halt.

In China, the mathematician-astronomer Ricci (1552–1610) worked his way into the ruling and intellectual classes because, by adopting Chinese dress and bringing gifts of clocks, maps, and Renaissance art, and by writing learned treatises in Chinese on religion, science, and friendship, he personified the best of two worlds. Five years after his death, the Jesuits were given permission by Pope Paul V to translate the Bible, breviary, and Mass into Chinese, but by the time they got around to discussing it again in the 1660s, the Jesuits were split over Ricci's methods, especially on accepting the Chinese rites honoring Confucius and their own family ancestors. Were these basically the rites of a false religion, or were they cultural traditions that could be reconciled with Catholic liturgy? Spanish Dominicans and Franciscans who arrived in China in the 1630s, who disliked the sight of Jesuits striding around in silk robes, joined the controversy. Rome changed its mind three times: condemning the rites in 1645, approving them in 1656, prohibiting them in 1715 and 1742, and authorizing them in 1939.

As early as 1536, Spanish Franciscans in Mexico opened a seminary to train native clergy; but because of the perceived poor quality of the candidates, the experiment did not succeed, and a variety of ecclesiastical laws, depending on the place and on whether the candidates were *indios* (purebred natives), *mestizos* (mixed European and native parentage), or *criollos* (born in the colonies of European parents) put up barriers to ordination. Nevertheless, the third Jesuit general, Francis Borgia (1565–1572), wanted native vocations. We do not know their racial mix, but in 1592, 61 of the 216 Jesuits in the Mexican province were born in America; in 1602, because of Valignano's leadership, the first two Jesuit Japanese priests were ordained. Over the next half-century, however, Japan declared itself a Closed Country and the shoguns sought to eradicate the Catholic Church in one of the bloodiest persecutions in history. They killed more than 13 percent of the Catholic population of 300,000 by cutting off their heads, roasting them at the stake, crucifying them, and hanging them over pits of excrement to force them to give up the faith. Although five Jesuits gave in to their torturers, 87 were martyred, including 44 Japanese.

The Jesuit arrival in what is now North America will present a different level of challenge. Some of the strategies that originate with Ignatius and the Constitutions will be familiar: attempt to influence the leadership—the king, the emperor, the tribal chief—as a way of attracting his followers as well, and search the local culture for ideas and images that match Christian theology. But now for the first time, young men in black robes with a dozen years of philosophy, theology, rhetoric, Latin, and Greek behind them must learn to sit painfully motionless for hours—even days—in a birch bark canoe.

2

The Maryland Tradition

The First Mass

Drive two hours south of Washington, D.C., through the lush, green farmlands of St. Mary's County to the southern Maryland peninsula, where the Potomac River empties into the Chesapeake Bay on the west, the bay reaches up past Annapolis and Baltimore on the east, and Maryland's Eastern Shore dangles down between the Chesapeake and the Atlantic Ocean. A few miles into the Potomac sits St. Mary's City, the first permanent settlement in Maryland, now a mini theme park, with reproductions, a gift shop, and skeleton replicas of original buildings, including a 17th-century chapel.

Then descend a few miles to St. Inigoes, where the first Jesuits, who had received from Lord Baltimore 2,000 acres for every five men recruited for the voyage, farmed about a sixth of the total 24,500 acres the Jesuits owned, not as formal chaplains but as participant "adventurers" in the founding of the colony.

Then turn north along the west coast into Charles County and to Chapel Point and Port Tobacco and St. Ignatius Church, St. Thomas Manor, possibly the oldest foundation in the world in continuous Jesuit possession.

In the ancient graveyard, fresh small Confederate flags stand by the graves of two Confederate spies. Some Union soldiers lie buried in the woods. This is the neighborhood into which John Wilkes Booth fled after Lincoln's assassination, and a new-looking gravestone is marked MUDD, descendant of the Catholic doctor, jailed as a conspirator, who treated Booth in flight.

A few miles away, on tiny St. Clement's Island at the mouth of the Potomac, on March 25, 1634, roughly 150 men, women, and children waded ashore from two British ships, the big 400-ton *Ark* and its pinnacle, the 40-ton *Dove*, and the Catholics in the expedition, a minority, gathered around a makeshift altar. There, Fr. Andrew White, age 54, of the Society of Jesus offered the first Mass as he said, "in this part of the world." Then assisted by the appointed governor, Leonard Calvert, the 23-year-old half-brother of the second Lord Baltimore, Cecil Calvert, they hewed a huge cross from a tree and erected it, reciting a litany "with great devotion."

White's Jesuit piety enabled him to interpret every event, particularly favorable ones, as if God's providential hand directly intervened day by day guiding His servants to their destiny. We do not know who named the ships; but the *Ark* was clearly Noah's ark, saving a chosen minority and bearing them into a new covenant; the *Dove* was Noah's dove sent out ahead to come back with the olive branch in its beak. Both ships had sailed from Gravesend, England, in the fall of 1633; but the three Jesuit passengers—White, a priest, John Altham, also a priest (alias Gravenor), and a coadjutor brother, Thomas Gervase—did not board until November 22 on the Isle of Wight in order to avoid the antipapist oath which colonists were obliged to take.

The next day it seemed to White that the sailors were conspiring to delay their voyage, but a combination of circumstances—a favorable wind and a near crash between the *Dove* and a French cutter—forced the party to set sail. It happened to be St. Clement's Day. St. Clement, a martyr, had been tied to an anchor and thrown into the sea. Thus, during their three-month voyage, St. Clement had guided the *Ark* and *Dove* to the island that today bears his name.

Andrew White is, in the judgment of one historian, a "mysterious" character. We have several writings and letters, especially one describing the voyage to America, but the drawings and idealized paintings that depict him saying mass and baptizing Indians give no consistent portrait. Born in London in 1579, he entered the English seminary at Valladolid, Spain, was ordained, and returned to England, only to be expelled in 1605 with 45 priests for some association with the Gunpowder Plot. He joined the Jesuits in Louvain, returned to England for a while, and then taught a rigid version of Thomistic theology at Louvain and Liège, where he several times complained to Rome that his colleagues, followers of Suarez, were not sticking to the *Ratio Studiorum*. So he lost his job at Liège and became eligible to be sent to the missions just when Cecil Calvert, Lord Baltimore, whose family had failed to establish its colony in Newfoundland and who had recently converted to Catholicism, was planning to fulfill his father's vision in the warmer climate of Maryland.

Whereas some English colonies, such as Virginia, replicated the state church of the mother country, and others, for example Massachusetts, established a congregational model, Maryland offered a different relationship: no established religion and complete tolerance for all Christians. Lord Baltimore wanted a unified community, loyal to himself, where men and women could prosper and pray without offensive public display, according to each one's conscience. The Jesuits would help by recruiting Catholic colonists and publicizing, with a pamphlet written by White, the project's virtues.

Like most immigrants, Maryland's first settlers, including the Jesuits, were not necessarily the elite of the mother country. In the minority were Baltimore's 17 Catholic "gentlemen adventurers," all but one in their twenties, second sons of English gentry, friends of the Calverts, seizing a new opportunity to both own property and practice their faith. Most of the others, including 20 brought by the Jesuits, were indentured servants who were promised 50 acres of land in exchange for five years of servitude. But few of the original party survived the hardships of the new life. Of the 17, after four years only Leonard Calvert and four others had not died or gone home, and the majority of the servants had died.

Over the years, numerous English Jesuits had written to their provincial to volunteer, but the provincial had his own criteria on who could be spared. In a typical letter, in 1640, Christopher Morris offers his three reasons for going: to save the souls of the Indians, for whom Christ has suffered as for Europeans; to use his skills in language and music for the "primitive church"; to die a martyr like his brother Jesuits in China and Japan. The provincial decided that these talents were best kept for Europe. Eight of the 14 sent between 1633 and 1645, including White's two companions, died—to be replaced over the years by a long string of men, some of whose names are lost and some whose names (including their aliases) line the memorial stones in the St. Thomas Manor graveyard.

Becoming Country Gentlemen

The mission's early history falls into two phases: the first dozen years during which the Jesuits—in a behavior pattern that will distinguish their efforts until the big institutions limit their mobility in the 20th century—restlessly reach out into new projects, like the conversion of the Indians; and the later years as gentleman-farmer circuit riders until the suppression of the Society in 1773 on the eve of the American Revolution.

Although the local tribe sold Calvert land for St. Mary's City, their enemies the Susquehannas and other tribes remained hostile. Defying the orders of civil authorities concerned about disease and danger to his life, in 1639 White went to live with the Piscataways. There, within a year, in a ceremony that Calvert attended, White baptized their chief Chitomachen, along with his wife and son, and learned enough of the language to prepare a dictionary, grammar, and catechism for his colleagues, who, for the most part, were forced to rely on interpreters when they taught.

According to the annual letters from Jesuit superiors to Rome, the Jesuits made many converts among the Protestant settlers, they cared for the dying, and they directed leading citizens in the Spiritual Exercises. On one occasion, White administered a "powder" mixed with holy water to a sick chief and bled him; the chief was cured and his family became Christian. On another, a Susquehanna caught a Christian Indian in the woods and plunged his spear in one side and out the other. Summoned to the dying brave, White touched his wounds with an alleged relic of the true cross he wore around his neck, prayed over him, and left directions for his funeral—only to meet him the next day paddling a canoe.

Providence, according to a 1640 letter, also occasionally punished the Jesuits' foes. One man who had been prepared for conversion suddenly reverted to his bad old ways. He ground his rosary into powder, mixed it with his tobacco, and smoked it in his pipe. His talk became ribald and sacrilegious. Until one afternoon, as he bathed in the river, a huge fish bit a big chunk out of his thigh and he died. It was fitting, the Jesuit wrote, that a man who joked about "swallowing" his rosary should "see his own flesh devoured while he was still alive."

Meanwhile tension between Lord Baltimore and the Jesuits developed on several levels. The Jesuits had received their 24,500 acres of farmland according to the same terms as other settlers so they could support themselves as farmers and not rely on the state for support; but to some degree they still imagined themselves as privileged— exempt from militia service, taxes, and restrictions on living and trading with or receiving land from the Indians. Although they reached a compromise by 1643, other forces were at work to shatter the Baltimore dream. The impact of England's Civil War, 1640–1649—the Parliamentary forces against the king—spread to the colonies. Puritans who had been welcomed to Maryland joined with Governor Claiborne of Virginia to overthrow the Calverts.

Catholics and Jesuits fled or died. Fr. Thomas Copley, White's successor as superior, and White himself were dragged to England in chains to be tried for breaking the law against priests entering England. White argued successfully that he had not come of his own free will and was banished again to Europe. Denied permission to return to Maryland, he slipped back into England where he served persecuted Catholics until he died at age 77 in 1656.

How Jesuits Are Organized

As pioneer Jesuits from Europe try to establish themselves in a new context, it might be helpful to describe the system of government within the Society of Jesus. In a way it seems hierarchical or military, with its emphasis on obedience and the willingness to be sent. Yet it is also paternal and fraternal in that the religious superior's style should be like that of a father and that, since terms run no more than three or six years, today's person in authority is also tomorrow's servant.

The father general in Rome is elected for life by the General Congregation, which meets regularly to elect a general or whenever representatives from the whole Society feel a need. The early American establishments were called missions, since they were sponsored and governed remotely by provinces in Europe. The province is the basic unit of organization. When Maryland, for example, became large enough to be self-supporting, it became the first American province.

The superior of the province is the provincial. He appoints, with the approval of Rome, local superiors of the various houses in the province. A rector is a superior of a major institution which consists of several residences. For example, the Fordham University community has a rector, but each of the four subcommunities on campus has a superior. An assistancy is the largest subdivision in the Society, and it may consist of an entire country or a number of countries combined. Today the American Assistancy has ten provinces, named for states, areas, or cities—New York, Maryland, New England, New Orleans, and so on. However, because of shrinking numbers, it may reorganize into four or five.

The priest's course of training goes through three major steps. When he enters he is a novice for two years of spiritual formation, including the "long retreat," being led through the Spiritual Exercises in 30 days, leading to taking the three vows: poverty, chastity, and obedience. Then he becomes a scholastic for approximately nine years of philosophy and theology education and teaching experience, leading to ordination. A few years after ordination he repeats the Spiritual Exercises and takes his final vows.

By 1648 Baltimore regained possession of his colony, and Copley and the Jesuits were able to return, to a new way of life, without the Indian missions, but as pastors to the Catholics spread throughout the colony and eventually reaching up into southeastern Pennsylvania, including the establishment of Old St. Joseph's Church in Philadelphia in 1732. They used their estates, such as St. Thomas Manor, as a headquarters and means of financial support, and, on horseback, rode hundreds of miles a week to offer Mass and hear confessions in tiny chapels and private homes for the faithful who were forbidden to attend Mass or Catholic schools by the Penal Laws that had been introduced in 1690 when the Calverts had been overthrown again and Maryland was once more a Royal colony.

During the 17th century, there were never more than five priests and four brothers to share the burden. So their social life was usually with secular neighbors, and in 1713 the provincial felt he had to warn his missionaries against elements in their lifestyle that might undermine their religious observance—like having many servants, card playing, associating too much with "seculars," and drinking alcohol.

From the beginning the plan had been to work the farm with indentured servants, and occasionally the Jesuits bought the contracts of Catholic servants in Virginia who might otherwise have lost their faith. Inevitably slaves replaced the servants. Even up to the Civil War there does not seem to have been a consensus among American Jesuits, most of whom were foreign born, that Negro slavery was immoral. Rather, they tried to treat them kindly, to pay them for extra work, allow them gardens whose produce the slaves sold, and to make them faithful Catholics. Lay catechists instructed the slaves in the faith. Slaves were allowed to attend Mass on Sundays and usually did not work that day or holy days, and usually—though not always—the

Jesuits tried to not break up the families when they were sold. Today a distinctive feature for the visitor to the old Maryland Jesuit churches is the upstairs balcony—for slaves and, until the mid-20th century, for blacks.

From a statistical point of view the accomplishments of the first Maryland Jesuits may seem modest, especially compared to their French contemporaries who spread down from the Great Lakes and deep into the Midwest. But the Society's commitment to Maryland was modest also. Although a total of 113 priests, one scholastic, and 30 brothers had served and 25 priests remained in 1773, during the first critical decade only 14 arrived and few endured. Unlike the French they did not master the native language, and between 1634 and 1643 they had converted fewer than 150. But this handful of Jesuits were, for all practical purposes, the roots and trunk of the colonial American Catholic Church, a struggling community without a bishop or the sacrament of Confirmation for 150 years; and they participated in an early experiment in religious freedom that set the stage for the First Amendment to the Constitution: "Congress shall make no law. . . ."

3

The Pioneers

Jogues and Brébeuf Suffer the Ordeal

It is January 5, 1644, and a ragged traveler knocks at the door of the Jesuit college at Rennes, France. He is gaunt, poorly dressed in clothes that do not fit him. He is bearded and young, 38 years old, but, with thinning hair and a lined face, looks much older. His hands are mangled stumps, his left thumb is gone, and his forefingers, from which the nails have been torn, useless. He asks the porter if he may speak to the rector, for whom he has news from Canada.

The rector is vesting for Mass, but he lays aside his vestments to hurry to the door. This poor man, he says, may be in need.

The visitor hands him a packet of letters, but the rector peppers him with questions. Has he heard anything of Father Isaac Jogues?

"I knew him very well," he answers.

"We have heard that he was taken by the Iroquois. Is he dead? Is he still captive? Have not those barbarians slain him?"

"He is at liberty," the stranger replies. "And it is he, my Reverend Father, who speaks to you now." Then he falls on his knees to ask the rector's blessing. Word spreads through the house and everyone rushes to see him. He is Lazarus raised from the dead.

In fact, he has less than two years to live.

Isaac Jogues, along with Jean de Brébeuf, is the best known of the eight North American Jesuits and their lay assistants who were martyred—Rene Goupil, Jean de Lalande, Gabriel Lallement, Charles Garnier, Noel Chabanel, and Antoine Daniel—in the story of the French penetration into New France. Their world, from the Jesuits' first arrival in French Canada in 1611 until their expulsion, in stages, in the 1770s, reached from the mouth of the St. Lawrence River in Northeast Canada down through the Canadian territory north of the river to and around the Great Lakes, in New England and upstate New York, and into the West and down the Mississippi River to Louisiana. Among the northern Indian tribes, they worked most often with the Hurons, Algonkians, Iroquois, and Mohawks; and though they were allied with the Hurons, their eyes were ever alert for the sick and about-to-die among their enemies, that they might administer the saving water of baptism.

Isaac Jogues was born the fifth of nine children in Orléans, France, in 1607, and entered the Jesuit novitiate at Rouen at the age of 17. As a young man he was small, delicate, sharp-eyed, and fine featured, but a vigorous swimmer and fast runner. For spiritual guidance he relied on Fr. Louis Lallement, his novice master, the uncle of several other Jesuits already working in New France. But the deeper scholarly issues of theology did not hold his attention; he wanted a theology he could preach simply to the "savages" of the New World.

When Jogues arrived in French Canada in 1636, France had already established a presence, after several unsuccessful attempts in the 16th century, when Samuel de Champlain, following a trail set by Jacques Cartier, set up a permanent post at Quebec in 1609. Two Jesuits had been assigned there but failed to establish a mission in 1611, and various groups of Recollets, an order of Franciscans, had labored with only modest success for years. Three more Jesuits, including Jean de Brébeuf, who came in 1625, were driven out when the English navy took Quebec in 1628–1629. Only when Canada was ceded to France in 1632 and the Jesuits were given responsibility for the settlers' religious needs as well as the evangelization of the natives did their efforts take hold.

At the time, four families or language groups of Indians, each family divided into several tribes, stretched from the Atlantic Coast to the Rocky Mountains, from the Hudson Bay to the Gulf of Mexico: the Algonkians, who included the Penobscots of Maine and other tribes scattered throughout; the intelligent and ferocious Iroquois, who included the Mohawks and the Hurons, with whom, along with the French, they were often at war; the Southern Indians, who had less contact with the Jesuits, except for their efforts in Louisiana; and the Dakotas, or Sioux, west of the Mississippi, with whom later generations of Jesuits would toil.

From the beginning it seems as if the goals of the French settlers and Jesuit missionaries meshed well. France pursued both territory and control of the fur trade; and they hoped the Catholic faith would pacify the natives and, as the missionaries spread across the country, bring distant tribes under French influence. But the Jesuits reconsidered their strategy. Often they joined the savages on their hunting parties and long periods in the wilderness, on foot and in canoe. Now they encouraged their converts to settle in established missions, like Sillery, four miles above Quebec, the large towns of Ihonatiria and Ossossane on Georgia Bay of Lake Huron, and Three Rivers, on the St. Lawrence, between Quebec and Montreal.

Here, surrounded by a palisade, the Indians could plant and harvest crops as well as hunt and fish, and receive religious instruction. The priests could celebrate Mass in a chapel decorated with vivid pictures of the Holy Family and the Last Judgment, nurse the sick, and baptize the dying. The Indians' new domestic lifestyle, however, angered the fur traders who counted on the wandering tribesmen to deliver pelts; the mutual relationship between France's economic ambitions and its religious zeal became strained.

When missionaries arrived in New France, also called Huronia, they sailed down the St. Lawrence River to Quebec and then to Three Rivers, from which they would set off by canoe to their mission stations. On August 14, 1636, young Father Jogues gazed up the river in awe as a flotilla of Algonkian canoes heaved into sight. The savages brandished 28 scalps from their poles, sang, and rapped the hulls of their birch-bark boats with their paddles. They had two prisoners—an Iroquois brave standing tall, proud, and naked in the canoe, and a native woman. As they pulled into the landing, the native women, many of whom had thrown off their clothes to swim out to the boats, surrounded the native prisoner, beat him with clubs, ropes, and chains, stabbed him with burning sticks, and crushed his fingers in their teeth. One who cut off his thumb had tried to force him to swallow it. When he failed to choke it down, she cooked it for the children to eat. Though he might not have realized it at the time, Jogues had been given a foretaste of his own future.

Ignatius, who had a sense of public relations that anticipated 20th-century practices, directed his missionaries to write detailed letters on their adventures that could be widely circulated to both Jesuits and benefactors. In 1632 Father Paul Le Jeune, superior of the Canada mission, had written a letter, a *Relation*, to his fellow Jesuits in France describing the country and the natives. All the men, he said, when it is warm, go naked, except for a small covering below the navel. They paint their bodies blue, green, and red, and their hair is black, long, greasy, and shiny. They are intelligent, patiently wait their turn to speak, and sing "oh! oh! oh! ah! ah! ah!" and dance by stomping their feet. They make their prisoners suffer all the cruelty that the devil can suggest. At last, as a final horror, "they eat and devour them almost raw." If they are captured by the Iroquois, he informs his brothers, "we would be obliged to suffer this ordeal."

Jogues had read this, and now he had seen an example. However, he noted that, though the "savages" were liars, thieves, and superstitious murderers with no moral sense, they were also gentle, wise, eloquent, and not to be condemned. He would learn to soften their hearts.

The following year his colleague and mentor, Jean de Brébeuf, a big strong man 14 years his senior, circulated a *Relation* advising new missionaries on how to deal with the Indians personally: Don't keep them waiting when embarking in the canoes. Carry a tinder box or burning mirror so you can light their pipes for them in the evening. Eat their dirty, half-cooked, tasteless food however they make it. "The Barbarians eat only at sunrise and sunset." Entering and leaving the canoe, tuck up your robes; your feet and legs should be bare. Don't ask a lot of questions. Bear with their imperfections without saying a word. Always be cheerful. Don't annoy anyone with your hat. Don't start something you can't finish: if you start paddling, paddle for the whole trip. The first impression you make will stay with you. "All the fine qualities which might make you loved and respected in France are like pearls trampled under the feet of swine, or rather mules, which utterly despise you when they see that you are not as good pack animals as they are."

On August 24 Jogues began a 19-day voyage on the Ottawa River, climbing up over rapids, crammed motionless and mute in a crowded canoe, and carrying his baggage and a sick 11-year-old boy on his back, to Ihonatiria, the Huron mission. Here he worked for six years, enduring sickness when the most popular "cure" was bleeding, and the ridicule and hostility of Indians and the medicine men who spread stories that the Blackrobes were responsible for the sickness and death that plagued their lives.

Progress was slow. For all the Jesuits' efforts among the Hurons, over a three-year period prior to 1640 they had "converted" only about 1,000 out of a population of 16,000, and most of those were sick infants and old people who died soon after baptism. The notion that the missionaries were responsible for various plagues, particularly smallpox, was not far-fetched, in that the European settlers may have carried to the New World diseases for which they had developed some immunity at home but from which the Indians had no protection.

Meanwhile, basic elements of the Indian worldview were so distant from a faith influenced by Greek and medieval philosophy that to accept baptism and the worldview that went with it was too great a leap for the native imagination. A brave asks where he will hunt in the afterlife if he is baptized and is told there is no hunting in heaven. He refuses baptism; how will he provide for his family if he cannot hunt? A woman's children die without baptism. Their mother refuses to be baptized; she does not want to go to the Christian heaven if her children are not there. Thus the Jesuits were conservative in determining whom to baptize; they baptized anyone, particularly children, in danger of death; but adults required a long period of preparation.

Father Jerome Lallement, superior of the mission, in 1639 wrote in his journal that he doubted they could succeed without shedding their blood, since it was a standard principle in the church that the blood of martyrs was the seed of Christians. He hoped that perhaps the daily sufferings of the missionaries could be accepted as a living martyrdom in its place. His hopes would be dashed.

On June 13, 1642, Jogues, with three Frenchmen and 21 Hurons in four large canoes, set out on a journey from Sainte Marie to Quebec, where Jogues was to deliver an ailing Jesuit to a new home, exchange messages, and bring back supplies. The return trip included, among the four Frenchmen, Guillaume Couture and a young former medical student, Rene Goupil, both of whom had joined the Jesuits as *donnés*, or committed lay helpers, and 40 Hurons, including two young children and a teenage girl. Among the Hurons were several outstanding Christians, dramatic evidence that gradually the fathers were having an impact; one may have had a foreshadowing of how their faith was to be tested.

On the first day of the return journey, Eustache Ahatsistari, one of the greatest Huron warriors, delivered a speech to his fellow travelers. If the Iroquois capture them, he said, he will tell them that the Europeans bring them axes and guns, but that they do not love them. The French, on the other hand, "tell us of an eternal life, of a God who has made all. . . . Then I will tell them that herein is my consolation: that

they may inflict all their torments on me, that they may by dint of tor-
ture tear my soul from my body, but not from my heart this hope that
after death I shall be happy. Thus will I preach to them, while they are
burning me."

On August 2 the Jogues party noticed footprints along the river
shore, left, in Ahatsistari's judgment, by a band of Iroquois braves,
traveling perhaps in three canoes—hostile, but less numerous than the
Huron party and therefore not a major threat. He was wrong. A mile
later, two waves of Iroquois, firing their muskets, overwhelmed the
Hurons and French. At first, Jogues, Ahatsistari, and Couture escaped;
but when Jogues saw that Goupil had been caught he gave himself up
rather than abandon his young friend, and then Ahatsistari and Couture also came forward, reluctant to abandon Jogues.

For over three weeks the Iroquois paraded their 22 captives
through the countryside, pausing in three villages to repeat the tor-
tures endured in each stop along the way. Stripped naked most of
the time, they would run the gauntlets, "caressed" by whips, knives,
stones, burning sticks, then stand displayed on platforms to be
taunted and beaten in the burning sun by whole tribes, or, their open
wounds now putrid, spread-eagled on the floors of their huts where
the children would come in and drop burning coals on their bare skin.

The Iroquois sensed that Jogues was the group's leader, so they
singled him out for special humiliation. They hacked off his left
thumb and chewed his fingers to the bone. Eventually the tribal elders
decided to spare the lives of the Frenchmen and all except three of the
Hurons, including Ahatsistari, who was burned at the stake. According to the Indian custom of giving captives to families who have lost a
brave in battle, Couture was adopted by a family in another village,
Jogues and Goupil stayed at the Mohawk village of Ossernenon,
"adopted," but more like slaves. Jogues wrote, "Our hands and fingers being all in pieces, they had to feed us like children. Patience was
our Physician. Some women, more merciful, regarded us with much
charity, and were unable to look at our sores without compassion."

Young Goupil, more zealous than prudent, did not last long. He
liked to caress and bless the little children. When an old man saw
Goupil make the sign of the cross on his grandson he was convinced he had put a curse on the child. "Go and kill that dog," he said
to his nephew. In Jogues's presence, the nephew sank his hatchet
into Goupil's head. For days Jogues struggled to retrieve and bury

Goupil's corpse. First he buried it temporarily in a creek, but a torrent swelled the creek and washed it away. Later he found the skull and bones in the woods and buried them secretly.

With nothing to wear but rags, not eating meat when he heard that the animals slain on a hunt were offered to the devil, Jogues lived largely on cornmeal. Extremely depressed, over 40 days he would finish his wood-gathering duties early and withdraw for eight or ten hours to pray alone in the woods. In a June letter, smuggled out to the French by a Huron, Jogues warns the governor that the Iroquois are about to launch a new campaign to kill all the Huron leaders and make the "two nations one people in one land." But he had become reconciled to his captivity and attached to his "aunt," who was kind to him. He says that he feels that God wills him to stay a prisoner because his presence "consoles the French, the Hurons, and the Algonkians," and that he has baptized more than 60 persons, "many of whom have already reached heaven." However, on August 18, 1643, informed of a plot to burn him alive, with the help of the New Amsterdam Dutch he escaped and was returned to France.

The Return

Jogues had long been thought dead; the word spread of his "resurrection," and much to his distaste he was revered as a martyr, a living saint. In Paris, the regent, Queen Anne, summoned him to the Palais Royal, where in the presence of Cardinal Mazarin and the five-year-old Louis XIV and others of the royal family, she took his mangled hands in her own and wept. He had but one yearning—to return to his Mohawk village.

Back in Three Rivers in July 1645, the French authorities had called the Iroquois, Hurons, and Algonkians together in an attempt to establish peace among themselves and with the French. They saw Jogues, who was now in America, with his experience, horrible as it had been, and his knowledge of their language, as their ambassador. The following spring they asked him to return for discussions with his previous captors. On route he and his French canoe companion paddled across Lake George, the first white men to see the lake, and Jogues named it the Lake of the Blessed Sacrament. The visit went well enough, and, expecting to return, Jogues left behind a closed box of winter clothes and Mass vestments. But he was not sent back until September.

Apprehensive, Jogues wrote to a Jesuit friend that he sensed he would have to stay longer, that he would have little freedom, be deprived of Mass and the sacraments, and would be held responsible for all incidents between the Iroquois and French and the Algonkians and Hurons. His heart told him that "I shall go but I shall not return. But I would be happy if our Lord wished to complete the sacrifice where he began it."

This time, with his young donné companion Jean de Lalande and Huron braves, as Jogues headed south toward the Mohawk River a band of Iroquois informed them that the peace had broken down. The Hurons deserted and Jogues and Jean continued alone. In his absence, the Mohawks had convinced themselves that Jogues's mysterious box held a demon who was killing them in an epidemic and ruining their corn crop. As soon as the Jesuits arrived, a renegade war party, streaked with red paint, seized them, stripped them naked, and dragged them to the village. There the Wolf and Turtle clans and his "aunt" gave them sanctuary, while the Bear clan called for their deaths. A group of sorcerers took his locked box down to the river and sunk it, drowning the demon. But they were not satisfied.

Jogues was allowed to address the chiefs. Quietly and eloquently he explained why he had come to them this third time, to show them the trail to heaven. He had showed them the contents of his box, he argued against their superstitions, and asked that they listen to his news about the great God who ruled all men. That night a young Bear brave invited him to his cabin, where, he said, they wished to talk to him. Jogues was suspicious, but he could not refuse a chance to win them over. As he put his head in the door a tomahawk cut his outstretched arm and smashed into his head. They cut off his head and pinned it on the palisades that surrounded the camp, and tossed his body outside the hut. Later they decapitated Lelande as well and stuck his head next to his friend's.

Today the town of Auriesville, New York, approximates the location of Ossernenon, and, on a hilltop overlooking the beautiful Mohawk River valley, pilgrims visit the Martyrs' Shrine and the grove by the stream where Goupil died and where, somewhere, Jogues buried his bones. Above, hundreds of simple headstones fan out over the graves of the Jesuits of the New York Province.

A Defiant Death Is Less than Human?

In 1645 there was a brief period of peace, and the Jesuits, who now had missions in five Huron towns and one with the Algonkians, renewed their hopes; but in 1648 the Iroquois returned to the warpath and drove the Hurons from their homes. In March 1649 they stormed the town named for St. Ignatius with a thousand braves, then went on to the town of St. Louis, where they captured Jean de Brébeuf, now 56 years old, and Gabriel Lallement, 39, the nephew of two other Jesuits, Louis and Jerome; they burned their huts, and dragged them back to the town of St. Ignatius to die. Their torments were particularly gruesome because Huron captives, who now hated the Blackrobes, joined in.

Their captors stripped them, tied them to posts, poured boiling water over them in a mockery of baptism, tied red hot hatchets around their necks, and sliced flesh from their legs and loins to roast. While Brébeuf, who uttered not a word except to encourage his friends, was still alive they cut his heart out and ate it, while, to somehow imbibe his courage, they gathered around to drink his blood.

The death of Brébeuf, in its extreme drama and brutality, cast Brébeuf in the mold of the legendary supermartyrs, the heroic model for the Catholic grammar school and high school students nurtured on the Francis Talbot, S.J., biographies, *Saint among Savages* and *Saint among the Hurons*, from the 1930s. To a few writers, however, his defiant death seems less than human. Francis Parkman, in *The Jesuits in North America* (1867), dwells on Brébeuf's frequent supernatural visions, which spring from the Jesuit's "deep nature like a furnace white hot, which gleamed with the still intensity of his enthusiasm." Demons appear as men, women, bears, wolves, and wild cats. Angels, St. Joseph, and Mary are there. Death, like a skeleton, threatens him but falls powerless at the Jesuit's feet. Parkman quotes a letter in which the Ursuline nun Marie d'Incarnation, herself a visionary, reports that, when God revealed to Brébeuf that he was to die, the Jesuits bled him and dried his blood so they would have relics, lest his body be burned to ashes.

The contemporary novelist and essayist Tobias Wolff discovered Brébeuf through Parkman, and, though he admires his courage, is repelled by his "unshakable certainty." Brebeuf, he says, scorned the Huron beliefs, shamans, healers, and their ceremonies to control nature, but he himself played the wizard with magnifying glasses that transformed a flea into a frightful monster. The Jesuits pretended that their clock was alive, and when it struck four times was telling the Indian visitors, who otherwise would hang around the Jesuit quarters all day, to "Get up and go home." Creatures of their own time, the Jesuits depended on France for logistical support; and, in Wolff's interpretation, the Huron-Jesuit alliance contributed to the tribes' eventual destruction. Finally, Wolff argues, Brébeuf went to his death without a second thought, while Jesus in the garden of Gethsemane sweated blood and prayed for "his cup to pass."

This was the end of the Huron missions and, to a great degree, of the Hurons themselves as a people, as they scattered to the West. Of the 29 missionaries who had been there over 35 years, seven lost their lives. The Jesuits in New France would regroup, return, move West and South; but for the time being they whiffed the smell of defeat.

Down the Mississippi

The specter of Jogues and his companions hovered over the next generation of French Jesuit missionaries, as had Xavier over the generation before. In 1653 a missionary from the Far East returned to Europe to recruit volunteers for Vietnam, and 20 came forward and sailed for the Far East. Jacques Marquette, the youngest of six children, born in 1636 to a Loan family of warriors that traced it lineage back to the 12th century, joined the Society at 17. He wrote to the general early that he had wanted to be a missionary all his life. When he heard of the Vietnam expedition, he pleaded, without success, to join. When Jogues died, Jacques was ten years old. Since, like Jogues, he had no disposition for abstract theological concepts, he argued, he would like to skip that part of his training and be sent abroad right away. On a visit to the Jesuit college at LaFleche his hosts showed him the room where Isaac Jogues had slept years before. In 1666 he found himself sailing down the St. Lawrence River toward Quebec.

As with so many ordinary men of those times who could not afford to have their portraits painted, we have very little idea of what Marquette looked like. When in 1952 his portrait was commissioned for a banking firm in Peoria, the artist visited the Marquette family's descendants in Loan for inspiration, and concluded that Jacques was tall and lean and blond with thinning hair. Though not by nature a theologian, he was eloquent and quick with languages, and people seemed to love him.

To visualize this young man's early apostolic work, it helps to see a map of Michigan sticking up like a gloved mitten with Lake Huron on the right and Lake Michigan on the left, and a thin, ragged Michigan land mass stretched above, with Lake Superior on the other side. In the upper right corner a strait linking Huron and Superior separates Canada from the Michigan land on Superior's south bank. On the strait is Sault Sainte Marie, where, after two years of learning the Huron language in Three Rivers, Marquette worked for 18 months. Far to the west on Superior's south bank is LaPointe (today's Ashland), where he toiled for another 18 months. Between the northern tips of Lake Michigan and Lake Huron sits Mackinac Island, near which he cared for the Hurons who had fled from Canada and upstate New York. To Ashland came Indians from the south, the Illinois, who spoke of a great river that flowed so far south that no one knew where it emptied out; and they asked him to come and teach them.

The discovery of the Mississippi River is due to the initiative of three men. Jean Talon, the scion of a French Gallican family, educated by Jesuits, and appointed entendant of New France in 1665, was informed there was copper ore on the shore of Lake Superior and wanted to establish France's influence beyond the Great Lakes. Twenty-seven-year-old Louis Jolliet, born the year before Jogues's death and educated in the Jesuit college in Quebec that replicated the education Marquette had received at Reims, had the entrepreneurial skills to win business backing for the trip and the frontier experience to lead it. He knew a priest always went along on these trips to meet the explorers' religious needs and to pacify the Indians. Who better than Jacques?

The trip in brief. On May 17, 1673, seven Frenchmen in two canoes set out. They paddled along the western shore of Lake Michigan to Green Bay, where they picked up the Fox River and fought its many rapids down to the Wisconsin River, which eventually shot out into the Mississippi. They rode the Mississippi around the whirlpools west of the Arkansas River, right before plunging into Louisiana. There they learned both that the Mississippi emptied into the Gulf of Mexico and that they were on the brink of Spanish territory and ought to turn around. A shortcut on the Illinois River brought them to a village of

Illinois Indians, who had originally invited Marquette to come and teach them, and then to the shore of Lake Michigan, where they became the first white men to encamp on the future site of Chicago. By the end of September they reached the mission of St. Francis Xavier near Green Bay.

"We joyfully plied our paddles," writes Marquette in his journal account of their expedition—a document that bursts with the optimism and enthusiasm of an idealistic young man seeing the heartland of the New World through the eyes of a scientific observer but with the zeal of an apostle. He records the fields of wild oats, then how the oats are harvested, cleansed, dried in smoke on a slow fire, buried in a skin bag, treaded with the feet to separate the grain from the straw, winnowed, reduced to flour, boiled, and seasoned with fat, and devoured with a taste "as delicate as rice." Using his six Indian languages he talks to natives along the way who warn them of warriors downriver who will kill them and of monsters known to devour both men and their canoes. He plucks a medicinal plant which, if masticated and placed on the wound, will cure a snake bite. On June 17 they enter the legendary Mississippi "with a joy that I cannot express."

The current flows gently. The landscape changes—a chain of high mountains on the right, beautiful land on the left. Once woods and mountains disappear, the islands become more beautiful. They behold deer and wild cattle, bustards and swans "without wings." A catfish so big that it might break the canoe slams against its side. A herd of 400 strange, humped, horned beasts roams the plains, so fierce that they toss a hunter in the air with their horns, then trample him to death. A tribe of Illinois welcomes them to their village, the chief gives the French his young son as a slave, as well as a "mysterious calumet," an elaborately decorated peace pipe. At the feast they feed their guests by placing the food—sagamite (corn mush) and fish—in their mouths "as one would give food to a bird." They encounter a class of males who from their youth assume the clothing and social roles of women, and huge, beautifully painted monsters on cliffsides along the river. Other cliffs are rich in iron ore.

At the end, Marquette records in his journal that if the voyage has resulted in the salvation of one soul it would have been worth it; and he concludes that as they passed through the territory of the Illinois a dying child was brought to him as they were embarking, and he baptized it shortly before it died. Thanks to providence, one soul had been saved.

True to his promise, Marquette set out in November 1674 to revisit the Illinois tribe that had pleaded with him to return. But he was a very sick man, suffering on and off from a bloody discharge from his bowels, made worse toward the end by diarrhea; and he knew it was time for him to die. He reached his old Indian friends and visited all their cabins, and then on Holy Thursday he called them all together on a beautiful prairie, spread with mats and bearskins and decorated with four large pictures of the Blessed Virgin. Five hundred chiefs and elders encircled him and 1,500 young men, and uncounted women and children, stood around as the weakened missionary preached to them of Jesus Christ and then said Mass and good-bye, promising this time that other Blackrobes would come back.

On the way home he was so weak that he had to be carried. As the party paddled up along the southern coast of Lake Michigan, Marquette pointed to a spot at the mouth of a river, near present-day Ludington, where he said he would like to be buried. He knew how his role model Francis Xavier had died and gave detailed directions on how he should be laid out and how his hands, feet, and face should be arranged, and how to ring the bell at his last breath. He heard their confessions, wrote down his own faults, asked for forgiveness, and removed the crucifix from his neck, asking that it be held for him to see.

Two years later his companions returned to his grave, dug up his bones and bleached them in the sun, placed them in a birch-bark box, and with a funeral flotilla of 30 canoes returned him to the mission at St. Ignace to be buried in a vault under the chapel. In 1877, after the chapel had been destroyed in a fire, a local priest excavated the site and found the remains of a box whose contents had been vandalized, including a few tiny fragments of bones believed to be Marquette's. Some fragments went to a monument at his burial site and the rest, in 1882, to Marquette University in Milwaukee. All the relics together weigh less than an ounce.

History, unlike Marquette and his brothers, does not judge his work on the number of baptisms. Though much of the Jesuit record in New France has the scent of failure, historian James Axtell, in *The Invasion Within* (1985), a study of the clash of cultures between Indians and Europeans on the frontier, says the French Jesuits, because they were better educated, learned the languages, and adopted the savages' cultural symbols such as peace pipes, made more converts than the English missionaries. Axtell also points out that "while being wracked by disease, war and dislocation, the Indians successfully conveyed to large numbers of adversaries, through a remarkable process of education, their own ineluctable pride, social warmth, and cultural integrity."

The Jesuits had approached the Indians with their own strengths and weaknesses. In their training, Latin exercises and religious drama had made them eloquent, a necessary skill in a culture where the Indians themselves, with a complex and highly structured language, were masters of rhetoric. For the Jesuits, the ability to address a tribal council in the midst of controversy could mean life or death. Their Ignatian spirituality enabled them to be in the world without being swallowed by it. They had a strategy: (1) get to the tribal leaders, (2) confront and defeat the shamans who controlled a superstitious religious culture, (3) give institutional support to new converts.

But the disadvantages were strong. Their long robes were effeminate and an obstacle in traveling; their beards and haircuts were, in the local view, ugly; they had no interest in women; their vow of poverty made them dependent on others, unable to dispense gifts other than trinkets. They didn't carry guns. The Blackrobes answered these objections by their moral probity. They were not after money or other men's women. Their donnés, laymen committed to the Society, helped with logistics and carried guns. They faced death with courage. When Jogues returned as a peace ambassador to the village that had tortured him, when Brébeuf suffered without tears, the Indians knew these men were special.

Axtell concludes, based on the work of other historians and his analysis of statistics in the *Relations,* that, putting aside the infant and deathbed baptisms, more than 10,000 natives, mostly adults, chose to become Christians. They made this choice because Catholicism, with its optimism, liturgy, art, music, and incense, appealed to the senses. Its attitude toward women, with the nuns and its cult of the Virgin Mary, gave women attractive role models. Most important, the Jesuits "practiced a brand of cultural relativism, without, however, succumbing to ethical neutrality."

Nevertheless, in the judgment of Francis Parkman, influenced by his progressive theory of history in which the French and Jesuits represented the forces of superstition and autocracy and the English represented the Enlightenment, the Jesuits' dream failed because they could not overcome the tomahawks and guns of the Iroquois. Had the Jesuits tamed the "savages," he predicts, the "savages" would have concentrated on agriculture, increased in population, enriched France with the fur trade, and established communities throughout the West ruled by the principles of Richelieu and Loyola. But Liberty, represented by the English colonies, would be sacrificed. For Parkman, the Iroquois were an instrument of Providence so that Liberty in time would prevail. "Meanwhile," he concludes, "let those who have prevailed yield due honor to the defeated. Their virtues shine amidst the rubbish of error, like diamonds and gold in the gravel of the torrent."

Meanwhile, in the Southwest

When Eusebio Kino was born in Segno, Italy, in 1645, Jacques Marquette was eight years old. When Marquette died in 1675, Kino had been a Jesuit for just three years and was studying mathematics in Upper Germany in preparation for what he hoped would be an assignment to China, where, in the footsteps of Matteo Ricci, he might gain access to the intellectual class and introduce them to Jesus Christ. Having dreamed of China, in a decision made by drawing lots with a friend, Kino was sent to Mexico, but, like many of his brother Jesuits, lost two years in Spain waiting to sail.

After years of delayed expectations, a group of 15 Jesuits led by Father Pedro Sanchez had arrived in Mexico City in 1572. Within ten years, they established the first Jesuit college in North America and a network of institutions that would spread in New Spain the missions of Arizona and California. The Franciscans had preceded them and reached out to the mountains to the north and east but left much of the western coast to the Jesuits. By 1654 the baptism registers for the whole mission system listed 400,000 names.

In 1681 Kino finally arrived in Mexico City, where, ever the mathematician, he quickly published a little book about the comet of 1680, which he had observed while waiting for a boat for two years in Cadiz. Thus he stumbled inadvertently into an academic cat fight, which missionaries, by vocation, usually avoid.

But Kino, Italian born and German educated, had first seen himself as an intellectual missionary and loved to express himself in print

—in a historical memoir kept from 1683 to 1711, in letters to distinguished persons such as King Philip V, and on a current controversy over how to interpret the mysterious appearance of a far-away speck of light in the night sky. While Kino was waiting in Cadiz, the noted Jesuit-educated Mexican scholar Siguenza y Gongora of the Royal University of Mexico had already published a learned and witty put-down of astrologers who interpreted their superstitions as natural phenomena. When Kino arrived, Siguenza befriended him and lent him maps of California. Kino did not mention his own pamphlet, already in press, until the day he left. There he argued that comets are warnings of events to come, and this was clear to everybody, "unless there be some dull wits who cannot perceive it."

As he prepared to leave town, Kino handed his colleague a copy, told him it would "give him something to write about," and headed for mission country. Siguenza exploded, griped that Kino had failed to return his maps and left them tattered and torn, and wrote a bitter reply—which did not appear for eight years.

From 1861 to 1685 Kino worked in Lower California, first at LePaz and then at San Bruno. Here he developed his expertise in map making, wrote, and drew close to the Indians, especially the youths, who were his pastoral responsibility. His preference for the exotic East, the footsteps of Francis Xavier and Matteo Ricci, died hard, and he corresponded with a noblewoman who might be able to help him get a better job. But he was captivated by the land, the geography, which he recorded meticulously, and the pearls, the key to this territory's future. But a combination of factors—hostile Indians, drought, epidemic, money problems, and leadership failures—led the Jesuits to withdraw and redistribute their manpower.

As with Marquette, we understand Kino's accomplishments best by consulting a map: one centered on the northern part of the Sea of California, with Mexico's Sonoma Province to the east, Lower California to the west. The Rio Grande flows across the top, separating Mexico from Arizona and New Mexico, and the Colorado River comes down from the north and joins the Rio Grande to flow south into the Gulf of Mexico. A dozen or so rivers flow down from the Mexican mountains and also empty into the gulf's east banks, while along the rivers' courses spread Indian villages and missions. Some, clustered around Our Lady of Sorrows, Kino's headquarters, between the 30th and 31st parallels, are as close as ten miles from one to another.

Superimpose on this the routes of Kino's 35 expeditions over 24 years from 1687 to 1711. In Kino's day this territory was called Pimeria, or Pimeria Alta, named for the Pima tribes, the objects of Kino's apostolic work. The Pimas were considered more peaceful, docile, and amenable to the mission's goals than their warlike neighbors. From the east came hostile Apache tribes, into whose territory the Spanish troops and Pima warriors would ride to punish them for their raids. Kino, by his extraordinary energy and organizational skills, soon made himself at home in and to some degree the master of this land.

In 1708 Kino, now the religious superior, writes to the missions' sponsor, King Philip V of Spain (1700–1746), to report on their progress and to ask His Majesty to furnish "about fifty missionary fathers, all with their customary alms or necessary supplies," to achieve the "extensive conquests" Kino has laid out. He has baptized in 21 years 4,500 souls. He could have baptized many more had not the conquest of California been suspended. Borrowing from Columbus, who referred to "Seven Cities" in the West Indies, he describes "Seven New Kingdoms" in the vicinity waiting to be developed, including New Mexico; Lower California; Upper California, which is California today; and Gran Teguayo, which today is Utah, and in those days, says Kino, reached to the sea discovered by Henry Hudson in 1612.

Kino's biographer, Herbert Eugene Bolton, the University of California at Berkeley professor who has been described as having done for the Southwest what Francis Parkman did for the French, has in several works spelled out Kino's achievements in a way that justifies the Kino statue in the National Statuary Hall and leaves his readers in awe. He was the first to thoroughly explore the Pimeria Alta country to which he was assigned. He made at least 14 expeditions into what is now Arizona. He had come to America thinking that California was a peninsula, only to find that conventional wisdom here was the opposite. Provoked by the local discovery of blue shells, which he had originally seen on the Pacific Coast, he made several trips down the Colorado River in 1700 and 1702 and observed the position of the sun to become convinced that there was a land route to California.

Kino was one of the first great horse and cattle kings of the West. Beginning with small herds collected from older missions, he established the stock-raising industry that still remained in over 20 locations in the early 20th century—all not for private or Jesuit profit but to feed the Indians at the established missions and give them financial independence. As a horseman, in his 50s, he would ride 800 miles in 30 days, 1,500 miles in 53 days, an average of 30 or more miles a day for weeks and months at a time. One morning in May 1700, he received word from a Jesuit colleague that a poor Indian they knew was about to be executed the following day at San Ignatio, 70 miles away. Riding through the night, Kino made the trip in less than a day and saved the Indian's life.

Inevitably, with his strong personality, Kino stirred up controversy. The fire for martyrdom that had inspired so many French Jesuits was shared in the Spanish missions. When young Francis Xavier Saeta, described as "of the best blood of Sicily," arrived in Caborea to establish a new mission called Conception, Kino furnished him with cattle, sheep, goats, and horses. Saeta was an enthusiastic apostle and successful fund-raiser. His mission boomed. When Kino invited him to his headquarters for Holy Week, Saeta was too engaged with his flock to accept. Suddenly, because of a local squabble between Pima Indians and their overseers, a band of Pimas went on the warpath, killed several people, and headed to Conception. First they pretended to Saeta that they were peaceful. Then they drew their bows and, as he knelt, pierced him with two arrows. The arrows sticking in him as he got up, he ran to his room, embraced his crucifix, and fell dead. The warriors finished him off with another volley of 22 shots as he lay at their feet.

Kino was determined that the culprits should be punished, and the army, by raids, arrests, and rewards, induced the natives to offer up the guilty. But the next phase of arresting the accomplices got out of control. At a "peace" meeting of 50 Indians and soldiers, the soldiers surrounded the Indians and began making arrests. One Indian suspect was peremptorily beheaded. The soldiers shot 48 natives, most of them innocent of the crime. The uprising spread for several months, until Kino helped establish a peace in which the killers and accomplices would be handed over and the missions that had been destroyed would be restored.

Meanwhile, the spreading news of Saeta's martyrdom was interpreted as an occasion to rejoice. Kino wrote a book and drew a map boldly exploiting Saeta's death to publicize the mission and its needs —for more young men like Saeta generous enough to die. Kino's Jesuit superiors were told by his many critics that he didn't really know the Pima language well, and that he baptized without proper instruction;

but Kino survived the criticisms, much of it from jealous men or Spaniards or Mexicans who resented an Italian, whom they often called a German. But Kino overreached in his efforts to assure the punishment —and execution—of Saeta's killers. The provincial forced their release, and eventually they were pardoned.

The priest who succeeded Kino when he died in 1711 described him as tough and very humble. He would weep while reading his breviary. He would angrily reprimand a sinner, but humbly absorb all criticism of himself. After supper, when others went to bed, Kino would retire to the chapel and often spend the whole night there. Sometimes he would have himself whipped for penance. He took his food without salt or seasoning so it would taste bad. He took no tobacco, snuff, nor wine, and slept not in a bed but on a horse blanket with a saddle as a pillow. Sick with fever for days, he would just say Mass and get back to bed. He died at 67.

For another 50 years or so, at the request of local Spanish bishops and the virtual command of the King of Spain, the Society sent men of various nationalities to continue Kino's work, with varying degrees of success. Beginning in 1759 and culminating with a decree of the pope in 1773, the crown heads of Portugal, France, Naples, and Parma, and finally the Vatican, became convinced that the Society of Jesus was a threat to the established order and was to be suppressed. Throughout the world Jesuits were deprived of their property, herded into ships headed they knew not where, and forced to create new lives for themselves as laymen, diocesan priests, or Jesuits in exile wherever they might find a haven.

A *Relation* by Francis Philibert Watrin, one of those expelled in 1762 from Louisiana, may be typical of what his brothers experienced throughout the country. The royal decree was presented to the council of New Orleans, composed not of scholars but of shopkeepers, businessmen, and army officers, to execute. The council decided that the Society of Jesus was "hostile to the royal authority, the rights of the bishops, and the public peace and safety," and their vows were now officially nullified. Their property was to be auctioned, their chapel ornaments given to the Capuchins, their chapel demolished. They could keep their clothes and their books and board the first boat to France.

With them sailed 48 Negroes, their former slaves who now belonged to the king. But with no one to care for them, the slaves clung to their former masters, who shared whatever they had.

PART II

Suppression and Return

4

Death and Resurrection

How Could This Happen?

How could it happen that a powerful international religious society of almost 20,000 men, faithful to the pope, confessors to kings, with colleges and mission outposts all over the world, ceased to exist in a four-stage process over 14 years?

Historians suggest three reasons that are intellectual, political, and personal: the rise of the Enlightenment—the Age of Reason—an intellectual force contrary to the Jesuit mindset which took its basic inspiration from the classical tradition and the Middle Ages; the emergence of the nation-state and the resurgence of the conflict between the Gallicans, who were loyal above all to the monarch, and the Ultramontanes, faithful to the Roman pontiff; and the weaknesses within the Society itself in terms of vocations, training, imagination, and leadership.

There were other factors as well. Jansenism, a rigoristic spiritual doctrine which argued, contrary to a more optimistic Jesuit theology, that very few souls were destined to be saved, was still influential in the Low Countries, in France, and in Italy. Jesuits, on the other hand, held a moral system called probabilism, which allowed a person the freedom of conscience to form a moral opinion and act on it if the opinion was probably true, even if a contrary moral opinion seemed more true. The opinion was considered probable if either the reasons were cogent or several reputable authors, though not the majority, held the same opinion. Thus the enemies of the Jesuits charged them with moral laxity. Furthermore, the Spanish Jesuit theologian Francisco Suarez's rejection of the divine right of kings and his theory that civil authority emerges from the people won the Jesuits no friends at court. But, as William Bangert says, the crushing blow was the Enlightenment, personified in Locke, Diderot, Hume, and Voltaire—Voltaire and Diderot were Jesuit educated—and identified by Peter

Gay with the rise of modern paganism, which "swelled to flood tide the waters that swept away the old order. Among the more considerable victims was the Society." Numerically, the Society had been growing, but "its roots were being washed loose by the rushing waters of the new age." The Enlightenment philosophers, Bangert suggests, were alienated from the spiritual tradition of the Middle Ages and the reform movements, Catholic and Protestant, of the 16th century and united in a pact to destroy revealed religion.

Meanwhile, although the Society had an impressive list of scientists and astronomers such as the great Croatian Roger Joseph Boscovich and some Jesuits sought to harmonize Enlightenment thought with Catholic tradition, it had failed to adapt to a changing world. The *Ratio Studiorum,* the official guide for Jesuit educators, had not been revised since first issued in 1599. The Society opened two elite schools in Spain specifically for the sons of the nobility, signaling a blindness to the more democratic social movements that would soon erupt. Because it was stuck with the ossified formulas in their old textbooks, a more serious problem was the Society's failure to deal with theological issues posed by the deists. Overly reliant on the Greek and Roman classics in their humanities classes, the Jesuits did not teach their students to write their own vernacular languages well. Pupils untrained to write a good letter were ill-prepared to defend the faith.

Ironically, Portugal, the first nation to sponsor Jesuit missionary expeditions to India and the Far East, had hatched a nemesis—Sebastiao Jose de Carvalho e Mello, better known as Pombal, Portugal's chief minister in 1750—who would put in motion the Jesuit exile. When some Jesuits suggested that the Lisbon earthquake of 1755 was a punishment for Portugal's sins, when 29,000 Guarani Indians in the Jesuits' Paraguay reduction under Portuguese jurisdiction resisted their new rulers and got Jesuit support, when someone shot and wounded the king in 1758, Pombal's propaganda machine riled public opinion against the Jesuits. Outlawed in 1759, in 1762 all 1,100 Jesuits were banished from Portugal and 250 were thrown in prison.

In 1764 the Society was dissolved in France, though its members could still live there, and in 1767, in Spain, then in Naples and Parma. Finally in 1773, Pope Clement XIV's brief, *Dominus ac Redemptor,* abolished the Society altogether—without explaining why, except to say for the sake of Christian peace. The most recent Jesuit history, Jonathan Wright's *God's Soldiers,* concludes that the "suppression might be best understood as a naked act of 18th century statecraft" that "didn't have to happen and that its agents would come to regret."

John Carroll and Anthony Kohlmann

When the 37-year-old Maryland Jesuit John Carroll learned of his order's suppression, he was at the English Jesuits' college in the beautiful medieval Belgian town of Bruges. He had returned not long before from a nearly two-year tour of Europe as mentor-companion of a young English nobleman, Charles Stourton, age 18. He had witnessed the last gasps of the old regime. And in Rome he had also heard rumors that the new pope was committed to the Society's suppression. He wrote to his Jesuit brothers in Liège that their fate seemed sealed. After the final word reached Bruges on September 5, he wrote to his brother Dan that "our long persecuted, and I must add holy, Society is no more. God's will be done." The greatest gift God could give him, he added, "would be immediate death." If God were to deny him this comfort, "may his holy and adorable design on me be wholly fulfilled."

Carroll's father had died shortly after he left Maryland in 1748, and he had not seen his home or family since. After a brief childhood education at a short-lived Jesuit school at Bohemia Manor, he had said farewell at age 12 and sailed with his cousin Charles Carroll, future signer of the Declaration of Independence, to France. There at St. Omer's, the English Jesuit refugee school for some of the upper-class and wealthy American Catholic landowners, he and Charles prepared for what would inevitably be leadership roles in the emerging American nation. When Charles returned home, John remained and joined the Society of Jesus, went through its long course of studies, taught school, and was ordained, as far as records can tell us, probably in 1769.

The Maryland to which John Carroll returned had changed in that it was on the brink of a revolution to which his family was committed, but the anti-Catholic laws were still on the books, and some of the Founding Fathers, including Samuel Adams, John Adams, and John Jay, were steeped in bigotry. Nevertheless, in April 1776, Congress asked Carroll to join a delegation of Benjamin Franklin, Samuel Chase, and his cousin Charles on a generally unsuccessful diplomatic mission to gain Canadian, support for American independence, mainly from Quebec.

After the war, Carroll, who had ministered to Maryland Catholics with his mother's home as a base, began to assess the broader needs of the American church and to take some initiative. For the most part, his fellow ex-Jesuits were aging, indolent, living in the past. One father, John Lewis, acted as religious superior under London's nominal jurisdiction. Collectively they did not want a bishop because one selected by British church authorities would compromise the new rapport between Catholics and other patriots which the Catholic contribution to the American Revolution had established.

If the image of John Carroll is strong today it is because of the majestic statue that greets visitors inside the front gate of the Georgetown University campus and the Gilbert Stuart portrait showing him in his ecclesiastical robes that hangs in the university president's office. In 1789, the same year in which he was elected by his fellow priests as bishop of Baltimore, Carroll founded Georgetown College so that Catholic boys like himself would not have to go abroad for a Catholic education, or to Philadelphia to attend the nonsectarian University of Pennsylvania, the only American school at the time to welcome them. Meanwhile, the Society would be partially restored in the United States through its affiliation in 1805 with the remnant that had survived in Russia thanks to the patronage of the empress, Catherine the Great. Carroll had supported the petition of his fellow ex-Jesuits to reassemble under Russian protection; but when it came to his actually signing the pledge to join them, he backed down.

Yet, whatever his ambivalence, he was quick to call on the reactivated Jesuits for manpower. He had had bad luck staffing the small parish of St. Peter's in New York, until the arrival in 1808 of fathers Anthony Kohlmann, an Alsatian who had joined the Fathers of the Sacred Heart, one of the several associations former Jesuits had formed to anticipate the Society's return; and young Benedict Fenwick, a descendant of an old Maryland family, who had entered the novitiate at Georgetown in 1806. Four Jesuit scholastics also arrived and quickly revived the failing parish. They preached in English, French, and German, and the New Yorkers flocked to Mass and communion and contributed alms for the poor.

The Jesuits' accomplishments reached even the famous patriot-deist Thomas Paine. Dying in agony in Greenwich Village and having been advised that the fathers might help, he summoned them to his bedside. The housekeeper warned the priests that Paine at one moment cried to God for help and in the next denied his existence. When the learned Kohlmann tried to open a discussion on Paine's *Age of Reason*, Paine told him to be still. When Fenwick tried to prove God's existence, Paine cursed and told the men to get out. Being reminded that he had invited them, Paine calmed down. Finally, when it dawned on the missionaries that Paine mistakenly believed they had some special medicines that doctors lacked, Fenwick confessed they had cures only for the soul. Adding a few more "blasphemies," the forgotten hero of the Revolution told them to go home.

Kohlmann's proudest project was the foundation of the New York Literary Institution, a boy's boarding school outside the city on the site of the present Saint Patrick's Cathedral. It had an enrollment of between 30 and 40 boys who were taught English, Latin, Greek, French, and possibly Spanish and Italian, and were given a strong course in mathematics. Tuition, room, and board were $200 a year, and the clientele included the sons of New York governors. The Institution's brief existence is one of the intriguing might-have-been tales in American Jesuit history. In 1812 John Anthony Grassi, an Italian who arrived in the United States in 1810, was appointed superior of the American Jesuits and rector of Georgetown College. Perhaps under the influence of three old Maryland Jesuits, brothers in the Neale family, and certainly acting under the direction of Archbishop Carroll, Grassi decided that there were not enough Jesuits to staff both schools and closed the new one in New York. Under protest, the bitter Kohlmann was brought back to Georgetown to teach theology.

Before leaving, however, Kohlmann enjoyed the limelight in a famous criminal trial. After hearing a thief's sacramental confession, Kohlmann served as an intermediary for him in order to make restitution for the penitent's theft. Later questioned by the police, grand jury, and the court, Kohlmann refused to reveal the penitent's name, using the sacred seal of confession as his defense. To Kohlmann's disappointment, after two Protestant lawyers spoke in his favor the district attorney decided to not pursue the issue. Kohlmann wanted to use his day in court to deliver an oration on the virtues of auricular confession and to publish a pamphlet on confessional secrecy, which he would sell to raise funds for a new Saint Patrick's Cathedral. Under pressure from the Saint Patrick's trustees, the district attorney relented, and for two days Kohlmann debated the issue before a bench of four judges headed by DeWitt Clinton, mayor of New York. Clinton delivered the unanimous ruling of the bench. In the ruling which Clinton later put into law, "no minister of the Gospel, or priest of any denomination whatsoever, shall be allowed to disclose any confession made to him in his professional character." The logic of the decision, however, was based not so much on the nature of the sacrament as on what the priest would suffer—in the violation of his conscience, in the punishments to be administered by the church, loss of income, alienation from his congregation, and the fear of hell—if he broke the seal.

Once John Carroll became bishop and got older and thought back on his life as a Jesuit, the Society's faults—its own responsibility for its suppression—moved to the front of his mind. Why did many Catholics as well as the enemies of religion hate them? What was gained by the Jesuits' strict adherence to Thomistic philosophy rather than allowing a variety of opinions? Where were the men who really knew the mind of Ignatius? Why had not the English provincial sent their best men to the American mission? Did the Society have full canonical rights—that is, since the Society had been disbanded by a papal decree, to what degree were their previous rights, such as their property rights, still protected?—during this period of partial restoration, 1806–1814, or was it subject to the bishop himself during these times? When Jesuits who had waited in Russia moved to the United States and impatiently demanded repossession of the properties the suppression had absorbed, Carroll replied that if it were not for him these Jesuits would not have had a Russian haven. Had the suppression perhaps been providential?

What Happened to John Carroll's Vision of America?

In a historian's broader perspective John Carroll is important beyond his relationship with the Jesuits and Georgetown. As the first American bishop, he brilliantly read the role of Catholics as both American and Catholic and boldly tried to build a new Church as loyal to the spiritual leadership of Rome but on independent native structures.

Following a meeting with clergy representatives in 1783 at the Jesuit plantation at Whitemarsh, the group drew up a constitution to govern themselves and preserve their property. If they were to have a bishop he must be an American. Rome agreed, and following some unsolicited advice from Benjamin Franklin, in 1784 appointed Carroll to direct the mission until the election, which in 1789 chose Carroll.

In *The American Catholic Experience* (1985), Jay Dolan lists five elements of Carroll's vision, parts of which he labels the American Enlightenment, the adaptation of some 18th-century democratic ideals to Catholic progress: (1) As *independent,* loyalty to the pope as spiritual head was to be their only connection with Rome. (2) They were a *national* church that would reflect the national spirit. In practice that meant a native clergy, not an imported priesthood; so Carroll established both Georgetown and St. Mary's Seminary in Baltimore. In the meantime, he demanded that Europeans both learn English and study our Constitution, laws, and customs. (3) Following the example of Lord Baltimore in the 17th century, who refused to allow the Jesuits any special privileges and was stung by how the Protestant takeover of Maryland killed religious toleration, Carroll insisted on separation of church and state. The Catholic Enlightenment started in Europe and England to bridge the gap between Catholicism and the Age of Reason.

In Carroll's perception, America was proving to the world that "general and equal toleration, by giving a free circulation to fair argument, is the most effectual method to bring all denominations of Christians to a unity of faith." Dolan observes that it took about 100 years before the church, at the Second Vatican Council, would endorse the position of the Catholic Enlightenment. (4) Prospective converts had to be persuaded by reason. Therefore, worship services should be in English, not Latin. The Philadelphia publisher Mathew Carey put out an English Catholic Bible in 1790. (5) Finally, the trustee system, a movement that came from Europe, gave the laity unprecedented participation in local church governance. In practice, the paying pew holders made major decisions, including buying the property, building the church, and sometimes hiring and firing the priests. Conflicts between bishops and trustees would tear apart the church for the first half of the 19th century, until the new dominance of the Irish immigrant church, with its traditional respect for the priest's authority, plus the you-do-what-I-say personality of New York's Archbishop John Hughes, would kill the movement.

In 1790, when Carroll traveled back to England to be ordained bishop of Baltimore, there were about 35,000 American Catholics, mostly in Maryland and Pennsylvania, and a few in New York and Boston, plus some who had migrated to Kentucky or as far west as Detroit. In 1791, when Carroll convened a church synod in Baltimore to set procedures for the country, with 22 priests attending, nothing innovative came out of it. As Dolan concludes, the hoped-for new relationship between the Catholic Church and the modern world "never happened." John Carroll, once he became bishop, frightened by the anarchy of the French Revolution, began to think in terms of preserving his own authority. He turned against the vernacular liturgy and no longer supported the election of bishops.

Carroll's desire for American priests was shattered. In the 1790s the overwhelming majority of American priests—in synods and seminaries—were foreign born. Many were refugees from the French Revolution seeking asylum, and most Jesuits were Europeans whose ideas would clash with those of American Jesuits. How could the Society of Jesus revitalize itself while divided by both language and political ideology?

In Dolan's analysis, when Carroll died in 1815 Catholicism was predominantly a Southern church stuck in the slave-holding culture, with membership concentrated in Maryland and Kentucky, both states with slave-based economies. James Hennesey, S.J., writes in *American Catholics* (1981): "Jesuits bought, kept, and sold black slaves . . . never was there an indication that either priests or lay people saw slavery as morally wrong." Carroll reported that there were about 3,000 Catholic slaves in Maryland. Carroll, in defending clergy accused of mistreating their slaves, was content to say that priests "treat their Negroes with great mildness and guard them from hunger and nakedness. They work less and are much better fed, lodged and clothed, than labouring men in almost any part of Europe."

At Carroll's death the question was whether the American church would forge a unique identity for itself or imitate the Rome-centered church of Europe. The answer would come from a century of immigration, 1820–1920, and from the Jesuits who came, fanned out across the country, and built their parishes, schools, and universities.

"I Do Not Like the Late Resurrection"

Not all the American leadership class was happy about the Jesuits' return. John Adams and Thomas Jefferson, intellectuals as they were, were interested in everything; and in a correspondence which sealed the friendship of former rivals until their deaths within hours of one another, they often wrote about what they were reading; but they sometimes wrote about religion and Jesuits. On May 6, 1816, Adams wrote:

> I do not like the late Resurrection of the Jesuits. They have a General, now in Russia, in correspondence with the Jesuits in the U. S. who are more numerous than every body knows. Shall we not have Swarms of them here? In as many shapes and disguises as ever the king of the Gypsies . . . assumed? In the shape of Printers, Editors, Writers School masters etc. I have lately read Pascalls Letters over again, and four Volumes of the History of the Jesuits. If ever any Congregation of Men could merit eternal Perdition on Earth and in Hell, According to these Historians though like Pascal true Catholicks, it is this Company of Loiola. Our System however of Religious Liberty must afford them an Asylum. But if they do not put the Purity of our Elections to a severe Tryal, it will be a Wonder.

On August 1, 1816, Jefferson replied:

> I dislike, with you, their restoration; because it marks a retrograde step from light to darkness. We shall have our follies without doubt. Some one or more of them will always be afloat. But ours will be the follies of enthusiasm, not of bigotry, not of Jesuitism. Bigotry is a disease of ignorance, of morbid minds; enthusiasm of the free and buoyant. Education and free discussion are the antidotes of both. We are destined to be a barrier against the returns of ignorance and barbarism. Old Europe will have to lean on our shoulders, and to hobble along at our side, under the monkish trammels of priests and kings, as she can.

Without intending to do so, the founders were laying out a formula by which Jesuit education might succeed.

5

The New America

Into Missouri

The period in which the Jesuits reestablished themselves in the New World has been called the Age of Jackson, an era of growth and confidence in which America, having defeated Great Britain more decisively at New Orleans in the War of 1812, was born again—this time in the image of a democrat and frontiersman. It was the era of the industrial revolution, the factory, the urban immigrant and working man, the penny press—the birth of daily newspapers like the New York *Sun, Herald,* and *Tribune*—of a literary renaissance, and social and religious reform. Wagon trains went West, and the great moral issue was whether it is right for one human being to own another. The French aristocrat Alexis de Tocqueville traveled throughout the country for nine months in 1831–1832, ostensibly studying the prison system but also drawing conclusions about the relationship, or tension, between democracy and religion. Equality, he says in *Democracy in America,* tends to both isolate men from one another and to "lay open the soul to an inordinate love of material gratification. The greatest advantage of religion is to inspire diametrically contrary principles."

The Society was restored very much in the manner it had been suppressed—gradually—as year by year each country that had expelled the Jesuits saw fit to bring them back. Three factors contributing to the restoration were the breakdown of the Bourbon opposition, the success of the Society in Russia where it had been protected, and the election of a new pope, Pius VII, who was determined to sanction the return. He did so on August 7, 1814, in the bull *Sollicitudo Omnium Ecclesiarum.* Historian Fr. William Bangert points out that in its absence the Society had missed the French Revolution and the rule of Napoleon Bonaparte, one of the great turning points in world history, and asks how well they would have weathered the storm.

In Europe, the restored Society often remained tied to the world that was gone. In America the separation of church and state gave it a rare opportunity to thrive in a new spirit of freedom. The 600 men who constituted the Society in 1814 were old men from 1773, former members of associations formed in anticipation of the Society's return, men who allied themselves with the remnant in White Russia, and secular priests who recently joined. All suffered from lack of strong leadership. The 18th general, Lorenzo Ricci, had been imprisoned in Rome's Castel San Angelo, where he died in 1775.

Not until 1829, six generals or vicar generals later, did a strong enough man emerge to get the Society moving again: Joannes Roothaan, the 21st general, a 44-year-old Dutchman. He concentrated on the basics: deeper study of the *Spiritual Exercises;* a return to the missionary spirit; and updating the *Ratio Studiorum* to emphasize vernacular language, modern philosophical trends, mathematics, history, geography, and science. Nevertheless, the Society was continuously harassed, and over the next 50 years from time to time was expelled from Italy, Spain, France, Germany, Switzerland, Guatemala, and Nicaragua. All of which made more Jesuits available for North America.

Consistent with the frontier spirit, their strategy worked swiftly. Step 1: start a school—or, as most often happened in the beginning, take over a school that either a local bishop had begun or another religious order had founded and wished to pass along. Step 2: get a reputation for good teaching, discipline, and personal attention. This attracts the leading families. The schools' success was often due to the enthusiasm of the "regents," the Jesuit scholastics who were between their philosophy studies and theology who teach and mentor in the "colleges." In the 19th century, before Jesuit schools conformed to the American accreditation system, a college could mean seven or more years from grammar school through a Master's degree, where the boys would be formed into young Christian gentlemen by a combination of classical literature, rigid dormitory rules, study halls, academic competitions, religious exercises, and sports. The tradition carried on into the 20th century, as Campion High School at Prairie de Chien, Wisconsin, advertised in the 1960s: "Send us a boy, get back a man."

Once the school was underway, the Jesuits branched out into other activities. For example, in 1846 New York's Archbishop John Hughes brought the French Jesuits from the failing St. Mary's College in Kentucky to take over struggling St. John's College and seminary in the Bronx, the future Fordham University. No sooner had they arrived than they fanned out into surrounding localities to set up new projects. Among them were parishes in Manhattan, where they were resented by local clergy because their sermons were better prepared than those of the parish priests, and because they sought out community leaders to gain influence and to start another college, Xavier, with a new church, on 16th Street. Xavier grew and for a while surpassed St. John's in prestige and enrollment. In the 20th century it retained its high school status as a military school. Typically, what began in the 19th century as a college in the middle of a city would grow into either a large urban or suburban university by the mid-20th century. Fordham began in the Bronx, which was then the country, remained there as the urban Bronx surrounded it, then in the 1960s reached back into Manhattan and built a second campus.

The revised *Ratio* was mainly a manual of practical pedagogical principles, some still operative, which have traditionally made Jesuit teaching special: (1) *Eloquentia perfecta:* write and speak well; (2) pray for knowledge, but work as if learning depends on you; (3) make a daily schedule, including breaks, and stick to it; (4) don't be late, and come to class prepared to contribute; (5) talk with friends about what you learn; (6) do more, *magis,* than what is assigned.

John O'Malley, S.J., in *The First Jesuits* (1993), summarizes the basic ideas underlying the developing system. Because the schools were endowed, they charged no tuition. American schools, for many reasons, had to be exempt from this rule. Though they attracted the sons of the elite, they accepted those of every social class. They stressed character formation, which was often achieved through the learning environment and religious exercises rather than through class assignments. The curriculum moved students systematically through higher and higher stages of learning. Jesuits loved their students and treated them as individuals, trying to influence them by example rather than words.

Although the schools spread as the work of distinct groups of immigrant Jesuits—particularly those from France, Germany, and Italy—many communities were mixed. By fall 1846, for example, the Fordham Rose Hill (Bronx) residence housed 47 men, of whom 25 were working at St. John's College, and 18 of these had come up from Kentucky. Of the others, some were community support men and others used Fordham as a springboard for other projects. Of the original 47, six left the Society; of the remaining 41, 19 were French, 11 Irish, 6

Canadian, 3 Germans, only 3 Americans, and one each from England, Spain, Belgium, Haiti, and Czechoslovakia.

We can only guess how well they got along. The rules said to speak English, but a few spoke it so badly that other students had no idea what they said. When Edgar Allan Poe, a recent widower who lived nearby, visited the manor house for intellectual conversation and a glass of wine, he enjoyed long walks with 23-year-old Edward Doucet, to whom he unburdened himself in French.

Meanwhile, the vast spreading-out of the society began in 1821 when Kohlmann, superior of what would in 1833 be designated the Maryland (or mother) Province, discovered that the seven Belgians he had admitted to the Whitemarsh novitiate were starving, living on potatoes and water. Should he dismiss them because he could not afford to feed them? Coming to the rescue, Bishop William DuBourg of St. Louis had learned of their plight and invited them west. With their novice master, Charles Van Quickenborne, three brothers, and another priest, they sailed down the Ohio River in 1823 on rafts to the confluence of the Ohio and the Mississippi and walked up to St. Louis. This group would grow into the Missouri Province. In 1820 the diocesan priests of St. Louis transferred their 1818 Saint Louis Academy to the Jesuits at Florissant; this would become Saint Louis University, the second oldest Jesuit university, and for generations of Jesuits it was a center of research on Jesuit spirituality and a school of philosophy called Missouri Thomism.

The Staging Areas Were the Basis of the Developing System

This was the beginning of a process which Philip Gleason describes as "staging areas," a deliberate pattern of growth in which Jesuit education, during its first century in America, fanned out across the country from nuclei—first in a border state (Maryland) and the Mississippi Valley (St. Louis), then in urban centers with high Catholic populations. As the list of Jesuit institutions grows, it begins to resemble the genealogies in the Bible in which one patriarch "begat" 12 sons and each of them "begat" more. Like the seeds sown in the gospels, a number of institutions were short-lived, several merged or took other forms. Some retired when they had accomplished their purpose.

This overview will not account for high schools, since what were originally called colleges were, in contemporary terms, often high schools that gave birth to modern colleges and universities. Nor will it account for the Jesuit seminaries and theologates, which have histories of their own. It will concentrate on those that have survived as colleges and universities, though not necessarily under the same name they had at the start. For the most part, each name represents not just an institution of higher learning but also a university or parish church with its own preachers and confessors, its grammar school and host of spiritual programs, retreats, and charitable and social societies. One motif is the missionary impact—English, French, Italian, and German. Another is the sense of a national network in which the great majority of these men are involved, shuttled from place to place whenever a Jesuit authority decides Father is needed somewhere else—or is causing too much trouble where he is. (Each school is here referred to with the founding date it officially claims.)

The first patriarch or staging area was Georgetown (1789), with offshoots in the Northeast—Holy Cross in Worcester (1843), Saint Joseph's University in Philadelphia (1851), Loyola College in Baltimore (1852), Boston College (1863), and Saint Peter's College in Jersey City (1872).

In stage two, Saint Louis University (1818), a spin-off from Georgetown, led to Xavier University in Cincinnati (1831), Loyola University in Chicago (1870), the University of Detroit-Mercy (1877), Creighton in Omaha (1878), and Marquette in Milwaukee (1881).

When Italian Jesuits who were originally attracted to the Rocky Mountain missions moved down to San Francisco during the Gold Rush, the third staging area gave birth to Santa Clara (1851), San Francisco (1855), Gonzaga in Spokane (1887), and Seattle (1891). Loyola in Los Angeles (now Loyola-Marymount) was given by the Vincentians to the Jesuits in 1914. A different group of Italian Jesuits started Regis in Denver (1888). Rockhurst (1910) in Kansas City, Missouri, stems from Missouri Province interest in Indian missions and the Great Plains.

Fourth, before the Civil War, French Jesuits who came to Kentucky in 1831 spread out to New York to take over St. John's College (Fordham) in 1846, to the Gulf Coast and Spring Hill in Mobile (1830), and to Loyola in New Orleans (1912).

Fifth, the German Jesuits of the Buffalo Mission started Canisius College, named for a Jesuit apostle to Germany (1870), and John Carroll in Cleveland (1886).

While the staging areas explain the first hundred years, in relatively recent years the various provinces have simply seized opportunities to open new colleges where the soil seemed rich and the need real: Scranton, which the Jesuits took over from the Christian Brothers in 1942, Fairfield (1942) in Connecticut, LeMoyne in Syracuse (1946), and Wheeling, West Virginia (1955). And it is good to remember that with the exception of Holy Cross and Marquette, the first rector of every college established in the 19th century was a foreigner. For a long while the spirit of "old Europe" set the tone for the system.

The Legacy of Pierre-Jean de Smet

One of the new young men on Fr. Van Quickenborne's raft to arrive at Florissant was Pierre-Jean de Smet, age 22, educated at the Belgian seminary in Malines, who came to America in 1821 and joined the Society at Whitemarsh. Today the young de Smet might be called a student athlete—smart, strong, capable of enduring long, painful trips without complaint. Although an idealized statue on the Saint Louis University campus depicts him as tall and thin, the mature de Smet was short (five feet, six inches) and stocky at 210 pounds. He wore his hair long and had luminous eyes that radiated attention and spirituality. He was to become one of a familiar but rare species of Jesuit—the public man. Known and revered throughout America and Europe, at ease with prelates, popes, army generals, Indian chiefs, and warriors as well as Abraham Lincoln, and an early master of the art of public relations and fund-raising, he was not universally revered by fellow Jesuits. They might not have shared his enthusiasm for traveling in blizzards or appreciate his naive tendency to promise the Indians more resources than he could deliver.

Ordained in 1827 and becoming a naturalized citizen as Peter John de Smet in 1833, he was from the beginning drawn to work with the Indians at a time when the relationship between government and the tribes was being redefined. Missouri, particularly St. Louis and Westport, which today is in Kansas City on the Missouri River, was the open door to the West, the start of the Oregon and Santa Fe Trails. An earlier government policy, according to which no Indian lands would be taken without their consent, had become an aggressive shove. President Thomas Jefferson took advantage of the Indians' tragic flaw:

their desire for the material goods the white man could supply. To meet the demands of the fur trade, the Indians would decimate the beaver and buffalo populations that had sustained their way of life. The Jesuits had come to St. Louis with two goals: caring for the Indian missions and meeting the needs of the white population. The time would come when they couldn't do both.

Returning to Belgium for four years, depressed and tired during two of them, 1835–1837, de Smet withdrew from the Society. After he was granted readmission, he returned with the self-appointed apostolate as peaceful ambassador to the local tribes. Although he never learned an Indian language and always wore his long black robes and crucifix, he adapted instinctively to their ways, to their protocol and ritual. Occasionally he would take out his piccolo and entertain them. In 1840, told that the Flatheads wanted a Blackrobe, he traveled with a wagon train north and west into the Rockies, to Jackson Hole and across the Grand Tetons, and up to northwestern Montana. Welcomed by the tribes, he joined 400 horsemen on a buffalo hunt and, in the course of his visit, baptized nearly 600.

From this excursion came his dream, which Father General Roothaan backed. He wished to reproduce in the Oregon Territory or in the Rocky Mountain Mission, which included Washington, Oregon, Idaho, Montana, and Wyoming, the famous 17th-century Jesuit reductions of Paraguay—the paternalistic, agricultural, self-contained, and isolated communities where religion, the arts and music, and peace would thrive. Roothaan had the missionaries read the reductions' history and apply the basic Jesuit principle of adaptation used in India and China to the American frontier. With the first mission established, St. Mary's in the remote Bitterroot valley near present-day Missoula, Montana, de Smet declared the Flatheads "the elect of God" and the model for more missions he would set up from the Rockies to the Great Plains. The exact number of missions depended on who was counting. De Smet's successor in 1846, Joseph Joset, reported four: St. Mary's among the Flatheads, Sacred Heart among the Coeur d'Alenes, St. Ignatius among the Kalispels, and St. Joseph's among the Okanogans. In 1863 de Smet enumerated 18 missions or stations with chapels. Sometimes missions moved, and some lasted only a few years.

For six years de Smet struggled to keep the project going, including repeated fund-raising trips around the United States and 19 abroad. On a trip in 1843 by way of Cape Horn and up the west coast, he brought back Jesuit recruits and five Notre Dame de Namur nuns, the first sisters in Oregon. On a boat to Europe he met New York's archbishop John Hughes traveling with politician Thurlow Weed and collected donations from their group. In Rome he convinced Pope Gregory XVI to appoint a bishop from the Oregon Territory and Roothaan to provide more Jesuits. He published in five languages a pamphlet on his experiences with the tribes in the Rocky Mountains in preparation for his European lecture tour. The eternal optimist regardless of the evidence to the contrary, de Smet wrote glowing reports on thousands of baptisms and communions and promised Indians and whites alike in his travels that he would send Blackrobes who would tend to their needs.

But in the testimony of many of the 23 Jesuits whom Roothaan had assigned to the mission, they did not admire his leadership skills. De Smet, addicted to travel, was always on the road, reaping acclaim, while they were stuck in the wilderness, diverting their pastoral energies to the white settlers impinging on the missions. They were starving, bored, lonely, suffering from cabin fever and cultural shock. As they saw it, de Smet soaked up public attention, and they were regarded as nobodies.

Finally, Roothaan decided that de Smet was guilty of the Missouri Jesuits' common fault: he overreached. Both Roothaan and de Smet were also blind to imagine that the Paraguay experience could be repeated in America. Indians whose lifestyle was built around hunting buffalos could not settle down and farm. Nor could they resist the good life which this early stage of the American consumer society waved before their eyes. The Flatheads, once the imagined exemplars of a Christian community, went sour. Some who had counted on the Blackrobes' medicines to cure their ailments found the potions didn't work. An old man who defended the Blackrobes was eaten by a grizzly bear. Not a good sign.

The Jesuits faced reality with regard to the reduction dream. Some villages remained as missions, but most Indians remained nomads, returning to the compound for feasts. Now the Jesuits found themselves torn between their original commitment to the Indians and the increasing demands of the white immigrant population. The Jesuits had introduced some gifts of modernity to the tribes—such as vaccination against smallpox and cholera, and gunpowder to ward off their enemies; but other whites introduced liquor and compulsive gambling.

De Smet himself, though his official job was as province treasurer, now launched a second career. From the 1850s to his death in 1873 the army called on him and on other Jesuits for a series of trips to the Great Plains to help them negotiate with warring tribes. His travels have been compared to those of the pope, as if his mystical presence and transparent kindness could achieve what government agents could not.

In the view of one de Smet biographer, the Jesuit Indian strategy changed from one based on social justice and Indian rights to a combination of "Christianizing and civilizing." In other words, its goal, like that of the government, was to transform Indians into white Christians.

These peace expeditions, most of them sponsored by the U.S. Army, were ambiguous experiences for de Smet and the other Jesuits involved, especially because they often sympathized with the Indian point of view. Robert Ignatius Burns, S.J., in *The Jesuits and the Indian Wars of the Northwest* (1966), answers that "the Jesuit, like every white man, could see how completely helpless the Indian military situation was in nineteenth century America." For the Indians to continue war against the American military was suicide. As mediators the Jesuits did their best to limit bloodshed and protect Indian rights when they could. De Smet had stated publicly that "it is always true that if the savages sin against the whites it is because the whites have greatly sinned against them." But he saw the officers who worked with him as men of integrity, and they knew that the Indians trusted him more than they did any other white man.

De Smet's final effort was his 1868 journey—now 69, half deaf, overweight, weak, and wearing a long white beard—into the camp of 5,000 Sioux warriors to confront Sitting Bull. De Smet had received word that Sitting Bull would accept him only if he came alone (without soldiers) and would keep secret the location of their camp, which was 300 miles away, on the Powder River, in the spectacular setting of the Yellowstone Valley. He set out from North Dakota, with his interpreter and 80 Indians, holding high a special peace banner with the name JESUS on one side and the Virgin Mary on the other. He had sent messengers ahead with gifts of tobacco to smooth his welcome.

Over two weeks later, on June 19, over 400 warriors on horseback galloped out to meet him and escort him into the camp with shouts of joy. The weary priest went right to sleep in his lodge, only to be awakened soon by Sitting Bull, wearing only the warrior's breach cloth, accompanied by three other chiefs, at his bedside. "Blackrobe," said Sitting Bull, "I can hardly sustain myself beneath the weight of white man's blood that I have shed." But the whites had provoked the war.

The next day at the great council, de Smet raised his hands to heaven, said a prayer, and spoke for an hour. His message: both sides were guilty of atrocities; the Great Father (in Washington) wanted to help them; it was useless to fight. Four chiefs replied, listing their grievances. One, Black Moon, concluded: "The buffalo, the elk, the big horns and the deer have quitted our immense plains. . . . May it not be the odor of human blood that puts them to flight?"

On July 2 a peace treaty was signed at Fort Rice. In reality these treaties were a ritual by which the government promised food and support in exchange for Indians' agreement to stay peacefully on their reservations. In fact, hordes of settlers would pour into Dakota and Montana and drive the Indians out. By 1870 President Grant assigned the 43 missions authorized in the reservations overwhelmingly to Protestant denominations, leaving the Catholics only four. In effect, de Smet pointed out, he denied the Indians their free choice of religion.

On May 23, 1873, de Smet went to bed in his little room in St. Louis and died. Historian Bernard de Voto, faced with the mystery of how this physically unimposing man who didn't know the language could speak with Indians for half a century and be so universally respected, concluded that somehow de Smet managed to let them know he loved them.

The Jesuit mission effort in the Northwest certainly did not live or die with de Smet. In 1854, because of the enthusiastic response to a call for volunteers, the Turin Province was given the administration of the Rocky Mountain Mission. By 1895, of the 160 priests, brothers, and scholastics in the territory, nearly half were Italians or Americans, with 40 percent from France, Germany, Ireland, or Holland. Only four of the 50 who were priests were born in the United States. In a way their foreign origins helped their relations, particularly as mediators, with the Indians, who were intrigued by Blackrobes but who had learned not to trust American whites. In 1876, when the government asked Fr. Giuseppe Cataldo to help negotiate a treaty with the Nez Perces, he replied that he had promised the Indians never to ask them to make their reservations smaller. If he cooperated, he would lose their respect.

Like the French in Canada and New York, the Italian fathers learned the Indian language fairly well because, trained in Latin and Greek, and as Europeans who had to learn the language of their neighbors, they were not intimidated by the challenge. On the other hand, while some studied Indian dialects and English at the same time, many failed to master English, so their communications world was restricted to Indians and fellow Jesuits. Like the French, the Italians translated the popular piety of their home country—communal worship, a vision of the world in which supernatural forces were at work, and magical practices inherited from ancient ancestors—into mission rituals. Both Indians and Italians loved to sing. When they heard the priests sing, whether Italian street songs or Gregorian chants adapted to Indian hymns, said Fr. Filippo Rappuglioso, the Indians were "in ecstasy."

In catechism class, the scholastics used the competitions prescribed by the *Ratio*, with trinket prizes for the winners. For the liturgies—candles, lots of candles. For Christmas, New Year's, Easter, feasts of Joseph and Mary, and Corpus Christi—more candles, bonfires at night, long processions into the church, ceremonial handshakings, and more songs. By the turn of the century, most of the western slope of the Rockies was Christianized; but on the eastern side, the shortage of priests and Indian poverty and starvation stymied religious progress. As one missionary said, there were good Indians, but "a hungry belly has no ears."

By 1900 the Indians sometimes had assimilated more rapidly than did the missionaries, so that priests from Europe were no longer welcome in either Indian or white parishes if they didn't speak English very well. Finally, as the Maryland Province demonstrated under different circumstances, the Society had shifted its priorities to the colleges. Gonzaga College opened in Spokane in 1887, and Seattle College opened in 1891. When American Jesuits offered to take over the Rocky Mountains Mission, the Italians resisted. The Turin provincial said bluntly that no American "thinks the missions are worthwhile." Americans, he felt, were prejudiced against native people, but even the best could not put up with the rigors of missionary life. Among Italian Jesuits, the old passion to confront the Rockies waned. They were no longer either dangerous or glamorous. Alaska was now the preferred missionary frontier.

The Jesuit mission to the Indians and to the Lakota Sioux did not end with the closing of the frontier and the pacification of the Indian tribes, but it continues to the present day. During the 20th century the emphasis was on the development of the early conviction that their pastoral ministry was not one-sided but a conversation, in which the Jesuits entered the Lakota culture and learned from them how to transmit the gospel. A key participant was the German-born self-trained anthropologist and linguist Eugene Buechel, who was born in 1874, the year after de Smet died, came to the Rosebud Reservation as a scholastic in 1900, and, with an interruption for theology and ordination, worked there until he died in 1954.

Buechel's sermons, 300 of which survive, emphasize work. Sloth to him was a mortal sin. His 300-page anthology of 1924 translated condensed Old and New Testament selections so the Lakotas could read the scriptures in their own language. He translated hymns and prayers, a grammar, and a Lakota dictionary was completed after his death. He also recorded Lakota legends, not fearing that their representations of native culture were a threat to the Christian faith.

By the 1930s most Lakotas spoke English. The younger Jesuits had less contact with them and, by the 1950s, the provincial told the young men there was no need to learn the language. In the 1940s Jesuits wondered about dances—whether the dances themselves or the customs they accompanied were a danger to the faith. But they kept adapting to the needs of their congregations, with outdoor liturgies that might have seemed a radical accommodation but were consistent with what De Smet had done 100 years before—as well as the chaplains in the Civil War. Today, students from Jesuit high schools and colleges journey to the Rosebud Reservation for summer camps and social service projects.

Is It Wrong to Sell Slaves?

While De Smet was beginning to act out the Society's dream of replanting Paraguyan communes in the Northwest, the Maryland Jesuits were fighting one another over whether they should sell their slaves to get money for Georgetown. Holding approximately 400 slaves at one time, the Jesuits were among the largest slaveholders in the United States.

For some of the fathers, this was a moral issue, but not in the same terminology that makes slavery unquestionably immoral in the 21st century. The papacy had several times condemned slavery—Pope Benedict XIV's *Immensa pastorum* in 1741 and Pope Paul III's *Sublimus Deus* in 1537 condemned not only slave conditions but slavery itself, based on the humanity of the slaves. In 1839 Pope Gregory XVI in *In Supremo apostolatus* condemned all involvement in the slave trade, in which "Blacks, as if they were not men but animals . . . are bought, sold, and devoted sometimes to the hardest labor." But the American bishops, led by John England of Charleston, treated the papal decree as if it had nothing to do with them. It condemned the slave trade, they said, but not "domestic slavery." Scripture and tradition allowed slavery, they said; and both Catholic laymen and bishops owned slaves.

While Protestant abolitionists crusaded against slavery, Catholics were free to oppose it, but without support from the church. The bishops saw tolerance of this practice as immutable doctrine, a political rather than a moral question, on which they were reluctant to speak. Besides, they argued, the slaves were not ready for freedom. For example, Fr. Auguste Thebaud, S.J., a brilliant French scientist and Fordham's first president, was not an abolitionist, but he was devoted to the Union cause. He supported the Emancipation Proclamation, but he wished the church had more time to make Negroes Christian. Many feared the social impact of thousands of free, ignorant blacks.

Most important, the idea that religion is a force for social reform was mostly a Protestant phenomenon, exemplified in the Christocentric saga of *Uncle Tom's Cabin*. The concept would take deeper root in the Social Gospel movement late in the century; but it had yet to make inroads on Catholic parish life.

Mid-19th-century Catholic piety, including Jesuit piety preached by conservative immigrant priests, displayed itself in the week-long parish missions aimed at getting congregations into the confessional, saying the rosary, revering relics, telling tales of miraculous cures, and promoting devotion to the Sacred Heart and the saints. In the Maryland area, John McElroy, an immigrant from Northern Ireland in 1803, was one of the leading figures of the first half of the 19th century. Even before joining the Society as a brother, he had mastered the spiritual literature from Augustine on. Determined to become a priest, he taught at Georgetown, was made a pastor in Frederick, Maryland, and from there, over 23 years, traveled 10,000 miles on horseback and carriage preaching to poor Irish immigrants from Baltimore to Boston and giving the Spiritual Exercises to priests and laity.

Fr. Francis X. Weninger, S.J. from Austria, preached 519 missions in his lifetime. The zealous Fr. Bernardine Wigel, S.J., a Swiss, rounded up 400 Boston sodalists, all wearing religious medals, to carry the corpse of young sodalist John Kelly from his home to the church to the miles-away grave, singing hymns and praying the rosary in the procession. It was a drama to demonstrate Catholic solidarity in what they considered a hostile environment; but it was over a hundred years away from the late 20th century Jesuit commitment to social justice.

In some ways this parish piety carried over to Jesuit treatment of their slaves. They saw slaves as fellow Christians, members of the body of Christ, to be treated with charity. They baptized slave children, tried to keep families together, taught them catechism, urged them to attend mass and receive the sacraments. When the "mission band" would come through the parishes, there are records of slaves, along with free blacks, joining the faithful for the sermons, exercises, and lining up to go to confession. They encouraged slaves to develop skills, hold land, plant gardens, sell the produce, and raise livestock. Like the Jesuits themselves, they had the right to protest mistreatment by appealing to a higher Jesuit authority. Maryland Jesuits, just as they saw their farms as integral to their mission, in the "Maryland tradition," saw slavery as part of the heart of that tradition.

Nevertheless, slaves were property, objects of the same racism that pervaded slave-holding society. John Carroll once wrote to a Jesuit in Virginia to applaud his zeal in instructing poor Negroes, "Diamonds are sometimes found in dunghills." In a treatise defending slavery, Brother Joseph Mobberly, the manager of St. Inigoes from 1806 to 1820, offers a list of Christian slave-holding saints. He believed that as descendants of Noah's son Ham, who saw his father's nakedness and who settled in Africa, they were doomed to inferiority. He linked their skin color to their vices. "The better a negro is treated," he wrote, "the worse he becomes." It is not clear how often it happened, but Jesuit owners approved the corporal punishment of slaves, though a brother or an overseer, not a priest, was to administer the lash. But not to a pregnant woman.

Technically the slaves belonged to the Corporation of the Roman Catholic Clergymen, the legal entity established by the former Jesuits in 1783, calling themselves the Select Body of the Clergy, so that their apostolic work could continue while the Society of Jesus was suppressed. This was the body which selected John Carroll as the first American bishop and head of the corporation. Carroll was quick to use the resources of the corporation, including income from the farms, to support Georgetown and the diocese of Baltimore. This was the first step in the critical shift of direction in the church's pastoral policy from the varied sacramental ministry of parishes and missions to urban education.

In the 1830s Georgetown was in a bad way. Under the leadership of a small group of young Irish American Jesuits who had returned from studies in Rome in 1828–29 with ambitious building plans, Georgetown began to transform itself from an academy into a university, open to all religions and with an elite enrollment in schools of science, medicine, and law. Thomas Mulledy, known for being proud and quick tempered, had asked while studying in Rome to be sent to the Indian missions; but in 1829, at the age of 35, he was named president of Georgetown. Immediately the college thrived; it tripled its number of boarders to 60, attracted the ward of Andrew Jackson and the son of Martin van Buren, and added a library, museum, and chapel. Mulledy also moved to get rid of the day students because they were from a lower social class.

But things began to fall apart. Mulledy lost control of student discipline and college finances. His health weakened by the 1832 cholera epidemic and his nerves were shot by three weeks of student riots in 1837, for which 21 students were expelled. With fellow Jesuits put off by his autocratic rule, he was ready to step down. But there was no one to take his place. His fellow Irishman William McSherry, now provincial, warned General Roothaan of the college's impending collapse and pressed for the sale of the plantations, which were no longer profitable, and of the slaves.

In the internal debate over the sale, the lines between the parties, both generational and national, were not clearly drawn. The older American Jesuits, in the "Maryland tradition," saw their apostolic work rooted in the land, of which slavery was a necessary component. These men and some foreign members argued paternalistically that they owed it to the slaves to keep them, lest they lose their religion under strange new owners. The younger Jesuits, for pragmatic reasons, favored selling the land and slaves in order to move on to other ventures. Some saw the Civil War and even a slave revolt looming ahead. Better to get rid of them now.

Finally Roothaan gave in, under three conditions: that free expression of religion be guaranteed; that spouses not be separated; and that the old and sick not be sold. The money was to go not for province works or debts but as capital investment to support the formation of young Jesuits. In 1838 Mulledy sold most of them, 272, to two Louisiana landowners for $115,000. Of this $90,000 went to Jesuit formation. The rest went to pay off Georgetown's building debts and to Baltimore's archbishop to settle claims he had on the land. Some slaves were urged by their Jesuit masters to escape. Those sold lost their opportunity to practice their faith. Mulledy, who had switched jobs with McSherry, went to Rome in disgrace. A local European Jesuit wrote to Roothaan, "This will be a tragic and disgraceful affair."

Out of Town on a Rail

If the period between the Jacksonian era and the Civil War was one of social reform and religious revival, it was also one of extraordinary bigotry directed against both the immigrants, especially the Irish who flooded the cities, and the priests, especially the Jesuits who served them. Anti-Jesuit books and pamphlets and anti-Jesuit lecturers toured the eastern coast. One, Joseph F. Berg, described Jesuits as men with "a will strong as iron, and a heart as cold as marble and as hard." Samuel F. B. Morse, inventor of the telegraph, portrayed Jesuits as enemies of freedom who conspired to manipulate the votes of millions of urban immigrants to elect Jesuits to the United States Senate and gain control of the nation. In the 1840s some Protestants were especially alarmed by the spread of Jesuit schools in the West, and the Society for the Promotion of Collegiate and Theological Education in the West urged the building of a school system to match college against college and annihilate the rival system of Jesuit education. In the 1850s the new Know Nothing Party published anti-Jesuit novels, including one that imagined an evil order of female Jesuits and another in which a Jesuit kidnaps and murders an innocent maiden.

This is the world which a 34-year-old Swiss, Fr. John Bapst, joined when he stepped off the boat in New York in 1848. He was on his way to Old Town Maine, an island in the Penobscot River, to minister to its

Indian tribes. This was the last place he wanted to be. When his religious superior had called him in and told him to pack his bags and leave for America that afternoon, he broke into tears. He had not wished to be a missionary. He loved Switzerland and spoke no English, much less an Indian dialect. But Jesuits go where they are sent.

The Old Town Indians had not seen a priest in 20 years—their last one had been murdered by Protestants—and they welcomed him with a celebration. However, they had forgotten all their catechism, fallen into drunkenness, and were at constant war among themselves. Within two years Bapst had learned enough of the language, which he imagined to be derived from Hebrew, to hear confessions, start a temperance society, and struggle, with little success, to establish peace. He fought to avoid despair and clung to the dream embedded in the European Jesuit imagination of reestablishing the reductions of Paraguay in North America. Then he moved his headquarters to Eastport, from which he served 9,000 souls riding hundreds of miles between Eastport, Bangor, and Ellsworth.

Though he proclaims his happiness in his work, his letters reek of loneliness, fatigue, and disappointment in his own failures. He has heard that over the years his Indians have killed ten priests, and he doubts he has the courage for martyrdom. For a while he has three co-workers, but some leave or are sent elsewhere. All are overwhelmed. It is 1852 before Bapst knows English well enough to write an English letter. On April 27, 1850, he begins to exult a little in what he perceives as progress. The Protestants, he feels, are ripe for conversion. He has baptized two Protestant women. He has proved to a Universalist the existence of hell. He tells of a Protestant gentleman who delivered an eloquent lecture in Bangor, a Protestant town, in praise of the Jesuits, to frequent applause. If Bapst was present himself, with his limited English, he might have mistaken criticism for praise; but he was assured by a priest who was there that it was a correct and lofty tribute.

"The United States is the freest country in the world," writes Bapst. He can establish as many schools as he wishes and no one will interfere, he says. "I could preach the doctrines of the Catholic religion in the most Protestant town," he says, and never be interrupted.

Reestablished in Bangor in 1853, with Ellsworth, 30 miles to the southeast, under his responsibility, Bapst set up a small church and school there. The presence of the school particularly enraged the Know Nothings who harassed Bapst; and in June 1854, they threw a bomb into his school. In a resolution passed at a town meeting, the inhabitants warned him that should he show his face there again they would provide him with "an entire suit of new clothes such as cannot be found in the shops," and a "fine ticket to leave town" on the "first railroad."

He ignored the threat and kept coming back. Some details differ on what happened next. In one account, on the night of Saturday, October 14, 1854, he was yanked out of the confessional, in another he was captured in the house of parishioners where he was hiding in the cellar. The mob stripped him naked, covered his body with hot tar and feathers, put him on a rail and rode him through the streets, bouncing the rail to increase his pain. They debated whether to hang him, but dumped him on the ground with a threat to kill him if he dared to say Sunday Mass the next day. Friends found him and peeled off the tar. And the next morning he went right to the church and said his public Mass.

The Protestants of Bangor did not share the bigotry of their Ellsworth neighbors. They denounced the affair and gave Bapst money and a gold watch, which, because Jesuits did not own gold watches, the father general gave him special permission to wear.

The rest of John Bapst's life was more serene, filled with accomplishments, and ultimately sad. He kept working in Bangor and Ellsworth for five years, became the spiritual father at the College of the Holy Cross in Worcester in Massachusetts in 1859, then went to the Boston College Jesuit scholasticate, where in 1864 he became rector of the College when it opened to lay students.

In 1869 what used to be known as the New York–Canada Mission, which since the days of Isaac Jogues had been under the jurisdiction of the French Province of Champagne, was made an independent mission responsible to Jesuit headquarters in Rome. This meant that the American Mission was coming of age, no longer "missionary territory." Rome put in charge the man who 22 years before had broken into tears at the thought of going to America.

Invited by the bishop of Newark to accept St. Peter's Parish in Jersey City in 1870, Bapst visited the site, a few blocks from the Hudson River waterfront. From the docks and railroad yards that received the tide of immigrants pouring into New York harbor, he glimpsed the future. He wrote to the Father General on October 16, 1870, that Jersey City had a population of 100,000 of whom 30,000 were Catholics.

"Conditions there will soon make it one of the most important cities in the union. The Church of St. Peter's is situated in a central part of the city and easily accessible. . . . All that we have to do is build the college."

In 1879 Bapst's health, both physical and mental, began to fail. Over the years he was moved around to various villa houses and infirmaries where the view of the Hudson Valley would remind him of the Swiss Alps or the presence of novices would cheer him up as his memory faded to the point that he did not know his own name. Brutally, his past returned to haunt him. He imagined that the mobs of Ellsworth were chasing him through the corridors of the infirmary. His older brother had left the Society in his first years because he could not control his attacks of scrupulosity. As if the gene had resurfaced in John, when he could no longer say Mass himself because he didn't know what he was doing he would attend daily Mass—but only after throwing himself at the feet of a fellow priest to confess the imagined sins of the last 24 hours. In 1887 he was buried in what was still a small cemetery at Woodstock College, the first Jesuit theological seminary in North America, on the Patapsco River, in the hills and woods outside Baltimore. Several hundred young men in black stood by.

6

A Nation and Faith Divided

"Glory"

In October 1850, 13-year-old Robert Gould Shaw, son of a wealthy Boston antislavery family, sat at his desk day after day in the study hall at Fordham, as the former St. John's College was already called, and wrote angry, whining letters home with one dominant theme. He hated the school and wanted to come home. The other boys, he complained, are lazy louts and troublemakers. They disrupt study hall with foot stomping and yelling just to intimidate the young Jesuit prefect who does not know how to intimidate bad boys. The other boys broke his violin, and he was attacked by a neighborhood dog. He and his 114 fellow students, which include some well-behaved seminarians and many from the Deep South and Latin America, live under a French and Victorian discipline, which includes whippings, intended to build character but builds resentment as well.

Robert was not even Catholic. He was stuck in the Bronx because his uncle, Coolidge Shaw, who joined the Jesuits after converting to Catholicism, convinced his parents to send him here.

In January his parents gave in and sent him to a boarding school in Switzerland, where he read *Uncle Tom's Cabin* and grew to the height of five feet, five inches. Unlike his parents, he was neither an abolitionist nor religious; and he never forgave the Jesuits, who, he was convinced, never forgave him for not converting to Catholicism like his uncle. He went to Harvard, from which he sent home letters that read much like his letters from Fordham. "I hate Cambridge," he moaned. As the Civil War loomed, he was indifferent to the fate of slaves. Let the Union split; that way slavery would be a Southern, not a national, disgrace.

But when Fort Sumter fell, Robert Shaw joined the renowned Seventh Regiment of the New York National Guard. In his letters home he complained about the Irish troops who "seem sometimes utterly unable to learn or understand anything." But, by February 1863, the governor of Massachusetts offered young Robert a commission as colonel and commander of the new Massachusetts 54th Colored Regiment of volunteers. He turned it down, then changed his mind. He wanted to prove that Negroes could be good soldiers. Shaw knew little about black people and referred to them as niggers and darkies and was surprised to find some of them "gentlemanlike." By March, however, he was bragging about them to his mother.

Later that year, in an event portrayed in the film *Glory*, Shaw and his regiment were ordered to lead the assault on Fort Wagner, which defended the entrance to Charleston Harbor. As expected, the first wave of the assault was wiped out. Half the regiment was killed, and Shaw fell with a bullet in his heart. When the Union Army asked for his body, a Confederate officer replied, "We buried him with his niggers."

"They Know How to Die"

Most likely, Shaw never knew that among the Jesuits who collectively made his life miserable two had, as chaplains, followed the Union troops into battle. Michael Nash, at 20, had been one of the vanguard of six Jesuits to arrive at Fordham on August 9, 1846. He had come to America from Ireland with his father in 1825 and remained here, the ward of Jesuits in Kentucky, whom he ultimately joined when his father returned to Ireland. At Fordham they worked him to the point of exhaustion, until he was diagnosed as suffering from consumption and was sent to France in 1856 to die. Rather than die, he saw a better doctor, got ordained, returned to America, and in 1861 was ordered by superiors—though he still felt sick—to join the Union Army as chaplain.

Assigned to the Sixth Regiment of Infantry, the "Zouaves," who wore colorful baggy-pants uniforms modeled on those of African tribesmen, he sailed in mid-June with sometimes rebellious troops, sons of Catholic families who knew nothing about their religion, to Fort Pickens on Santa Rosa, an island off rebel-held Pensacola in the Gulf of Mexico.

For summer months they endured the blazing sun, torrential rains, mosquitoes, alligators, and poisonous snakes. Jesuits had accompanied the troops during the Mexican War and, given no training, saw themselves as missionaries, determined to risk their lives to administer the basic sacraments—baptism, penance, and the Eucharist—often at the moment of death. Like Francis Xavier, Isaac Jogues, and their contemporaries, they were convinced, according to the theology of the day, that without baptism and/or confession of sins the troops would go to hell. The moody Nash suffered his ups and downs—one minute too worn out to preach at a Sunday Mass, the next, in the midst of a rebel invasion, running from one dying man to another, Union or Confederate, offering prayers. His letters, which gave evidence of Nash's later reputation for exaggeration, bristle with poignant scenes. A dying Protestant soldier begs, "Father, do not leave me." Nash explains that "many others are stretched out on the sand." "That is true," the lad replies, "but they are Catholics, Father; they know how to die."

Peter Tissot, who arrived from France as a 23-year-old scholastic, impressed students with his lofty manner and well-knit physique that enabled him to beat them at handball and football. In 1861, assigned to the Irish Rifles regiment, he moved to Washington, and in March of 1862 joined the 100,000 men who marched off in the Peninsula campaign. In May, knee deep in mud, on the eve of the battle Williamsburg, Tissot warned a soldier who had not been to confession in a long time that if he died and went to hell he had no one to blame but himself. "You're right," the boy replied, "I take the whole blame on myself." But when the boy wasn't looking, Tissot, hoping he had repented in his heart, gave him absolution anyway. The boy was struck down in the battle's first minutes.

Jesuits Hold Their Tongues

One day General Philip Kearny, a divorced man whose wife and daughter were Catholics, treated Tissot to wine and a cigar and entertained him with his romantic ideas about the church. The Catholic Church, he said, had the power to stop the war. Unfortunately, the church had no unified position on the war. In *Catholicism and American Freedom*, John McGreevy places the American church's intellectual disarray in the context of the parallel struggle in Europe between the Ultramontanist Party and the liberals or revolutionaries. Polemicists on both sides of the Atlantic continually linked the Jesuits with the forces of reaction, proponents of slavery, and enemies of freedom.

At the same time, American bishops, for example Archbishop Hughes, tended to support the Union, but not abolition. In Rome the Jesuit journal *Civilta Cattolica,* which spoke with the Vatican's voice, traced the origin of the war to the mania for liberty, referring presumably to the abolitionists, who, as Protestants, were considered enemies of the church. According to McGreevy, "Only one Jesuit, Father Weninger, publicly defended abolition, perhaps because he had personally witnessed the horror of a New Orleans slave auction." Orestes Brownson, the great Catholic and transcendentalist philosopher, who had sent his son to Holy Cross but had an up-and-down relationship with the Society, wrote in the last issue of *Brownson's Quarterly Review* (October 1864) that the Jesuits were "a society so destitute of loyalty that it could look on with indifference and see a nation rent asunder."

Perhaps the perceived lack of "loyalty" was due to their own immigrant status. For the recent arrivals, their concept of liberty was untouched by the unique Revolutionary experience. Their concerns were pastoral. Jesuit chaplains served in both armies. And they kept their opinions on the controversy to themselves; the war became a forbidden topic in Jesuit communities, lest it rupture the bond of fraternal charity and revive the anti-Catholic crusade that nativism had mounted in the 1850s.

When the war broke out Boston College was the scholasticate for 46 scholastics and eight brothers from all over America and the Old World, including France, Germany, England, Ireland, and many more countries. On March 3, 1861, the rector, Fr. Bapst, wrote to a friend that "we are just at this moment resting upon a volcano," referring to Lincoln's inauguration. When the silence on the war in the community was broken, it was Bapst's role to restore peace.

Of the colleges whose enrollments were most vulnerable to the impact of the war—including Loyola in Baltimore, Saint Joseph's in Philadelphia, and Holy Cross in Worcester—Georgetown almost closed. In the fall of 1861 only 50 students enrolled. The following fall only 17 returned for the start of class. The doubling of the District of Columbia's population, however, brought an influx of day students; as a result, Protestants and Jews, including many Germans, constituted over a third of the student body. While a majority of the Jesuits and students favored the South and students yelled "Three cheers for

Jeff Davis" when two Union officers reconnoitered the campus, the Jesuits held their tongues, and the campus endured the brief billeting of Union troops on campus without incident. When the army set up temporary hospitals on campus, in Trinity Church, and in the novitiate at Frederick, Maryland, the Jesuits ministered to the wounded and converted hundreds to Catholicism, 120 of whom died.

In St. Louis the mixed allegiances of Missouri residents were exemplified in two Jesuits. De Smet supported the Union and, like a contemporary lobbyist, he used his contacts in Washington—which included Abraham Lincoln, with whom he spent an hour to get government money for the Indians—to gain favors for the Jesuits. While keeping a diplomatic silence in Missouri, he wrote political analyses to his friends in Europe. The cause of the war, he said, was disagreement on slavery. The emancipation proclamation convinced him that slavery would be extinguished. Hardly heavy punditry; but peacemaking was his gift. Father William Stack Murphy, on the other hand, a thin, white-haired man who spoke seven languages and who had moved all over the East in different administrative posts, was convinced the South had every right to secede. The state draft law and the federal draft law of 1863, which demanded universal conscription, applied to the Jesuits in St. Louis and Cincinnati as well. Jean-Pierre de Smet wrote carefully reasoned pleas to New York's Thurlow Reed, who did not answer, and, while in Washington on other business, talked Secretary of War Edwin Stanton into granting Jesuits exemption from the draft and from paying the 300 dollar fee, which, he argued, would impoverish the Society and threaten its charitable works.

In Cincinnati, Archbishop John B. Purcell was one of the few to take on slavery as a moral issue. "It was Christ's mission to set men free," he said, "and Christian people disregard his precepts and principles and example, when they seek to uphold or perpetuate involuntary human servitude." But for the most part that was not a line of argument the Jesuits embraced. At the war's close, a radical wing of the Republican Party in Missouri passed a state constitution demanding a sweeping loyalty oath stating that its signers had never sympathized with the South. The Catholic clergy disapproved and no Jesuit signed.

One of the five recruits De Smet brought back from Europe in 1844 was Giovanni Nobili, who followed the Gold Rush to San Francisco in 1849, which resembled, he said, "either a Madhouse or Babylon," he wasn't sure which. At the bishop's request he took over the formerly

Franciscan Santa Clara Mission and started a school. The fourth president of Santa Clara College, Swiss-born Fr. Burchard Villager, had just escaped from Baltimore, which was then torn by riots in April 1861, to make the trek across the country. Though disappointed with the unimpressive campus of adobe constructions, he was determined to give it some tall, nonadobe buildings that would project a new prestige. He would succeed because he developed Santa Clara's science program and dormitories, because the new railroad was coming through, and because their life was relatively unaffected by the Civil War.

The usual propaganda that Jesuits were somehow pulling strings to influence war policy showed up in California, but it was ignored. Yet, one Santa Clara Jesuit, Joseph Bixio, an Italian from Turin, felt called to service at the front like his brother Jesuits in the East. Accounts of this chaplain's career are contradictory, since he seems to have told different stories to different people; but somehow he served in the armies of both the North and South, and was almost hanged as a spy.

Back at Santa Clara the closest the campus came to wartime status was the full dress parade of the cadet corps down the Alameda San Jose, parades which, according to one student wit, displayed his classmates as "invincible in peace, and invisible in war."

The French Rebel Priest

Behind Confederate lines, the urbane and occasionally pompous Louis-Hippolyte Gache, who had joined the French Jesuits in Savoy in 1836 at age 19, was having the most satisfying experience of his life. He had arrived in Mobile in time to participate in the founding of Spring Hill College in 1847, but had been transferred instead to the beautiful rural flatlands of towering oaks at St. Charles College in Grand Coteau, Louisiana. Its founder was the temperamental Jesuit artist Nicholas Point, who would depart to become a missionary companion of de Smet but leave him when their personalities clashed. Things were happening fast in what is now the New Orleans Province, and Gache helped plant the seeds in New Orleans of what are now the Church of the Immaculate Conception on Barone Street, Holy Name Church on St. Charles Avenue, Jesuit High School, and Loyola University. At Grand Coteau, however, parents complained that he was too strict, and he was bounced back to Spring Hill in 1849. In his wartime letters he would disparage *"les têtes louisiannaise."* Before he could settle in, he was yanked back again to Baton Rouge to start still another college. There he fought with Methodists who opposed the project, and he bragged that he had a pistol to greet the first Protestant to touch his fence. By 1852 he was fired as president and again recalled to Spring Hill.

May 1861 found Gache a Confederate Army chaplain in Pensacola, across the water from Fort Pickens on Santa Rosa Island, which his troops would one day bombard and invade and where some would come face to face with Michael Nash.

For the next four years with the 10th Louisiana Regiment, Gache served contentedly throughout Virginia. There he encountered the notorious Father Bixio, the chaplain who served both sides, whom a Jesuit scholar describes as "the incarnation of the tartuffish Jesuit, every bit as ingenious and resourceful as he was double-dealing and cunning." Like most Civil War chaplains, Gache wore his black robes and not, unlike a few Jesuits who scandalized him, an army officer's uniform. In the Richmond prison he found three captured fellow Jesuits, including Tissot, whom he had taught as a student in France and who assured him of the North's determination to conquer the South. Three years later, on July 18, Gache wrote a mournful but generous letter to his Jesuit brothers at Spring Hill describing how, as Jefferson Davis abandoned Richmond on April 2, the city went up in flames and the throngs surged into the streets with their possessions, and "no one spoke." "Everywhere there was grim silence, drawn faces and a sense of hopelessness and horror." The Union Army, he said, "convinced citizens they had fallen into the hands of the best of enemies" because so many Union officers were Catholics.

For the rest of his life Gache bounced around the Northeast— Holy Trinity in Georgetown, Old St. Joseph's in Philadelphia, Holy Cross, and, in 1904, St. Andrew-on-Hudson, the new novitiate of the combined New York and Maryland Provinces, which had opened with 54 novices, moving up from Frederick, Maryland, the year before. But it seems from his 1865 letter from Richmond that "nothing so captivated my heart as [Baltimore's] Loyola College. It had only a hundred students . . . but they are the most admirable young men. . . . One could see at a glance that they were from the best families in town."

A Black Jesuit

In 1853 a young Jesuit in his first assignment at Holy Cross wrote to his Jesuit mentor Fr. George Fenwick. Fenwick had helped guide him both into the church and the Society when he and his three brothers—James, Sherwood, and Michael—were students there a few years before. Patrick Healy was doing well and, though a strict disciplinarian, was popular with the students. But one thing was bothering him—the family secret. "Remarks are sometimes made (though not in my hearing) which wound my heart. You know to what I refer." The problem had become acute with the arrival of his 14-year-old brother, Michael, who might become the victim of gossip. The Healy boys, plus their three sisters, looked white but were legally black slaves, children of the white immigrant planter Michael Healy and his slave common-law wife Mary Eliza.

The father had systematically slipped his children into the North, where they could assume new identities and be free from the past. Three of the four brothers and the three sisters reaffirmed their new personae by becoming priests or joining the religious life. James became bishop of Portland, Sherwood vice chancellor of the archdiocese of Boston, and Patrick, who as far as we know was probably the first black American Jesuit, became president of Georgetown.

Patrick escaped the Civil War—during which his brothers declined to condemn slavery—by studying theology in Europe. There, working his way for the second time through the Spiritual Exercises of St. Ignatius, he underwent a strong transformation, a conviction that he had become a "new person." In 1864 he wrote to a friend that he prayed "the Society may never have reason to regret of having allowed me to be . . . one of its children," in spite of the risk that he might tarnish "its good name by my irregularities." In the interpretation of James M. O'Toole, the Healy family biographer, the words in the ordination liturgy from John's gospel, "I no longer call you slaves, but friends," had other meanings for Patrick Healy.

American Jesuits have a mixed history on the issue of racial integration, but there was no policy excluding black persons from membership. Jesuit superiors had the confidence to send young Healy right to Georgetown, first to the low-profile job of teaching philosophy to Jesuit scholastics, then to become prefect of studies in 1867. Over the next 12 years his efforts to downplay the classics while emphasizing

English literature and especially the sciences were part of his long-range project of making Georgetown a real university, in the same sense that Harvard and Johns Hopkins (the latter was established as the first primarily research institution) were called universities. Named president in 1875 at the age of 39, Healy knew that the American bishops, egged on by intellectuals like Isaac Hecker, founder of the Paulist Fathers, and Orestes Brownson, had begun thinking about a national Catholic university. So he was determined to simply forge ahead and make that university Georgetown. To attract and hold onto students, this meant lots of changes in the standard Jesuit formula: an elective system, commercial and science courses, dormitories with private rooms, an endowment, a network of prominent alumni, and, in Healy's personal vision, a big, towering, multipurpose building that would stand out atop the Potomac cliffs, against the skyline, and say notice us. He had in mind the Romanesque style; and it would not face the river but the city, to tell the Washington population where St. Ignatius believed the Society's mission belonged.

Now he had to raise the money. But Healy was a sick man, suffering headaches and weakness that would keep him in bed for days, very possibly due to an undiagnosed form of epilepsy. Nevertheless, he set out across the country for 18 months, combining a sea voyage for his health to San Francisco and a begging tour among alumni in Denver, St. Louis, Chicago, Milwaukee, Detroit, Buffalo, New York, Philadelphia, and Boston, nearly all of which now had struggling Jesuit communities of their own. He raised less than $60,000.

Although his term would have ended in 1880, Healy stayed on to complete the building, got sick again, fell in his room in 1882, and was compelled to resign. For the next 30 years he traveled the globe, tried to keep his family together, and settled into the quiet life of a parish priest. He had not transformed Georgetown to fit his dream; but he had raised standards and had gotten the medical and law schools on their feet. Today the Healy Building towers pierce the skyline, one mimicked by a modernistic version on the university library, as jets roar over, taking off from National Airport just a few minutes away. It was the 1950s before Georgetown talked publicly about having had a "black president." Ironically, today both Georgetown and Holy Cross have buildings named after both Fathers Mulledy and Healy—for the Jesuit who sold the slaves and for the Jesuit who was once a slave himself.

7

Schoolmasters and Preachers

"They'll Study or Kill Themselves"

Jacques Barzun, in *From Dawn to Decadence,* his cultural history of the West, delivers this assessment of the mid-17th-century Society of Jesus:

> Meanwhile, by care and thought and continually revised methods, the Jesuits shone as schoolmasters—unsurpassed in the history of education. They taught secular subjects as well as church doctrine and did so with unexampled understanding and kindness toward their pupils. Their success was due to the most efficient form of teacher training ever seen. They knew that born teachers are as scarce as true poets and that the next best cannot be made casually out of indifferent materials, so they devised a preparation that included exhaustive learning and a severe winnowing of the unfit at every phase of a long apprenticeship.

This was the presuppression Society at the height of its influence, when it had set up so many schools in Europe that there were almost too many, in fact more than in the mid-19th century. But the improvisational context of establishing schools in what was still a frontier mission made exhaustive preparation an unattainable goal. When Michael Nash and Edward Tissot proctored study hall and played football with the boys at Fordham, they were still, as Jesuits, students themselves, with Latin theses in philosophy to memorize for the next day. Colleges for scholastics opened and closed according to how vocations rose and fell and where the men were needed, and the scholastics had to cheerfully pack and shuttle to another home.

The system was hard on their health and detrimental to their intellectual development. Ideally the formation process was supposed to move through graded steps, phases of action and contemplation, each building on the previous. First came two years of the novitiate, strict spiritual discipline, methods of prayer, Society rules, and the 30-day silent retreat with the Spiritual Exercises. Next, a two-year classical curriculum, Greek and Latin literature, rhetoric, and science, followed by three years of philosophy, taught in Latin, centered on St. Thomas Aquinas's thought organized into theses, in which adversaries of truth are set up and refuted. This culminated in an oral exam designed, allegedly, to gauge the student's knowledge and quick wits. It also determined, depending on the score, whether the student stayed "up" and continued in a "long course" of studies that would qualify him for the fourth vow of obedience to the pope or went "down" into "short course." The long course also made him eligible for "profession," to be named superior of a house or for other leadership positions. All this presumed a connection between the ability to do well in a philosophy oral in Latin and the ability to lead men.

Thus prepared, he was ready for regency, to teach high school—to engage the 14-year-old mind—for three to five years, depending on the school's needs and whether his performance was up to snuff. He was presumed ready to teach anything—religion, history, language, literature, science—whether trained in it or not. Generally, young Jesuits loved teaching. They submitted humbly to professors for seven years; then they had adult responsibilities. Boys looked up to them, tried to outsmart them, to "break" them. And both students and teachers thrived in the relationship of challenge, attention, and affection.

Then, after years of "action," they went back to "contemplation," four years of theology—scripture, sacraments, dogma, and morals, with ordination after the third year. Theology also climaxed with an oral exam on "everything," in which one could stay "up" or go "down." The overall assumption of the whole process was that the philosophical system called neo-Thomism was a sort of wax that links philosophy and theology to each other, wherein answers to theological questions on how Christ is present in the Eucharist or how God can be three persons in one nature were anticipated in the philosophy courses on the distinction between essence and existence, and between "virtual" and "real," learned five years before. This inspired jokes about the scholastic asking a question during philosophy and being told it would be answered in theology. And when he asked the question in theology, he was told . . .

But so far the American Jesuits lacked the money, place, and manpower to make this sequence happen. They were in a mix of missions, floating across the map, taking courses in small groups at Fordham, St. Louis, Georgetown, or Laval College in Montreal. Without a central training camp to make them emotionally one as a generation of American Jesuits, they depended on Europe.

In 1859–1860 the superior general, Fr. Peter Beckx, sent a visitor, or investigator, to solve the problem. He ordered that, with Boston College a temporary seminary, the North American provinces should build a common seminary at Conewago, Pennsylvania. The Boston project died in debt in 1863, and the young men spread out again. Meanwhile, Conewago, which was near Gettysburg, became a potential battlefield. Finally, under the leadership of Fr. Angelo Paresce, the Maryland provincial, with financial backing from Missouri, they discovered a beautiful, hilly track of farmland a short train ride from Baltimore, on the Patapsco River in Maryland. The woods were lush with cedar, oak, hickory, and maple trees and the river slopes with laurel that the seminarians would gather at Christmastime. The quarry from which they would hew granite for the house would, over the century, fill with water in which the men would swim. Paresce pulled a faculty and library of 45,000 volumes together from Georgetown, Boston, Fordham, Canada, France, Spain, and, above all, Italy.

On Thursday morning, September 23, 1869, the bell that drove 47 groggy scholastics out of bed, down the hall to the common bathroom, and down the stairs into the chapel for morning visit rang at 5:00 for the first time at Woodstock College. For many it was the first time they had their own room and their own stove heater. Whether the rural isolation and the pedagogical system based on memorizing Italian manuals in Latin would sit well with young men in their physical prime would be another question. According to legend, one Italian professor looked up at the imposing four-story rectangular structure surrounded by hills and woods and said, "*Aut studium, aut suicidium*," they'll either study or kill themselves.

At 11:15 the prefect of studies, Italian theologian Camillus Mazzella, age 36, summoned his students and told them that their books are like swords, the Jesuits' weapons. Just as the Roman College, later the Gregorian University, launched the Counter-Reformation in the 16th century, Woodstock College must send leaders into the American church. After dinner, all retired for music and cigars.

As the college grew in size and prestige, more specialized science courses, for example astronomy, were added to the required physics and chemistry classes. A print shop was set up, and, beginning in 1872, the college published, until 1969, the *Woodstock Letters,* a journal of living history—letters, obituaries, memoirs, original documents, statistics, local reports, book reviews—as a bond of union among American Jesuits. It featured from time to time photographs of new Jesuit buildings around the country. They suggest something like an imported "Jesuit" style—big, bulky, granite, Italianate-Renaissance, four-story constructions with white granite bordering the tall windows, high ceilings on the first three floors and low on the fourth.

The college also published theology tracts, texts covering the whole of the discipline, in Latin by the faculty. Some were sold commercially and read by diocesan priests. Fr. Mazzella sent his to Rome, to Pope Leo XIII, who sent him a "We have received with great pleasure" letter. The pope summoned him back to Rome to teach at the Roman College, where, based on his ten years in America, he was considered an expert on American culture, including what Rome considered dangerous "American" ideas. Then the pope made him a cardinal.

In the mid-1880s the "perfect" professor, by popular acclaim, was Fr. Aloysius Sabetti, who tested his own book, a manual on moral theology, on his students before having the press run off 2,000 copies for public sale. Born in 1839, the last of 15 children in an Italian family where the father died before Luigi was born and his mother died a few years later, Luigi wanted to be a Jesuit from the time he first heard how they were kicked out of Italy and returned. The Society became his family from the moment it let him in, and, though only in his early 30s, he became a father–big brother figure to the Woodstock scholastics who lined up outside his room for guidance and who loved to kid with him in class.

Class was all a Socratic back and forth. Don't take notes, it's all in my book, he said. Class was all in Latin—except for his English interjections of "Quick now!" "If you hesitate, you are lost!" "Yes or No?" In one class described in *Woodstock Letters* (Vol. 29), apparently recorded verbatim, he challenged his class with: "Here is my case: There was a marriage between the Sun and the Moon in a balloon near Cincinnati twenty or thirty years ago. Was it a valid marriage and what can be done about it? That's the problem. Don't laugh! This is serious business."

He darted around the room teasing his pupils. "Such problems come up every day in the confessional or the parlor. Don't laugh. . . ."

Students attempted humorous responses. History does not record his answer; but it seems that the process of thinking through and applying canon law to obscure situations—jurisdiction, whether the sun and moon were both baptized, and whether the priest, if there was one in the gondola, had delegation from the Cincinnati parish over which they floated—is what mattered for the moment. In his spare time over 30 years, Sabetti raised funds to personally landscape the Woodstock campus, lovingly planting flowers and trees. In the same spirit—and as an emotional release—in the 1940s a student-faculty team turned some rolling fields into a primitive golf course.

By 1885, with 213 Jesuits and 28 in the ordination class, Woodstock claimed to be the "largest Jesuit community in the world." The numbers of the scholastics were doubling every five years. It was time to split. The New Orleans Mission, the Mission of California and New Mexico, the Rocky Mountain Mission, and the Missouri Province agreed to build another seminary in St. Louis.

Meanwhile, in Washington, D.C., with Bishop John J. Keane of Richmond as rector, the Catholic University of America opened its doors in 1889 with a faculty of 12. Its founders were to become known as "Americanists," a vague term that came to connote too great a readiness to adapt Catholic piety to American culture, a vision the Woodstock faculty did not share.

In America What Language Shall We Speak?

In the summer of 1907, young John LaFarge—son of the American painter and stained-glass artist John LaFarge, friend of William and Henry James—who, after graduating from Harvard and his ordination in Europe had joined the Jesuits, was sent to teach freshman "humanities" at the new Jesuit school, Canisius College, in Buffalo. "One taught English, Greek, and Latin to the freshmen as a coordinated whole," he wrote in his autobiography, *The Manner is Ordinary*. "To me it was an entirely new and difficult experience."

There were other difficulties. This was the last year of a short chapter in American Jesuit history, the Buffalo German Mission, created in response to the pleadings of bishops in the northern corridor, from up-state New York to the Indian territories, for priests to preach to German Americans who were slow to assimilate. LaFarge, an American "blue blood," whose father had attended Fordham in its founding years, had studied at Innsbruck; so he could sympathize with both sides in a community split over how much they should adapt to or oppose the influence of American culture in an American school.

John Timon, first bishop of Buffalo, had sought Jesuit help since taking office in 1847. He had inherited a rebellious parish, St. Louis, where Archbishop John Hughes of New York had fruitlessly put the trustees under interdict to bring them into line. When a preached Jesuit mission failed to soften them, in 1851 Timon created a new Jesuit parish nearby, St. Michael the Archangel, which drained off a majority of St. Louis's congregation, though the rebels stayed firm. Finally, the Jesuits and Timon played their strongest card. In 1855 they imported the famous German preacher Francis X. Weninger to preach a St. Louis mission, as Timon lifted the interdict and revoked the trustees' excommunication. The schism ended. Hard feelings remained. And the Jesuits were confident enough to build another church, St. Ann's in 1858, which served as a catalyst in developing a new German neighborhood.

As they continued to talk about the future college as a priority, the fathers took on all kinds of other work that would distract them from a single goal. To the three parishes they added parochial schools, chaplaincies at convents, hospitals, the poor house, and the insane asylum. Plus they built a new and magnificent St. Michael's Church, with seating for 1,750 congregants and a dozen confessionals, though they had only three priests to hear confessions. As work piled up, the new superior of the New York–Canada Mission, James Perron, called on the general in 1867 to establish a German-speaking mission in the United States. There was only one dissenting voice: by one of the oldest fathers, Thomas Legouais, a pioneer Jesuit at Fordham, physically so small he was occasionally mistaken for a child by lay visitors to the St. John's College campus. Yet he was considered a spiritual giant by the boys who loved him and his peers who sought his advice. It did not seem wise, he wrote to the general, to erect a Jesuit apostolate in America on the basis of a foreign language.

On July 4, 1869, 18 new Jesuits arrived in Buffalo from Germany, and the New York men gradually withdrew, gone by July 26, 1870. Six weeks later, Canisius College offered its first classes. In August 1871 the provincials past and present of Maryland and Missouri and the superior of the New York–Canada Mission met at Woodstock and assigned to the Germans the dioceses of Buffalo, Rochester, Erie, Cleveland, and parts of Michigan, Minnesota, and Wisconsin. True to nature, the Germans reached out in every direction, and a number of projects failed. They entered and withdrew from churches and schools in St. Paul, Minnesota; Burlington, Iowa; and the Indian Mission in Wyoming. They started a college in Toledo, which closed during the Depression. They prospered, however, in the Rosebud and Pine Ridge Reservations in South Dakota, where they established boarding schools for boys and girls.

In Prairie de Chien, Wisconsin, the fathers accepted a property, an old hotel, where a Christian Brothers school had failed and opened the College of the Sacred Heart, a boarding school, in 1880. By 1886 they had about a hundred students, but as a whole the school wasn't working. These were not boys with whom Jesuits usually worked. Only a few, those in the seminary course, followed the classical curriculum; most took commercial courses, fooled around, couldn't learn correct English, were rude to professors, and, when disciplined, simply quit. The fathers closed the school, reopened it as a novitiate, moved the novitiate to Cleveland, and, to fulfill a promise to the bishop, reestablished the high school in Prairie de Chien. By 1907 the students numbered 125.

In a shift of the wind, Jesuit authorities, because of renewed persecution under the *Kulturkampf* in Bismarck's Germany, were suddenly stuck with a surplus of men without work. So they turned again to Cleveland's Bishop Gilmour, with whom they had been dickering for years over where, when, and how they could set up shop. They finally opened St. Ignatius College in 1886. Progress at both Canisius in Buffalo and St. Ignatius in Cleveland, today known as John Carroll, came by inches; by 1906 one had 48 students, the other 77.

In the long run, little old Father Legouais's advice was prescient. Three principles are fundamental to Ignatius's vision: be willing to go to various places; adapt to the circumstances one finds; retain enough emotional detachment from the work to allow you to give it up. The German Jesuits, exiled from their homeland, had come with an expectation of sustaining German culture on the American frontier. As LaFarge recalled, "They had been buoyed up by a great hope for a new Germany in the new world." But they clashed from the beginning with the other major local immigrant group, the Irish, who built part of their spirituality around taking the temperance pledge. For Germans, beer was basic to the good life. In an unfair twist of history they were needed because they spoke German and were ultimately rejected because they failed to master English. Jesuits from New York came up to help temporarily with the teaching, and the Germans were always glad to see them leave. Furthermore, when Father General Beckx in 1872 appointed Henry Behrens president of Canisius College, he said, "I entreat you not to begin too many things. We cannot do everything that needs doing in this boundless land. Let us do well whatever we do." That advice didn't sink in.

In 1907 the German Mission was dissolved. The German fathers actively involved in the mission stayed where they were, and the American-born scholastics studying in Europe returned to America. Their work was split between New York, California, and Missouri. LaFarge remembers that one of the fathers, a Swiss but a German nationalist, confided that "the saddest event in American history was the refusal by the Wisconsin legislature to sanction the use of German as the official governmental language of the state of Wisconsin." Some Canisius fathers thought classes should be taught in German. "English was discouraged because . . . once you learned English you absorbed strange American ideas and departed from the orthodoxy."

The second semester of 1908, LaFarge moved to Loyola College in Baltimore, which he loved. When he walked into class the boys walked up one by one and said, "Good morning, Father."

Since LaFarge had entered the Society already ordained, he had missed the standard Woodstock regime; so in 1908 he slipped off to the woods for two years of philosophy review, which, writing in 1954, he recalled as "the greatest natural intellectual satisfaction I have ever experienced." Especially the study of "being." In the light of new-Thomism he reviewed his Harvard and Innsbruck years.

How "American" Were the Jesuits?

Charles R. Morris, in *American Catholics,* calls this end-of-the-century chapter of American Catholic history the "grand American Catholic compromise," because during it Rome and the American church locked horns again and again over just what form this rapidly growing church would take—how much of it would be "of Rome" and how much would be special to a democratic culture. In many ways it was also the period of the nation's greatest contrasts and transformation. As immigration swelled to 8.2 million in the first decade of the 1900s, America moved from an agrarian to an industrial society. The mass media boomed under the sensationalist, crusading inspiration of Joseph Pulitzer and William Randolph Hearst. The great muckraker Jacob Riis exposed to the world the underside of the Gilded Age in the overcrowded tenements of New York's lower East Side in *How the Other Half Lives* (1890), and Upton Sinclair's socialist novel *The Jungle* (1906) revealed the corruption and brutality of Chicago's meat-packing industry.

This same city sponsored the 1893 World's Fair, America at its best, the World Columbian Exposition, whose 250-foot-high Ferris wheel challenged the Eiffel Tower of Paris. It was here that the historian Frederick Jackson Turner delivered his landmark address, "The Frontier in American History," with its thesis that the frontier movement made possible by open land had closed. The fair also glorified the nation's accomplishments in science and technology, a social change Jesuit schools had not yet absorbed.

Liberal Protestantism's answer to the injustices of the age was in the social gospel movement, influenced to some degree by socialism, with the doctrine of the kingdom of God, where the kingdom about which Jesus preached was seen not as an other-world reality, but as a visible, just society that Christians collectively were called to create. Catholics were well aware of the needs of the poor; but, devoted to the principle of private property, the church shrunk from theories and movements inspired by socialism. The church served the poor in its institutions—schools, parishes, orphanages, homes, and hospitals.

A few liberal, or "Americanist," ecclesiastics, including James Cardinal Gibbons of Baltimore and Archbishop John Ireland of St. Paul, concerned with the status of the workingman, were more directly involved in social issues. In 1887 when, because of alleged socialist influence and secrecy, Pope Leo XIII was reportedly about to condemn the labor union, the Knights of Labor, of whom two-thirds were Catholics, Gibbons rushed to Rome to stop him. Gibbons's letter excoriates the "heartless avarice," which through "greed of gain" grinds down working families. Leo's act would risk "losing the love of the children of the church." In 1891 Leo XIII produced the landmark *Rerum Novarum*, "On the Condition of the Working Classes," which, while supporting private property and repudiating socialism and class warfare, asserted the right of workingmen to organize into unions. The state, it said, should use the law to regulate working conditions and to protect the health and welfare of the workers.

The day of the Jesuit political activist was a half-century away. The piety Jesuits promoted during these years was consistent with its mission of preaching and popular devotion to the Sacred Heart and the Blessed Virgin Mary before the Civil War, including an emphasis on the miraculous. *Woodstock Letters* (vol. 19) in 1890 recounts the miraculous powers of St. Ignatius water, created by blessing water with a relic or picture of St. Ignatius and using it, depending on the country in which it is applied, to save a Swiss from fire, a Frenchman from temptation, a Spaniard from the Burgos plague, and, in Pittsfield, Massachusetts, sufferers from sciatica.

A small group of Catholics associated with Isaac Hecker, the founder of the Paulists and influenced by American transcendentalists, gradually developed an alternate spirituality that relied less on emotional devotions and more on internal, quiet reflection. The hierarchy remained split on how to relate to Rome while forging a distinctly American church. At the Catholic University, within a few years, the Paulists, Dominicans, Franciscans, and other religious communities clustered around it, giving the church a forward-looking intellectual center of its own. The Jesuit parallel institutions, Georgetown and Woodstock, were but a car or train ride away; but since Catholic University was considered a product of the Americanist wing, they and the Jesuits were not to be friends.

For ten years, a sniping war waged as American bishops and Vatican authorities traded barbs. Bishop John Ireland in 1896 praised separation of church and state and criticized the Jesuits. Finally, Archbishop Francesco Satolli, who had been the first apostolic delegate to the United States, joined forces with Cardinal Mazzella, whose congregation supervised Catholic educational institutions, first to remove Bishop Keane from Catholic University, and then to draft, for Pope Leo XIII, the 1899 encyclical *Testem Benevolentiae*. Based on an interpretation of a French biography of Hecker, the encyclical condemned ideas for the most part inaccurately attributed to misguided Americans. It warned against the church's adapting itself to an advanced civilization in order to make converts, against trying to do without spiritual direction, and against the idea of establishing a national church. The pope addressed it to Cardinal Gibbons, an occasional visitor to Woodstock. *Woodstock Letters* (vol. 29) in a note following Mazzella's death, said the pope was so pleased with Mazzella's draft of the encyclical, referred to as the encyclical on Catholic unity, that he put his own pectoral cross around Mazzella's neck. The note concluded that Mazzella remained loyal to the Society, even though this was not always clear. Although the writer does not say so, it is possible that Mazzella's involvement in Vatican politics made him an ambiguous figure in his old home.

The Legendary Father Damen

Jacques Marquette passed through what is now Chicago in his expedition of 1673 and returned to live there during the spring of 1675. When the first Midwestern Jesuits reached St. Louis in 1823, its population was 5,000, while Chicago was a village of 60 to 70. Over the years, Missouri Jesuits, like Fr. Weninger, preached missions and gave clergy retreats in Chicago, and in a pattern repeated all over the country, anxious for religious-order priests to meet their shortages, bishops negotiated with Jesuits for a church or school. The Chicago breakthrough came in 1856, when Fr. Arnold Damen of St. Louis and three associates conducted a series of missions, which drew overflow throngs to the biggest church in the city. Thousands of Germans and Irish immigrants had flooded the city without priests to meet their needs.

Responding to the bishop's pleas, Damen moved to Chicago in 1857, immediately put up a small, temporary church, which he packed to overflowing with penitents and communicants—30,000 the first year—while he raised funds for a "pure Gothic" Church of the Holy Family, to be "one of the largest and most beautiful in the United States." Also in his plans was a college to rival Georgetown. Not all Chicago welcomed his plans. The *Chicago Tribune* (May 25, 1857) may have been speaking for the Protestant leadership. The facts show, says the *Tribune*, "that the Society of Jesus is the most virulent and relentless enemy of the Protestant faith and Democratic government . . . the embodiment of despotism."

Who was this Father Damen? His career demonstrates that although in the public mind the Jesuit mystique may focus on the uni-

versity, the typical Jesuit is not the university professor. He is more a
hybrid—the pastor who teaches, a teacher who preaches, an entrepre-
neur, organizer, or fund-raiser who also fasts and prays. Born in a little town in DeLeur, Holland, in 1815, he was studying at a classical
school at Turnhout, intending to enter the priesthood, when Jean de
Smet, who had returned to Belgium to regain his health and rethink
his vocation, met him and convinced him to sail back to America with
his three other recruits in 1837.

At Florissant, which was then a small enterprise with only four
novices, Damen made good progress in learning English, but, to the
disappointment of his mentors, did not display much talent for other
things Jesuits are supposed to do—teach, preach, or learn philosophy
and theology. Nonetheless, he was ordained in 1844 and spent two
more years half-employed, an assistant pastor at the college church,
but was not trusted to preach. Indeed, since the course of studies was
yet to be structured by the Woodstock routine, it was 1859 before
Damen, who would lock himself in his room to study in two-hour
daily spurts, completed his theology and took final vows.

Beginning in 1846 Damen's career began to turn around. Dejected
by the minor tasks superiors gave him to keep him useful, Damen, according to legend, made a private vow to never decline any little job
he was given; in return he asked God for the gift of preaching. Gradually, as he gave the instructions following Sunday afternoon vespers,
the crowds were moved by his words, struck by his dignified manner,
impressive physique, and stately figure. As a friend described it, audiences were moved by "his powerful and musical and sympathetic
voice, and above all, his heart strong in his affections." Those are
terms used by his contemporaries. Today's observer of his photograph
would call him handsome but heavy. Others were more refined as
speakers, but he was more effective. He had studied the great speakers from Greek times to the present. His biographer, analyzing rhetori-
cal style, compared one of his fellow missioners to Daniel Webster and
Damen to Abraham Lincoln. He was practical and direct, and his ex-
amples were easily absorbed.

Damen caught fire. He organized the Young Men's Sodality with
members from the better families and extended its influence throughout St. Louis. He offered the Spiritual Exercises to both individuals
and groups, and every year some who had made them joined the Soci-

ety. His administrative skills flourished as he opened parochial schools and hired religion teachers. When the Asiatic flu struck in 1849, he ministered to the victims. Then, in 1857, he moved to Chicago.

Damen chose the lakeside site for his church because, though it was then north of the central city, he saw the population, particularly the poor people, moving in that direction. He identified with the energetic spirit of the city and dared to give it an extra push. At the same time, he pushed himself in a variety of directions. He begged money from his rich friends in St. Louis, then in 1858 went South to work among laborers building dikes on the Mississippi. He dedicated the church in 1860, then enlarged it at the transept in 1866, making it 186 feet long and 125 feet wall to wall.

His missionary travels—a significant innovation in that part of the country because they were in English—multiplied. They met the needs of great numbers who had fallen away and not seen a priest in years. To finance these expeditions, Damen mastered the literary form of the begging letter—to Superior General Beckx in Rome and his provincial Fr. John Fruyts—in which he enumerates his victories (9,000 confessions in Chicago, 4,000 in Dubuque); dramatizes the need ("My voice has given out, I am so hoarse I can hardly he heard"); and asks for something. He asks Beckx not for money, but for 14 paintings of the Way of the Cross for the church. To Druyts, "In the name of God, send me Fr. Smarius."

In the summer of 1861 he did get Cornelius Smarius. This was a turning point in the development of the mission, in that now it was no longer Damen's personal apostolate but a formal part of province policy. As a team their impact doubled. At Cincinnati Cathedral in 1863, Fr. Smarius preached upstairs and Damen down. In two crowded side chapels men and women, some in their 60s, prepared to receive first communion, and 12 priests heard confessions. Some presentations were considered lectures, with a broad topic, "The Catholic Church," and aimed to win over Protestants in the audience.

> It is love for your salvation, my dearly beloved Protestant brethren, —for which I would gladly give my heart's blood,—my love for your salvation has made me preach to you as I have done. "Well," say my Protestant friends, "if a man thinks he is right, would he not be right? Let us suppose now a man in Ottawa who wishes to go to Chicago, but takes a car to New York." The conductor asks for his

ticket, and at once says: "You are in the wrong car; your ticket is for Chicago, but you are going to New York." "Well, what of that," says the passenger, "I mean well." "Your meaning will not go well with you in the end," says the conductor, "for you will come out at New York instead of Chicago." You say you mean well, my dear friends, but let me tell you that meaning well will not take you to heaven; you must do well also.

Since Protestant theology emphasized the individual interpretation of Scripture, in his approach to Protestants, Damen downplayed its importance. After all, he said, Jesus did not tell the apostles to write, he told them to preach. The church taught very well for 1,400 years before the printing press made the Bible available to the public. Then what happened? Disagreement and confusion.

As might be expected, Damen was criticized in letters to superiors, including the general, for a list of "violations": he sold books, collected admission for lectures, and gave a talk on purgatory and venial sins. He faced these head-on and wrote that the books were sold by the parish, not him; the admission, 50 cents, to the extra lectures went to alms for the poor, and what's wrong with talking about purgatory and venial sin? His biographer, who absolves him of even minor faults, like being too severe a superior, admits one limitation: he did not relate well to inner-city Chicago tough adolescents, who, unlike youths in the rest of America, had minds of their own.

In 1871, as the Chicago fire roared through the city, leveling it in three days, a writer to *Woodstock Letters* (vol. 11) on November 12, 1871, proclaimed, "Chicago is proud Chicago no longer. The fire-king has robbed her, not only of her pride and wealth, her pomp and luxury; but also of her many sanctuaries and shrines, of her monuments of Christian charity and devotion." The cathedral, monasteries, convents were all "buried in one promiscuous grace."

But all was not lost. "By the favor of God, our home and parish still stand on the very borders of the smoldering waste, as a monument of his impeachable mercy towards us." Classes at his St. Ignatius College, which had opened in 1870, resumed after two weeks, and the students "who had lost everything but their lives" came seeking consolation from their professors and were "anxious to get back to their books." The bishop, burned out of his house, moved in with the Jesuits and made himself at home. None of the 98 students in the first year were ready for college-level work, and Damen, though president, spent two-thirds of his time on the missions. In 1872 he resigned, and his successor built up its academic status so they could grant six Bachelor of Arts degrees at their first commencement in 1876.

As expected, Damen kept working to the end. Up at four, he started hearing confessions at five. After saying Mass, he attended another one or two out of devotion. He preached at 9:00 P.M., after dinner, and at 10:30 finished the day in the confessional. In observing obedience, he presumed to act only when he could still ask permission. As he got older his austerities increased, adding to the personal list of days on which he must fast. An altar boy sent to his room to bring him down for his mission sermon had to pause outside the door as he heard the sounds of the whip as Damen scourged himself. At first the boy was frightened, then he remembered that that is what saints do. Inevitably, miracles were attributed to his intervention: a woman with a "spiritual derangement" was declared a hopeless case by her doctors. Damen arrived and applied a relic. She was cured. When superiors in the summer of 1888 sent him to Omaha for its "healthy climate," he gave missions in Nebraska until he was felled by a series of strokes within the year and died on January 1, 1890. He was buried in the Florissant graveyard, near his old inspiration, Jean de Smet.

In 1970, when the school he founded celebrated its 100th anniversary as Loyola University, the *Tribune* editorial praised the institution for its "knowledge in the service of man." It had grown to be the "largest Catholic university in the country," training the area's doctors, dentists, lawyers, and social workers.

The parish mission in Damen's day was to some degree a descendant of the revivalism of McElroy and related to the second Great Awakening of Methodist and other evangelical itinerant preachers of the early 19th century, which began in 1800 and ran right through the Civil War. All aimed at the conversion process, the final commitment to Jesus as savior. The Jesuit missions wanted to save by rescuing the Catholic masses from both unbelief and Protestantism.

Today's Jesuits have replaced this not by preaching to large groups but by a variety of group experiences. Marriage Encounter, with psychological questionnaires and shared wisdom from those married successfully, prepares young couples for the sacrament; 12-step retreats combine insights form the Spiritual Exercises with the rules of Alcoholics Anonymous. Retreat houses and faculty retreats at colleges return to the original method in administering the Spiritual Exercises one on one. In the high schools and colleges, the retreats are built around group dynamics—such as depriving retreatants of their watches—exhausting late night conversations, and the experience of community, which, built by these techniques, they hope will hold over when they return to school.

But Father Damen lives on in stories like the following.

Late one night in the midst of a terrible storm, two children knocked at the Jesuit residence and pleaded for a priest to come and care for a dying woman. Damen himself roused up and took the call. He followed the poor waifs into the stormy night to what seemed an abandoned shack in the poorest part of town. Leaving his guides behind, Damen climbed the stairs to find an old woman at death's door. He gave her comfort, heard her confession, administered the last rites. Then she asked, "How did you find me? No one knows where I am or that I was sick." He described the two children who had dragged him forth. And she died in peace. But as she died she whispered, "The children you described are mine. But they died many years ago."

8

The Turning Point

"It Is a Perfect System"

It is 1892. Two young Jesuits, Philosopher and Theologian (not their real names), on a break from Woodstock and on an after-supper stroll, are on a summer visit to St. Inigoes, the Maryland countryside where Andrew White landed in 1635. They have been reading the latest *Woodstock Letters* (vol. 121) with its annual fold-out pages with charts showing the enrollment statistics on the number of students in U.S. and Canadian schools for 1890–91. It lists 28 institutions, 11 of which are boarding schools. The largest of them is the thriving St. Francis Xavier in New York City, with 509 students; the smallest, Gonzaga in Spokane, with 62.

The total is 7,086, an increase of 582 over the year before. Philosopher, says the anonymous author of "About Teaching," a speculative essay, is "full of ardor" for the teaching experience he is about to begin, but is at a loss to explain why our schools are so successful. Fortunately, his older companion, Theologian, whose learned conservatism has tamed his impulsiveness, has all the answers. "The reason is not far to seek. Our system must always prevail in as much as it is a system, but chiefly because it is a perfect system. Our success may for a time be slow, but under ordinary circumstances doubtful never," he tells philosopher. For a while, prestige had slipped, he said, because they had been forced to employ laymen; but now that there are enough Jesuits, the "keen eye of the American public has sent enrollment up." Following the Ratio is the key. Soon "even Protestant universities will not be ashamed to imitate us."

As they stroll along, the experienced teacher explains to his rapt audience of one how to prepare the prelection, where the teacher explains the assignment by demonstrating how to best translate the text. Translate not word for word, theologian says, but by phrases; and above all be elegant. In your spare time this summer, "translate Ovid as Irving would, Cicero in Newman's style, or a speech by Demosthenes in the Gladstone or Macaulay manner." He explains how to correct themes, the importance of discipline, the necessity of learning not many things—as do some colleges—but a few things well.

"What about the English course?" asks P. Some say there should be one in every college. Surely not, replies T., "for by persevering in our system which has been so eminently successful for three centuries we shall in the end attract more students than by trimming our sails to every popular breeze, thereby forgetting our reputation as conservative teachers, who are convinced that the ancient classics are the best means of educating the spiritual nature of man."

As they approach the villa house, the sunset on the river reminds them of Homer's "wine dark sea." The *haustus* bell rings—from the Latin *haurior,* to draw water. Which translated means: it's time for a beer.

Two Jesuits on the Road

Let us imagine that the two young men spend the rest of the summer on railroad trains and river boats as they visit some of the colleges where most likely P. would never work, before returning to the Maryland–New York–New England area where he will.

In St. Louis, the college had closed its boarding department abruptly in June 1881, after 16 of its 51 boarders, went out to the local taverns for the rest of the night rather than return to the dormitories after commencement exercises. Step by step, the college was moving to new quarters on Grand and Lindell Avenues. When P. and T. arrived, the building of the new Gothic church was still in progress, ending when the tower went up in 1916. The new classrooms were ready in 1888, with 435 students enrolled, far more than the 284 in the old neighborhood. In September 1889 the scholastics from Woodstock had returned to their home province. Now St. Louis was growing dramatically—a school of divinity in 1899, a medical department in 1903, law in 1908, and finance in 1910.

In Cincinnati, St. Xavier College (est. 1831) had barely survived its first decade, with location problems, a series of summer cholera epidemics that killed several Jesuits, closing the boarding school in 1854, and an ongoing struggle against poverty. But with new construction at

Sycamore and Seventh after the Civil War, the college had flourished but had not tried to expand. During P. and T.'s visit, it is likely they heard discussions of some extension lectures with which Xavier Jesuits would experiment in 1894.

In Milwaukee, Marquette, which had opened in 1881, had almost closed in 1885. The staff of three priests, three scholastics, and three brothers had worked furiously to be ready for the 100 boys they expected to swarm through the door on opening days, but they were disillusioned to greet only 28.

Edward and John A. Creighton were Omaha brothers and entrepreneurs largely responsible for the overland telegraph system to the Pacific, who also made their fortunes in banking, selling goods to Montana mining camps, and cattle raising. When Edward died suddenly at 54, he left no will, but, having no education himself, wanted to found a college. So, his widow in 1876 left $100,000 to the diocese, and Bishop James O'Connor turned to the Society of Jesus. In 1878 Creighton College opened with 120 students. When P. and T. visited, there were 240. Desperate for Jesuits in the 1880s and drawing students from the poorer classes in what was still a pioneer town, the college was almost given over to the Buffalo Germans; but they turned it down. For a while it shelved the classics and offered business courses to hold their students. The classics restored, they graduated their first Bachelor of Arts in 1891. Thanks to several gifts and the work of two Jesuits, brothers Joseph and William Rigge, the college was well equipped in physics and chemistry and, in 1885, with an astronomical observatory. A medical school opened in 1892.

When P. and T. arrived in Detroit, where the college had opened in September 1877 with 84 students, they were in time to enjoy the new combined college and Jesuit residence building, praised in the press as "a college building that would compare favorably with any similar institution in the land." By the time of the visit, enrollment had reached 289.

On the last leg of their return trip to Baltimore and then out to the Woodstock station, T. talked a lot less than he had on the way west. Somehow he had come to see that the situation on the ground was more complex than the positive statistics in *Woodstock Letters*. P. had brought his Latin texts with him and a copy of *Newman's Idea of the University* to prepare himself to face the 14-year-old mind wherever he was to be sent. There was a letter waiting for him from the provincial.

He was being sent to Boston College. He was in for a shock. During the next five years he would, perhaps without realizing it, witness a turning point in American Jesuit history.

Harvard versus Brosnahan, S.J.

The Society of Jesus at the close of the century had many reasons for hope. Yet, thanks to what began as a minor controversy in Boston but grew to involve the image of the Society in America, the next decade would demonstrate that its situation was more precarious than imagined.

Few institutions are more conservative, more stuck in doing things the way they did them the year before, than the university. The Jesuit universities, founded as they are on the Society's principles of adapting to the needs of a culture and a time, theoretically should be open and flexible institutions. But Jesuit education was wedded to the method and content of the *Ratio Studiorum*. How could this document speak to the age of Darwin, to the new biblical criticism that challenged the traditional historical interpretation of Genesis and the Gospels, to the social movement of once immigrant Catholics into the middle class and their embrace of middle-class aspirations, and to the educational "reforms" that made college a social rite of passage rather than a process of indoctrination, that made college "fun"?

The trouble began in June 1893 when Charles W. Eliot—president of Harvard University (1869–1909) and leader of a reform group including the presidents of Johns Hopkins, Cornell, Michigan, Stanford, and Chicago—published new rules on who would be admitted to Harvard Law School. The list included Harvard seniors and graduates of 69 other colleges. No Catholic or Jesuit schools made the cut.

By no means, said Eliot, was the exclusion anti-Catholic bigotry. It's just that the Jesuit program of studies was so different than that of Protestant and nondenominational colleges that its students would enter law school unprepared. Far from being anti-Catholic, Harvard welcomed Catholic undergraduates and had invited Bishop Keane, rector of the Catholic University (1889–1896) to lecture at Harvard three times and had just awarded him an honorary degree. Keane welcomed invitations to speak to Protestant audiences because he saw them as apostolic opportunities to soften interreligious tensions and enhance Catholicism's status in Protestant America. At Harvard's alumni dinner during his 1893 guest appearance, Keane said, the "old period of hostility and suspicion" had passed; "a new era of trustfulness and love has taken its place."

Jesuits would not agree. Eliot, from one of Boston's wealthiest families, a religious Unitarian, trained in chemistry rather than in the classics, spearheaded an educational reform agenda—raising academic standards, expanding electives—which in some areas, particularly student life, moved 180 degrees from the Jesuit philosophy.

For Eliot and his colleagues the scientific method was the only method worthy of respect; law was considered a science, and so the case method was deemed a method of scientific research. With the expansion of many disciplines, science courses flooded the curriculum. By 1907–1908 when Eliot retired, Harvard offered 254 semester-long and 189 year-long courses. Add to this the spirit of liberty that breezed through the new generation of students from the upper, middle, and even laboring classes, many from Irish Catholic families, overwhelmed by new courses that pushed the classics to the sidelines.

What to take? Let the student decide. The elective system grew out of the spirit of individual liberty and responsibility instilled by the Protestant Reformation, a rebellion against the old system, which, as stereotyped, treated students as children rather than as men. As it played out, the lack of restriction on student behavior—including their self-segregation according to wealth and class into expensive housing, fraternities, and clubs and their plunge into sports and partying—was all part of "becoming a man."

For the Jesuits, the *Ratio* and the inculcation of religious attitudes by catechism, public piety, strict dormitory surveillance, and frequent sacraments built character to enable the Christian gentleman to do battle against Protestantism and secularism.

Havens Richards, S.J., president of Georgetown, who had studied science at Harvard for a year, protested in a letter to Eliot, sending information on the Georgetown curriculum. Eliot relented and added Georgetown, Holy Cross, and Boston College to the list—though he dropped Boston College and Holy Cross in 1897–98.

With the renewed exclusion, relations between Harvard, the Jesuits, and their Massachusetts constituency continued to deteriorate. But the debate hit its nadir in 1899 when Eliot published an essay, "Recent Changes in Secondary Education," in the *Atlantic Monthly.* In a text where he was proposing that the elective system should be extended to high schools, he said that those who argue that authority should lay out a prescribed course of studies follow "precisely the method followed in Moslem countries, where the *Koran* prescribes the perfect education." This system goes from primary school to university, he said, and cultivates nothing more than memory. The same system, he said, was followed by Jesuit colleges, which had not changed in four hundred years, "disregarding some trifling concessions made for natural science."

Selected to reply was Fr. Timothy Brosnahan, recent president of Boston College and now philosophy professor at Woodstock. Brosnahan, a slender man of 42, had spent his whole life between Washington, where he went to Gonzaga College, Boston College, and Woodstock. But he was then and in the following years the most consistent Jesuit voice opposing any change in the *Ratio*. *The Atlantic* declined to publish his reply, but it ran in the Catholic weekly, the *Sacred Heart Review* (January 13, 1900), in a widely circulated pamphlet reprinted in both Catholic and secular papers across the country, and in *Woodstock Letters* (vols. 29, 31).

Brosnahan's article, which exceeds 5,000 words, opens with a mix of politeness and irony. Harvard has prospered because of Eliot's "executive ability," he says. He presumes Eliot would not criticize a system he had not studied. Then, in the logic of a Woodstock Thomistic disputation, he argues that if Eliot wants to extend the elective system to high schools it follows that he would extend it to little eight-year-old "tots" who would pick their grammar school courses without the guidance of their nurses. Eliot claims the Ratio has not changed in 400 years. Brosnahan marches the reader slowly through the *Ratio*. He shows that in the 17th century students gave 25 hours a week to Greek and Latin. Today they give them only 53 percent of a 27-hour week; the rest go to English, mathematics, modern languages, and science.

The quality of a student's education, says Brosnahan, should be measured by which courses he has taken, not by the number of courses offered. After all, with the Harvard elective system, a young man could graduate with no science at all. Indeed, until 1872–73, Harvard prescribed the same courses for all students; only recently has the elective system become "an educational fetish, which whoso does not reverence is deserving of anathema." Eliot claims his system respects "the sanctity of the individual's gifts and powers." Brosnahan concludes that the Jesuit respects the individual too much "to make the plastic souls and hearts and minds of those entrusted to their care the subjects of untried, revolutionary and wholesale experiment."

The public reaction favored Brosnahan. And when the Holy Cross and Boston College alumni gathered for their banquets, speakers, especially at Holy Cross, hit Eliot. Dr. Francis Barnes, who lectured at Boston College and was active in the alumni group, declared that Eliot "appears in his true character—a dogmatizing bigot."

Why Must We Be Strangers in the Land?

Whatever the acclaim for Brosnahan's reply, the whole episode had far-reaching effects unforeseen when the quarrel began. The weaknesses of the system of which the Jesuits were smugly proud were laid bare.

First, the seven-year structure of the *Ratio* was incompatible with the new four years of high school leading to four years of college structure mandated by the accrediting agencies. Some of the Jesuit colleges offered a course of studies of nine years: two of grammar school, four called academic, and three called college. Some tacked on a 10th year for a Master's degree in philosophy. In reality, the seven-year continuity was a façade. Very few stayed the whole course. At Boston College, graduation classes in 1877–1900 ranged from nine to 29. In 1900 no job required a college degree. Students stayed an average of three or four years. Only a third of the students taught by Jesuits in the 1890s were doing college-level work. At Xavier in New York, only 9.6 percent completed the course; at Fordham, only 6.7 percent. Obviously, parents did not share the Jesuits' idea of what the *Ratio* was worth.

Second, following the controversy, enrollment in Jesuit colleges declined. The feeling spread among the more successful Catholics that they should send their sons to nonsectarian colleges. The number of Catholics at Harvard College rose from 325 in 1893 to 480 in 1907. For them the college experience was more than the degree—it was the development of friendships, the network of associations that would determine one's future. An 1897 study by Dr. Austin O'Malley, a literature professor at Notre Dame, based on data from 35 Catholic colleges, estimated the total number of collegians (excluding prep students) at 4,764. O'Malley also concluded that many colleges were so weak that only 973 students were getting a college education. Another survey showed 1,452 Catholics in just 5 percent of the nation's non-Catholic institutions.

Third, the Jesuit response to this shocking realization was weak and confused. College presidents urged bishops to pressure families to send their sons to Catholic colleges, but the bishops declined. Catholic critics spelled out the dangers of non-Catholic campuses—opposing philosophical ideas, cheating scandals, sexual escapades, violence, drunken parties. Jesuit Rudolph Meyer, Missouri provincial and rector of St. Louis University in the 1880s, was the kind of theologian chosen 20 years before at Woodstock to make "The Grand Act," a public display of erudition, in which the actor defends all of theology for a full day before an audience of all his peers, the faculty, and visiting dignitaries including the Cardinal of Baltimore. So his pronouncements on morality carried weight. In standard theology, to place oneself in the "proximate" occasion of sin can itself be a serious sin. To him, non-Catholic schools were "usually proximate dangers to faith and morality." Thus, parents who sent their sons to these schools commit a sin— unless they have taken precautions to make the danger remote.

One of the biggest obstacles to the Ratio's reform, indeed to any modernizing ideas, was the general of the Society, Luis Martin Garcia, elected in 1892. A friend of Leo XIII and Pius X, he was a major force in what they collectively saw as a war against "the spirit of the age." As a Spanish monarchist infuriated over Spain's loss of the Spanish-American War in 1898, he was ill-disposed to comprehend any American Jesuits who wanted to adapt to a democratic society. Martin and Meyer were instrumental in drawing up *Pascendi Dominici Gregis,* the 1907 encyclical condemning modernism. The follow-up was the oath against modernism (1910), which every priest up to 1967 was required to take before ordination. The gist of the oath, read today, is to offset the intellectual threat posed by historians who, applying the principles of new history and new biblical criticism, would question the authority of Rome in interpreting biblical and theological propositions.

In 1903 the Maryland–New York provincial, Thomas Gannon, strove without success to open Martin's mind. When Europe drove the Jesuits out, he said, America let them in. Unfortunately, the governance of American Jesuits was in the hands of Europeans who didn't understand the country. He asked: "Why should our Society alone hold itself, as it were, aloof and remain a stranger in the land?" But American Jesuits would plead with Rome for permission for the simplest things—for the debate team to travel overnight—and be refused.

For the next 30 years, a series of committees attempted to reform the *Ratio*. Progress was very slow. The four-four system was adopted in 1896. When one committee suggested a few significant changes, conservatives shot them down. By 1915 Jesuits admitted they could no longer teach philosophy to boys in Latin (though they continued it in the seminaries through the 1960s). In 1923 they adopted the term "semester hour" to mean a unit of credit, introduced majors, and made Greek optional. Athletics flourished, discipline loosened.

But why did Jesuits have to be dragged through this critical turning point in their history? Several studies published within recent decades make the case that, with possible exceptions, American Jesuits were just not very intellectual. One of the modernists, William Laurence Sullivan, wrote in 1895 that the Roman system of theology was articulated by Jesuits "whose reputation for scholarship is one of the most extraordinary delusions of the pious." We have already seen that the books published by Woodstock Press were teaching manuals rather than contributions to new knowledge. A study of the scholarly output of the Boston College Jesuits at the turn of the century finds the output negligible. Occasionally, one of them wrote under a pseudonym articles critical of Harvard professors for the *Stylus*, the college magazine. They gave popular lectures on apologetics to policemen and labor leaders and recommended books Catholics should read. Rather than address larger issues, they reinforced their separate enclave.

At Catholic University an effort was made to hire Scripture professors in tune with the latest scholarship, which meant men influenced by the German school of Tübingen or its disciples or critics. In 1835 D. Strauss published the influential *Life of Jesus,* suggesting that a traditional biography of Jesus could not be written because the Gospels give us only unconnected fragments on which each evangelist imposes his own order. In 1900 Adolph Harnack's *What Is Christianity,* making strict use of the critical historical method, reduced Jesus' teachings to the fatherhood of God and the brotherhood of man. In 1910 Albert Schweitzer's *The Quest for the Historical Jesus* criticized his predecessors and concluded that Jesus was a heroic fanatic who identified his messiahship with the coming end of the world. These men and their contemporaries stressed the close analysis of texts in their historical settings, the interrelationship of various texts, and the variety of sources contributing to each document. In Catholic circles this tradition was the object of suspicion; it was not until Pius XII's 1943 encyclical *Divino Afflante Spiritu* that Catholic biblical scholarship came of age.

At Woodstock, Anthony J. Maas, S.J., set the tone of Jesuit biblical analysis with his 1891 *Life of Christ According to Gospel History,* which ignores the evidence that each Gospel has its own theology and harmonizes the four often contradictory accounts into one continuous narrative, eliminating the individuality of the evangelist. Maas's spirit was continued at Woodstock, in a column in the *American Ecclesiastical Review,* and in popular lectures by Walter Drum, S.J., son of a captain killed at San Juan Hill and brother of a general. He carried a personal military spirit into his biblical research and teaching. Drum mastered, he said, 29 languages in his studies in Beirut and Innsbruck and in his extensive travels throughout the Holy Land. Woodstock scholastics found him distant, as if "over their heads," but his principle influence was as a polemicist, a scourge on scholars, including Jesuits, whom he considered heretical. Though he collected notes on various topics, by his death he had never published a book.

Drum was an example of a phenomenon among Jesuits well into the 20th century, when the course of studies developed a man's ability to criticize the work of others but not the desire or ability to create something new and personal of his own. There are a number of explanations, though some might not apply to various individuals. Their spiritual and intellectual training had squelched the assertiveness that writing demands. They feared the editor's rejection slip. Men in their 30s and 40s were already too old to take even minor risks. They were complacent in the illusion that the Jesuit course of training had taught them all they would ever need to do God's work. Meanwhile, at the St. Andrew on Hudson Novitiate, until the late 1950s Maas's *Life of Christ* was required reading for all.

PART III

Engaging the World

9

The Social Question

A New Jesuit Voice

It is fitting that the name of the American Jesuits' new flagship magazine should be the one proposed by Thomas Gannon, former Fordham rector and the Maryland–New York provincial in the first years of the 20th century.

Gannon was most conscious of the negative aspects of European control of American Jesuit enterprises and was forthright in his efforts to break from European restrictions on an appropriate American lifestyle. His 1903 letter to Father General Martin was typical. European meddling was out of step, he said, with "our principles and spirit and in response to the requirements of time and place." In 1905 he wrote Martin it was futile "to restrain . . . the liberty of American college students," who were "18 to 23 years of age." They are men in "habits, dress, and social life" who attend dinners, receptions, and theater. He himself as a Holy Cross student 25 years before had gone out to dinners and lectures and returned quite late. Students should have their own rooms; otherwise Jesuit schools would lose them. He proposed a revision of the *Ratio* that would keep its spirit intact but be open to "all that is best and really valuable and progressive in our modern civilization."

When he heard of the new weekly magazine, to be modeled on the London Catholic *Tablet*, he proposed they call it *America.* In the first issue on April 17, 1909, the lead editorial spelled out its goals. It was to take the place of a monthly, *The Messenger,* to meet the needs of the time:

> Among these needs are a review and conscientious criticism of the life and literature of the day, a discussion of actual questions and a study of vital problems from the Christian standpoint, a record of religious progress, a defense of sound doctrine, an authoritative

statement of the position of the Church in the thought and activity of modern life, a removal of traditional prejudice, a refutation of erroneous news, and a correction of misstatements about beliefs and practices which millions hold dearer than life.

The editor emphasized that *America* stood for both North and South America, that, with both Jesuit and lay correspondents, the review would try to cover the world, especially Europe. In tone it would be without bias, prompt, fresh, accurate, and courteous, "a bond of union among Catholics and a factor in civic and social life." The editor was John J. Wynne, already the editor of the monumental *Catholic Encyclopedia* (1909), so far the towering scholarly achievement of the American church. Wynne lasted but one year, to be succeeded by Maryland–New York provincial Thomas Campbell, the man responsible for the timing of Walter Drum's vocation. (Drum had thought of pursuing a PhD at Harvard before joining the Society. Campbell told him, "If you are going to be a Jesuit, enter the Society now, and don't waste two years at Harvard.") From 1914 to 1924, throughout World War I and its aftermath, Richard Henry Tierney brought to the office what Thurston N. Davis described, in the 50th anniversary issue (April 11, 1959) as "a polemic spirit, a readiness for controversy, and a deep concern for the international responsibility of American Catholics."

In its almost century of life, *America* has survived a series of minor and major controversies. Two editors have been removed for having followed policies that most historians today would judge prudent, brave, and correct, but which displeased authorities in Rome. Readers impatient with its moderation have called it "the bland leading the bland," but its overall impact in the careful education of the Catholic public, particularly on issues of social justice, has been enormous. Appearing when it did, it was also a signal to Jesuits born in the previous century but now coming into maturity that they now had a national voice that would carry their words around the world.

Anyone who worked at *America* or has followed it carefully over the years could read the 28 pages of the early issues, in their large format and columns of solid, unbroken, small typeface, and see characteristics embedded at birth that have hung on for a century: a consistent civil tone; a steady respect for authority, especially the hierarchy; and a quaint preoccupation with New York, particularly its own neighborhood. For Jesuits are walkers, and some imagine that what strikes them as amusing on the street will interest their readers as well.

The early issues, especially with the Chronicle section at the beginning (now called Current Comment) and the short news items in the back, indicate that its purpose is to inform more than to persuade. The first Chronicle item remarks on the 100th anniversary of the cornerstone laying at Old Saint Patrick's Cathedral, across the street from the home where Anthony Kohlmann, S.J., and Benedict Fenwick, S.J., future bishop of Boston, opened a school on Mulberry Street in 1808.

We learn that France is celebrating the beatification of Jeanne d'Arc; there's a cabinet crisis in Newfoundland; in Russia the decree of toleration has sent perhaps hundreds of thousands swarming from Orthodoxy to Roman Catholicism; in the United States there is little support for women's suffrage. An editorial says the church is right to excommunicate Professor Schnitzer at the University of Munich for calling the resurrection a legendary addition to the Gospel and for criticizing the encyclical against modernism. An article asks whether a Catholic can be a socialist and answers that one cannot deny the right of private property and remain a Catholic and adds that nearly all socialists are antireligious. The books section reviews three books on Jeanne d'Arc by non-Catholics—Mark Twain, Andrew Lang, and Anatole France.

The news items report that E. H. Shackleton has arrived at a point 111 miles from the South Pole. Another item, as if in answer to its own article, quotes a speaker who says: though fundamental principles of socialism cannot be accepted, there is a bond of sympathy between all right thinking people and socialists, the desire to come to the relief of the oppressed and poor. On September 18, 1909, a reviewer reports: "Mr. G. Bernard Shaw has written much that is wicked." He wrote a blasphemous play lately. Lord Chamberlain refused to license it in England, but W. B. Yeats and Lady Gregory sponsored it in Ireland. *America* never tells us the play's name.

LaFarge's New Education

In November 1910 the Woodstock rector, Fr. Maas, awakened John LaFarge in the middle of the night to tell him his father had died; he had to get the early morning train from Baltimore to get to New York in time for the funeral at the Church of St. Francis Xavier. When he returned to Woodstock, it had become clear to Maas and the provincial that LaFarge's health was not robust. He had tried to cure himself with long walks and rest, without success. Maas called LaFarge in and told him with a peculiar metaphor that it was "better to be a live jackass than a dead lion." This meant they judged that, since LaFarge lacked the stamina for a life of scholarship, they were sending him into parish work at St. Thomas Manor, St. Ignatius Church, Charles County, Maryland. He would begin his priestly career in the footsteps of Andrew White.

As things worked out, he was moved first quickly from St. Thomas Manor to Philadelphia's Old St. Joseph's Church at Willing's Alley, only a block from Independence Hall, and from there to the hospitals and prisons on Blackwell's Island (later Welfare Island, then Roosevelt Island) in New York City's East River. There, for eight months, he ministered to the city's most forsaken—900 drunk and disorderly sentenced to the Work House, 3,300 in the City Home, 300 neurologically ill, and 1,000 tubercular in the Metropolitan Hospital. He also got a sense that those who served the poor were a "great and rather jovial family." The pastor had organized the nurses into a sodality, and the warden set up shop work to rehabilitate the prisoners. During these months LaFarge administered the sacrament of Extreme Unction 3,000 times. These men and women had no one but their Creator, wrote LaFarge in his autobiography, and at death their Creator was "there" in a dramatic manner that took his breath away. LaFarge had been judged not fit for higher studies, but be was being schooled. "Innsbruck and Woodstock were schools of knowledge," he wrote, "but Blackwell's Island was a school of life and death."

In September 1911 he reported as assistant pastor to the Church of St. Aloysius in Leonardstown in St. Mary's County, one of three centers serving 22 missions or parishes. The churches, a handful of which still stand, were small and white—simple in décor, without many statues that would offend their 18th-century Protestant neighbors—with balconies where slaves once sat and where their descendants still worshiped. The white citizens were descendants of the *Ark* and the *Dove* period, who had forgotten their origins and were now just conservative, passive Catholics.

In an interlude that reconnected this now country pastor with his aristocratic past, in 1913 LaFarge revisited his old family friend Henry Adams, great-grandson of John Adams, grandson of John Quincy Adams, and son of Charles Francis Adams, Lincoln's ambassador to Great Britain during the Civil War. His *Mont-Saint-Michel and Chartres* (1904) and his autobiography, *The Education of Henry Adams* (1907), represented a religious and philosophical yearning for transcendence and unity he could never satisfy. Eliot had brought him to Harvard to build its history department. At the visit, LaFarge was 33, and Adams, 75, was living on H Street in Washington. Sitting at the piano, LaFarge helped Adams's secretary decipher Gregorian chant manuscripts for Adams's medieval research, then sat by the fire with him, a stroke victim, and talked about their families. LaFarge sensed that Adams wanted to talk about his own search for religious faith, but it was in Adams's character to put up a wall against questions. LaFarge could not break through. Adams died in 1918. In 1905 he had written to his niece, "Perhaps John will kindly stick me into his Mass."

In 1915 when LaFarge moved to St. Inigoes Manor he got a better sense of how the Negroes interpreted their history. They remembered 1838 as if it had happened to them personally, when Fr. Mulledy sold their ancestors to slave merchants who carried them to Louisiana and Georgia; and they remembered Father Carberry, who fought against the sale and then warned them in time for some to escape into the woods.

As he made his rounds, usually in a horse and buggy, LaFarge had time to think, to come up with ideas to deal with two big problems as he saw them: (1) to improve the condition of poor Negroes, mainly with education; (2) to deal with the problems of Catholic farmers and the need for an association to help them. He saw the two as connected. Priests could help rural whites and blacks to unite, to petition government agencies for assistance. After a one-year interruption for tertianship, a third probation during which Jesuits prepare for final vows, LaFarge was reassigned to a new residence, St. Michael's at Ridge, for four years, 1918 to 1922, which he described as "the hardest years of my life, certainly those in which I felt helpless and abandoned by everything human." Also: more stomach problems.

He begged for money from wealthy friends to support his projects, recruited white and black nuns to set up schools, and established in 1924 the Cardinal Gibbons Institute, a vocational school for black boys and girls, which was a lot of trouble, both because of the lack of funds and disagreements with the black educators the trustees had chosen to direct it. It had to close during the Depression in 1933; but LaFarge's successor, Horace McKenna, reopened it as a day school in 1936.

In 1926 LaFarge left the Maryland Counties to become an associate editor of *America* in New York City. There he would set out from the America staff residence, Campion House, on West 108th Street, where he never felt at home. For 15 years in Maryland he could speak to everyone on the street. Even his horse knew automatically when to stop at the sight of a new person to allow him to strike up a conversation. This didn't happen on the upper West Side.

For a man with a frail constitution, LaFarge began, at 46, a double career: as editor and writer, and as a speaker and social activist involved in a list of causes—interracial relations, liturgical arts, Catholic rural life, international peace, and anticommunism. Though he was most identified with race relations, anticommunism stirred him in special ways. He often argued against racism because he feared the communists could exploit it for their purposes. His *America* responsibilities, which included editorials, articles, and a personal column, gave him infinite opportunities to pour out convictions he had held for years, way back to his opposition to Eliot's elective system at Harvard.

Yet he was constantly sensitive to the spoken and unspoken restrictions in the office—the feelings of the provincials, fear of offending bishops, and the domineering presence of Paul L. Blakely, S.J., a conservative Southern states-rightist, who by force of personality tilted the editorial board during the 1920s and 1930s. Their tasks compartmentalized, each editor took responsibility for a big topic or part of the world and developed a level, sometimes amateur, of expertise for "his" area"—the East, Europe, Africa, and soon. LaFarge was the "Negro expert," so he opened with a four-part series repeating themes he had developed in the Counties. David W. Southern, in *John LaFarge and the Limits of Catholic Interracialism, 1911–1963*, enumerates them:

> Education is all important in solving the race problem, the Negro is
> the ward of the white man; blacks are more susceptible than whites
> to materialism and radical movements; blacks are better off on farms;
> black vocations are needed to convert the race; only Catholicism has
> a clue to the solution of the race question, though Protestants have

more racial achievements; and finally, all must have the patience of
Job in the face of the racial dilemma.

Although the heart of LaFarge's philosophy was interaction between
blacks and whites, this raised two problems: since the associations
were initiated by white Catholics, the blacks could feel like secondary
members; LaFarge could be uncomfortable with aggressive, militant
blacks who lacked his patient spirituality. Constance Daniel, the black
woman who directed the Gibbons Institute, had the nerve to write
LaFarge letters attacking what she saw as the racism in the Catholic
Church. LaFarge tended to attribute the Institute's problems to her
management rather than to the failure of the trustees to raise money.
Meanwhile, the Daniel family who lived in the building lacked heat
and food, and their daughter died of pneumonia.

The Daniels had become devotees of Thomas Wyatt Turner, a
Howard University professor and founder and president in 1924 of
the Federated Colored Catholics (FCC). LaFarge and William Markoe,
S.J.—who, unlike LaFarge, was bold, loud, charismatic, and willing to
tangle with superiors—both became active in the FCC. In 1932 they
conspired to remove Turner because, in Markoe's words, he had "a little of Black Muslim in him." They changed the name to the softer National Catholic Federation for the Promotion of Better Race Relations.
In a last-minute coup, LaFarge also changed the name of the Federation's magazine from *The Chronicle* to *The Interracial Review*.

Southern concludes that LaFarge's "'humble and dignified manner' . . . should not obscure his determination to act as the key Catholic spokesman on racial policy in the United States." In place of the
FCC, in 1934 LaFarge created the Catholic Interracial Council of New
York (CICNY).

One of the church's embarrassments during the 1930s and 1940s
was that, in spite of special interest in the doctrine of the Mystical
Body of Christ, which teaches the dignity of every individual and
the unity of the human family, Catholic schools were still segregated.
LaFarge was exceedingly moderate on desegregation—don't force it
where it's illegal or strongly resisted. Yet he was very angry in 1934
when Fordham turned down Hudson J. Oliver, Jr., the son of his
friend and "almost entirely white in appearance." In a letter to the
provincial, LaFarge went so far as to accuse Fordham's rector of "mortal sin" and threatened to "denounce Fordham in public" or "quit all

my colored work forever." Of course, with his rules against criticizing religious authorities, he had no such intention. The solution was to order Saint Peter's College to accept Oliver. Ironically, the Saint Peter's dean, Robert I. Gannon, S.J., was soon made president of Fordham, where he welcomed the CICNY conference in 1936 with the assurance that "no student would be denied admittance to any department of the university because of race prejudice." As things worked out, young Oliver did not do well at Saint Peter's, and, though blacks had been in Fordham's other schools for years, it was not until 1947 that a black face appeared among the graduates in the Fordham College Yearbook.

That same year Francis K. Drolet, S.J., published in *Woodstock Letters* (vol. 76) "Negro Students in Jesuit Schools and Colleges, 1946–1947." There had been in recent years, he said, "much discussion on the moral problem whether or not Jesuit schools, as private institutions, were bound to admit members of any specific race; and this meant, usually, the Negro race." Of the 64 high schools and colleges surveyed, 47 had or would admit Negroes, 6 would not, 11 didn't answer. Of the high schools, 4 did not. Of 8 who did not answer, most were in the South. Of those who would admit, most had one or none. Out of a total of 23,494 students, 20 were black. Among the 21 colleges that replied, 436 of the total 81,794 students were black. St. Louis University had the most with 150, then Fordham with 102. Georgetown, LeMoyne, Saint Peter's, and Santa Clara had none. The large numbers were due to the professional schools rather than the college. With unintended irony, Drolet ends on the hopeful note of Pius XII's 1939 letter, *Sertium Laetitiae*, addressed to the people of the United States. The pope expressed "special paternal affection, certainly inspired by Heaven, for the Negro people dwelling among you." John LaFarge had read the letter looking for something more.

As in the 19th century, during the slavery issue and the Civil War, in the first half of the 20th century there was no Jesuit consensus on race, just as there was no consensus on fascism or the Vietnam War. As usual, some brave men spoke out on all these issues and paid for it with ostracism, imprisonment, or death. On race in particular, Jesuits were not well ahead of the public. When John LaFarge, for example, argued for the admission of a young black man to the Society, the objection was that it was not clear where this man could be sent to work and be accepted.

The "Secret Encyclical"

In 1931 Wlodimir Ledochowski, son of a Polish count and general of the Society from 1915 to 1942—a period that included the end of the Old Order with World War I, the rise of fascism and communism, and the beginning of World War II—was asked by Pope Pius XI to direct the preparation of a new social encyclical. Celebrating the 40th anniversary of *Rerum Novarum, Quadragesimo Anno,* written by German Jesuits, condemned the excesses of both capitalism and communism and was widely accepted in the United States as another papal defense of the rights of the working man. Catholic social activists found it consistent with the 1919 "Bishop's Plan for Social Reconstruction," drawn up by Catholic University theologian Msgr. John A. Ryan—which called for housing for working people, a legal minimum wage, and social insurance—and with programs of President Franklin D. Roosevelt's New Deal. In short, the American church was slowly developing a social program.

But Ledochowski's personal concern was the threat of Marxism. At his order, in 1934 the Maryland–New York provincial appointed Georgetown Foreign Service School founder Edmund Walsh, S.J., assisted by LaFarge, to plan a response to the general's wishes. In 1935 a national group of Jesuits gathered at the former West Baden Springs Hotel, in West Baden, Indiana, then the philosophy-theology school of the Chicago Province, to draw up a social action plan. Walsh was a very conservative, single-minded anticommunist, not much concerned with other social issues, while LaFarge sought to link anticommunism and interracial relations. Not much came of the effort, although in 1940 the general appointed another Jesuit, John Delaney, to develop the Institute for Social Order, which would go through several forms in different homes. Meanwhile, LaFarge had another opportunity on the horizon.

In 1938, as LaFarge concluded a fact-finding tour of Western Europe, including Germany and Czechoslovakia, Pope Pius XI stunned him by calling him to a secret meeting at Castel Gandolfo. LaFarge had sent him a copy of his new book, *Interracial Justice;* now the pope wanted him, "as if you yourself were the Pope" to write an encyclical on racism and fascism, including anti-Semitism. When LaFarge informed Ledochowski, the general exclaimed, "The Pope is mad!" afraid that a condemnation of Germany would strengthen Stalin. For three months LaFarge, assisted by a German priest-economist, settled in the Paris residence of the Jesuit magazine *Études* and, pushing himself to the point of collapse, wrote the encyclical.

Called *Humani Generis Unitas*, the first 75 pages, written by his coauthor Father Gustav Gundlach, repeated ideas from previous encyclicals on the unity of the human race. LaFarge's 50 pages on totalitarianism, racism, and anti-Semitism were sharper. He condemned Nazism as contrary to natural law, and, concerning the United States, condemned lynching and public distinctions based on race. Although he said racial segregation caused harm, he backed off from an absolute condemnation, allowing for "social separations" where "brotherly love and prudence" might require it. Anti-Semitism, he said, was "totally at variance with the true sprit of the Catholic church." But he worried about "misguided" Jews who were attracted to communism.

On September 20, for personal reasons that are not clear, LaFarge delivered the manuscript not to Pius XI but to Ledochowski, who sat on it for months, in effect suppressing it; and there is no evidence Pius XI even saw it before he died on February 10, 1939. When Pius XII issued *Summi Pontificatus* (the *Unity of Human Society*) in October, LaFarge looked in vain for his ideas on racism. The best he could get was the greeting to blacks in *Sertium Laetitiae*.

The Showman

LaFarge's contemporary, Chicago-born (in 1888) and St. Louis–based Daniel Lord, had a totally different personality. He was a wide-open, gregarious showman and dealt with some of the same issues with very different tactics. He is best known for his revitalizing of the sodality of the Blessed Virgin Mary by publishing a flood of books and pamphlets—90 books, 45 dramas, 13 musicals, and nearly 300 pamphlets with provocative titles like *Christ and Women, Fashionable Sin, Murder in the Classroom,* and *Has Life Any Meaning?*—by touring the high schools and colleges, writing and producing original musical shows on religious themes with student casts, establishing a series of Summer Schools of Catholic Action to train thousands of priests, nuns, laymen and women and student sodalists to transform their own communities, and by revamping *Queen's Work* as the national sodality magazine.

Without theoretical discussions on the prudence and timing of integration, he would simply crowd his musical stages with young black faces as well as white. Without preaching on the subject, if asked his stand on war he would reply that he himself could never kill another person and would have to refuse to serve. His efforts were resisted by bishops who resented so dynamic a presence in their dioceses and by other priests and fellow Jesuits who may have been jealous of his huge popularity and/or were convinced he harmed the sodality movement by making it an everybody-welcome mass movement rather than a disciplined cadre of the spiritual elite.

In Hollywood he advised Cecil B. DeMille on the silent version of *King of Kings*, said Mass on the set, convinced DeMille to drop the scripted love affair between Mary Magdalene and Judas, and wrote the first version of the Motion Picture Code. Pius XI consulted him on an encyclical on the movies, and FDR sought his ideas on Social Security. In 1943 he replaced Fr. Delaney as head of the Institute for Social Order and called another conference at West Baden to seek ideas that would point ISO in the right direction.

It didn't work. The participants knew they lacked the training in the social sciences to speak authoritatively. Some, including Zacheus Maher, the general's visitor, were disturbed by tendencies they saw in the younger Jesuits who were vocally dissatisfied with their training —intimations of the generation gap of the 1960s. Finally, as head of ISO, Lord's talents were more those of a cheerleader than executive director. Staff who wanted to consult him found him hard to talk to. Visitors with personal problems would gobble up his office time while a staff member working on a deadline would cool his heels. Lord explained, "When I'm dealing with a soul, the whole world can wait." Given an opportunity to socialize, Lord would head for the piano to lead the party in a community song fest, oblivious that some would rather just talk. Worse, he did not supervise his staff but simply gave them jobs at the beginning the year and left them alone. By 1947 the finances were in disarray, and Lord was removed, replaced by Leo Brown, S.J.; but, like Lord, Brown would have limited resources to work with. The American Society still lacked the trained manpower to do social research as well as the times demanded.

What had been the sodality, technically the Congregation of Mary (CM), was transformed in a series of meetings between 1948 and the early 1950s, with the initiative coming from Jesuit headquarters in

Rome, into a more international and social version of the movement called the Christian Life Community. In the late 1960s the CLC profited by the rediscovery of the original form of the Spiritual Exercises. And its members experienced the Exercises with one-on-one direction. Today the CLC is also a Non-Governmental Organization affiliated with the United Nations, which works on the grassroots level for peace and justice.

China

When George Dunne entered Los Angeles Loyola High School in 1918, the school was in its very early years. It would quickly expand into a college and in 1929 move to a beautiful campus at Playa Del Rey and become a university; but for George it was a "microschool," where the high school, college, and Jesuit living quarters were all crammed into one building, with a couple of Jesuits living in classroom clothes closets. The college graduating class in 1929 numbered ten. Academic standards were flexible: George went to college in the morning, worked in a fruit and vegetable store in the afternoon, and attended the law school in the evening. Colorful Jesuits included the 250-pound Fr. Fox, who easily drifted from his philosophy notes to gossip about glamorous movie stars who sought his advice. The first person George met on his first day was Zacheus Maher, S.J., who would rise quickly in the Jesuit power structure and with whom Dunne would cross swords in later years.

George entered the novitiate at Los Gatos, California, in 1926. For several years he fought depression and struggled with the obligation of celibacy, but somehow it never entered his mind to leave. He just knew he had been called by God to this life. When California Jesuits were given responsibility for the mission in China, Dunne volunteered and sailed in August 1932. The mission—which included a cathedral-sized church, schools, an observatory, orphanages, major seminary, a publishing house, and the Jesuit school of theology—was centered in the village of Zikawei, on the edge of the French concession, today a booming commercial neighborhood of Shanghai. Dunne quickly sized up the political situation and drew up a proposal for an institute in Nanking, then the capital, to train leaders dedicated to democratic ideals in economics, politics, and education. Dunne saw that the present Kuomintang leadership was corrupt; and unless the current structure could be reformed, China would go communist within 30 years.

Dunne of course saw himself working for the rest of his life in the Nanking project, but a number of factors interfered. He suffered from asthma and chronic diarrhea and periodically would retreat to a downtown Shanghai French Jesuit infirmary to recuperate. There he had the occasional thrill of meeting and serving Mass for the paleontologist Pierre Teilhard de Chardin, discoverer of Peking Man and already a hero to young French Jesuits. Meanwhile, the local superiors had already decided to make Dunne a theology professor. To rescue him from that fate, California Jesuits engineered his temporary return to Los Angeles, with the expectation of later going back to Nanking. Once back in Los Angeles, invited to address the meeting of the American provincials on the Chinese situation, he discovered that, in spite of Pius XI's social exhortations, they weren't remotely interested. Dunne learned what LaFarge and Daniel Lord were learning during those years of the West Baden meetings, with their visions of new institutes and social reform: the grassroots American Jesuits lacked the training, confidence, and imagination to tackle big issues of justice, race, peace, and war. Pearl Harbor shattered Dunne's dreams of returning to China and accelerated the events that led to communist rule. But this young Jesuit had several bigger emotional shocks ahead.

"A Man of Principle"

In 1943, as the recently ordained Dunne was finishing his doctoral studies in international relations at the University of Chicago, but before his final vows, he was asked to give the annual retreat to the Jesuit theology students at Alma College, the California province theologate. At retreat's end, when Dunne entered the dining room, the young men broke into applause, and many of them wrote letters of praise to both him and to the provincial. But hardly had he returned to his dissertation, which he was writing in a cabin in the Michigan woods, when he received a letter from Maher. Because he represented Rome during World War II, Maher was the virtual head of the America assistancy and now accused Dunne of disrupting the lives of the young Jesuits, throwing even the best of them "off stride" with what he had said during the retreat.

In the Spiritual Exercises, during the contemplation on the Incarnation, Ignatius asks that we "look out over the face of the earth" and see various persons, "some white and others black, some at peace and others at war, some weeping and others laughing, and some healthy and others sick, some being born and others dying," in preparation for how the Divine Persons will plan the redemption of all. Today it would be common to introduce social issues at this point or at the Sermon on the Mount. In 1943, even with World War II waging, it was not. When Dunne got to the Sermon on the Mount, he talked about anti-Semitism, Hitler's holocaust, racial segregation, the rat-infested tenements of New York, the exploitation of migrant workers, the Spanish Civil War, and the world's poor. Dunne knew there were a few anti-Semites and pro-Franco men in the group, but he was shaken to think their complaints, if indeed they complained, would swing Maher against him. Yet he knew Maher as a man deeply pessimistic about the nature of the Jesuits under him, predisposed to think the worst, "a man often in error, but never in doubt," and he was disillusioned about a governance where people can make accusations and remain anonymous to the accused. Dunne later discovered that only one man had complained, the rector, a conservative man incapable of discussion. He had been annoyed at Dunne's request to say a "dialogue mass," a modest 1940s liturgical adaptation during which the congregation answers many of the prayers.

In September 1944, with PhD in hand, Dunne reported to Saint Louis University, where the province had established an Institute for Social Science (ISS), a new research arm of the ISO. He quickly learned he had to tread softly after his six-minute radio homily on the Sacred Heart program got him called before the president, Patrick Holloran, S.J., to explain himself. The talk, on racial integration, said the president, could be interpreted as an attack on John Glennon, the archbishop. While St. Louis was still a segregated city, a small group of Jesuits—including LaFarge's colleague William Markoe, his brother John, and archeologist Claude Heithaus—had been agitating to integrate the university. On February 11, 1944, Heithaus, after having rewritten his talk 20 times and clearing it with three Jesuit faculty, had preached on segregation. If Muslims and Hindus are welcome at Saint Louis U., he asked, why are not Negroes? At the end, the congregation of over a thousand joined him in a pledge never to injure a black person. Published in the *University News*, of which Heithaus was moderator, and reported in the *St. Louis Post-Dispatch*, the sermon had a strong positive effect on local blacks and many Jesuits. But not on the archbishop. Following a tumultuous meeting between the archbishop, Holloran, and Heithaus, it was agreed that the university would be allowed to integrate, but that Heithaus would be silenced.

Later, Dunne discovered that Maher had fully supported Holloran in his resistance to integration, and Dunne challenged his judgment. Maher replied, "George, we cannot take positions on social subjects which run counter to the positions held by the society in which we live." As a matter of fact, when ISO was getting started, Daniel Lord consulted the provincials on whether ISO should shy away from controversial issues out of fear of alienating benefactors. The provincials promised to support ISO on issues of social justice and conscience. Dunne sensed that Maher was out of step with the Society and with his own conscience; for Maher had told Dunne when he was in high school, "A Jesuit is a man of principle," that the teachings of Christ can contradict social mores. Maher and Dunne could never look one another in the eye again.

For a while integration at Saint Louis was a success. Blacks and whites shared classrooms, the gym, the pool, and activities. *Life* magazine did a photo story on Saint Louis as the first Catholic university to admit Negroes. But in spring 1945 Holloran, a month before the major student ball, backed off from social integration and ordered the student council to pass a resolution forbidding Negro student participation in extracurricular activities. It meant the annual student ball would be a "whites only" affair. Heithaus, obliged to break his silence, published a protest in the *University News* on March 16 and refused to require the paper to print the restriction on the student ball. The provincial tried to get Maher to make Heithaus leave the Society, but Maher did not go along. Dunne, writing about the event in his 1990 autobiography, saw it as a case showing no one, even a Jesuit superior, can require another to go against his informed conscience.

Nevertheless, Holloran determined that Heithaus must be punished, publicly humiliated by the dinnertime ritual in which a reader in the pulpit proclaims a *culpa*, a condemnation of the Jesuit for his offense—in this case, refusal to publicize a segregated dance. In the presence of over 300 Jesuits, including all the scholastics in studies, Heithaus stood holding his biretta in his hands and was publicly reprimanded for ignoring the wishes of his superior.

Dunne resisted the temptation to dump a soup tureen on Hollo-ran's head. As they filed silently from the dining hall, Dunne grabbed Heithaus's hand and said, "It's an honor to know you."

Heithaus was expelled from the university, sent first to become an army chaplain, then to Marquette, then back to St. Louis to die. When Dunne wrote to the Missouri provincial that he would have a problem in conscience working at a resegregated school, he was shipped back to California. He had been invited to join the *America* staff, but LaFarge wanted to wait until the "heat was off." It was 1967, after La-Farge's death, before the invitation was renewed. At the time, Dunne was at Georgetown training Peace Corps volunteers.

On August 27, 1970, Jesuit General Pedro Arrupe wrote to Hei-thaus, "I must not forget to allude to the farsighted efforts on behalf of civil rights and equality of opportunity for Negroes. The Christian justice of your position has never been in doubt; its timeliness has been authenticated in more recent years."

10

At War

"I'll Meet Him in Hell"

After the bombing of Pearl Harbor, when George Dunne spontaneously told his provincial he wanted to enlist as a chaplain, the provincial told him he had already recruited three, and that's all he could afford. The impulse to be a chaplain was another lingering spirit from the Society's first century, of the zeal to be a missionary, to throw oneself into a situation that demanded the most generosity, and in which one might be killed.

The missionary zeal was a constant until after Vatican II, when the purpose of mission work shifted from conversion to inculturation. The French, Spanish, Italian, and other missionaries sent to the Indians risked their lives because they were convinced the native people would never see heaven unless they were baptized; so the goal was to change them—socially and culturally—even give them an economy that would enable them to lead good Christian lives. More recent theology calls for adapting to a culture, absorbing its wisdom, truly respecting, for instance, Eastern religions as a means toward salvation.

But the challenge to military service usually comes only once in a generation; and in the 20th century the notion that one has not lived if he has not shared in his generation's war has hung over Jesuits as over any young man of age during World War I, World War II, Korea, and Vietnam. Daniel Lord, who could tell us he would have refused to don a uniform and kill another human being, also was embarrassed during World War I to appear in public in a cassock when other men his age were on the battlefields in France.

But, as we saw during the Civil War, for those who volunteered as chaplains, even stronger than patriotism was the conviction that young men must not die without a chance, even at the last minute, to be reconciled to God. True, 17th-century Jesuits accompanied the Spanish Army in imperialistic expeditions into the New World to serve Spain as well as God, but as Diego Laynez, second general of the Society, spelled it out: "By prayer and good example, by preaching and hearing confessions, by nursing the sick and helping the dying, these men will do a tremendous amount of good. They will teach the soldiers proper motives for fighting, keep them from quarrelling among themselves and will call them to task for blasphemies and gambling. Finally, I know that the soldiers will profit from this, for by their peace of mind and confidence in God they will better fulfill their duties in war."

Jesuits plunged into American wars from the beginning. During the Mexican War (1846–48) the U.S. government was anxious to have Catholic chaplains for the expeditionary force, both because nearly half the men were Catholic and because the war was against a Catholic power. John McElroy, whose physical strength matched his zeal, gave up his roles as pastor and church builder to join Zachary Taylor's forces. His companion in Mexico, Anthony Rey, S.J., was killed by guerrilla forces. During the Civil War, Jesuits served on both sides. During World War I, 39 Jesuits were commissioned, though some served only a few weeks or months. Their letters, like the letters of their contemporaries, narrated months of routine and days of horror. One writes frustrated in 1918 that he is stationed behind the lines in a quartermaster's camp with 150 Southern Negroes, none of whom are Catholics when "thousands are needing us vitally up nearer the front in the hospitals." Another at the front says their main duty is to administer the sacraments no matter what uniform the penitent wore:

> A wounded and a dead man could be found everywhere. German, American, French and Algerian all were visited by me. The regimental surgeon of the 18th, a good pal of mine, protested when I assisted a German.
>
> "Father, let him alone."
>
> I smiled and answered. "If I do, Major, I'll meet him in hell along with you."

As the war ended, provincials quickly recalled their men to work at home. But when World War II broke out, Jesuits had men from the various provinces in missionary war zones all over the world. When the Philippines fell to Japanese invaders, Jesuits were marched into prison camps, where they survived until rescued by American troops at the end of the war. By then, 243 Jesuits had served (181 Army, 60 Navy, 2 Merchant Marine), and their experiences were a cross section of the war itself. Jesuits in Manila saw their islands fall. A Navy Jesuit chaplain was the first American into Tokyo at the end of the war. Fr. Berkeley Kines (Md) landed in Algiers in 1942 and was with his troops at the Kasserine Pass. Wounded at El Guettar, he rejoined American forces to invade Sicily. Fr. Thomas B. Cannon (NY), in Italy with the 10th Mountain Division, saw two division chaplains killed and the third a casualty in the first weeks of combat.

Fr. James A. Gilmore (Ore) went ashore at Normandy. In December 1944 Fr. Paul W. Cavanaugh, his regiment ambushed during the Battle of the Bulge, was imprisoned until rescued in April 1945. On May 3, 1945, Fr. William Cummings (Md) walked into a mine field to help a wounded man, and the mine exploded, hospitalizing him for three months. In the Pacific, in the Gilbert Islands, Fr. Stephen J. Meany (NY) was wounded four times in his attempts to help a wounded soldier. On Iwo Jima in 1945, after the raising of the American flag had been photographed, Fr. Charles F. Suver (Ore) raised the host at Mass on the same mountain. Off Kobe, Japan, when a bomb hit the *U.S.S. Franklin* and 700 men died, Fr. Joseph O' Callaghan (NE) heroically tried to minister to them all.

The bond of union among Jesuits during the war was *Woodstock Letters,* and the men poured out their major and minor experiences in letters to friends that also ended up in print. Fr. Herbert P. McNally, S.J., began his account as a chaplain at the U.S. Naval Training Station in Norfolk, Virginia, in June 1941 and ended at Reykjavik, Iceland, in January 1942. We don't know to whom the letters were addressed but deduce he was a fellow Jesuit, stationed at Georgetown, a faithful correspondent, who sent him magazines and newspapers, though their letters took weeks to go back and forth.

McNally's tone is consistently up-beat. He tells his friend again and again that he is "happy," though the months and days in Iceland pass slowly, and if told he had to leave in an hour he would be ready in 15 minutes. Each day is a routine of Masses, confessions, talks, shuttling from one camp to another to offer the sacraments. At Norfolk, up at 4:30 A.M., he hears confessions before the 6:00 o'clock Mass, then hears confessions before and after the Mass he says at 8:15. The general strategy is to find out who are the Catholics—he refers to them as "lads," "youngsters," and "kids"—get them in for an interview, as in taking a parish census, assess their religious needs (have they made first communion, been confirmed?), then hope they show up for Mass. If only a handful show up, he will get to their Catholic officers, with the hope they'll nudge their troops into church. In July we learn that the tan he hoped to acquire is "behind schedule," that sea nettles keep him out of the surf. He learns he's being sent to Iceland with the marines. "The prospect of Iceland appeals to me a lot." He's told they are a "swell crowd," and as the only chaplain he'll have his work cut out for him.

In Iceland it rains nearly all the time, the wind blows at gale force, and the landscape is drab and bare. The good days are clear and crisp with the gaunt mountains all around. On Sundays he drives to three Masses in an open truck with the rain in his face. On December 18, 1941, he writes: "Japan has been spoiling for a fight with us for a long time. She succeeded in getting in the first wallop—and what a wallop it was—but she is in for a terrible trouncing." He adds that "we will come out on top—especially if the home authorities get serious about the subversive elements in the States, and stop coddling them." At Christmas midnight Mass, he has 300 in the church by 11:50 P.M. and a line of 45 waiting for confession. What can he do? He calls them to the front, gives them all general absolution, and urges them to go to confession later. Most of the choir members are Protestants who after Mass drive to sing again at Protestant services. After dinner he drives out in a storm to bring gifts to the "lads" in the hospital. "It was awful driving, but the reaction on the sick lads was worth all the inconvenience. So that was my Christmas. I think you will agree a very happy one."

In November 1944 another Jesuit writes anonymously describing a twelve-day battle in Holland where his unit is under constant German artillery barrage as they make their way across field and ditches from one town to another. The chaplain travels with the medics, and when a medic is hit he becomes a stretcher bearer himself. "It is hard to give you a true picture," he concludes. "Pardon my scrawl." But his account is gripping:

> Then the order came to go forward and we started off. You can get some idea of the war's destruction from pictures but nothing can give you a picture of the fear and tensions in every heart. Even such things as a wandering cow, ludicrous enough in retrospect, can

freeze your heart in no joking manner. So on through the dark, past barns and houses, awaiting the enemy fire. . . . We were exhausted from the effort of wading, and my heart seemed ready to burst, yet we couldn't stop. Dawn was getting brighter and we were clearer targets with each minute. Finally we reached the steep bank where our men lay. They had to haul us up for we were done in. Then one of the two medics broke and I lay beside him, shaking and scolding him to get him out of it. . . . The next day the mortar fire slackened but snipers hung on our flanks. One fired at me a couple of times but missed so badly I felt contemptuous of him—yet the same one later got two of our boys through the head. . . . The people welcomed us into the houses and we heated our food on stoves and made coffee. I went to the church to receive Holy Communion and found the pastor dying, his arm torn off by a German shell. The curate gave me communion. The nuns here did a good job caring for the injured civilians. I was told of a wounded German in the house and got him to our aid station. He was young, handsome, but the paleness of death was on him. . . . I met some of the seminarians when I went to receive Holy Communion, and these men were very kind. I must have been a disgrace to the Society, dirty and unshaven, my clothes filthy. The medics moved to a Franciscans Sisters' school and I had a room that night and said mass the next morning. Later my seminarian friends heated a pot of water and I got a bath. . . . Pray for me, especially for faith and trust in the Sacred Heart. If I can only have that vivid faith then I won't hesitate to be where I should be. Courage is needed here and for a priest courage is sublimated into faith.

"The Groans, the Cries, the Agony"

For the most part, bringing forgiveness and peace to men on the brink of death also brought peace to the chaplains themselves; but some of what they witnessed challenged their confidence that men, especially young "lads," are basically good. As Donald Crosby, S.J., describes the Normandy situation in *Battlefield Chaplains: Catholic Priests in World War II*:

The battle for Normandy entered a decisive phase on July 5, 1944, when the drive on St. Lo began. The Allied plan was to capture this key transportation center and then use it as a staging point to aim a knockout blow against the enemy. If all went well, they hoped to chase the enemy across France into Germany itself. The Germans, however, close to follow another scenario. Although they were hopelessly outmanned, outbombed, and outgunned, they continued to maintain a precarious hold on the city, putting up the kind of still resistance that the allied forces had seen earlier in North Africa, Sicily, and Italy. Even so, it was too late for the Germans to maintain a protracted defense, since by mid-July the Allies had landed over 900,000 troops.

The horrors of the hedge row campaign ended with the liberation of St. Lo on July 18, 1944, but the Americans had been forced to annihilate the city in order to take it. As one GI put it, "We sure liberated the hell out of this place."

Crosby wrote that sentence in the 1990s, years after the Vietnam quote "destroyed the city to save it" had entered the vocabulary of moral irony.

Chaplains especially were appalled by what our bombardment had done to what was once a beautiful medieval city, as American bombers flew over again and again and the earth shook and the fires raged, and the acrid smoke enveloped the countryside. Children, old people, young people drifted up and down the highways, nowhere to live, nothing to eat. As one priest described it, the older ones "stare with haunting eyes" while "the filthy gaunt bodies of children are covered with sores. Poor people!"

California Jesuit John Bradstreet was among the witnesses as American soldiers roamed the streets and machine-gunned German soldiers who tried to surrender. As one German sergeant, unarmed, standing alone raised his arms to surrender, Bradstreet saw an American private gun him down. The private searched the corpse and found a letter the man had just addressed to his wife and baby. The private admitted to Bradstreet that the German was "a handsome young fellow" but "if I hadn't killed him he would have killed me." Not so, said Bradstreet, since the man was unarmed. Another time Bradstreet witnessed a group of Americans with machine guns shoot three captive Germans already in custody. One of the killers quipped, "Well, that's the easiest guard duty I've ever had."

Crosby describes the terrible psychological burden on the chaplains who get to know the troops so well, only to see them die. Not just see them die individually, but to stand by at mass burials and see hundreds of men, row by row, side by side, each wrapped in his own parachute, ready for the grave. By the end of the Normandy struggle, chaplains were working to the point of exhaustion and breaking down, with no one to replace them. "The Catholic church's hierarchy in America simply would not send its quota of chaplains, arguing that the needs of the home front took first priority. As a result, the priests at the front had to do the work of two men and even three or four."

From one point of view, the little island of Iwo Jima, a miserable pile of gray, volcanic ash with a 550 foot volcano jutting up from a treeless landscape, did not seem worth a single human life—much less the 45,000 killed or wounded on both sides. But unfortunately it sat halfway between the Mariana Islands and Japan in the air route the long-range B-29 Superfortresses flew on their bombing raids in the summer of 1944. The combined impact of swarms of Japanese fighter planes and the island's radar antennas, which warned Japan of the coming attacks, meant the island would have to be taken. So on the landing day, an armada of 500 ships delivered three Marine divisions of 70,647 men, with 58 chaplains, 19 of whom were Catholics, including two Jesuits—Charles F. Suver (Oregon Province) and James J. Deasy (California)—to the beaches.

On the 600-mile voyage to their target, the men studied maps of the island, of the cliffs and caves where 23,000 Japanese ready to die were dug in, awaiting them. Anxiety mounted on the ships as the young men turned to their chaplains and the sacraments for strength. Two marines on Deasy's transport threw themselves into the sea rather than face certain death on the beach. On the eve of the landing, a cluster of men gathered in Suver's cabin started to brag. One said if he could get a flag maybe someone could hoist it on the top of Mount Suribachi. The next lieutenant said, "OK, you get it and I'll get it up there!" And Suver had to add, "You get it up here and I'll say Mass under it."

Landing day, February 19, was a bloody disaster, with the 30,000 men who hit the beaches taking 2,500 casualties, 12 percent of their force. By the end of the assault, casualties would reach 30 percent. Charles Suver said Mass at 5 A.M. and climbed down into the landing vessel at 7:30. As the shells fell into the water around the boat the men did not curse or joke. They hit the beach at 9:40, and Suver had to decide how to dodge bullets and shells and carry an unwieldy box with his Mass kit at the same time. He left the box on the beach with the hope that someone would see his name on it and deliver it the next day—and someone did. Then he and his chaplain's assistant got lost, stumbled behind Japanese lines, got out and found an aid station, a makeshift hospital, where they stayed and worked for the next three days.

James Deasy's boat was held up because so many landing craft had been destroyed by Japanese fire. As his craft plowed through the surf, the severed arms and legs and heads and bloated bodies of their comrades greeted their arrival. Deasy walked the beach giving absolution, last rites, and communion to the dying. "Men were dying right on the water's edge," he remembered. "What a horrible sight! . . . trucks and ammunition blown up, bodies burning alive, the groans, the cries, the agony." For five miserable days and nights, sleepless and starving, he crawled from one foxhole to another, covered with a thick layer of dirt, praying with each mortar blast or sniper's bullet, "Is it my turn, O Lord, is it my turn?" Because all the men were fighting for their lives there was no time to bury the dead, and the stench of the rotting corpses hung in the air. For Deasy the smell came from the bodies of men who had become some of the best friends he had ever known. One was a Santa Clara College student he remembered from before the war when he was dean of students. Before the young man headed out to take over a section in the front lines, Deasy heard his confession. Less that 24 hours later, a sniper got him.

On February 21 an all-day torrent turned the volcanic ash into mud. At 4 A.M. a 700-pound Japanese mortar shell landed next to Deasy's foxhole, blew him up in the air, and, when he came down, the dirt and mud buried him alive. By sheer luck his helmet fell over his face, capturing enough air to let him breathe, and his right hand was reaching up with a few fingers above the earth. By 7:30 A.M. the firing had let up enough for men to dig him out.

On the fifth day, Suver and his assistant saw four men making their way up the mountainside, remembered their commitment to say Mass at the top, and followed them up, arriving just as the flag began to flap in the breeze. With the permission of the commanding officer, he spread a board across two gas drums for an altar, had two marines hold up a poncho to protect the altar from the wind, placed men with their rifles to hold off any Japanese still lingering in the caves a few yards away, and began, *"In nomine Patri, et Filii, and Spiriti Sancti.* Then,

> *Introibo ad altare Dei.*
> I shall go to the altar of God.
> And the ex-altar boys among the 15 answered:
> *Ad Deum qui laetificat juventutem meum.*
> To the God who gives joy to my youth.

The battle continued for another month and the casualties and corpses piled high. At the end, Deasy looked out over the field of nearly 6,000 crosses of the fallen with mixed feelings. He was happy to be alive, but he sometimes wished he had been worthy to have died with so many of these men.

The famous battle of survival of the aircraft carrier USS *Franklin* was part of the April 1945 battle for Okinawa, one of the bloodiest of the Pacific war. The job of navy Task Force 58 was to attack the Japanese airfields on Kyushu, the southernmost island of Japan, lest these planes threaten the Okinawa invasion. But the Japanese planes also inflicted heavy damage on four of the 16 carriers in the fleet and so damaged the *Franklin* that only miracles of heroism allowed it to persevere.

In his memoir, *I Was Chaplain on the Franklin,* Joseph T. O'Callahan, S.J., describes in slow-motion detail the March 17 gathering of 1,200 young American men ranging from 17 up, more than a third of the ship's force, for the Mass before combat. He describes each vestment —the amice, alb, cincture, maniple—and the prayer uttered as each goes on, followed by the Latin of the liturgy and the responses. In his homily he frankly reminds the men that they have had ample opportunity to go to confession during the week, and now it is too late. Too many waited too long. But then, so everyone can go to communion, he gets them off the hook by granting a general absolution, with the condition that they will confess later.

O'Callahan, a talented athlete at track and tennis at Boston College and teacher at Holy Cross, was in graduate studies in mathematics at Georgetown when he decided his vocation was in the naval chaplaincy rather than the classroom. He joined the year before Pearl Harbor.

On March 19, 1945, the feast of St. Joseph, the *Franklin* fought off an attack of Japanese planes without noticing one had returned. O'Callahan and other officers were eating French toast when, *bang,* a terrible explosion shook the ship. An enemy 500-pound bomb had hit and exploded deep within. A series of watertight doors slammed shut, trapping hundreds of men in various compartments. A series of explosions followed one after another, men were instantly burned to death and clouds of smoke billowed through the decks. O'Callahan immediately sprung into action. With the Protestant chaplain as a companion, he made his way through the various passageways seeking out the wounded, offering comfort and encouragement as medics gave sulfa powder, burn jelly, and morphine. O'Callahan held several men in his arms as they died.

Another plane appeared overhead and dropped two more bombs that exploded on the hangar deck and flight deck. Panic-stricken sailors bunched around the only ladder leading up, but O'Callahan calmed them: "Here, boys, single file." On the flight deck he encountered a blazing inferno out of control, burned and bleeding bodies everywhere, the stench of burning flesh, and the groans of the dying. On the top deck a pile of five-inch shells was growing hotter, in danger of exploding. The chaplain, acting now like a commanding officer, organized volunteer groups of men to dump the shells overboard, passing them along from one man to the next in line to the railing and into the sea. One sailor quipped that this was a variation on the popular wartime song, "Praise the Lord and *Dump* the Ammunition!" Next, they cooled a stack of 1,000-pound bombs by hosing down the hot shells, careful to bounce the water off the deck rather than strike the bombs directly. A flying fragment cut O'Callahan's leg, but he ignored the wound until a doctor friend took him aside to treat it later.

Finally, the cruiser *Sante Fe* pulled alongside and evacuated 800 wounded, and later the *Pittsburgh* took the *Franklin* in tow. By then 770 men had died. By 10 P.M. a group of exhausted officers gathered in their wardroom for a minute's relaxation. O'Callahan left briefly to get some "religious books" from his cabin and returned with a quart of whisky, which he passed around. Whisky is forbidden by navy regulations on ships at sea. O'Callahan obviously decided that under the circumstances he could get away with it; and he was right. His citation for the Congressional Medal of Honor concluded: "Serving with courage, fortitude and deep spiritual strength, Lieutenant Commander O'Callahan inspired the gallant officers and men of the *Franklin* to fight heroically and with profound faith in the face of almost certain death and return their stricken ship to port."

Crosby's research confirms that the chaplains overwhelmingly supported World War II as a just cause, and when the atomic bomb was dropped on Hiroshima and Nagasaki, 65 percent of the 200 who responded to Crosby's survey supported its use. If one would think that priests should show greater moral sensitivity when today both moral theologians and pubic opinion widely question the bomb's use, it's important to realize that many chaplains, including Suver and O'Callahan, deeply hated the Japanese. One angry priest said in the survey that bombing Hiroshima was a good way to get even for Pearl Harbor. For another, whatever weapons did the job were morally acceptable. But 15.5 percent opposed the use of the atomic bomb. Among those who visited the sites of the bombings it took only a few minutes to decide that America was guilty of a "moral monstrosity." The failure to see the Japanese as fellow human beings was a prejudice fed by atrocities the chaplains had witnessed, and some failed to match their love for the "lads" with Christian forgiveness of those who killed them.

An exceptional response was that of Jesuit William Leonard of Boston following the battle for Luzon. Assigned to burial duty in a temporary cemetery only a few miles from the beaches, Leonard stared at the 3,500 new white crosses, then was overcome by the "disgustingly sweet" smell of the young men's corpses. He walked the rows noting the ages of the men who lay below. Most were 18 or 19. "For this, some poor woman labored for nine months, brought the child into the world, took care of every need, watched him grow up, proud, and this is the way it ends? There's got to be a better way," he told Crosby. "I became a pacifist, and still am."

Beware the "Spirit of the World"

During the war, and especially after the 1942 death of Fr. General Ledochowski, when it was impossible for the Society's delegates from all over the world to meet in Rome to elect a successor, Zacheus J. Maher, who had been appointed Visitor, assumed an unusual leadership role in the American Assistancy. A Visitor is a representative of the general who travels throughout the country, analyzes a situation, and makes recommendations to correct apparent faults. Maher set himself up for the duration at St. Andrew-on-Hudson, the novitiate north of Poughkeepsie, New York, sitting high on the bluffs over-looking the Hudson River and the New York Central Railroad tracks, where the luxury trains with bar and dining cars rumbled by in the evening and the scholastics stood above in the gazebo catching a glimpse of the outside world.

In the winter when the river froze over, occasionally a foolish novice would risk his life to cross on the ice. In the summer they would take a motor boat, allegedly an old lifeboat from the *Normandie*, up the river to tiny Esopus Island for a swim. On afternoon walks in bands of three, some would stroll up the road to Franklin D. Roose-velt's estate. According to legend, one afternoon Eleanor Roosevelt met a little group and invited them in for tea, which she was about to serve to a small group of women friends. Though nervous and untu-tored in tea-time etiquette, the novices accepted. At the end the ser-vant brought each guest a finger bowl. Never having seen a finger bowl before, a novice picked his up and drank it. For Mrs. Roosevelt there was only one thing to do. To save the boy embarrassment, she picked hers up and drank hers too. And all the ladies did the same.

In August 1943 Maher sat in his spare room with only a crucifix on the wall and wrote a *Memoriale* of his visit, a 38-page report, including previous documents from Ledochowski, to be read aloud at table in every house in America. For the first eight pages, single spaced, he de-scribes Fr. Ledochowski on his deathbed, "the frail, wasted frame, worn with years of toil and suffering," "always a gentleman, every inch a nobleman," who "next to Holy Church and the Holy See" loved the Society "with a strong manly, paternal love." Father General, says Maher, held the American Assistancy in high esteem. "But he knew too that precisely because of the American outlook we were exposed to influences which, unless carefully guarded against, would work harm to that genuine spirit of the Society, the maintenance of which was his supreme objective."

· According to Maher, Ledochowski prayed that "we might be less *effusi ad exteriora* [absorbed in external, material things], less caught up with sports . . . more embracing in mortification." He lists the accom-plishments of the American Jesuits under Ledochowski's rule: assign-ing the China Mission to California, Jamaica and Iraq to New Eng-land, Patna to Chicago, Ceylon to New Orleans; establishing *Jesuit*

Missions magazine, the Fordham intellectual quarterly *Thought*, the *Jesuit Educational Quarterly*, *Theological Studies*, *Review for Religious*, as well as encouragement to *America* and its documentary spin-off, *The Catholic Mind*, and Daniel Lord's the *Queen's Work*. He recalled the General's words to the last General Congregation: "*Executio! Executio! Executio!*" Meaning, we need no new rules. We must enforce the rules we have.

In the following pages Maher gets into the nitty-gritty of broken rules. The subtext: the Spirit of the World—American popular culture—is undermining traditional Jesuit life. To the 21st-century reader Maher's attention to apparently trivial spiritual violations may seem extreme—even humorous. They probably also seemed so to some Jesuits at the time. But they are consistent with the worldview that sees two cultures—the religious and secular—at war. These strictures speak for a spirituality in which every detail matters, perhaps equally. Some Jesuits incorporated this attitude into their daily lives; some bore with it, accepting odd regulations with a sense of humor. When the naval chaplain at Norfolk drove to Virginia Beach to work on his tan, he might not have known about Fr. Ledochowski's 1938 letter warning against sunbathing. If so, he might have smiled. Ten years later, when another letter from Rome was read prohibiting sunbathing in a New York house with a beach, the superior considered it *Romanita*, that is, a typical Roman regulation that does not apply to America, and deliberately spent the afternoon on the beach.

"Away games" for athletic teams are too long and too many, according to Maher. They are to be limited to two four-day trips a year, including the weekend. Jesuits attend too many sports events and waste too much time reading sports pages in newspapers. Nor may Jesuits listen to professional sports on the radio. Ours [a term meaning "We," as distinguished from non-Jesuits] use too many cars. Our cars should be less expensive. Buicks give scandal. The coadjutor brothers (Jesuits who choose not to be priests) are to be treated well, but should not expect the same recreation and holidays as scholastics. Priests may play cards during recreation, novices never.

Reading novels and magazines, watching public movies, visiting externs (non-Jesuits), and associating with girls endangers chastity. "Men accused of these faults are not to be readily believed if they deny them. . . . Anonymous letters, though *per se* they do not merit credence, may nevertheless afford the occasion of prudent investigation." There are too many dances at our schools and too many of Ours attend them. Men are wearing brightly colored sweaters and sweatshirts with numbers on them at recreation. They are not to play games in shirtsleeves. Men who drink too much are to be punished and warned that they must amend their ways or leave the Society. Golf is to be played only on the courses of our institutions, not on public courses. The common rule that "no one may touch another" must be observed in sports, including "touch" football.

In yearbooks, pictures of girls at dances must show them modestly dressed. In posed sports pictures the swim team must wear shirts. Even though the superior is not obliged to read all the incoming mail of his subjects, he should at least open the letters before delivery. At breakfast, Ours are not to order what they please but all eat the same thing. "It savors of the club, of a freedom and independence which are not becoming." Customary table penances, such as the *osculation pedum* (one gets on his hands and knees, crawls under the table, and kisses the feet of the man on the other side), have been neglected. Maher is concerned about what he calls the "group spirit" among the younger men. It starts in philosophy "among a few men of inferior ideals" but who have influence by expressing themselves forcefully, and grows in evil—it begins with self-gratification, the cult of comfort, neglect of penances, disregard of the modesty in "managing the body," then cigarettes.

A separate seven-page document focuses on smoking, a habit Ledochowski had been writing against for ten years, not because of health—in fact, it was commonly believed to be a "medicine"—but because it symbolized worldly pleasure. The rules had been laid down: smoke only with the provincial's permission and only in one's own room; novices and juniors may not smoke, philosophers only for grave reasons. But the vice hung on. Maher paints a gruesome picture of the dissolute priest administering the Eucharist and the holy oils of Extreme Unction with hands stained with nicotine and reeking with the nauseating stench of tobacco. The exhortations had little effect. In 1956 Pope Pius XII delivered an exhortation to the Society, "Let them give up smoking." An attempt was made to enforce the ban. During studies they would sneak in contraband cartons (a violation of poverty) and smoke in secret small groups—or get a note from a doctor. Today very few Jesuits smoke, and only in their own rooms; but the motives for not smoking have changed.

Reading these 38 dense pages one would never guess it was written with the nation at war. Maher mentions the war only insofar as it impinges on the Jesuits' daily order. Ours were allowed to listen to radio news only 15 minutes a day; this was extended during the war but would be cut back as soon as the war was over. Our houses have been forced to hire women as secretaries and cooks because the men are away at war; but "war or no war," male secretaries and cooks must be found.

Again and again Maher returns to the same theme. We face a crisis of the spirit, the same crisis about which Fr. Luis Martin warned us 40 years before—the spirit of the times.

11

The Cold War

A Church Strong, but Weak

If the late 19th century was an era in which the American Catholic Church took root, the first half of the 20th century, culminating in 1960, is the age in which it began to bloom. The election of the first Catholic president seems an apt climax for this long process during which, beginning with the American Revolution and summed up symbolically on the deck of the USS *Franklin* and in the fields of white crosses over Catholic graves in Normandy and Iwo Jima, Catholics had had to prove that they were immigrants and patriots too. This efflorescence of Catholic institutions and culture has been described in various ways, as a maturing process, a coming of age, and even as a period of triumph. In the years following World War II, several of the social justice initiatives begun in the 1930s—retreats, labor schools, racial integration, and the confrontation with communism—came to the fore again, sometimes in new forms, and showed signs of both unresolved conflicts and progress.

These gains were made possible by a postwar leap in the Catholic population, which doubled between 1940 and 1960. In the Northeast, Catholics amounted to almost 40 percent of the population, and, in the nation as a whole, 23 percent. On this base, with vigorous clerical leadership in the population centers like New York, Philadelphia, Chicago, and Detroit, parishes, more than ever, became prosperous social and cultural centers with convents, grade schools and high schools, athletic teams with their own leagues, social clubs, Holy Name Societies, and sodalities—all geared to nurture, protected to some degree from secular corruption, a parish child through youth and adolescence, and into a Catholic college. At the same time, though this was not foreseen, as Catholics participated in the postwar economic boom, they jumped from the center cities to the suburbs where, as New Orleans Jesuit social activist Louis Twomey pointed out in his newsletter,

Christ's Blueprint for the South, in 1958, they often forgot their Catholic working-class origins and became affluent political conservatives.

John Tracy Ellis, in *American Catholicism* (1967), lists the main evidences of this new maturity, beginning with Pope Pius X's 1908 declaration that America was no longer to be considered mission territory. Although there were probably 40,000,000 Catholics in America in 1956, they were concentrated, at 82 percent, in the cities, while John LaFarge's concerns that rural Catholics needed more attention had been justified by a "leakage" in country areas. And, for many reasons, large numbers drifted away from the city churches as well. On the other hand, there were signs of strength: increase in foreign mission work; an international eucharistic congress, which gathered participants from all over the world to Chicago in 1926; more Americans in the College of Cardinals (8); an increase in contemplative religious orders like the Poor Clares and Trappists; increased liturgical participation, as in the dialogue Mass; finally the higher profile of the National Catholic Welfare Council (NCWC), the association by which the American bishops have coordinated their teaching, especially on social policy.

Nevertheless, there remained ways in which the Catholic Church and the Society of Jesus might always be both at home in America. The tension between church and state on the theoretical level was being worked out in Rome during Vatican II's deliberations on the Constitution on Religious Liberty. But in other ways, any American religion or religious order might remain at odds with American society. Christianity has always had a countercultural streak. If the dominant culture is perceptibly corrupt, violent, racist, or otherwise abusive of human dignity, the Jesuit's conscience should lead him to stand against it. The mid-20th century offered several opportunities.

The Labor Schools Open

One of the elements in the Catholic "triumph" during these years was the positive image of the church and the Catholic priest, especially as they appeared in a long string of Hollywood movies: Gonzaga University alumnus Bing Crosby as Father O'Malley in *Going My Way* and *The Bells of St. Mary's;* Pat O'Brien as a football coach—as Notre Dame's *Knute Rockne* and as Frank Cavanaugh, Fordham's *The Iron*

Major—and as chaplain to *The Fighting 69th;* and Spencer Tracy as Father Flanagan in *Boys' Town* and the dynamic priest in *San Francisco;* and Karl Malden as the labor priest Father Barry in *On The Waterfront.*

The general religion-friendly tone of movies during the 1940s and 1950s owed much to the influence of Martin Quigley, publisher of the *Motion Picture Daily* and the *Motion Picture Herald,* a graduate of Catholic University who had a Jesuit son and was convinced that in the long run indecent movies were bad for the motion picture industry. The code drawn up by Daniel Lord had failed to make an impact; but Quigley was determined to try again. This time he got help: from his friend Wilfred Parsons, S.J., editor of *America;* from the American bishops, working through the NCWC, with the establishment of the Legion of Decency in 1935 with its rating system; and from a Catholic, Joseph I. Breen, the head of a reorganized Production Code with teeth. It was Breen who suggested adding a boxing match between Tracy's priest and the gambler Clark Gable to *San Francisco.* Gable hits Tracy later in the film, and it had to be made clear to the audience that the priest could really fight.

Budd Schulberg's script for *On the Waterfront* was significant for several reasons. Consistent with the social encyclicals, it identified the church strongly with the plight of the working man. At a time when the worker-priests movement in France, in which priests actually took factory jobs, was being curtailed, it documented an American movement with similar goals, the labor-school priests; and this story was based, sometimes using his very words, on New York Jesuit John "Pete" Corridan. Corridan and Philip Carey, S.J., the New York Jesuit who more than anyone else came to personify the labor school tradition, ran what was called the Xavier Labor School, at the parish of St. Francis Xavier on 16th Street, not far from the Chelsea piers; and they were allied with another movement, the lay-operated Association of Catholic Trade Unionists (ACTU), established at the Catholic Worker house on Mott Street in 1937. While ACTU established over a hundred chapters around the country, the Jesuit labor schools were limited to about 12.

The labor-school movement traces its roots back to Fr. Terence Shealy, one of those Jesuits who, though they have no particular professional credentials such as a doctorate, are very good at getting things done. Born in County Cork, Ireland, in 1863, he was a popular athlete in school, but his main gifts were personal, a feeling for others' needs that led friends to come to him for advice. He joined the Jesuits and came to America with the hope of bringing Americans into the faith. Teaching at Fordham, he organized its law school and, though he had no legal training, he taught jurisprudence and then medical ethics at the medical school. Asked how he could qualify himself to teach technical subjects with little training, he replied, "I had to sweat blood to do it."

What became known as the retreat movement, in which selected groups of laypersons—businessmen, professional groups, working men—go to a special house and for several days, keep silence and listen to talks based on the Spiritual Exercises on sin, judgment, forgiveness, and the life of Christ, had recently spread from France, Belgium, and Holland to the United States. In 1909 Shealy gathered 18 men at Fordham to inaugurate the movement in America. Shealy's rhetoric stressed manliness and military anecdotes. "We belong to a militant church and we must be up and doing," he said. "A great general was asked by a young officer what he must do to win distinction, and the general replied, 'Try to get killed as often as you can.'" He was well-read enough to inform and uplift his audiences, but, like some of his contemporaries, Shealy saw the faith as threatened by modern ideas. "What is the latest fancy of a fad-seeking world, a world ever ready to grasp any theory that will dull the voice of conscience: that man is descended from a beast."

The retreats initiated by Sealy were popular and moved to Manresa, a Jesuit house on Staten Island. As an offshoot of this Retreat League, Shealy established the School of Social Studies, a series of free lectures in 1911 at Fordham's downtown Law School offices. Anticipating the later labor schools, they centered on the dangers of socialism and on Leo XIII's *Rerum Novarum* on the rights of labor. Shealy's published lectures reveal the mind of a man not ahead of his time: "Women talk a great deal of their rights and very seldom of their duties," he said. He feared the "tyranny of the lower classes . . . the autocracy of the gutter" more than he feared the tyranny of the ruling class. He predicted that Prohibition would lead to Bolshevism in America because it would encourage working men to defy the law. For him, "the revolt against authority" was the worst evil that plagued the modern world.

The step from Shealy's retreats and lectures to the formal labor schools required a new initiative and level of organization. The first two Jesuit labor schools, established in the mid-1930s in response to Ledochowski's anticommunism commitment, were at Xavier in Manhattan and across the East River in Crown Heights, Brooklyn. An experiment in adult education, they focused on the adult male working classes, who came one evening a week from 8:00 to 10:00 to acquire basic moral and legal principles and practical skills that would enable them to understand the rights of both labor and capital. Then they would use parliamentary procedure, rhetoric, and bargaining and organizing techniques to enhance the union's influence and sometimes promote reform. In Philadelphia the school took a different emphasis, and both city officials and management attended the classes.

The schools had an additional agenda: to offset the influence of Communists in the labor movement. The participants learned Communist techniques for dominating a union meeting—like strategically placing their members around the room to yell out objections at crucial moments and dragging out the meeting until late at night when most had left before taking a vote—and imitated them or adapted to offset Communist maneuvers. Most of the lecturers were experienced laymen, and after a while the workers and the union leaders took over many of the classes, and the Jesuits could serve as counselors or chaplains. The schools were an example of a phenomenon that became more pronounced as priests played both social and pastoral roles. The working man was an individual with both economic and personal problems and brought both to his encounter with the Jesuit.

Phil Carey told a historian that the motivation for working in these schools "was that horrible, terrible thing that came from the Depression—the absolute collapse of a whole society. The fact was that a lot of men were walking around "like zombies." His father was a streetcar conductor. His own brother, a Fordham graduate, walked the streets every day failing to find work. He'd come home and throw himself on the couch in desperation. Carey knew that for the men "the encyclicals were dusty books on the priest's shelf." Carey was a low-key, seemingly shy, sensitive, compassionate man, the kind of priest to whom the working men would unburden themselves discussing family problems. While Corridan carried the bigger public image, Carey was for years one of he most successful mediators or behind-the-scenes figures in the New York labor scene. By training small groups in pro-democracy tactics, he set up the circumstances in 1948 where the Catholic and anticommunist members of the Transport Workers

Union forced boss Mike Quill to clear the Communists out of his leadership group. Carey started at Xavier in 1940 and stayed until he died a half-century later.

The Priest Takes on "Mr. Big"

When *On the Waterfront* was about to be filmed, Karl Malden approached "Pete" Corridan for advice on how to portray him, and Father Pete replied, "Karl, don't play me like a priest, play me like a man." He told Malden that he was born in a neighborhood where there were two ways to grow up, "Become a priest or a hood." Malden's reflection was that Corridan had become the priest but had retained the personality of the alternative lifestyle, and he had stayed in the neighborhood as a way of reconciling the two forces through his role as a teacher.

John "Pete" Corridan (1911–1984) was born in Harlem, the eldest of five sons of a New York City policeman who died when John was nine. John claimed his father had left no money because he was an honest cop, relegated to pounding the beats in remote places because he would have cramped the style of cops on the take. He went to the Jesuit Regis High School and New York University at night while working at a Wall Street firm during the day. Impressed by Rene Fullop Miller's *The Power and Secret of the Jesuits,* he joined, taught at Canisius College in Buffalo, and worked at the Crown Heights Labor School during regency and, after ordination, was sent to the Xavier Labor School in 1946.

Even during his Crown Heights experience he had studied the scandal-ridden International Longshoreman's Association. He had read Father Edward A. Swanstrom's *The Waterfront Labor Problem* (1938) and the research of Staten Island's Father John Monaghan, the chaplain of the New York ACTU, and concluded that the basic problem, which violated the rights of the longshoremen, was the "shape-up" (which simply means lining up with the hope of being hired) system. Twice daily the hiring foreman, actually an agent of the union bosses and burdened with his own criminal record, met with a semicircle of expectant laborers and, with a mere gesture, looked around and hired You, You, You, and not all the rest of You. In an *America* article (November 20, 1948), Corridan declared that "Men are hired as if they were beasts of burden, part of the slave market of a pagan era." He meant that because of the concentration of power in the hiring boss, the workmen had no rights.

One of the obstacles—sometimes traumatic—of Jesuits in the social apostolate who take their roles as prophets seriously is the discovery that their opponents are fellow Catholics who supposedly have read the same gospels and shared the same teachings of the church. In reality, in the 1940s the waterfront was dominated by Catholics, from the longshoremen to the rich men who owned the ships and the docks. In the case of the International Longshoremen's Association (ILA), the "president for life" was Joseph P. Ryan (1884–1963), who was under the control of the waterfront bosses, and William J. McCormack (1890–1965), the multimillionaire businessman dubbed by journalists the "Mr. Big" of a mysterious business empire. Corridan saw them as two sons of Irish immigrants in collusion to exploit the dockworkers. In 1948 Corridan told the Jersey City Knights of Columbus: "You want to know what's wrong with the waterfront? It's love of the lousy buck. . . . In many ways you can't blame the mob . . . even if the mob is Catholic. They see supposedly Catholic-educated men chase a buck as if Christ didn't exist, and hide behind their professional Catholicity."

Corridan may have oversimplified the situation a bit; many longshoremen were not Irish but Negroes and Italians, and the ILA consisted of 67 local unions in the Port of New York, many with their own agendas, rather than all under Ryan's thumb. When Ryan got resistance from the ranks, he blamed the Communists; but Corridan, like his fellow labor priests in other parts of the country, faced with the same accusation, replied that "communism thrives best where conditions are unhealthy, and they are plenty unhealthy on the docks." Daniel Patrick Moynihan, who had worked briefly on the docks as a young man, wrote that the Irish on the docks had emerged "egalitarian . . . tough . . . and defiantly democratic." But they had "established a singularly dispiriting regime of political, business, and trade-union corruption."

When Malcolm Johnson, an investigative reporter for the *New York Sun*, began a series in November 1948 entitled "Crime on the Waterfront," Corridan contacted him and began to feed him tips. Corridan got Johnson emotionally involved, as he said, "hoping that something would happen to free these men." In Johnson's series, the piers were

"controlled by mobsters and labor racketeers. Each gang rules a territory and rules it with an iron hand, its power enforced by strong-arm
squads." Corridan wrote to the *Sun* praising the articles and got
friends to do the same. The *Sun* ran a second series based on material
Corridan had sent to Johnson, published under Johnson's name but
with few changes from Corridan's text. From 1949 to 1953 Corridan
flooded reform-minded print journalists and TV personalities with
waterfront corruption material and testified before a subcommittee of
the Senate Committee on Interstate and Foreign Commerce.

The combination of Johnson's series in the *Sun* and a bitter 25-day
strike called by dissident ILA Local 791 longshoremen in 1951 led to
an investigation by the New York State Crime Commission. Corridan
visited the strikers daily and led them in prayer to end the strike without violence, a tactic to tame the hostility between the mob on one side
and the Communists on the other. Suddenly, on the 21st day of the
strike, Cardinal Spellman called Carey, Corridan, and the Jesuit provincial to his office; it was obvious that McCormack, "Mr. Big," had
gotten to the cardinal. Corridan's enemies had floated stories that he
used foul language, picked fist fights, and worked every other day as
a stevedore. Corridan easily refuted the slanders and turned on Spellman with a powerful argument that his prominent Catholic laymen
friends were creating the conditions that would allow a Communist
takeover of the docks. Spellman, a Fordham graduate who had almost
joined the Jesuits, accepted the defense and blessed Corridan and
Carey's work.

In January 1953 Corridan presented written testimony to the
Crime Commission in which he called for "a rank and file revolt
against the leadership of the ILA," which he called a "company union" dominated by "gangsters." The investigators established a Waterfront Commission to monitor the docks, and Ryan spent a brief term
in jail. Corridan enjoyed a brief taste of victory, but his hopes that the
1953 election would choose the AFL over the ILA were shattered. Even
Local 791 had formally rejected his endorsement of the AFL, which he
saw as the more honest union, and Corridan himself. He had been encouraged by men who once were afraid to talk to him and now came
to his classes at the school. But the ILA 791 held a meeting in which
they thanked him for his spiritual aid but added, "Please let us run
our union," and the union newspaper chimed in: "We regret very
much as Catholics that we are forced to publicly criticize a Catholic

priest [who] has seen fit to continue his political meddling into our union affairs." To his critics, Corridan had crossed the line which in their minds separated the priest from the political activist.

In January 1957 Corridan went to teach economics at LeMoyne College in Syracuse, and later at Saint Peter's College in Jersey City. Budd Schulberg had begun research on *On the Waterfront* in 1950 and became fascinated with this fast-talking, chain-smoking Jesuit who didn't match the Hollywood stereotype of the priest. He discovered that Corridan swore like a longshoreman and drank with them, "but he gave me feelings about Christ that I never had before." For his part, Corridan imagined that if the film had been finished sooner it might have influenced the ILA election in his favor; but he had to content himself with urging Schulberg to make *Waterfront* "a *Going My Way* with substance."

Integrating Jesuit Catholic New Orleans

It was characteristic of these years that issues of ordinary justice so often were tied to debates about communism. This happened on the New York waterfront, in the campaign for racial integration in New Orleans, and in other controversies that followed.

New Orleans novelist Walker Percy remembers the evening in 1964 when Louis Twomey, S.J., director of the Loyola University Institute of Human Relations, came to his house for supper before delivering a talk at the local high school. He was a "lank man: pale, long face, yet fit; big hands, bony knees riding high and a bit awkward like a Georgia parson come to pay a call in the parlor; chain smoker, big hoarse voice (one wonders whether it was the cigarettes or the public speaking)." Percy's daughter played the guitar and sang for him. He laughed a lot, passed up a drink, and talked a lot about communism and the social encyclicals. He himself had been called a Communist agitator by those who couldn't stomach his social message. At the lecture he talked "like an angry short-stop." Before he got going he looked around the room, then in a big loud voice said, "Why don't I see a single black face here?" Shocked students rose to defend themselves. He had their attention.

Lou Twomey had not always felt so strongly about the rights of black people. Born in Tampa, Florida, in 1905, his basic attitudes were southern. His family on his mother's side had fought for the Confederacy, and once as a teenager at a party he angrily tore the page of "Marching through Georgia" out of a song book. As a student at Georgetown his special joy was baseball; but when he graduated in 1926 he entered the Jesuit novitiate at Grand Coteau. At the end of his first year, Lou's father had a nervous breakdown and Lou had to return home for a year to run the family store. Back at Grand Coteau he focused on studying rhetoric. Then he went to Saint Louis U. for philosophy, still taught with the syllogistic textbook manual with its set answers to the "objections" of adversaries. The library shelves were well stocked with the works of the masters, but scholastics would go a full three years and never open one of them.

After teaching English and Latin and directing the debating society at Spring Hill College, Twomey did theology at St. Mary's College in Kansas. The college, whose remoteness can be understood only by experiencing the long drive across the flat Kansas terrain to reach it, had once been an Indian mission. Then it was a boarding school, the scene of the boys' novels of Fr. Francis J. Finn, a series in which Tom Playfair and Percy Wynn learned to play fair and win and be good role models for the Catholic school boys who read their adventures well into the 1940s. In the 1930s it became the theologate for the Missouri Province. During Twomey's annual retreats and his tertianship, themes that would recur throughout his life made their way into his spiritual notebooks: "To pursue staunchly unpopular causes, e.g., Labor and Race relations, when they seem to promote the Kingdom of Christ," and "sacrifice on smoking again."

After a short stay as principal of Jesuit High School in Tampa, in 1945 Twomey made a two-step move into the work which would command the rest of his life. First, two years at the Institute of Social Sciences at St. Louis University, where Fr. Leo Brown, S.J., directed his Master's thesis on FDR's National Industrial Recovery Act, and where he could collaborate with Daniel Lord, the Summer School of Catholic Action, and *Queen's Work*; then in 1947 he went to Loyola University's Institute for Industrial (later Human) Relations, where he stayed until the end.

There perhaps his most significant move was publishing a monthly six-page newsletter—a sort of Jesuit equivalent of *I. F. Stone's Weekly*—*Christ's Blueprint for the South*, loaded with facts, statistics, condensations of other articles, and Lou's opinions on social questions. Directed at Jesuits, the first issue went to only 50 of them in the South. By Lou's death, 3,000 had spread out across the country. In the novitiates, where theology was reading Anthony Maas's gospel harmony, a 20-year-old Jesuit would not see a newspaper or hear a radio broadcast for two years, and where letters were opened and news clippings removed, the *Blueprint* was often the only contact with the outside world.

The Institute, as a labor school, started with the Philadelphia model in which labor and management took the same courses; but soon it became more labor oriented as management sent fewer personnel to its programs. Convinced that the two great changes facing the South were industrialization and the need to readjust to a new climate of racial relations, Twomey made the dignity of the individual the underlying theme of his whole approach. But despite his attempts to approach controversial topics with fundamental appeals to patriotism and basic human rights, he was steadily attacked. When he criticized the National Association of Manufacturers at a sodality-sponsored Summer School of Catholic Action (SSCA) assembly in 1948 for opposing a housing bill before Congress and other social legislation, the NAM president called his thinking "pure socialism" " fuzzy thinking . . . responsible for the troubles in our country." When his address to the Sheet Metal Contractors National Association in New Orleans caused a stir, Twomey wrote to the executive secretary. He knew he had dealt with controversial matters, he said, and "I also know well that what I said did not please some in the audience. However, I have long since made up my mind that it served no useful purpose for people to hear only what they wanted to hear." When Twomey spoke before the Louisiana legislature to oppose right-to-work legislation, arguing that workers who share in the benefits of unionization should share the burden of maintaining the union, Catholics opposed to him published an anonymous advertisement in the New Orleans *Times-Picayune* denying that he represented the church's position. Another similar ad carried the signatures of 66 Catholics from the area.

C. J. McNaspy, S.J.—the musicologist, dean of Loyola's Music School, an *America* editor in the 1960s, mentor and patron of scores of young Jesuit artists and writers, and friend and biographer of Twomey—recalls visiting New Orleans in 1947, meeting a black priest friend at the station, and being unable to find any place where the two of them could sit together in public and talk. New Orleans was so bigoted that the huge, beautiful swimming pool in Audubon Park, right across from Loyola and Tulane Universities in the Garden District, was closed to all rather than allow black people to swim with whites. McNaspy's recollections put into perspective what may appear to be Twomey's tardiness in integrating the courses at the labor school in 1950. For most of his life, Twomey had accepted segregation as a given, and McNaspy speculates that it was the two years at Saint Louis University—1945 was the year Heithaus broke his silence and was punished with the *culpa*—that he thought deeply on what he had seen and turned around. As a regent and teacher of jurisprudence at Loyola Law School, he helped them integrate in 1952. Eventually the New Orleans provincial ordered the integration of all Jesuit parishes, schools, and retreat houses, though not until after the Supreme Court ruling. Loyola University dragged its feet until 1962.

While Twomey was getting himself established in New Orleans, so was his colleague Joseph H. Fichter, a new Harvard Jesuit with a PhD in sociology, assigned in 1947 to Loyola University. A northerner who had been turned down by the New York Province for not having had Greek and Latin, Fichter would soon become the New Orleans province's best-known Jesuit. At Harvard he had been intrigued by the church as a sociocultural system, which would supposedly "demonstrate an internal solidarity flowing mainly from its integrated core of values." He also wanted to study the effects of interaction within small groups. By participant observation he would ask and answer, "Does the informal practice of Catholicism differ from the formal expectations of the official church?" For his research project he carefully selected Mater Dolorosa Parish, under pastor Monsignor Joseph Pyzikiewicz, as a "good," "successful" parish where, not naming the parish, he would study over two years, with the help of ten Loyola research assistants, every aspect of parish life to determine the correspondence between its Catholic goals and parishioners' actual behavior. Fichter participated by saying the children's Sunday Mass for several months and by long conversations in the evening with the pastor.

Unfortunately for all involved in the parish research, the evidence did not show a correspondence between Catholic values and daily human relations. The parish was integrated in that a small group of black people attended the Mass and sat separately from the others, though there was another "black church" in the neighborhood. Parishioners bonded according to social status, educational background, or wealth, not according to the practice of their faith. The pastor referred in private to Negroes as "Mississippi niggers," and complained when Fichter addressed racial justice issues in his Sunday homilies.

Fichter and his team prepared four reports on their surveys, the first in a book called *Southern Parish*, published in 1951 by the University of Chicago Press. Fichter had passed his manuscript through an elaborate screening and censorship process, which involved the Jesuit censors, Archbishop Rummel of New Orleans, as well as the scholarly advisers of the Press. But once the book appeared, the pastor, though he and his parish had not been identified, found unflattering references to his Polish accent and his long, dull sermons, and launched a campaign lasting several years to suppress the study. Though the professional sociologists reviewed it well, the local clergy power structure in New Orleans wanted the book withdrawn. They succeeded in pressuring the Jesuit provincial and the president of Loyola to make sure the other three volumes never appeared. Fichter even traveled to Rome to appeal to the general, Jan Baptiste Janssens, who said he agreed with him and would follow up—but didn't. In 1957 Fichter accepted a visiting professorship at Notre Dame and returned to Harvard from 1965 to 1970 as the Charles Chauncey Stillman Chair of Roman Catholic Studies. Reflecting on his career, he conceded that almost every time he tackled what he thought was a worthwhile research problem he seemed to get "in trouble."

Parallel to his parish research, Fichter, in cooperation with the local chapter of the National Federation of Catholic College Students (NFFCS), became Loyola's most visible faculty member in the movement to desegregate the university. Also, as cofounder and chaplain of the Commission on Human Rights (CHR), a Catholic lay organization, he labored to offset the entrenched white supremacy most Catholics endorsed. In 1959, for example, Loyola cosponsored a production in Holy Week of a Passion Play at the downtown Poche Theater, which would not admit Negroes. Again and again they were rebuffed by the Jesuit community leadership, some of whom were outright segregationists, and some, including the president and the provincial, who described themselves as centrists, as "prudent" men who thought the two races were "not ready" to mix socially.

Prior to 1952 Loyola repeatedly rejected outstanding black candidates to the Law School, despite an eloquent letter from Mother Mary Agatha, S.B.S., president of the predominantly Negro Xavier University, on behalf of one promising student, Richard Gumbel, a married World War II veteran and father of two, to Loyola president Thomas Shields, S.J., "I have never asked you for a favor but I do beg you for this one—not so much for the young man in particular as for the cause." Rejected, Gumbel appealed to Shields, arguing that "if the courts of the land could force those state universities to admit men of all color, then most certainly an institution founded upon the philosophy of Jesus Christ, administered by men dedicated to the upholding of those principles, and in whose care Mother Church had entrusted the continuance of those teachings, would do so." Shields responded with a letter which rebuked Gumbel for his "implied insult to the Jesuit Fathers." Gumbel, with Twomey's recommendation, was accepted at Georgetown. When Loyola Law integrated in 1952, Twomey tried to win him back, but he declined.

In time, Twomey came to consider the race question more important than the union cause. In 1960 he had been asked to edit *Social Order*, the journal of the St. Louis–based ISO; then in 1963 the provincials decided to close it down and the staff of the ISO moved their small predominantly research operation to Cambridge. Twomey seems to have interpreted the move as more evidence that the Society was not sufficiently committed to social justice. He wrote in *Blueprint*: "American Jesuits as a whole have little to pride ourselves on when we examine our attitudes and conduct toward the Negro." McNaspy, with characteristic charity, commenting on his friend Lou's statement, enumerated over a dozen southern Jesuits who worked with Negroes, and he explains the extent to which Lou had enemies in the Loyola Jesuit community. McNaspy quotes Harold L. Cooper, S.J., who stresses how Lou always saw the *good* in people, even in those who hated him:

> He had three real adversaries among the Loyola Jesuits. To them Lou was a complete *bete noir*. They didn't fear him in the way they feared Fichter. They knew he was not an intellectual, a theoritician. They feared, disliked and avoided him because he actually practiced what he preached. Subconsciously, I feel, they sensed Lou was a reproach, unwittingly I'm sure, to them. It was N. who went farthest in that opposition, calling Lou a communist—and seriously meaning it. Still, Lou felt no personal animosity. He was not the subjectivist that many ardent men can be.

Fr. David Boileau, a diocesan priest who followed Lou at the Institute, observed that there were four major obstacles that hindered Lou's journey and continued to block a full understanding of his life: the anticommunist hysteria of the McCarthy years; the racism that was due to willful evil, and not only ignorance, as Lou thought; the southern culture gap, where the church was weak, the union movement disorganized, and New Orleans characterized by the lowest level of education in the country; and finally Fr. Twomey's health. He was seriously ill for the last ten years of his life and almost totally inactive for the last five. He died in 1967 at age 64 of emphysema. He had smoked himself to death. As Lou died, Ray Ariatti, a longtime labor activist, civil rights photographer, and dear friend, hovered by his bedside trying to piece together his friend's last gasping words.

> Lou whispered: "We . . . must establish our identity . . . in togetherness . . . (long, deep gasp for breath) . . . toward . . .
>
> Ray asked: "The social apostolate, Father?"
>
> Lips moved. No sound.
>
> Ray tried again: "Toward the dignity of the human person, Father?"
>
> Lou smiled and whispered: "Yes."

America's "Most Famous Jesuit"—for a While

When the young Bill Clinton arrived at the Georgetown School of Foreign Service in 1964, he tells us in *My Life*, he knew that its founder, Father Edmund A. Walsh, was a "staunch anti-communist" and that its faculty, many of whom had fled communist regimes in Europe or China, were still conservatives and "sympathetic to any anti-communist activity by the U.S. government, including in Vietnam."

The irony is that Walsh, who was one of the best-known, most influential American Catholics of his time, is already, only 50 years after his death, a forgotten man.

By any standard, Walsh's career dazzles. Born in Boston in 1885, he entered the Society of Jesus in Frederick, Maryland, after Boston College High School in 1902. From 1909 to 1912 he taught in Georgetown's high school division and was thus on campus in May 1912 to witness a scene which years later he told friends he could recall "vividly, as if it were yesterday": the dedication of the statue of John Carroll, seated as if he were a pope or president, in front of Healy Hall. The inscription read: "Priest-Patriot-Prelate." The main speaker, Chief Justice Edward D. White, struck two themes on which Walsh, according to his biographer, would build his career: "how Georgetown's and the nation's history intersected, and how democracy and religion mutually reinforce one another."

For the next three years Walsh studied and traveled in Europe, including attending lectures on international affairs at the London School of Economics, then theology at Innsbruck. As war broke out in 1914 his diary reveals the enthusiasm of a young man who has discovered his second vocation:

> Another week of thrills—a new declaration of war almost every day! . . . But the outlook is black indeed. That universal European conflagration, long feared, seems at hand. France is expected to attack Germany or Austria at any moment—and then Italy must thro' her treaty, join Austria and Germany. But Italy is not trusted—she may fail her allies at last moment for her own interests, but if she does sacrifices the last remnant of her national honor.

Ordained at Woodstock College in Maryland in 1916, Walsh was assigned to Georgetown in 1918. The idea for a foreign service school had been germinating for some time in the mind of John B. Creeden, S.J., Georgetown's president. He described his goal as a service to the country that would bring the Society into contact with prominent men in finance and government. But fulfilling this vision required the help of both Constantine McGuire, a State Department official with extensive international experience who provided the expertise, and Edmund Walsh as a "front man" who knew how to publicize the school, raise money, and recruit faculty. So, if the Foreign Service School had a "founder," it was the president, Creeden, who thought of it, assisted by these two key men.

Meanwhile, Walsh was already developing a persona that would serve him well for years. He had been an actor since high school. On campus he wore a long black cape and posed for photographs in front of a map or leaning on a globe. Like prominent Jesuit contemporaries

—Carey, Corridan, and Twomey—he was neither a scholar nor an intellectual; but he had presence, entrepreneurial skills, and a clear moral vision that drove him on.

Apparently because his diplomatic talents were evident, he was made director of the Papal Relief Mission to famine-stricken Soviet Russia in 1922 and went on to spend 20 months there, both distributing food and as an ambassador from the Holy See to the new communist government that was persecuting the Christian religion. Over three decades, stunned by what he had witnessed, Walsh made himself the most outspoken critic of the Russian Revolution, which he saw as a plot to enforce an immoral, godless system on an unwary world.

Walsh's Russian experience had two aspects. The first was his famine relief work, from July 1922 to March 1923, which was a great success. By 1923 the mission and its 2,500 employees had fed 158,000 Russians a day. The other was Walsh's role as a Vatican representative to report on the persecution of the church and the trials of Archbishop Jan Baptist Cieplak and his vicar general, Monsignor Constantine Budkiewicz, for their refusal to relinquish church property to the state, proselytizing minors, and counterrevolutionary activity. Both were sentenced to death. Walsh's request to administer the last rites to them was refused. Cieplak's sentence was commuted to ten years. Budkiewicz was executed. For Walsh this scene encapsulated the Russian Revolution. They had murdered a Catholic priest. What could be worse than that?

Though it was not widely known at the time, Walsh's diary entries reveal that he understood Soviet communism as a "wholly Jewish movement." Though Lenin was not Jewish, his upper echelon leaders were. When someone who had worked with Walsh in Russia complained to the Vatican about his brusque manner and insensitivity to Slavic culture, Walsh responded that his manner was an insistence on justice and the rights of religion: "It is not the Slav mentality which the Mission does not understand, but rather the Jewish greed for gold and hatred of Christianity, which I have found it necessary to combat."

Part of the secret to Walsh's influence is that he was a doer. He had traveled widely and learned to think big. Here is an example.

In the summer of 1992, the year after the first Gulf War, a lone Jesuit writer got a visa and took the 14-hour cross-desert bus from Amman, Jordan, to Baghdad just to educate himself on the impact of the war. Iraq was suffering terribly under the sanctions and large street demonstrations against America were regular occurrences. Arriving at midnight, knowing no one, directed by a fellow passenger to the Hotel Baghdad, the Jesuit discovered at the hotel desk that he did not have enough money to meet the cost of the room. Desperate, he explained that he was a Jesuit priest short on cash. The hotel clerk replied, "I was educated at the Jesuit Baghdad College. Let me see what I can do."

Since 1921 the Chaldean patriarch, who had graduated from the Jesuit university in Beirut, had been asking for a Jesuit college in Baghdad. By 1931, with the interest of the king, Rome agreed, and Pius XI asked Edmund Walsh to do the diplomatic work to get it started. Walsh's idea was a consortium of four American Jesuit institutional sponsors—Boston College, Georgetown, Fordham, and Saint Louis—which would help raise money and send faculty. The Iraqi government agreed. The Vatican's Oriental Congregation wanted only a boardinghouse, not a college. Walsh, by his diplomatic skills, prevailed; but the Vatican, as if to punish him for winning, excluded him from future negotiations. Baghdad College, although its pioneer founders were from New England, Chicago, and New York, eventually became primarily the responsibility of the New England Province and one of the great temporary success stories of the American missionary efforts.

The Jesuits eventually built a campus along the Tigris with over a dozen buildings, including a church designed by one of the Jesuits. The textbooks were in Arabic and English, all following the curriculum set by the Iraqi government. The students were Catholic and Muslim. The Jesuits, scrupulously neutral in political discussions, made no attempt to convert anyone. They were just delivering a Jesuit education to a Muslim culture, while, at the same time fortifying Iraqi Christians in their faith. Muslims were not required to take religion. The Jesuits designed a khaki cassock to ward off the heat and endure the dust storms, planted gardens around their residence, set up a minor seminary, and founded Al Hikma University as a higher education extension of their college high school. They introduced science labs, a science society and telescope, showered the boys with attention, sponsored debate teams, yearbooks, and basketball, soccer, handball, track, and tennis teams—all those things that seemed to work for American boys and which seemed to work in Baghdad, too.

By the time the Jesuits were expelled in 1968 there were 60 Jesuits in Baghdad, many of whom had been there for over 20 years. The college had 1,000 students and Al Hikma had 656. Why were they expelled? The Baathist Party won out after a series of coups, and they were by policy against private education. Several members of the Student Union, a political group of young men in their 20s, were antagonistic to the Jesuits for a variety of reasons. There was strong Arab resentment of American support of Israel in the 1967 war, and Al Hikma had a relatively large number of Jewish students. Students who had been expelled for academic or disciplinary reasons put slanderous articles in newspapers and magazines. Most of the Jesuits were reabsorbed into the New England Province, but 15 stayed on to work elsewhere in the Middle East. Those who served in Baghdad loved it and left with broken hearts.

Walsh, because he was a well-known, politically connected Washington academic with international experience, was chosen to advise the American prosecutors at the Nuremburg trials after World War II. During the Cold War he lectured nonstop to the FBI, war colleges, thousands of Georgetown elite in his open-to-the public evening course, and wrote books that got mixed reviews and soon disappeared. Of *The Fall of the Russian Empire* (1928), the *New York Times* praised his research and depiction of the Russian Revolution as a "long tragedy of mankind." The *New Republic* opined that "Stray facts float forlornly in a riot of fiction."

Ironically, the one event for which Walsh is most remembered may not have happened the way it was reported. On January 7, 1950, Walsh and Charles H. Kraus, a political science instructor at the Foreign Service School whose specialty was anticommunism and who was also a speech writer for Senator Joseph R. McCarthy of Wisconsin, had dinner at the Colony restaurant with William A. Roberts, who was also an attorney for the muck-raking columnist Drew Pearson, and Senator Joe McCarthy. After dinner McCarthy asked for advice on 1952 campaign issues. Some suggested the St. Lawrence Seaway or a pension plan for the elderly. Then Walsh asked, "How about communism as an issue?" The senator liked that. The government was full of Communists, he said, and he was going to hammer them. Drew Pearson reported the meeting in his column in March, and several books repeat the story. More recent studies point out that Walsh was strongly anticommunist but not necessarily partisan, that he denied having given the advice, and that McCarthy had shown interest in the Communist issue independent of any advice at the restaurant.

Psychologically, Walsh remains a mystery, though his biography provides clues that his obsessions may have exceeded his wisdom. The months in revolutionary Russia may have frozen his judgment. He was convinced the Communist revolution had been engineered by Jews. He was not a scholar, but he attached PhD to his title even though it was an honorary degree from his own school. He favored obligatory military service for all, but did not believe that conscripts should be paid. He taught that America had the right of nuclear "first strike" against Russia. Ultimately, his life had one message: we have moral values; Russia does not. Though Walsh is forgotten, some of his ideas survive. He painted a world canvas in two colors—black and white. Some contemporary political leaders see it the same way, and they miss his kind.

The Voice of *America* Is Silenced

America, under editor Robert C. Hartnett, S.J., a 1927 Loyola Chicago graduate, Daniel Lord sodalist, and 1946 Fordham PhD in political science, moved into the Cold War trying to speak for a church and for a Society of Jesus that was as torn apart as the rest of the country to whom it spoke. As Hartnett saw it, *America's* job was to apply church teaching to current events. Charles Morris explains it in this way:

> The intensity of Catholic Cold War anticommunism has been variously explained as an expression of status anxiety, as the hyperpatriotism of the ethnic outside, as anti-Semitism, as a reflection of traditional loyalties, or even as an artifact in the eye of the analyst. But these explanations typically miss the religious component of the Catholic stance. To Catholics Stalin was the antichrist, a satanic figure of biblical proportions.

As it happened, the peak of Catholic influence in popular culture coincided with mass opinion being strongly anticommunist. "It was a

watershed in American Catholic history: the nagging Catholic griev-
ance that their patriotism and Americanism had never been fully ap-
preciated was in Catholic eyes, finally and gloriously put to rest."

In Los Angeles, George Dunne discovered that when he spoke on
racial or labor issues in the 1940s and 1950s anonymous reports were
sent to the chancery suggesting he was a subversive, even dangerous,
character. He recalls:

> It is sad and deeply disturbing that otherwise intelligent people . . .
> are easily beguiled by such blatant propaganda. That they are is
> substantiated by the whole history of the McCarthy era. The key, of
> course, is the almost obsessive fear of communism peculiar to Amer-
> icans. To suggest that someone is a communist, or associates with
> communists, or is sympathetic to them is an extraordinarily effective
> way of condemning the accused and of mobilizing support for the
> accuser.

A complication for the Jesuits was that McCarthy was a Jesuit alumnus, from Marquette University, who touted his Catholicism, especially when Jesuits criticized him, and his Catholic supporters continually pushed the idea that somehow McCarthyism and Catholicism
were Siamese twins joined at the hip.

Young Joe McCarthy arrived at Marquette in 1930, one of a total of
3,000 students, when the university was celebrating its Golden Jubilee
year. Somehow he held several part-time jobs at once, moved into the
law school in his third year, started a boxing career, plunged into a
fraternity life that kept him up all night partying and gambling, and
prepared for exams by listening to his classmates run through old exams right before the tests. He profited slightly from a public speaking
course, but never learned to study and read. His biographer, Thomas
C. Reeves, concludes: "Joe's schooling had failed to provide him with
the solid educational foundation that a man of his later responsibilities
would find useful. He emerged from Marquette with only hazy and
simplistic historical and philosophical perspectives. He had not even
been required to write out his thoughts logically and clearly."

The McCarthy-Jesuit fight began during the 1952 presidential election when McCarthy delivered a speech aimed at destroying the reputation of Democratic candidate Adlai E. Stevenson, the governor of
Illinois. McCarthy deliberately referred to Adlai as "Alger," as if to

confuse him with accused alleged Communist agent Alger Hiss, and waved copies of the *Daily Worker*, which McCarthy falsely claimed endorsed Stevenson. *America* editor Robert C. Hartnett, whose natural sympathies were with the Roosevelt-Truman New Deal–Fair Deal tradition, felt an obligation to set the record straight and enumerated the lies and distortions in McCarthy's speech.

McCarthy struck back with a letter trumpeting his Catholicism: "Being an ardent Catholic myself, brought up with a great respect for the Priesthood, which I still hold, it is inconceivable to me that a Catholic Priest could indulge in such vicious falsehoods in order to discredit my fight to expose the greatest enemy of not only the Catholic Church, but of our entire civilization." The contemporary reader who reviews the "controversial" *America* editorials and articles of 1953–54 may well wonder what the fuss was all about. As a polemicist, Hartnett, who had been a college debater, was balanced, dry, and academic. He laced his editorials with references to Woodrow Wilson, John Henry Newman, and the latest scholarship on governmental theory. His main concern was the relationship between presidential leadership and congressional power; and he saw the danger, with the Eisenhower presidency passively, by irresponsible inaction, ceding too much power to the legislative branch, of a "peaceful overthrow" of the presidency.

But McCarthy and his followers—including Hartnett's fellow Jesuits—began a campaign barrage of letters to Hartnett's Jesuit superiors, first to the New York provincial John McMahon, S.J., and then to the general, John Baptist Janssens, in order to silence *America* on this issue. McCarthy also enjoyed the support of most of the diocesan Catholic press, especially the conservative, large-circulation *Brooklyn Tablet* and members of the hierarchy, who by their support encouraged the public notion that if you were a Catholic you had better like McCarthy too.

For *America* the highpoint came in May 1954 during the Army-McCarthy congressional hearings, prompted by a fight between McCarthy and Army Secretary Robert Stevens on whether David Shine, a former McCarthy aide who had been drafted and a friend of McCarthy aid Roy Cohen, had or had not been given preferential treatment. McCarthy produced a classified FBI document, given to him by an unnamed source, to support his case. This was a major breach of national security. The *America* editorial of May 22, 1954, concludes: "Mr.

McCarthy seems to think that all the operations of government boil down to one: eliminating people *he* judges subversive. . . . If he insists on his piecemeal and 'peaceful' overthrow of the Presidency, he may do great harm to U. S. policy by his so far very successful diversionary tactics."

The New York press picked up the battle. Because opinion was so divided, the Jesuit communities on their own, like those during the Civil War, thereafter decided McCarthy would be a forbidden topic of conversation. On May 29 the Jesuit authorities silenced *America* on that topic. Hartnett appealed and got a reprieve when the "good of the Church" might require them to speak. The American Jesuits seemed to have settled this among themselves when, in June 1954 Janssens, angry that *America* was involved in "political or secular matters" and very upset that Hartnett thought the magazine should have complete freedom of expression, clamped down. Harnett, exhausted by the battle, took a break and resigned. He insisted to Jesuit historian Donald Crosby that he had not been "fired." He was just worn out. Crosby concludes that Janssens's action "showed his authoritarian and regressive tendencies at their worst," consistent with Janssens's cooperation in suppressing such leading Jesuit intellectuals as Woodstock theologian on church and state, John Courtney Murray, the French ecclesiologist Henri de Lubac, and anthropologist Teilhard de Chardin.

When George Dunne was working at St. Francis Xavier Church in Phoenix, an "otherwise intelligent monsignor" told him that he could not understand why George was against McCarthy. "After all," he said, "he is against communism, isn't he?"

One night the senator himself, who had been visiting friends in Phoenix, called Dunne up and wanted to know why he was against him. Dunne recalls that his speech was slurred and that his well-known alcohol problem seemed to be taking its toll. Dunne replied to the senator, as he had to the Monsignor, that the end does not justify the means. McCarthy broke into a belly laugh and told him a joke about two Irishmen intended to refute that moral maxim. "This was evidently an ethical doctrine outside his ken," Dunne recalled. "I hung up the phone feeling sorry for McCarthy; a few months later he was dead of excessive drink."

The Cold War years for the American Society of Jesus, could, in a sense, have begun in the 1930s when Fr. Ledochowski determined that the Society's energies should be directed against communism—an attitude America did not adopt until after World War II. Progressive Jesuits like Dunne, Twomey, and Fichter found themselves smeared as "Communists" when they pursued social justice goals on behalf of black people. Walsh built a public persona opposing the Red menace, and Hartnett, who dared to confront the demagogue, was forced to fall on his sword. Conclusion: some Jesuits are very brave. Sometimes they cannot all count on broad Jesuit support.

12

The Golden Age

Death on a Winter Night

> The evening of March 9, 1956, was clear, cold and Lenten. The Bowl looked as it had since the first snow back in November. Stockbridge Mountain stood out against the faded blue winter sky, its long flank mottled with snow patches and the black of jutting ledges. The snow from several recent snow storms lay out over the frozen lake, bright in the weak sun, but dull and gray in the distance down by the island and Interlaken.
>
> —F. X. Shea, S.J., "The Shadowbrook Fire,"
> *SJNEews*, December 1973

It was about half past midnight, and Father Bill Carroll thought he smelled smoke. But he had been wrong before—last year he smelled something burning in the middle of the night, but the house had been searched and no evidence of a fire found—and maybe he was wrong again. Actually a second search, four days later that year, had discovered a hidden beam in the ceiling of the scholastics' toilets that had been smoldering for four days. But Bill Carroll had a tendency to be nervous anyway. Several years before, he and Father Stephen Mulcahy had been badly smashed up in an auto accident and both now lived conscious of the possibility that they could die at any moment.

They were among 16 priests in a community of 127, including priests, 100 scholastics—novices and juniors in their college courses— and 11 coadjutor brothers at Shadowbrook, the New England Province novitiate in Lenox, in the lovely Berkshire Mountains. Once dubbed the "largest family home in America," former summer "cottage" of Andrew Carnegie, the sprawling Tudor castle estate, with its own farm and livestock, was in its last years as a Jesuit house, and fund-raising had begun to build something more up-to-date. In fact, the house was a fire trap.

The men had ended a standard day of class, some skiing on a slight slope or slipping around on the icy paths during an evening walk, and were kidding one another at evening recreation. At dinner, Walter Young, a junior, had delivered a sermon honoring the fourth centenary of the death of St. Ignatius, entitled "Go Set the World on Fire," the words St. Ignatius reputedly said to Francis Xavier when he sent him to Japan; but, rather than comment on that, the fathers kidded Mulcahy, a Boston College man, about his having to sit with Holy Cross men at the upcoming Ignatian alumni dinner. After litanies at 9:00, the novices retired to their dormitories, where, three times a week, they self-administered the "discipline"—whipping their bare shoulders with a knotted cord for as long as it takes to say a quick "Hail Mary"—before bed. While the central wing housed the classrooms and ascetories, the common study hall where each one had a little desk, the west wing had the fathers' rooms with the novice infirmary on the top, third, floor, and the east wing had the chapel on the first and the juniors' and novices' dormitories on the second and third.

By now, however, Father Carroll knew he was right. He jumped up, crossed the corridor, and broke in on Father Sullivan, and he smelled smoke, too. Sullivan hurried down the stairs toward the kitchen to check and was confronted by a wall of flame. In this kind of crisis Jesuits, at least in New England in 1956, run to the men in charge —to wake the minister, Father Arthur B. Tribble, and the rector, Father Francis Corcoran; and then each man, without one duplicating another's efforts, took an initiative. They knocked on doors, remembered who was most vulnerable, sought them out, reminded one another to stay calm, called the fire department by means of the town switchboard, as the corridors quickly filled with smoke—first in a blue haze hovering about the ceiling light bulbs, then in dark, roiling clouds that plunged the corridors into darkness, then followed by the spreading flames.

Among the calmest was Father Tom Kelly, a quiet gentleman of inner intensity. He was the first to reach the novice dormitory in the far wing, which the smoke and flames had not yet reached. He woke the manuductor (in Latin, one who leads by the hand), the head novice whose bed was by the door, and told him there was a "small fire." The manuductor simply switched on the lights and told the novices, "Get up and go down the tower stairs," without telling them why. The novices and, a few minutes later the juniors, still in pajamas but wrapped in their blankets, were soon safe, out in the snow. And then, as the flames rose and the firemen and police and Red Cross and hundreds of townspeople began to arrive, the scholastics, pajama clad, did what they could to rescue those still trapped in the blaze.

Soon the stairways and airshafts and some of the corridors were blazing infernos, and the only escape was through the windows. Rescue teams with a few ladders ran back and forth, though not all ladders reached the windows, which were 40 feet above the ground, or the sloping roof where some had crawled out and were moving back and forth walking precariously in the gutters. Some tied sheets together and tried to shimmy down, others took their chances in perilous leaps, hoping to be caught in blankets their brothers held stretched out below them.

Father Mulcahy, age 58, totally bewildered, asked Father Carroll, who was moving in and out of hysteria, what was going on. Carroll told him the house was burning down, to get a blanket and get out. Mulcahy returned to his room, closed the door, and stayed there until the flames consumed him. As Carroll smashed a window to escape, suddenly Father Tribble, age 53, appeared and asked for absolution. Carroll threw himself out the window and smashed his heel on the rock-hard ice. He regained consciousness on the way to the hospital, with the words of absolution, "*Ego te absolvo*" ringing in his head. Father John Post, the novice master, not knowing the novices were already safe, was obsessed with rescuing them. His hands singed by flames and trapped in his room, he tried to lower himself on a rope of sheets. Below, novices called up to him to wait for a ladder; but Post was too confused to conclude that if the novices were outside he didn't have to save them. The flesh on his burned hands tore away, he lost his grip and plunged. He smashed two vertebrae and severed the motor nerves of his legs and hips.

Brother (novices were all called brother, partly to erase the individualism that goes with one's first name) Robert F. White, the youngest of the first-year class, had been sick and was staying in the infirmary on the west wing third floor. There, smoke billowed up from the windows below and flames crackled outside his door. As the smoke overtook him in his room he fell to the floor then crawled to the window for air. Below, his friends called up to him to jump, but he could not even see the ground. For 20 minutes he hung outside the window, terrified, fighting for air. Then he saw the red glow of the fire glistening on the snow, and somehow quietly realized that he must jump or die. He threw down a piece of bedding and asked where it had landed. In the middle of the blanket, they replied.

"All set?" he called. Then he jumped, tossed himself limp and relaxed in an act of faith that his brothers would save him. Novice Mike Connolly, holding the blanket, looked up and saw the body, arms and legs flapping, sailing down and knew to his horror that White would miss. So he pulled himself under him to break his fall. White hit Connolly's shoulder and almost tore off his ear, then slammed through the blanket tearing it like a tissue, and hit the pavement. He broke both legs and smashed his kneecap. The doctors said that if he had not fallen relaxed he would have driven his legs up through his chest.

Soon it became clear that the house was gone. Fathers Tribble and Henry Muollo, age 54, and Brother Henry Perry could not be found and were presumed, like Father Mulcahy, to have died in their rooms. Many days later, when the rubble was cleared and sifted, a few of their bone fragments were found and buried together.

The story first broke in the pages of the *Berkshire Eagle,* and radio and television quickly spread it across the country. The thousands who had traveled to the Tanglewood Music Festivals had seen the sprawling old mansion on the hill and wondered what went on up there. Millions had seen the recent romanticized photo essay in *Life* magazine by Margaret-Bourke White on the Jesuits; and here was a very different picture—Jesuits as victims of a terrible and dramatic tragedy. The town switchboard received hundreds of phone calls of inquiry and condolence. The local Red Lion Inn transformed itself into an instant seminary lodge, and the towns of Lenox and Stockbridge, where the Jesuits had been seen as aloof, suddenly became welded in spirit with the hundred homeless young men. These young men quickly found homes in the New York and Maryland novitiates at St. Andrew-on-Hudson, Plattsburgh on Lake Champlain, and Wernersville, Pennsylvania. The emotional bonds that link young men who share an isolated, highly structured, and spiritually motivated lifestyle are strong; and for some, being cast into the "outside world," even the world of another Jesuit novitiate, meant an unexpected bout with loneliness. At the same time, they experienced a Society bigger than the New England countryside—the first mini-lesson that the Jesuit's vocation is "to go to various places." Of the scholastics who survived, approximately half went on to ordination and stayed in the Society;

and in the spring of 2006, 16 of the 34 Shadowbrook Jesuits still alive came together for a weekend of remembrance.

A Picture of the "Old" Society before the 1960s

In 1955 John LaFarge had been a priest and a Jesuit for 50 years, and he celebrated by commemorating the Society in his book, *A Report on the American Jesuits*, in a collaboration with *Life* photographer Margaret Bourke-White, who had been assigned the story on the American Jesuits and who of course was taking many more pictures than could appear in the magazine. Bourke-White, who had known nothing about Jesuits other than that they existed, spent six months visiting Jesuit houses all over America and the St. Louis Province missions in Honduras. With Father Daniel Linehan, director of the Weston Observatory and a seismologist, she tramped through the Maine woods on the Canadian border as Linehan waded into the Kennebec River rapids and set off dynamite charges to test their impact on the river and on the plans for a new dam. Each morning he said Mass at a makeshift altar in the woods, and he explained to the journalist: "Think of all the energy stored up in the world—all that power. That is God. And I held Him in my hands this morning. That is why I am happy. That's why I'm a priest." The amazed Bourke-White watched the fully vested Linehan say Mass in the woods. Then she flew to Central America to click away in the Honduran hills as Father William Ulrich hoisted a huge fat hog on a scale. He had brought scientific agriculture to a Mayan tribe.

The photographs Bourke-White took are more iconic than journalistic. Handsome young men in well-pressed habits pray standing in the sun in front of a statue of St. Ignatius and staring into the distance clutching a rosary in both hands. Or they sit or stand in graveyards to read their books. Except for the seismologist, the men wear habits or collars all the time—to fly planes, feed chickens, weigh hogs, sail boats, harvest grapes, and sit in Greek class at Shadowbrook in a shabby classroom that was obviously once something like a millionaire's living room. But they get the idea across that Jesuits do a lot of things. Five University of San Francisco students look over Father Raymond Feeley's shoulder as he shows them a Communist newspaper; on a world map on the wall, the Red Soviet menace spreads into

Europe and Asia. On the Philadelphia docks, Denis Comey, S.J., climbs down into the ship's hold to inspect a questionable cargo. Explorer Bernard R. Hubbard, once the famous "Glacier Priest," has donned his old Eskimo furs and posed with binoculars. George Dunne and Alton Thomas, executive secretary of the Urban League in Phoenix, chat with an integrated group of high school students. A chorus of uniformed young women in the sodality of Our Lady sings, surrounding the cherubic, white-haired, beaming Daniel Lord as he sits at the piano, looks into the camera, and sings and plays.

LaFarge's text provides statistics that help us picture the mid-century Society. Of 32,899 Jesuits in the world, 7,751 are in the American Assistancy, with 4,204 priests, 2,919 scholastics, and 628 coadjutor brothers. Between 1880 and 1954 Jesuit high school, college, and university enrollments increased from 4,330 to 122,338. Add the students in mission countries for a total of 134,337. Of the 33 colleges and universities, including six seminaries, 15 are colleges only and 17 are universities. The law schools have 2,148 day students 1,840 at night. Georgetown, Creighton, Loyola Chicago, Marquette and St. Louis have medical schools.

LaFarge calls attention to the marked expansion of Jesuit institutions, a special characteristic of what has been called the postwar golden age of higher education, and to the challenge of training Jesuits to staff these schools. At the moment, 46 Jesuits were in doctoral degree studies; of these, 16 were pursuing their degrees in Catholic and 32 in secular institutions. In 1953–54, American Jesuits produced a total of 112 books, monographs, and scholarly articles. It is interesting to observe in the list of 28 colleges and universities and 40 high schools that the vast majority have at least one high school, now independent but attached to it historically, which also serves as a feeder school. New York City had five high schools, and the state of Washington, which, compared to the Northeast, does not have a high Catholic population, had two universities and four high schools.

LaFarge's metaphor for the Jesuit is the pioneer settler in the New World who comes to "implant lasting and fundamental principles." Though the pioneer stage has passed from public life, in spreading the Kingdom of God the frontier never closes. While the principles never change, the pioneer adapts his method to the world he finds. In America the "modern situation" has four aspects: men are ignorant of the truth; social and economic disorder hinder the spread of the truth; the vast outside world of other races knows not the church; there is a "supreme struggle" to ensure a Christian education for America's youth. He then, in strong language, says the church in the United States has been and must always be the church of the poor: "Were wealth, not the Faith, to determine the counsels of her leaders, it would be the beginning of the end, as it has been the downfall of the Church in times past." "If her voice were to be silent when Christian justice is violated, when discrimination and oppression are the fate of the weak, and wealth can control not only the social organism but the organs of public opinion itself, then it is but laying up anger for the day of reckoning."

To speak for the poor has been the mission of *America* magazine from the beginning, he concludes; but these ideas must be communicated to the individual. This is the role of the lay retreat movement, the Spiritual Exercises of St. Ignatius, and the Apostleship of Prayer, a spiritual movement that spreads devotion to the Sacred Heart of Jesus and the practice of receiving communion on the first Friday of each month. He seems to have placed the solution to a social and economic problem in the lap of the individual rather than in a call for broader reform of the social structures that oppress the poor. It will require another generation of Jesuits to reshape the Society's collective response to an unjust world.

The Fight to Face Facts and Raise Standards

In *Academia's Golden Age, Universities in Massachusetts 1945–1970*, Richard M. Freeland interprets the postwar years for a small group of New England universities, including one Jesuit institution, Boston College, as a "world transformed," an era in which a combination of political and economic forces radically altered the nature, scope, and mission of most of American higher education.

Though his study is focused predominantly on secular institutions, since the changes are the result of federal government policies their impact on the Jesuit system also was profound. Yet one man's gold is another's glitter—a sparkle in the sand of the academic mountain stream can be a temptation to adapt so quickly to an apparent bonanza that other, more basic investments may be squandered. The "gold" of this age was the combination of two gifts: the huge increase

in enrollments, sparked by the G.I. Bill, and the availability of government funding, partly for war-related and scientific research, but also
for social research, buildings, and other projects. Along with the influx
of G.I.s and federal investment in research, enrollments were boosted
by the prosperous economy and a surge in a middle class that was determined to enjoy the good things of life—from the suburban home
with the picket fence, barbeque, and new car and TV to social status
that comes with a college degree. Freeland describes the mood in this
way:

> The country's agenda was long. The human costs of the war, and the
> even more-frightening possibility of atomic conflict, made the impor-
> tance of maintaining peace evident. Europe had precipitated two
> wars in a generation and now lay in ruins. The United States, sud-
> denly the preeminent power of the globe, would have to pioneer in
> shaping a stable world order. In some, the nation's new international
> prominence aroused a sense of urgency about discrimination and in-
> equality at home. More broadly, world leadership implied a need to
> maintain military and economic power and the technological vitality
> on which they depended. Many educators believed they had im-
> portant roles to play in all these contexts—through training leaders,
> forming attitudes, and advancing knowledge. As one college presi-
> dent put it: "Events . . . have shaken the complacency of many uni-
> versity communities and compelled educators to . . . make [their]
> maximum contribution to a decent, well-ordered, free and peaceful
> society."

Government planners asked the American Council on Education
(ACE), headed by Dr. George Zook, to prepare a report on the impact
of the G.I. Bill. Zook's committee foresaw an enormous positive social
impact as a result of bringing higher education to a vast percentage
of the population that otherwise would never have gone to college.
Others, like Harvard president James B. Conant, who saw higher education as aimed at an elite, feared the consequences of multitudes
crowding courses for which they were unprepared. In fact, between
1945 and 1949, veterans poured onto the campuses in unprecedented
numbers. About 2.2 million—three times the number foreseen—enrolled. In 1950, about 50 percent of the college population was attending a publicly supported college; by 1970, 73 percent.

Another group, the Commission on Financing Higher Education, sponsored by the Rockefeller Foundation and the Association of American Universities, attempted to answer these questions: Who should go to college and for what? and, How would graduate education and research be developed? Unlike Zook, the Rockefeller group did not see educational inequality as a significant problem. Education was to "develop intellectual promise" and the capacity to deal with abstract ideas. For them, about 25 percent of the population was capable of profiting from college. Both groups believed in "liberal" education; but Zook thought it should be directed at life's problems, while the Rockefeller report would nurture personal qualities indirectly through the arts and sciences. Still another team, the Harvard Committee on General Education in a Free Society, published a very influential "Redbook," an argument that general education should be aimed at the student's life as a "responsible human being and citizen." The assumption of all this discussion is that education should meet the national needs, and government should direct funds to programs that responded to those needs.

What did this process mean to Catholic higher education and Jesuit colleges and universities in particular? For one thing, it meant that Jesuit institutions that were established as colleges began thinking of themselves as universities. The requirements to be a university may differ from one accrediting agency or state to another. It may designate a collection of several schools and programs under one roof, centered around a liberal arts college that gives the primary identity and provides the general education or "core" courses for the other schools of business, fine arts, music, social service, law, medicine, education, and nursing. It should have graduate programs and promote research, although the amount and quality of research at schools that call themselves universities may differ widely. And the long process by which American Jesuits in the intellectual apostolate have attempted to move from mediocrity to excellence was a slow one.

The transformation should have begun at the turn of the century when Harvard and Boston College squared off over law school admission requirements and the Jesuit core curriculum. A few farsighted Jesuits did take that conflict as a turning point and set the stage for the following steps. Beginning in the 1920s, in a process that would continue until the 1940s, the 26 Jesuit institutions of higher learning, enrolling 38,200 students in 1921, had to accommodate their structure and philosophy to the national accrediting agencies, the Association of American Universities (AAU) and the North Central Association of Colleges and Secondary Schools (NCA). In the midst of that exercise the American Society of Jesus was moved to ruthlessly examine its own institutions and prepare the Report of the Commission on Higher Studies of the American Assistancy of the Society of Jesus, 1931–32, a document known as the Macelwane Report, which called for radical changes in the way Jesuits are prepared for the intellectual life. But as we will see, the report was initially suppressed.

Finally, in the 1960s and 1970s Jesuit institutions separately incorporated their Jesuit communities from their universities, and the schools remade themselves into "nonsectarian" universities in order to qualify for more state and federal aid. They established lay-dominated boards of trustees as legal owners of the schools, and accepted national secular norms, based on the American Association of University Professors (AAUP), for the hiring and promotion of faculty. Opponents of these changes called them a "sellout," while proponents called them norms for excellence, responding to the mandates of Vatican Council II and playing in harmony with the modern world.

The Chicago Example

Let us consider the experience of Loyola University Chicago as one early example of the accreditation decision. While the AAU set standards for accrediting universities, the NCA set terms for affiliation for colleges. These included 120 credits required for a baccalaureate degree, courses of studies in eight departments, Master's or doctoral degrees for all faculty, and a faculty work load of not more than 15 to 18 credit hours (five to six courses) a semester. The Catholic Educational Association established similar but weaker guidelines in 1915. Faculty needed only a baccalaureate degree, since so many were foreign clergymen. Notre Dame, however, accepted NCA standards, while the Jesuits applied neither to the NCA nor the CEA.

At the heart of Jesuit resistance was a reluctance to submit to an outside authority and to change the way they prepared their own men to teach the *Ratio Studiorum*. Furthermore, one major purpose of Loyola (then called St. Ignatius College) was to prepare potential candidates for the priesthood, and moral development—chapel, the annual retreat, and monthly sacraments—was as essential as the intellectual. The effect on enrollment of Jesuit failure to adapt was swift and clear. In 1920 Notre Dame registered 360 arts and letters students out of its total 1,000 enrollment, while Loyola Chicago got only 124 within its 2,200. Other obstacles: a Jesuit school student needed 140 hours to graduate, thanks to the required Greek, Latin, and religion, and he couldn't get into an AAU graduate school without coming from an NCA institution.

Under the leadership of Alexander J. Burrowes, S.J., first as president of Loyola, which he rechartered as a university in 1909, and then as provincial of the Missouri Province, Loyola moved to accept the standards of the NCA. The Jesuit schools were expanding, adding law and medical schools, because Catholics were demanding more professional education; so Burrowes began thinking in terms of a "Jesuit university of high rank," and Jesuits were no longer modeling their schools on their secular liberal arts competitors like Oberlin or Amherst. By 1919 the new Missouri provincial was writing to Ledochowski asking permission to drop the Greek requirement and reduce the hours in Latin, English, and philosophy. The general's yes marked a new age in Jesuit education.

Presidents in other provinces followed the Midwestern example with hesitation, while the agreement to raise faculty standards presented another challenge. Ledochowski had been receiving complaint letters from America that the colleges were not Catholic enough. So the general responded with letters telling the presidents to stop hiring non-Catholics to teach and, where there were non-Catholic deans, to remove them. At the same time he ordered that standards be raised. Thus the Jesuit universities had to expand their graduate offerings to train a new army of Catholic PhDs, and the graduate schools, with their research requirements, became the new point of emphasis on the Jesuit campus. Between 1931 and 1937 Loyola University raised its total of PhDs on its own faculty from 37 to 72, and between 1928 and 1940 the number of PhDs it had granted went from two to 16. Nine of these were in education.

Thus this accommodation project was strung out over almost a generation of Jesuits. The next major stimulus was the Society's response to the bombshell report of the American Council on Educations (ACE), which had surveyed 77 graduate schools offering doctorates in 1934. Of the 66 programs it approved, the only Catholic programs were those at Catholic University and the University of Notre Dame. No Jesuit doctoral program made the list. When the *New York Times* printed the news, it was clear that the Jesuit schools were in for another round of self-examination. Actually, the examination had been conducted, but Ledochowski had buried the Macelwane Report, named for its committee chairman and principal author, in his files for four years. Now was the time to dust it off.

The Bad News and What to Do about It

A commission of six Jesuit administrators, headed by James B. Macelwane, an outstanding physicist at Saint Louis University, surveyed the whole assistancy and produced a 234-page study that compared Jesuit institutions of higher learning with the secular and other Catholic institutions on their academic standards, the qualifications of their faculties, the depth of their teaching, membership in associations, and library holdings. They concluded with 12 pages of specific recommendations, which, if followed, would have produced a significantly different Society of Jesus than the one that moved into the 1960s and that lost many members in the shock of the '60s storm. Several of its findings were very embarrassing.

Jesuit education, the report begins, is to "educate the whole man for a definite philosophy of life . . . not merely for the present world but for the world to come, 'eternal in the heavens,' " and to create leaders, "whose wisdom, prudence and sincerity will place them at the head of every important endeavor." The authors make it clear that they fear their report will be ignored and they call for an appointed *commissarius* with power to accomplish its goals. "The inertia of local traditions, the inbred opposition of Ours to any change, and the prevailing ignorance of conditions among both inferiors and superiors, all call for energetic action, which can only come from a head exercising inter-province power."

Why are non-Catholic institutions more successful than ours? They built up their prestige in the public eye. "They do not cover their deeds with a veil of mystery." They recruit the "highest type" of faculty who do research and write for publication. They are well organized with statutes and laws. The Jesuits' Catholic competitors also have better-trained faculty who write books and articles and participate in the Catholic Philosophical Association and the Catholic Historical Association. In Jesuit schools Jesuits are appointed who not only lack PhDs but lack any training in the subjects they teach. In other schools, upper-division courses are intrinsically difficult and require maturity to master, such as "Roman Satire" or "Victorian Poetry" or "The French Revolution" or "Theoretical Mechanics." The authors conclude, "With the exception of philosophy one will look in vain for such courses in many of the Catholic colleges, including our own."

Jesuit libraries are far behind those of others. Typical non-Catholic liberal arts colleges have well over 100,000 volumes. While Holy Cross has 150,000, John Carroll has 40,000 and Canisius has only 18,900. In a questionnaire answered by 621 Jesuit teachers in seven provinces, only 9 percent had the PhD and only 9 percent had published research. However, 57 percent thought the PhD was necessary. Leadership has been poor because incompetent, untrained Jesuits were named deans and rector-presidents. In the Missouri and Chicago provinces, from 1917 to 1931, 50 men served as deans—18 for one year, 14 for two years, 11 for three years, 6 for four years, only 7 for more than 4. To serve as community rector requires one set of qualities, as president another. Few men have both.

How can we establish our superiority? The obvious answer is to produce gentlemen distinguished by "virile Catholicity"—culture, scholarship, and leadership ability to fearlessly attack "all current evils." How is this to be done? In one recommendation, the establishment of a central office to unify, monitor, and support the network of institutions, the Jesuit Educational Association (JEA), was born, bore fruit and evolved into today's Association of Jesuit Colleges and Universities. In another, a "commissarius" was appointed to direct change, but he did not last long. Four other major changes, if accepted, would have had a major impact. First, all Jesuits should enter the Society with the understanding that all Jesuits should earn the PhD. This would have several good effects, from raising the professionalism of the graduate programs to elevating the intellectual atmosphere in the Jesuit community, where the more serious scholars sometimes felt isolated and discouraged.

Second, standards for admission to the Society must be tightened. It is not enough that the applicant wants to be a priest or save his soul or the souls of others, or frequents the sacraments to please his teachers, or wants to turn his back on a world he fears. The Society already has too many "pious but useless men." It may be technically true that the Society is not a teaching order, but 90 percent of its activities in America make it so. Therefore, the young men should enter only after two years of college, when one's academic maturity is more tested, and they should be trained in the novitiate in a way that develops their potentials from the start. One paragraph is especially devastating:

> Again and again our Fathers who had taught certain novices during their college days have been dismayed by the effects of novitiate training on these students. Those who had been sane and normal as students, developed in the meantime, a warped and distorted view of life in general, and of life in the Society in particular, that threatened to minimize, if not ruin entirely, their future usefulness in the Society in any capacity.

Third, all scholasticates should be on or near universities with graduate programs, so that from the beginning the young man is looking ahead, developing his specialty, seeing himself as a serious scholar. The third year of philosophy should consist of graduate courses, and while the Thomistic system must remain the core of the program, more modern philosophers must be added. Fourth, all should join and fully participate in both the national and regional accrediting agencies. In short, profit by, rather than be threatened by, the professional standards of the non-Jesuit world.

Over 30 years would pass before these recommendations began to be part of Jesuit training. Universities are by definition conservative institutions, as part of their mission is to preserve and pass along the best traditions of the past. That universities are to generate new knowledge was for Catholic priest-professors a "new" idea. Even John Henry Cardinal Newman in the Bible of Catholic intellectuals, *The Idea of a University* (1852), did not see research and the dissemination of new knowledge as part of the Catholic university's role. The American Jesuits in the 1930s agitating for reform were a distinct minority. Paradoxically, although the 1920s and 1930s were an era of literary flowering now considered a "Catholic Renaissance" and *America* and the newly founded *Commonweal* were publishing articles calling for the revival of Catholic scholarship, most Jesuits don't seem to have noticed. In 1923 Richard Tierney, S.J., editor of *America,* had complained that articles Jesuits submitted were unpublishable because the men didn't keep up on literature and philosophy.

Fordham's president in the 1930s, Aloysius Hogan, S.J., used to call the coaches in on Monday mornings and tell them how they should have played their games; but in 1933 he simply refused to fill out a questionnaire from the American Council on Education because he didn't like the question about how many books the faculty had published. He did, however, want AAU approval as a "University of Complex Organization" and pushed for it, though, he was warned that Fordham wasn't ready. In 1935 Fordham lost approval for both the graduate school in Manhattan and the college at Rose Hill. Both libraries were inadequate, reference books were locked in cases. Father Robert I. Gannon, Hogan's successor, who came to Fordham from Saint Peter's College to clean up the mess, wrote in his Fordham history, *Up to the Present*, "It was one of the darkest single days in 125 years."

In the Society LaFarge describes, new Jesuit faculty with PhDs from Harvard, Yale, and Paris are filtering into university departments; but the novices are overwhelmingly right out of high school. Seminaries are still in the woods. Following a decision process that began in 1945, when there were signs that so many men were joining the New York and Maryland provinces that Woodstock could not house both the philosophers and theologians, in 1957 they opened Loyola Seminary, a sleek new philosophate, not near Fordham, where the faculty wanted to go, but at Shrub Oak, in the remote hills of Westchester County in New York, to protect the young men from the evil influence of the city. The physical and emotional isolation, the dated textbook Thomism delivered from mimeographed notes in thesis form, the rules and surveillance used to control college boys a hundred years before tended to break the spirit. Of 136 who were there in 1968, three-quarters left the Society. When the generational revolt swept the world, including the seminaries, the Shrub Oak scholastics boycotted exams. The province sold the building to a Bible school and the scholastics and faculty moved to Fordham in 1969.

An Imaginary Tour of the Midcentury Jesuit West

Let us imagine that a half-century after Woodstock's Philosopher and Theologian took their trip through the colleges and universities of the

Midwest, two more, in 1957, have gotten special permission to spend their summer on the roads of the West, taking a Trailways bus up the California coast, where the Pacific Ocean washes the beaches on their left and the Rocky Mountains rise to the east and north. They have brought LaFarge's book along for spiritual reading. Philosopher Frank, who reveres the scholastics who taught him at St. Joseph's Prep in Philadelphia and owes his vocation to his senior retreat, likes to remind Theologian John that neither Francis Xavier nor Isaac Jogues ever got PhDs nor taught in a university. For him, a high school regency is the time to prepare for becoming a priest, in the pastoral rather than the academic role. He's slated to teach religion, world history, public speaking, Latin, and homeroom, and moderate the booster club, the sodality, the Apostleship of Prayer, the baseball team, and the drama club at his alma mater, and he can't wait to get started. Throughout the course, Frank has been a standout in seminary shows. He can sing. He knows no world history, but he will stay up late reading the textbook the day before the class.

John has spent two summers at Fordham. There he has talked to Father Joseph Donceel, the Belgian philosophical psychologist who is working the theory of evolution into his classes in spite of the fact that another Jesuit is reporting him to Rome for his dangerous ideas, and to J. Franklin Ewing, S.J. a very heavy man, an archeologist, who has been digging both for early human fossils in Lebanon and for Rene Goupil's bones at Auriesville. Like Donceel, he was a friend and advocate of the controversial Teilhard de Chardin, who wrote on evolution. John wants a doctorate in theology. He is developing a "process theology" wherein God himself does not know the future but evolves along with and parallel to his creation, suffering with the pains of the created world; but he's not sure the church or the Society, which censored the evolution chapter out of Donceel's textbook and silenced Teilhard, will support his ambition.

Loyola and Santa Clara

When Frank and John pulled into Loyola University of Los Angeles, they left their bags in their rooms and walked down the hill through the lovely neighborhood of Del Rey Hills for a plunge in the surf. This is the university where George Dunne had started high school and which had moved and changed its name twice and almost died once. During World War II the campus was down to 100 students with only one graduate in 1944. Only an army contract to train officers saved it. When they arrived, Charles Casassa, S.J., the first president with a PhD, was in the eighth year of his 20-year term, and the campus was very much alive. Casassa had opened a graduate division in 1950, terminated football in 1951, opened an Institute of Human Relations to promote racial relations in business and government in 1953, started an honors program, and constructed a chapel; and an engineering building and a student center and new library were on their way. In the early 1970s Loyola would merge with Marymount College, which already shared the campus, to become Loyola Marymount University.

Moving up the coast, in their visit to Santa Clara, Frank was, in a sense, connecting with his own roots. For much of the Society's history, competent administrators have been in short supply, and the top ones have played musical chairs—from provincial here to president there and then president somewhere else. Saint Joseph's Prep and College in Philadelphia first opened its doors in 1851 at Old St. Joseph's Church in Willing's Alley, in downtown Philadelphia, just a few blocks from Independence Hall. Burchard Villager, S.J., a rotund and decisive man with gray hair, had come from Switzerland in 1848 and served as prefect of studies at St. Joe's before becoming Maryland provincial in 1858. Named superior of the California Mission in 1861, he looked at the shabby Santa Clara campus, already in deep debt, and declared: "You must show yourself above the fence, show yourself to the world and strike their senses with a decent appearance." The gamble paid; new buildings brought more students.

In 1868 Villager returned to Philadelphia as fifth president of St. Joe's and engineered its move to 17th and Stiles Streets in North Philadelphia. Thinking big again, Villagers gave priority not to the new college buildings but to the magnificent Church of the Gesu, a cathedral-sized Baroque Revival red brick edifice that would fill with awe the Prep adolescents who were marched in weekly to prepare for confession in its pews. As a result, the college itself lay dormant for almost 30 years before funds were available to get it working again. By the time Frank was a student, the Prep and College had split. The neighborhood was inner-city black where, said one of the Jesuits, there was probably a murder a week. The Prep was a quadrangle in which the Gesu was one wall and the Jesuit residence another. A marvelous marble staircase greeted students inside the front door. The senior smoking room was down the hall; and the crew team would jog down the street to the Schuylkill River waterfront to the boathouse for practice. The college had moved to the suburbs on City Line Avenue.

Frank strolled across the Santa Clara campus. Somehow it seemed fitting to him that the same man who had built *his* campus on the other side of the country a century before had also had a hand in building this one.

Like Loyola, Santa Clara had gone through a series of near-death experiences of its own. The California Mission had both prospered in that it had two colleges fairly close to each other—Santa Clara and St. Ignatius College (later the University of San Francisco) a few hours away. St. Ignatius, with 700 students in 1884, was the largest Jesuit school in the country; Santa Clara had a third that number. A total of a hundred Jesuits served the two schools and a score of parishes in the region. Overworked, the men declined to rethink their situation and consider some changes. To solve the manpower problem the province lowered standards for admission to the Society and got a reputation for taking men everyone else had refused. At the turn of the century its buildings declined again, the local neighborhood spawned saloons on too many street corners, and to protect their students from temptation, the college tightened the rules until the Santa Clara became known as a prison. Fund-raising drives sputtered and failed. In 1906 shock waves from the San Francisco earthquake shook the boarders out of their beds, and in 1909 a fire gutted the faculty residence. They planned moves to Los Angeles or San Francisco.

In 1910 a new young president, James P. Morrissey, S.J., after much consultation, determined that Santa Clara would stay where it was and become the "great Catholic university of the West." He fixed up the campus, gave senior students individual rooms, put indoor toilets and running water in the dorms, raised entrance standards, expanded the curriculum, and, though the only graduate degree was an M.A., felt he could start calling it a "university." But, in a pattern that does not do the Society credit, though Morrissey was loved for his enthusiasm, industry, and character, a group of older Jesuits of European origin, described as "in their dotage," were shocked by his innovations and his loosening of the discipline. They bombarded the general's office in Rome with their letters of complaint. They criticized his every move until they won a letter of warning from the general to Morrissey to "govern according to our laws." Morrissey did not have a thick skin. With little sympathy from his fellow Jesuits and no support from the provincial, he fell into a deep depression, offered several times to resign, and, driven to the breaking point, quit in 1913 and in a few years left the order. He had tried to change some Jesuit educational policies and had been broken.

The college scraped through other disasters. In 1926, the old mission church, which went back to 1825, was reduced to ashes. The flames were discovered during the seven o'clock mass, and the bells rousted students and faculty to fruitlessly fight the fire. To turn a tragedy into an opportunity, the president determined to rebuild the church to its original form, since the lost church had been embellished to the point that it no longer resembled the historic site. In 1933, Brooke Hart, a student from a wealthy family who had just graduated, was kidnapped and murdered; and, with the encouragement of the governor of California, James Rolph, Jr., a mob of vigilantes battered down the door of the San Jose jail, dragged out the two alleged slayers, stripped them naked, and strung them up in the nearby trees. To what extent were Santa Clara students involved? Various newspaper reports make it clear that students were members of the mob, though the *San Francisco Examiner* concluded that the lynching had not been "organized and carried through" by Santa Clara students.

"The Glacier Priest"

In the 1940s the one priest, other than the Hollywood film priests, known to most American grammar school students was the one with the airplane who wore furs and had all those dogs. In December 1955 Bernard Hubbard, S.J., the "Glacier Priest," on his way to a lecture in Hartford, Connecticut, went by way of Newark, New Jersey, where he had friends and wanted to say Mass. Mass and his breviary were essential to him, and this most-traveled man tried to avoid travel plans that would interfere with either. But his leg had been numb since getting out of the taxi, his head was buzzing, and, while vesting, he couldn't get the chasuable over his head. He had had a stroke. He heard the doctor say he would not make it to the next morning, and he muttered, "Yes, I will, Doc." He had climbed and photographed too many mountains in Alaska—indeed all over the world—to let one stroke knock him out.

When Frank and John arrived at Santa Clara, which was Hubbard's home base and where he was recuperating, he was almost normal, except for a dragging right foot and a weak right hand. In some ways he was a role model for both young men. Frank could identify with Hubbard in that that Hubbard never got a PhD and taught a long list of courses when he was not trained to teach them all. He was, like Pierre-Jean de Smet, a public man, a favorite of the military to whom he lectured on his travels and who made promises he could not always fulfill; but millions of young people who read his books, like *Mush, You Malamutes,* and in grammar school saw those 16 mm films of him landing planes on dangerous glaciers, concluded that here was a priest who was also an explorer and a moviemaker. Maybe they could do some of those things, too. Meanwhile, if John had poured a late night Irish whisky with Father Ewing at Fordham, Ewing would have told him to put aside a lot of that "docility" he was taught in the novitiate and make up his mind on what he wanted to do and pull every string, write every letter necessary until he could do it. Hubbard's career demonstrates that even in the 1930s an enterprising Jesuit could do what he wanted.

Hubbard entered the Society in 1908 at the age of 20 after a youth of climbing the local mountains. In Innsbruck for theology, he picked up the "Glacier Priest" title for climbing and photographing the Alps. Assigned to teach at Santa Clara, he took the summer of 1927 to become the first man to tramp across the Alaskan Mandenhall and Taku glaciers. The next year he explored Kodiak Island and found mountains 6,000 feet high. He traveled both with rugged Santa Clara athletes for research companions and alone, as when he drove a dog team 1,600 miles from the Alaskan interior to the Bering Sea. In the 1930s he concentrated on volcanoes, like Aniakchak, which had erupted spectacularly in 1931 and whose smoldering crater he explored and described for *National Geographic.*

Since, as a scientist, Hubbard was largely self-trained, the scientific impact of his explorations was not great; but his public impact as a promoter of Alaska, Santa Clara, and the Catholic Church was remarkable. When, during World War II, General George S. Patton, Jr., led his army into Vienna and rescued for the West the famous Lipizzaner horses at the Vienna riding school, Hubbard was with him to entertain his troops. When Hubbard met General Douglas MacArthur, then military governor of Japan, MacArthur confided to Hubbard that his problem with Jesus Christ was that Christ's life was a failure. "No great man," said the general, "should be a failure even in Christ's circumstances. His crucifixion is a stumbling block to me." Hubbard told the general that there is a crucifixion, a failure, in every life. "I will pray that some day you will understand Christ's failure as a success." Several year later MacArthur met Hubbard in New York and said that now he understood.

After the war, at the request of Father General Janssens, Hubbard toured the world filming the Jesuit schools, missions, and apostolates; and later Hubbard enlisted George Dunne to write the narrative for two documentaries on Alaska and Japan. Dunne wanted to say no because he knew Hubbard made promises about his projects and didn't come through. But Dunne said yes, and, not to his surprise, Hubbard neglected to credit him in the films. Although Hubbard thought he had recovered enough from his stroke to go back on the lecture circuit and fly back to Alaska in 1962, in May he was stricken again. By chance, Dunne, who had been recuperating in the Santa Clara infirmary right across the hall at the same time, heard his gasps in his last days. "He had been a great human being," wrote Dunne, "who could charm blackbirds out of the trees."

At the end of the 1950s Santa Clara was finally ready to make the transition from a school where in 1948 the president, Fr. Charles Walsh, had declared that the university "holds that the theory of evolution is but a theory . . . so certainly false that it would be extremely rash to maintain it," and which *Time* magazine described in 1951 as "a place apart from the rest of the brash and bustling state," to a university widely accredited. The Jesuit theologate Alma College, in the Santa Cruz Mountains, became affiliated as its graduate school of theology, where future and former Jesuit, governor, and presidential candidate Jerry Brown had joined the student body. But in changing it was not keeping pace with the valley—today's Silicon Valley—which surrounded it. That would come.

"Shifting Smoke and Lurid Flame"

The University of San Francisco places its own golden age next to America's end-of-the-19th-century Gilded Age, symbolized in San Francisco by the mansions of the railroad barons on Nob Hill. It was the era when the Statue of Liberty was dedicated in New York Harbor, when the Spanish-American War marked the beginnings of an American empire, and when, in 1880, St. Ignatius College and St. Ignatius Church moved from their Market Street address to their new home on Van Ness Avenue at Hayes Street. The school traces its origins to the 1855 founding of the one-room schoolhouse, St. Ignatius Academy, and so climaxed this period in its imposing new quarters marked by new laboratories, a college orchestra, a gym with an indoor running track, and an enormous church containing one of the nation's finest organs with a week-long Golden Jubilee celebration and a Mass of thanksgiving on October 15, 1905. Within six months all was dust.

When the first tremors of the great San Francisco earthquake of April 18, 1906, first hit at 5:12 A.M., thousands of sleepers were thrown from their beds; but the 44 Jesuits at St. Ignatius were already up. The City Hall collapsed, the Palace Hotel turned on its axis, huge fissures opened up on the streets. As the president of St. Ignatius, John Frieden, S.J., described it, "The great strata of rock and conglomerate that form the peninsula on which San Francisco stands rotated, tilted, twisted, sank and heaved in veriest agony. The massive buildings of St. Ignatius seemed like a piece of shrubbery in an autumn storm." But the buildings did not fall. Hundreds flocked to the church for a series of Masses and confession. The priests hurried to the makeshift hospital to minister to the crushed and broken dying. Then things got worse.

In the city, since the earthquake had broken water mains, the firemen had no water pressure to hose the fires that destroyed the Hearst Building, the Opera House, Chinatown, and hundreds of other neighborhoods. On Hayes Street, a woman cooking breakfast sent flames into a fire-damaged chimney, which spread quickly to St. Ignatius Church and lit one of the towers. With thousands of others, Father Frieden, carrying some clothing and the archives, headed for the beach, escaping "one vast mass of shifting smoke and lurid flame"— flames visible from 50 miles away.

The college relocated to a hastily built temporary campus, which, they said, looked like a "shirt factory," rebuilt the church on a hill at Fulton Street, started a law school, and survived an enrollment plunge (down to 24 students) and money crisis during World War I. In 1930 it changed its name to the University of San Francisco. During World War II, USF alumnus and Associated Press photographer Joe Rosenthal scaled Mount Suribachi with the marines and shot the pictures of the flag raising.

From the 1920s to the 1950s, ahead of Jesuit schools in the Northeast and South, black faces appear in the yearbook on the boxing, basketball, and football teams. The 1951 football team was undefeated, and nine of its starting players were drafted into the NFL. For some reason, however, USF did not get invitations to bowl games. When the Orange Bowl expressed interest, USF would be invited only if it left its two black players behind. The students refused, preferring to be known as the team "undefeated, untied, and uninvited." When Philosopher Frank and Theologian John stopped by, USF was still in a glow from its basketball team having won NCAA championships two years in a row.

The Singer with a Classical Education

Understandably, any Jesuit institution in the Northwest, the frontier of the Rocky Mountain Mission, which had become the special apostolate of the Italian immigrant Jesuits, traces its origins to de Smet. But the lesser-known second founder was Father Joseph Cataldo, whose first work was to build up the neglected Indian missions during the early 1880s. His ultimate accomplishment was the establishment of the small school that became Gonzaga University in 1887. Then with reluctance he gave a start to the future Seattle University in 1891. Born in Sicily in 1837, he entered the Society at 16, and when Garibaldi invaded Sicily he fled to Belgium, was ordained in 1862, then came to America and the Rocky Mountain Mission. He was frail throughout life. As an infant he had been pronounced dead but recovered as his burial was being prepared. As a boy his father warned him that the Jesuits would have no use for him because he was too weak to work. During studies he sometimes had to withdraw from school to recover in his native air. Photographs show him as a tiny, feeble old man in a wheelchair; but despite his frailty he became not only a pioneer missionary but a linguistic scholar, master of 20 European and Native American languages. He continued to pull himself together to appear at Gonzaga celebrations and fund-raisers until he died at 92.

In 1877, appointed head of all Jesuit projects in the Northwest, on a return trip to Europe in 1885, Cataldo set out to recruit more Jesuits to staff the nine major missions for which the Society was responsible and establish new Indian schools where they were needed. Though he was not eloquent, his simple logic which warned of the hardships and promised the consolation of some spiritual victories helped to recruit 31 young men: eight Italians, 13 Frenchmen, four Germans, a Belgian and one from Holland, and four Americans. Most were still seminarians. He had almost doubled the number of Jesuits in the Northwest. Some left the Society, some returned to Europe; but enough stayed to make a difference. Without them Gonzaga would not have gotten off the ground. Meanwhile, by 1890, Seattle had become Washington's largest city, with a large, mostly Irish immigrant Catholic population. In 1891, in response to the bishop's pleas and with Gonzaga and his Indian missions already overburdened with only 150 Jesuits at his disposal, Cataldo said yes to Seattle. He sent Fr. Victor Garrand, who had been complaining that Cataldo's devotion to his Indian tribes was out of date, to establish a church and school.

If the University of San Francisco's "golden age" ended with an earthquake, Gonzaga's, in the judgment of its historian, Wilfred P. Schoenberg, S.J., ended with a song. The years 1930–58 were the years of the Glee Club, climaxing in an all-star Gonzaga-produced television spectacular—and a new library. The music department had been started in the school's second year, and from then on the chorus and orchestra gave both concerts, some as long as three hours, and "musical interludes" during oratorical contests and stage shows. In 1893 even Shakespeare's *Julius Caesar* was interrupted eight times for music. The first minstrel show was in 1912. The music department rose and slumped during the late 1920s; then Lyle Moore, who had been a part-time voice teacher and basketball coach at another college and was part time also at Gonzaga, took charge. He developed the 30-voice Glee Club, which for the next several decades traveled up and down the West Coast in a Greyhound bus, giving sometimes three concerts a day and clocking 5,000 miles a season.

"Where the Blue of the Night Meets the Gold of the Day . . ."

Bing Crosby, writes Gary Giddins in the first volume of his biography, was "the only major singer in American popular music to enjoy the virtues of a classical education. It grounded his values and expectations, reinforcing his confidence and buffering him from his own ambition. As faithful as he was to show business, his demeanor was marked by a serenity that suggested an appealing indifference. He had something going for him that could not be touched by Hollywood envy and mendacity." Whatever the weaknesses in the Jesuit colleges nationwide in the early 20th century, the Jesuit formula seems to have been working well for the Crosby family in Spokane. Somehow his poise, calmness, and cool demeanor may have been the product of what Ignatius called "indifference," a sense of priorities that allows one to accept defeat but retain one's integrity. In 1942, informed that his family was safe but his house had burned to the ground, Bing asked, "Were they able to save my tux?" As his brother Bob put it, "The Jesuits trained him to weigh the rewards of this world versus those of the next and to keep his own counsel."

At Gonzaga High School, part of a still very small Gonzaga University, before and during World War I, Harry "Bing" Crosby, though he lived a block away, was often late for class, though he would come early on Monday mornings to entertain his friends with the songs and sketches he had memorized at the vaudeville show over the weekend. He served Mass regularly as a boy and occasionally as an adult, having remembered the prayers at the foot of the altar, "*Ad Deum qui laetificat, juventutem meum.*" But his passing desire to become a priest had to compete with the day when he was 14 and saw Al Jolson in blackface playing a clever black servant in *Robinson Crusoe, Jr.* To Bing, Jolson was "the greatest entertainer who ever lived." Though a marvelous whistler and singer, Bing, who also got good B/B+ grades, made his name in debate and elocution, which taught him to enunciate and analyze a text at the same time. At graduation from the high school in 1920, Bing, who had chosen to follow the classical course at the university, delivered a speech on "The Purpose of Education."

As a college student, Bing did well for a while, but there was the constant tug of the theater, the shows with the Drama Club where, in emulation of his hero Jolson, he mastered the art of blackface, and continued perfection of his elocution. But the day when the extraordinary quality of his voice first got noticed was when he sang *"Panis Angeli-cus,"* and "Oh Lord I am Not Worthy" in the college chapel for the Feast of the Immaculate Conception in 1922. One of the Jesuits Bing admired was the down-to-earth prefect of discipline; but he may have learned one lesson too well. Although St. Ignatius from the beginning forbade Jesuits to administer corporal punishment—he let the lay teachers do it—this man carried a big leather strap with which to beat misbehaving students. Bing did not object; indeed he applied the same rule with his sons. A series of distractions, including varsity baseball and an outside job as a drummer in a band, made him less motivated to study law, the concentration he had decided on in junior year. Also, playing and singing with the Musicaladers kept him away from home. He was drinking more than he should. With only a few months to go, after having posed for his senior yearbook picture, Bing dropped out of Gonzaga in 1924.

Crosby's tradition of giving money to Gonzaga began as a high school sophomore with a gift of one dollar to a fund drive in 1919. In 1937 he celebrated at the Gonzaga Homecoming in four days of shows, dances, and a football game—a visit rivaled only by the two-day stay of Daniel Lord and the "largest Catholic youth convention in the history of the West." In 1947 Frank Corkery, S.J., Gonzaga's president and Bing's old buddy from high school days, wrote to Bing about building what would be the Bing Crosby Library. From then on Bing threw his time and money into the drive, boosting the fund with gifts ranging from $60,000 to $160,000 to a final $700,000. In 1949 Bing invited the Glee Club to appear on his Easter program on ABC. The climax of the drive was the October 13, 1956, "Bing Crosby and Frank Sinatra Show," Bing's first live major TV appearance, a benefit for Gonzaga. The library was dedicated in October 1957. On stage in his doctor of music academic gown, with his new wife of ten days, Kathy Grant, and twin sons, Crosby received the long applause of 5,000 spectators, stepped to the rostrum, and said, "Oh, I wish Bob Hope could see me now."

The traveling scholastics, Frank and John, had not been given permission to watch the Crosby TV show in 1956, but they saw the new library rising in their summer visit of 1957.

The golden age of Jesuit higher education expansion came to a close with the founding of the last three new institutions—Fairfield University in 1942, LeMoyne College in Syracuse in 1946, and Wheeling College, later University, in 1954. All were in suburbs rather than cities, in very beautiful settings, with, inevitably, modern buildings built on hilly land where architecture and landscaping could provide that welcoming atmosphere, a message to a student that he or she will both be breaking into a strange new world and yet feel at home. Fairfield's campus, less than a mile from U.S. 95, combined the properties of two old estates. LeMoyne, named for the Jesuit missionary Simon LeMoyne, a contemporary of Issac Jogues, is in Syracuse, upstate New York, not very far from the Mohawk Valley and Auriesville, where Jogues and Goupil were killed. The Maryland Province accepted the invitation of Wheeling's Bishop Swint because they shared his conviction that the coal-mining country of West Virginia should have a Catholic university. Now it was as if the academic frontier had closed. America had as many Jesuits colleges and universities as it could absorb. Now the system could not expand; but, in many ways, it still had to grow.

In 1991, William Sullivan, S.J., Seattle's 20th president, finished his 20th year in office on the university's 100th anniversary. He spoke for many presidents in the introduction to his own university's history:

> Almost the entire first century of Seattle university has been a time of struggle. The lack of resources from the beginning, the dearth of students, the exodus to Roanoke Street for 13 years, the impact of world War II and the Vietnam War, the rapid turnover of presidents in the late Sixties and early Seventies—all these factors paint a picture of adversity far greater than that experienced by many other American universities.

The one clear lesson of this history, he says, is that the will to survive and faith in a mission can carry through troubled times. Since 1941 the G.I. Bill and the Second Vatican Council have brought irreversible changes. Meanwhile, a university is necessarily dynamic, but it must preserve the way in which it differs from other institutions like itself. What he wrote about Seattle in 1991 described the past and the future of perhaps all the other Jesuits across the country at the end of their common golden age of growth.

PART IV

The Modern Society Emerges

13

Freedom from Fear

Shaking Off the Suppression

In general, novices in the late 1950s knew nothing that was going on in the "outside world," outside the gates of the country novitiate, until the novice master at the morning conference dropped headlines on them from papers they were not allowed to read and radio reports they were not allowed to hear. But 1958 was a "hot news" year by any standard.

On October 9 they learned that Pius XII had died. Those who had been reading the secular press before they came in may have known two things: this pope had been most unsympathetic to the movement of the worker priests, where, in Europe, priests took off their collars and took on factory jobs as a way of reestablishing contact with the working masses alienated from the church. He had also, in 1955, in an exhortation to the Society, said: "Among the superfluous things that a Jesuit could very well do without is the habit of smoking tobacco." Clearly, this was something which Jesuits who had his ear had asked him to include in his talk, to give teeth to the injunctions Fathers Ledóchowski and Maher had proclaimed to deaf ears. Novices who had read *Time* magazine before entering knew that two Vatican stars named Tardini and Montini, Montini the more "liberal" of the two, were in the wings as a future pope.

On October 28, 1958, Cardinal Angelo Roncalli, 77 years old, of whom no one had heard, was chosen. At first, hearts sank. How could this old man give vigorous leadership? Then the letters from home snuck in old photos of Roncalli the diplomat at a reception in Turkey with a cocktail in one hand and a cigarette in the other. There was hope.

On July 25, 1959, Roncalli, now John XXIII, announced that he was calling an Ecumenical Council, Vatican II, the first since Vatican I, in 1870, which, against resistance from some of the American hierarchy, had proclaimed the doctrine of papal infallibility and set the tone for the defensive, walled-off mentality which was to characterize the church until this moment. Now he famously "opened the windows" and let in the intellectual and cultural history of the last hundred years—the impact of Darwin, Marx, and Freud, and also John Dewey —categorized in philosophy classes as "adversaries" to be refuted rather than as geniuses with insights that must be understood. Within a few years the Society of Jesus the young men had joined would be radically changed.

Statistically, the American Society of Jesus was at its apogee. In 1950, there were 6,897 American Jesuits; by 1960 the number rose to 8, 338. It never reached that peak again. In 1970, there were 7, 055. While the number of priests from 1960 to 2000 was well over 4,000, the number of scholastics plummeted precipitously from 3,116 in 1960 to 714 in 1980. Ironically, however, regardless of the dramatic plunge in membership, which can be explained in many ways, the perspective of history marks these years as a "revolution," "renaissance," "rebirth," as in the Greek myth of Anteus, who, every time in combat he was slammed down against his mother earth, gained new strength for the battle.

The principal catalytic element, from one point of view, was Vatican II and Jesuit participation in this astonishing event. But the seeds of the flowering had been planted years before. A fundamental step for American Jesuits in joining the silent revolution was shaking off the psychological wounds of the 19th and early 20th centuries that had rendered them timorous and unmanned.

Samuel K. Wilson, S.J., a president of Loyola University Chicago who was most instrumental in making Loyola a respectable research institution, wrote in an article, "How Modern Are the Jesuits?" in *Manners* 1 (December 1936)," that "the Jesuits are not modern at all."

> Moreover, it must be remembered that in the eighteenth century the Jesuits were suppressed by no less an authority than the Catholic church. The fact of the suppression had very real and lasting results, even though it was dictated less by principle than by policy, and when expediency ceased, the Society was restored. But no man brought back from the grave ever completely forgets the agony of death, and the corporate body of the Jesuits has never quite forgotten the suppression. It is more cautious and conservative, more safe and

sane, more fearful of making mistakes than the average corporate group which has existed several centuries.

Somehow, gradually, by the 1960s, Jesuits had begun to free themselves from this fear and to move into an era when, though its numbers fell, its integrity rose. Part of it was response to exterior challenges, and a great part was due to the example of fellow Jesuits who stuck their necks out, were hurt, but did not leave.

French historian Jean Lacouture, in *Jesuits, A Multibiography*, sums up the transition:

> The great Jesuit adventure of the twentieth century, necessitated in part by the Company's spinelessness throughout the nineteenth, found specific expression in the great *aggiornamento*, the opening up, the bringing up to date, of the Catholic Church proclaimed during the Second Vatican Council of 1962–1965. If the Jesuits of the twentieth century were as a body (and some out of deep personal conviction) very different from their recent predecessors, it was partly because the whole Catholic Church was being nudged into profound mutation by the good-natured man elected in 1958 under the name of John XXIII.

Writing as a Frenchman, Lacouture attributes the cosmic shift from the grip of ultramontanism to Vatican II Catholicism to the influence of four great Jesuits: Teilhard de Chardin, who placed Christianity within the timeless history of the cosmos; Karl Rahner, who, with his notion of the "anonymous Christian," freed the church from its "monopoly on salvation"; John Courtney Murray, who reconciled the church to the principles of pluralism and religious freedom; and the general, Pedro Arrupe, the visionary who "embodied the principle of charity in justice." But these were men forged in the fires of the previous generation, whom history had prepared, often through suffering, for this moment.

Seven Steps toward Freedom

As a general rule there have been few great and famous Jesuits. The Society's impact has been collective and anonymous rather than through brilliant individuals; and novices have been cautioned that celebrities have been few in the 1950s—like John Courtney Murray and Thurston Davis, though most novices had heard of neither—and it would be unrealistic to expect to match their fame.

Of the men who led not the "revolt" but the reshaping, some were famous and some where less so. The 1960s were possible, insofar as the Society of Jesus was concerned, because of several interlocking movements.

First, the spirit of self-criticism in the church, while not strong, was loud enough to get attention. *America* and the independent, lay-edited *Commonweal* (which would have two Jesuit book editors in the 1970s and 1980s) engaged in controversies over the Spanish Civil War, fascism, and American involvement in World War II, as well as the changes in Catholic higher education. Historian Theodore Maynard concludes *The Story of American Catholicism* (1942) with an assessment of the church's contribution to culture. He is wary of the proliferation of professional schools which, though they bring in money, drain energies from other works and attract non-Catholic students and professors who are not dedicated to nor influenced by the Catholic ethos. He recalls as notable the Catholic poets Jesuits Leonard Feeney and Alfred Barrett, whom Margaret Bourke-White later depicts teaching on a Fordham lawn; and he singles out the quarterly, *Thought*, whose editor, Wilfred Parsons, S.J., was simultaneously editor of *America*. He rates three Jesuit historians: Thomas J. Campbell, who he says is "hardly a Catholic Parkman"; Gilbert J. Garraghan, author of the three-volume *Jesuits in the Middle United States*; and, the "most brilliant," Thomas A. Hughes, an Englishman who taught at American colleges and author of the four-volume *History of the Society of Jesus in North America* (1907). Jesuit editor John J. Wynne's *Catholic Encyclopedia* he calls "by all odds the greatest monument of American Catholic learning."

Maynard considers the liturgical movement, which he sees as teaching the faithful how to assist at Mass, the "most memorable of all Catholic developments of our time." He excuses Jesuits for not being conspicuous as liturgists on the grounds that, unlike other religious orders, they do not recite the office in choir; but the best popular book on the liturgy is by Jesuit Gerald Ellard, *Men at Work and Worship*. Also, Jesuits have been outstanding astronomers. None of this modifies Maynard's agreement with George N. Shuster writing in the

American Scholar (1940–41) that "Catholic writing has seldom been at so low an ebb. The educated Catholic has never been so much alone in the midst of his fellow men."

An even more damning portrait, from Catholic University's leading historian, is John Tracy Ellis's "American Catholics and the Intellectual Life" in *Thought*, at this time published at Fordham and edited by William F. Lynch, S.J., later author of *Christ and Apollo*. Ellis begins with Cambridge University's Denis W. Brogan's 1941 judgment, "In no Western society is the intellectual prestige of Catholicism lower than in the country where, in such respects as wealth, numbers, and strength of organization, it is so powerful." Then he explains how this came about. Early Catholic immigrants were poor and illiterate, and Americans in general are wary of scholars. Ellis recalls that when 15-year-old John LaFarge, the artist, father of the Jesuit, was at St. Mary's College in Emmitsburg, he asked his father to send him the works of Herodotus, Plautus, Catullus, Theocritus, Dryden, Goldsmith, Michelet, Moliere, Corneille, and Victor Hugo. The family passed on its love of books. But 20th-century Catholic families do not know how to do that. The only leadership Catholics have shown, says Ellis, is in business. And, with few exceptions, these rich Catholics do not support Catholic colleges with big gifts. Few clergy have higher degrees in the humanities, and the intellectual culture in seminaries is low.

Ellis boldly charges that Catholic intellectuals have "betrayed" that which is "peculiarly their own." He echoes Maynard's description of Catholic colleges that "in a mad pursuit of every passing fancy" have spread out into secular fields—engineering, business, nursing—where they have little competence and have neglected scholastic philosophy and the liberal arts. The second "betrayal" is in establishing competing graduate schools without the libraries or scholars to justify competing programs. (Though he does not say so, in this he appears to support a Catholic University specific complaint against the Jesuits whose new programs were competing with CU.)

Finally, our scholarship is weak because of a misguided spirituality embedded in spiritual "classics," like the *Imitation of Christ*, over which many a seminarian has prayed that "I had rather feel compunction than know its definition," without a counterbalancing emphasis on the evils of intellectual sloth. Ellis concludes that Catholics "have suffered from the timidity that characterizes minority groups, from the effects of a ghetto they themselves fostered, and, too, from a sense of inferiority induced by their consciousness of the inadequacy of Catholic scholarship." He cites two Catholic scholars—Francis B. Wilson and John Courtney Murray, S.J.—who have broken through to influence the secular world by being quoted in Walter Lippmann's *The Public Philosophy.* "Yet," says Ellis, "an effective result of this kind is only attained through unremitting labor, prolonged thought, and a sense of the exalted mission of the intellectual apostolate on the part of the Catholic scholar."

The second movement was the vigorous bursting forth of biblical studies, given a green light by Pius XII's 1943 revolutionary encyclical, *Divino Afflante Spiritu.* It called for scholars to apply the historical method to the sacred books, to dig back into the original languages rather than draw their conclusions from the Latin Vulgate. The main breakthrough was in its recognition of ancient literary forms, thus freeing the exegete to distinguish between what is literal history and what is historical only in the broad literary sense. Whereas in the modernist era scholars had been intimidated into studying only "safe" topics, now they were urged to take on the difficult problems posed by the texts.

This led to the founding of the Catholic Biblical Association and the *Catholic Biblical Quarterly,* where soon a whole generation of outstanding Jesuit writers—Weston's Frederick J. Moriarty; Woodstock's Joseph Fitzmyer, later an authority on the Dead Sea Scrolls, expert of Luke, and an editor of the *New Jerome Biblical Commentary;* Canadians David Stanley and Roderick McKenzie; and John L. McKenzie, author of *The Dictionary of the Bible.* Gradually new ideas sunk in. The process of inspiration was not God whispering in the ear of the sacred writer or guiding his hand across the page; it was the community, guided by the Spirit, discerning which books belonged in the canon. When did the apostles finally recognize the divinity of Christ? Most likely at Pentecost. A clue to the change in atmosphere is the fate of John L. McKenzie's very widely read study of the Old Testament, *The Two-Edged Sword.* When the provincial sent the manuscript for censorship to the old-school professor at Woodstock, he rejected it. Sent on appeal to Stanley and Moriarty, it was approved. By the time of the Council the writers of *Verbum Dei,* the declaration on revelation, were able to say that Scripture *contains* revelation, in the form of a written record, but that not all Scripture *is* revelation—a distinction that frees interpreters from a rigid, noncontextualized reading of every text.

Third, the American labor priests, parallel to their brother "worker priests" in France who took off their collars to work on an assembly line, dramatized the church's commitment to a "worldly" problem—poor people. Both Heithaus in St. Louis and LaFarge at *America*, although LaFarge could not countenance the "imprudence" of Heithaus's rebellion, put the church on the front line on racial issues.

Fourth, the university presidents who, from the 1930s, knew that only high standards would make the Jesuit message credible, and kept pounding away on their basic message, which would bear fruit only in the 1970s.

Fifth was the influence of French Catholic intellectualism, which had fostered a literary renaissance with François Mauriac, Paul Claudel, and the George Bernanos novel and film, *Diary of a Country Priest*, and which now surged ahead with the "nouvelle theologie." Led by a small groups of Jesuits and Dominicans, and given voice by neo-Thomist philosopher Jacques Maritain, they employed the tools of modern scriptural criticism, in that they examined the historical roots and contexts of theological ideas: What did the relationship between church and state mean to the early church, the Patristic Age, Thomas Aquinas and other medieval theologians? These men, including several Jesuits, and along with existentialists Jean-Paul Sartre and Albert Camus, strongly opposed fascism in all its forms—including the capitulation of much of the French church to German occupation of Vichy France, and the international Catholic cheerleading for Franco's Spain.

In years in which Catholicism, with some reason, was perceived as in league with totalitarian regimes, Maritain and his American counterpart, Woodstock College professor John Courtney Murray, struggled to develop a theology within traditional Thomism, which was both consistent with American democracy and with the international dedication to human rights that was emerging from discussion at the United Nations after World War II.

As war loomed in Europe in 1938, antifascist German and French intellectuals found new homes on American Catholic campuses. In 1940 Maritain, who had already published 60 books that would rank him as one of the greatest minds of the century, sat down with Fordham president Robert I. Gannon to discuss the possibility of his coming to Fordham as chair of the graduate philosophy program. At the moment, Maritain was opposed to the relationship between the Vatican and the Mussolini fascist government. He wanted assurance from

Gannon that he could speak out on political issues that were not governed by the content of revelation. Gannon, a pro-Franco conservative, refused. Thus the greatest living Catholic philosopher went on to teach and lecture at a dozen other universities, finally at Princeton until 1960. Gannon, as a conservative spokesman, was typical of his era, but not representative of the momentum in the church.

Sixth, perhaps the patron "saint" of the French spirit infusing the American church had been dead only a few years—Teihard de Chardin, whose manuscripts on evolution and the relationship between spirit and matter, suppressed by his Jesuit superiors but handed over to his secretary, began to appear in books immediately after his death.

Born in 1881, Teilhard, who had the blood of Voltaire in his veins from his mother's side of the family, was raised in a house once frequented by Pascal. He entered the Society at 20 and in studies on the Isle of Jersey and at Hastings, and during two years teaching in Cairo, came under the influence of progressive Jesuits who chafed under the strictures of Pius X's antimodernist crusade. He devoured Henri Bergson's *Creative Evolution* (1907) and the works of geologists and prehistorians who led him into a career in paleontology. During World War I he refused a commission and toiled alongside Moroccans and Zouaves as a stretcher bearer and won the Legion of Honor. After the war, in his writings, lectures, and in teaching geology at the Catholic Institute in Paris, his reputation spread; but while the evidence for evolution was widely accepted in the secular intellectual world, for church authorities in Rome it could not be reconciled with the Genesis stories of the Garden of Eden and Original Sin. Word reached the Vatican that Teilhard's ideas were suspect and Ledochowski exiled him to China.

Many of Teilhard's friends urged him to leave the Society that squelched his talent, but he submitted; and ironically the years in China, marked by his role in the discovery of the Peking Man, only enhanced his reputation. In 1948 he appealed personally to Father General Janssens to allow publication of the *Phenomenon of Man* and to let him accept a university chair. Janssens would not take the risk of giving Teilhard freedom in a church where evolution was only a theory. Teilhard moved to New York where the Werner-Gren Foundation for Anthropological Research had offered him an intellectual home.

Young American Jesuits tempted to leave the Society in the turmoil of the 1960s, years in which a thousand possibilities seemed to beckon, knew his story and prayed about it as they asked themselves where the talents God gave them could best be used. Though written in the 1920s, his major works, *The Phenomenon of Man* and *The Divine Milieu*, which provides a spirituality of work, spoke to the American 1960s. *The Divine Milieu* offered encouraging reassurance to men and women sucked into the competitive vortex of law, medicine, teaching, farm and factory labor, and raising a family. If we understand our role in the creative process, in Teilhard's view these struggling people are being sucked into God, not alienated from the source of all creation. Thomas Merton, Graham Greene, and Flannery O'Connor testified to his influence, and Mario Cuomo said Teilhard convinced him that "God did not intend this world only as a test of our purity, but rather as an expression of his love; that we are meant to live actively, totally, in this world and in so doing make it better for all whom we can touch."

One of the controversies during the 1950s and '60s, inspired partly by the worker priest movement, was the identity crisis of the so-called hyphenated priest. One French theologian even suggested that every priest should have a secular job. If the modern priest, in order to partake in the rebuilding of the secular city, is also a lawyer, doctor, professor, congressman, psychiatrist, or circus clown, how does he retain his "sacred" character? Are there some jobs beneath his dignity? One article suggested the priest could not be a garbage collector. For many young Jesuits, Teilhard resolved this tension, and they printed his prayer on their ordination cards: "To the full extent of my powers, because I am a priest, I wish from now on to be the first to become conscious of all that the world loves, pursues and suffers . . . to become more widely human and more nobly of the earth than any of the world's servants."

Though he had died a decade before, in 1955, Vatican II's Declaration on the Church in the Modern World rings with his influence. It opens: "The joys and the hopes, the griefs and the anxieties of the men of this age, especially those who are poor or in any way afflicted, these too are the joys and hopes, the griefs and anxieties of the followers of Christ. Indeed nothing genuine fails to raise an echo in their hearts." On the relationship between human activity and the paschal mystery, the Council says:

Appointed Lord by his resurrection and given plenary power in heaven and on earth, Christ is now at work in the hearts of men through the energy of His Spirit. He arouses not only a desire for the age to come, but by that very fact, He animates, purifies, and strengthens those noble longings too by which the human family strives to make its life more human and to render the whole earth submissive to this goal.

Until St. Andrew-on-Hudson closed and the novices moved to the LeMoyne campus at Syracuse, they had the privilege of cutting the grass around Teilhard's grave.

The seventh movement that set the groundwork for the emergence of a new Society of Jesus was the theology of the German Jesuit Karl Rahner. As Teilhard de Chardin reconciled the worlds of science and religion, Rahner was able to rescue Thomistic philosophy and theology from the stale notes from which they had been taught by restating basic principles enriched by the terminology and insights of Belgian Jesuit Joseph Marechal, the founder of Transcendental Thomism, who was influenced by Maurice Blondel and Emmanuel Kant. To this he added the existentialist metaphysics of Martin Heidegger, with whom he studied in Freiburg and who taught him to read texts in a new way, asking what is behind the text, and above all to confront the radical questions of existence.

Rahner's essays, which, beginning in 1954, have been collected in over 20 volumes called *Theological Investigations*, can be heavy going. But they were essential to the Jesuits of the pre- and post-Vatican II years for several reasons: they begin with the analysis of human experience and move from that to a grasp of God's presence and love; they are ultimately inspired by the principles of the Ignatian Spiritual Exercises and the ability to "find God in all things," which also animated Teilhard; and they deal directly with pastoral problems—like the inspiration of the Bible, freedom in the church, justice, peace, marriage, prayer, and death. In Rahner's view we are spiritual beings; that means we are transcendent, able to reach beyond the limitations of time and space in our search for truth. As we reach out, God is constantly open to receive us, and we may even grasp him unknowingly, "anonymously," and in the act of our loving of other persons—which is the same as our love for God—we are really loving God. This basic human experience can be that of the "anonymous Christian." As Fr. Richard McBrien describes Rahner's idea in *Catholicism*, "God is always present within us, even before we begin the process, however tentatively and hesitantly, of trying to come to terms with God's reality and our knowledge of God."

Like Teilhard, Rahner suffered from the Roman censors, but when Vatican II was convened, he became, working on numerous committees behind the scenes, in the words of one observer, the "most powerful man" at the Council. In the judgment of theologian Ronald Modras in *Ignatian Humanism*, Rahner's greatest contribution was "his theology of universal grace and its implications for the Catholic relations to other churches, to the world religions, and to the modern secular world. One relates differently to people if they are viewed as kindred spirits within a community of grace rather than as outsiders." We have only to think back over the Society's missionary efforts—to the Mohawks, the Chinese, to the Civil War soldiers, and even those of World War II—and the perceived need to baptize and absolve, to sense how both radical and liberating Rahner's worldview can be.

The Excommunicated Poet

Then there was the strange case of Jesuit Father Leonard Feeney, one of that handful of Jesuits who become "famous," but whose careers end in an odd mix of obscurity and shame. Born in 1898 in Lynn, Massachusetts, the son of Irish immigrants and the youngest of three brothers, all priests, he entered the Society at 16, studied at Woodstock and then at Weston College, the new philosophy-theology school of the New England Province, which opened in stages in the 1920s to absorb the growing overflow at Woodstock. Feeney was quickly perceived as brilliant, witty, charming, and a gifted writer and poet. In the 1930s he became a Catholic best-selling author with his "Catholic verse," which was taught to Catholic schoolchildren, and his collection of stories, *Fish on Fridays* in 1935. Elected president of the Catholic Poetry Society and named literary editor of *America*, by the 1940s he had published a dozen books and was accepting invitations to speak and preach all over the country. When he preached at Saint Patrick's Cathedral in New York in 1937, Cardinal Hayes sat in and *Time* magazine took note of his wit.

In the early 1940s he began to visit the St. Benedict Center, a meetingplace for Catholic students and professors at Harvard, Radcliffe, and other local secular colleges. It was slowly evolving into a cultural and accredited academic oasis where young people presumably threatened by the non-Catholic environment of their schools could strengthen their faith. A regular visitor was Avery Dulles, son of John Foster Dulles, a Navy veteran, Harvard Law School student, and recent convert to Catholicism. The Center had no chaplain; but Feeney began coming in almost every day from Weston, where he was teaching, to preside at tea parties and sit down privately with those who wished spiritual direction. In 1943 he was named their full-time chaplain.

Within a few years, the small, lovable figure of Feeney began to change. He was a very clever mimic whose crowd-pleasing routines included imitations of Katherine Hepburn broadcasting a Joe Louis prize fight, Fulton Sheen as the prophet Isaiah delivering a Coca-Cola commercial, Al Smith lecturing on scholastic philosophy, and Eleanor Roosevelt broadcasting her regular radio show from Calvary on Good Friday. Then as his theology began to harden and his relationships with his religious superiors became strained, his humor sharpened and was pointed at those, including bishops, whom he considered doctrinal liberals, and became downright mean.

Feeney, who was not known for his theological depth, held the strictest interpretation of *extra ecclesiam nulla salus*, or outside the church there is no salvation, first proclaimed by Boniface VIII in his bill *Unam Sanctam* in (1302), in which he held that papal authority extended over all creatures in the world. This idea had returned most recently in Pius IX's 1864 Collection of Modern Errors, one of which was the belief that men can "attain eternal salvation in the practice of any religion whatsoever." Feeney's targets included Boston's Archbishop Cushing and William L. Keleher, S.J., president of Boston College, where Feeney had also taught and had gained a following among a few professors, who pushed "no salvation" in their classes. *Commonweal* executive editor John Cogley said he could hardly recognize this "angry, splenetic man" as the author of *Fish on Fridays*.

The atom bombing of Hiroshima threw Feeney and his cultlike followers into an apocalyptic fervor, a conviction that the world was doomed. He lashed out at Harvard as a "pest hole," Boston College as in "heresy" for teaching that non-Catholics might be saved, and accused Cushing and Bishop John Wright of diluting the faith by dining or speaking at Harvard. In 1948 Jesuit superiors, to shut him up, ordered him to move to Holy Cross. He refused. Now, while he had been demanding a doctrinal hearing on the subject of *nulla salus*, heresy was sidetracked and the issue became religious obedience. St. Benedict's was placed under interdict, four of his faculty followers were fired from Boston College and Boston College High School, and his ideas were condemned by the Vatican. On October 28, 1949, Feeney was sitting in the Center, reading, surrounded by students at work, when he received a registered letter. Without even opening it, he announced, "My dear boys and girls, I have been dismissed from the Jesuit order."

Feeney's response was to get nastier. His anti-Semitism became more virulent as he and his followers, some of whom were physically abusive, appeared regularly on the soapboxes in Boston Common calling Cushing the "archdiocesan ragman," and Jews "filthy demons." Young Jews from Brandeis drove in to harass him, but he refused to be silenced. Eventually he and his followers wore themselves out. In 1953 he was excommunicated.

For those who had admired the early Feeney it was a sad and inexplicable affair. Whether the church and the Society handled it well is another question. Perhaps authorities could have used it as a "teaching moment" and sponsored an open forum in which theologians, using the historical criticism that had been introduced by Protestant biblical scholars in the 19th century as well as the leaders of the "nouvelle theologie," explained the contemporary doctrine on salvation by putting Boniface VIII and Pius IX in context. But America was just coming out of World War II, Jews were only five years out of the holocaust, and Catholics were backing the United Nations' development of human rights and finally feeling at ease with their non-Catholic fellow citizens. The last thing the church could afford was the perception that Catholics thought all non-Catholics were going to hell. So they handled the Feeney case in the usual way.

Americans and Catholics Hold the Same Truths

The task of the third great Jesuit "reconciler" of the 20th century, John Courtney Murray, was, like the others, very broad, in that it required the contemporary church to use the tools of modern history to come to terms with an idea, a system of thought, which had both served and enslaved it for centuries. For Teilhard, the literal interpretation of the creation story in Genesis; for Rahner, the rigidity of a formulaic neo-Thomism; for Murray, both the Feeney trap of *nula salus* and the medieval political theory in which, since Catholicism is the one true faith, the ideal state is one in which the church is the established state religion. His task was narrow in that, as an American Jesuit, he needed to demonstrate that Catholicism and democracy were not only compatible but actually made for each other.

He did this in a life that was relatively anonymous, extremely rich, and tragically short. Born in New York City in 1904, John thought of becoming a lawyer like his father, but joined he Society at 16. He studied at Weston and Boston College, taught in the Philippines, was ordained at Woodstock, did his doctorate at the Gregorian in Rome, then returned to Woodstock to teach in 1937, where, except for a 1951–52 stint at Yale, he stayed until he died in New York of a heart attack in 1967. During most of that time (1942–67) he was editor of the extremely influential quarterly, *Theological Studies*. Founded in 1940, with patristic scholar and renowned orator Walter Burghardt, S.J., as managing editor and later editor, *TS* over the years became the cutting-edge journal of the American Catholic theological community.

Murray was a tall, stately man, with a bald head, dark-rimmed glasses, and a deep, powerful voice that gave weight to his words carefully spoken and deliberately delivered, with a demeanor which some found haughty, signifying an impatience with lesser minds, but which his friends saw as shyness. Sometimes his earned impatience could evoke a caustic wit. When Paul VI kept rewriting minute details of a document, Murray quipped, "What does he think he is, a managing editor?" But in his dealings with others he personified Newman's definition of a gentleman, one who does not inflict pain.

In *Theological Studies* and *America* and other professional journals, Murray evolved and tested the ideas that would find their epitome in the Council's Declaration on Religious Freedom. Meanwhile, in 1948, his friend Gustave Weigel, S.J., returned from Chile, where he had been teaching dogmatic theology for 12 years. Weigel's first article for *TS* when he returned reported on "Theology in South America" (1948), in which he said, basically, that there wasn't any. There were no "great movements," no scholarship because scholarship was not esteemed. Ironically, after Weigel's death in 1964, Latin America would rock the world with its "theology of liberation." But Weigel was Murray's colleague in reaching out to non-Catholics and encouraged Catholics to study original Protestant sources. He considered himself a "middle generation" ecumenist, between those who would not talk theology with Protestants and those who would achieve deeper levels of Christian unity.

Murray's starting point, as he says in the foreword to *We Hold These Truths* (1960), a weaving together by editor Phil Scharper of a decade of published Murray articles, is to show how both America and American Catholicism are built on the same beliefs, principles of natural law expressed in the Declaration of Independence:

> The life of man in society under government is founded on truths, on a certain body of objective truth, universal in its import, accessible to the reason of man, definable, defensible. . . . For the pragmatist there are, properly speaking, no truths; there are only results. But the American proposition rests on the more traditional conviction that there are truths; that they can be known; that they must be held; for if they are not held, assented to, consented to, worked into the texture of institutions, there can be no hope for the founding of a true City, in which men may dwell in dignity, peace, unity, justice, well-being, freedom.

Perhaps freedom was the troublesome word, but inevitably Murray made enemies within the church. Ironically, his opponents were based in the Catholic University—Father Joseph C. Fenton, editor of the *American Ecclesiastical Review*, and Francis J. Connell, C.SS.R., first president of the Catholic Theological Society of America—where in the 19th century Catholic University had been more progressive compared to Woodstock's ultramontane conservatism. Their ally in Rome was the head of the Holy Office, Cardinal Alfredo Ottaviani. An internal battle waged over ten years, during which Murray was ordered to submit to stricter censorship. It ended in 1958 when the Jesuit office in Rome ordered Murray, whose health had been slipping since 1950 because of a heart condition, to "sideline" his writings on church and state.

Walter Burghardt recalled the "bleak spring day" in 1955 when Murray sifted through the hundreds of books on his floor-to-ceiling shelves, keeping those on grace, the Trinity, social issues, humanities, or the new atheism and shipping the ones on church and state back to the shelves of the Woodstock College library. As if he could expunge the central issue of his life by this act of religious obedience.

But Murray did not disappear. The John F. Kennedy campaign for the presidency, in which the Kennedy speech writers had checked their church-state formulations with Murray, and the publication of *We Hold These Truths, Catholic Reflections on the American Proposition*, brought Murray to the cover of *Time* (December 12, 1960). Daniel Callahan in *Commonweal* called his book "the most profound attempt yet made to establish the compatibility of American pluralism and Catholicism." His "silencing" did not last long. The Apostolic Delegate to the United States, Archbishop Egidio Vagnozzi, squelched a Murray invitation to the first session of the Vatican Council in 1962, but New York's Francis Cardinal Spellman brought him as his *peritus* (expert) to the second session in 1963. It took two years, over 600 written interventions, 120 speeches, and five corrections of the text before, on September 21, 1965, the Council approved the text of the Document on Religious Freedom by a vote of 1,997 to 224. On November 18, in the company of other priest-scholars who had been silenced and sidelined before the Council, Yves Congar and Henri de Lubac, he stood tall on the altar in St. Peter's Basilica to concelebrate with Pope Paul VI the Mass of reconciliation.

In his introduction to the text published in *The Documents of Vatican II* in 1966, Murray writes that the document is hardly a milestone in human history, because the idea of religious freedom had long been recognized, even by Marxists. "In all honesty it must be admitted that the church is late in acknowledging the validity of the principle." But it was significant because it deals with the "development of doctrine," and it still remains to be explained by theologians how the gap between the *Syllabus of Errors* (1864) and *Dignitatis Humanae Personae* (1965) has been bridged. In a later footnote he suggests that the passage that reads, "For the rest, the usages of society are to be the usages of freedom in their full range. These require that the freedom of man be respected as far as possible, and curtailed only when and in so far as necessary," may be the most significant sentence in the Declaration. Paradoxically, says the Council, freedom is both threatened and freedom itself is a threat. Where freedom is responsible, it calls for "rightful response to legitimate authority."

In August 1967, in a taxi on the way from his sister's house in

Queens to the *America* residence in Manhattan, Murray was stricken with a heart attack and died. His funeral Mass was in St. Ignatius Loyola Church on 83rd Street, the same church in which a small crowd had said farewell to Teilhard de Chardin a dozen years before, and his body made the trip back to Woodstock for burial.

Before he died Murray had planned to update in the spirit of Vatican II, for publication in *Woodstock Letters* (vol. 96, Fall 1967), an extraordinary talk he had given to fellow Jesuits in 1947. Year after year the third-year scholastics about to be ordained had asked him to give their ordination retreat; so he was known to the younger men not just as a "famous" theologian—for Jesuits are seldom very impressed with the "greatness" of one another—but as a wise man who knew a lot about life. The talk, "The Dangers of the Vows," warns young Jesuits about the "risks of religious life," especially the "one supremely perilous risk—that of losing your manhood." Both the world and religion put obstacles in the way of manhood, and too many succumb. Look around, he says, and see men damaged by the way they react to the vows of poverty, chastity, and obedience; and we see men unorganized, and intellectually and emotionally immature. They lack responsibility, integrity, and purpose. This is because they have failed to encounter and master the three elemental forces—with the earth, with woman, and with one's own spirit.

"Man is not a man until by his own hard work he has bent stubborn earth to his own purposes." Woman offers two things to man: the possibility of procreation, in which man becomes a father, and thus more fully like God; and the "possibility of headship," wherein Adam's fault was in allowing Eve to "rule" him into temptation. (Obviously, Murray wrote this decades before *Theological Studies* had published its articles on feminist theology.) Finally, by giving in passively to Jesuit obedience, one loses the power to choose a destiny, "to summon all his energies for a pursuit." By entering religion we avoid these encounters. Under poverty, the community takes care of us, and we risk becoming childlike in our dependency. With chastity, "sex is dead," "man risks becoming a disembodied head, that fancies itself a whole thing when it is not." "Your typical bachelor is proverbially crotchety, emotionally unstable, petulant, and self-enclosed—small and childish in the emotional life."

Obedience, like poverty, throws one on the collectivity, and on the will of another. There is no need to search one's heart to decide what to do. "In a word, one can live through one's public life, and spare oneself the lonely agony of the desert struggle." Your obedient man can become less a man.

One can imagine Teilhard, Rahner, and Murray all submitting in obedience to silencing they knew to be unjust, realizing as well that being a Jesuit had brought them to whatever eminence they had attained, and asking themselves whether their manhood was at risk.

14

The Arrupe Era

Another Resurrection

On October 11, 1963, word reached *America* magazine that a Jesuit had risen from the dead. The editor, Thurston N. Davis, a Harvard PhD in classics who had been dean of Fordham College in the 1950s but had left that post to replace Robert Hartnett as editor, was, above all, a man of moderation. But here was a scoop, relayed from a provincial to a former provincial who relayed it to him. And although *America* was only a weekly magazine, Davis responded like a deadline reporter. He called in Robert Graham, a California Jesuit historian whose specialty was the Vatican, and Eugene Culhane, his former Fordham assistant dean and now *America* managing editor, who had covered the Castro revolution with some sympathy. Together they hustled out to Idlewild International Airport (now John F. Kennedy) to meet BOAC Flight 501 from London at 6:55 A.M., which would deliver two Americans from Soviet prisons who had been exchanged for two Russians in our jails.

Thurston Davis had known Walter Ciszek since they were novices together at Wernersville, Pennsylvania. He remembered him as a trim young athlete, a linguist, hard worker, quiet but outgoing. But he had not seen him in 30 years. A lot had happened since then. Ciszek had been inspired by a letter from the pope read to his novitiate class asking for volunteers to work in Russia, and he had built his vocation around responding to that invitation. This determination had led him to Poland when World War II broke out, and into Russia disguised as a workman in order to minister to Polish workmen, and, eventually, to Russian prisoners who had no priest. Arrested as a spy, he was jailed for five years at the notorious Lubianka interrogation center near Moscow, and then sentenced to 15 years of hard labor at Norilsk in Siberia. He had been presumed dead, and Jesuits had inserted his name into the list of the departed for whom they prayed. Later, cryptic letters signed with his name reached his family asking for a suit, a coat, some books.

And as the two freed men, the other a student, surrounded by State Department officials, whisked by them, the Jesuits barely recognized their old comrade. But, Davis wrote later: "He has come back to us from the mines and prison camps of Siberia—his hair nearly white, his hands gnarled from labor as a miner and mechanic, but unbroken, not brainwashed, and with a heart filled with compassion for the people to whom his whole adult life as a priest has been consecrated."

Ciszek's story is important not only because it is in the tradition of Isaac Jogues and other missionaries who suffered and often died to spread the gospel, but because it exemplifies a lesser-known theme in the Jesuits' history: their willingness to go to prison according to the pastoral needs of their time. Ignatius was twice jailed by the Inquisition. The English Jesuit martyrs were imprisoned and then disemboweled and hanged in public executions. Jesuits died in Dachau. Jesuits in the Philippines were imprisoned all during the World War II. Now, in the 1960s and '70s, Jesuits would go to jail deliberately in acts of civil disobedience to protest the Vietnam War. A prison term would become a badge of honor.

Ciszek told his story twice—in *With God in Russia* (1964) and again in a reflective meditation on the same events in *He Leadeth Me* (1973)—and in talks to fellow Jesuits. It is a tale remarkable for its simple directness, Christian charity, and lack of any Cold War rhetoric. For a while, as one of the more "famous" American Jesuits, who had probably suffered as much for the faith as any Jesuit alive, he remained outstanding by the manner in which he was ordinary.

As a novice he almost didn't make it. Born in 1904, the seventh of 13 children, son of a saloon-keeper father and a prayerful mother, he had grown up "a bully, the leader of a gang, a street fighter" in Shenandoah, Pennsylvania. He entered Sts. Cyril and Methodius Seminary, Orchard Lake, Michigan, where he continued to toughen up with 4:30 A.M. five-mile runs around the lake and cold swims in November. During one Lent he ate nothing but bread and water and ate no meat for a year. One summer he stayed at school and worked in the fields just to teach himself how to deal with loneliness and separation from family and friends. Reading the life of the boy saint, Stanislaus Koska, he saw him as a "tough Pole" and role model. He wrote to the Jesuit house in Warsaw asking to join, only to be referred to the Maryland–New York provincial. In 1928, at 24, he made his way to the provincial's office at Fordham in the Bronx and somehow talked his way into the Society.

At St. Andrew-on-Hudson, put off by the ostentatious piety of his younger fellow novices, Walter cut corners a bit on the rules. Until the novice master, Father Leo Weber, called him in and told him to leave. Walter assumed his stubborn Pole role and almost shouted, "I will not."

Weber got up and loomed over him: "What's going on here? Who do you think you're talking to?"

"I just won't leave, that's all," Walter replied. Then he dissolved in tears. They talked for a long time. He stayed. The following year a letter from Pope Pius XI asked for volunteers for Russia. Walter was in his second year at Woodstock when his answer arrived calling him to Rome to study at the Russian College. After his ordination in Rome, Ledochowski called him in.

The general, he recalled, was a small, frail man with a thin, ascetic face, sunken cheeks, high forehead, "and the most serene eyes I have ever seen." He "radiated peace and quiet," spoke in an abrupt, decisive manner, but was most charming and easy to talk to, even as he paced up and down the room. Unfortunately, conditions—the looming war—made it impossible to send a priest into Russia. Perhaps that day would come. But for the time being the Society's mission in Albertin, Poland, was flourishing, and a great source of vocations for the Oriental rite at the Russian College. Would Walter go?

Ciszek arrived in Albertin in November 1938. On August 21, 1939, the American Embassy telegraphed Ciszek that war might soon be declared and that he should prepare to leave Poland. But still holding his hopes of getting into Russia, Ciszek decided to stay. Hitler invaded September 1, and within days the Russian Army occupied the town and took over the Jesuit property. Warned again by the American Embassy to return home, Ciszek and a Russian Jesuit, Nestrov, devised their plan to slip into Russia disguised as laborers and to minister secretly to the Polish and Russian workmen who had been drawn or forced into service in the lumber yards of the Ural Mountains.

Together, in March 1940, they acquired false papers and identities —Ciszek became Wladimir Lypinski—got $15 from the lumber company, packed a secret Mass kit in their suitcases, and climbed into box-car 89725, full of laborers, for the two-week trek to Teplaya-Gora, 750 miles northeast of Moscow, a booming industrial area providing coal, iron, and lumber for the war.

There they worked and worked. Nestrov had an office job, but Walter hauled logs from the river and stacked them in high rows, sometimes diving under water to drag up water-soaked beams from muck and slime. Jesuit spirituality had taught them to be "contemplatives in action," that to work is to pray; but they had never expected to see this idea exemplified so dramatically. Their only consolation was to say Mass, secretly in the woods, one at the altar and the other standing guard, in the silence of the forest where chipmunks ran by and birds gathered overhead as signs of the presence of God.

Then in the middle of night, in 1941, when Germany had just switched sides and invaded Russia, the NKVD arrested them as German spies, confiscated their Mass wine and tooth powder as "nitroglycerin and gun powder," and threw them in jail. In fact, the police had been watching them for some time. As he was moved from place to place, Ciszek's interrogators told him bluntly to stop lying with his false name. They knew he was a Jesuit priest born in 1904 and now a spy for the Germans. Two or three times a month guards would take him aside and beat him on the head with rubber clubs—just to soften him up. Determined to break him, although he had simply been telling them the truth, his captors moved him to the dreaded prison, Lubianka, near Moscow, where he lived in solitary confinement in a six-by-ten foot room, allowed only 20 minutes of exercise a day, and was subjected to endless interrogation by gentlemen smooth, polite, naïve, and brutal, both experts in their trade and clumsy amateurs, for four years.

He kept his hope alive by organizing his day around his religious duties with the texts of Scripture, the liturgy, prayers, and hymns he had memorized long ago: morning meditation, the prayers of the Mass, the rosary, examination of conscience, and psalms from the breviary. In the afternoon he recited poetry he had learned in school—Wordsworth and Shelley—and made up jokes about Stalin to make himself laugh. But finally they broke him—with drugged food and drink, and electrodes. He remembered the walls and ceiling pressing in. Everything was burning. He shouted and shouted, huddled deeper in the corner, and fell asleep. He signed papers admitting that he had been found guilty and was thus being sentenced to 15 years at hard labor in Siberia.

But his captors held him for another four years, during which he was allowed to read, with a concentration on Russian literature, Dostoevski, Tolstoy, Turgenev, Gogol, Leskov, plus Jack London, Dickens, Shakespeare, Goethe, and Schiller, and even *Quo Vadis,* and a biography of Napoleon. He was reunited with Nestrov, who had also been interrogated at Lubianka and sentenced to 15 years, and with whom he could renew his sacramental life. When the war ended in 1945 there was a brief, false hope of freedom. But they had been convicted of spying for the Vatican. Their next endless train ride took them across Siberia and then to the far north to Norilsk, where the Yenisey River flows in from the Kara Sea.

For the next 15 years Ciszek lived in a variety of the camps, shifted from one job to another—he dug coal, built a copper factory, worked as a hospital aid, built barracks, welded steel, and crushed stones. They lived 150 men crammed into a room 100 feet long and 30 wide, with a bucket in the corner for a toilet. His companions were mostly political prisoners, but about 50 were criminals, thieves, who preyed upon the others until someone enforced the prison's primitive law by murdering the predator. Some plagued with scurvy, their breath stank, gums festered, lips bled, and teeth rotted. Their legs weak, they could stand no more than ten minutes at a time.

They sweltered in blistering heat, wearing only shorts, or shivered in cold winds and snow. The overwhelming primitive craving was for food. The basic meal was a piece of bread and a cup of thin soup, then they would scrounge, scrape, and beg for something more to survive. Through it, Ciszek's moods rose to a confident consolation that God was with him, then fell to depression and suicidal despair. Years later he told some scholastics what he declined to say in his books, that he was once tempted to throw himself over a staircase with the hope of being killed.

At long last Ciszek was able to do secretly what he had come to Russia to do—serve the people as a priest. For some years he and Nestrov had discovered, to their dismay, that the Russian men, raised in the Communist system, scorned religion and were repelled, rather than consoled, to find themselves in the presence of a priest. Now there were several priests in the camps and they cooperated in scheduling secret Masses and developed codes and signals that would allow them to "hear" confessions while appearing to work. The prisoners made wine from raisins and stole wheat to bake hosts, and a shot glass served as a chalice.

In 1953 conditions in the camp, disturbed by rumors that Stalin was sick, became much worse. The men grew restless and camp officials tightened rules. Groups larger than two were forbidden. The men protested being called by numbers rather than their names, officials ordered inspections to make sure numbers were in place. Guards confiscated metal objects, extra clothing, and holy pictures. Offenders were stripped and made to stand naked in the snow. In Ciszek's barracks, men suspected of "squealing" were hacked or stabbed to death. The news in March 1953 that Stalin was dead was the spark that lit revolts in prison camps all over Russia. Work stopped. While Moscow decided whether to send troops, camp officials negotiated with the prisoners' leaders and promised to use names, shorten work hours, and improve food. But finally Moscow decided the rebellion must be crushed and sent in the troops. The army burst into the factory where Ciszek and fellow prisoners had held out for five days and lined them up in the yard and leveled their machine gun sights at the prisoners. Ciszek made his last Act of Contrition, fully expecting to be shot.

Suddenly a car roared up, camp officials jumped out with papers in their hands, read out names, and put certain prisoners on a truck and had them taken away. An official walked over to Ciszek's group, telling them they had been spared this time but could not expect mercy again. But soon the revolt broke out again. A commission arrived from Moscow and again promised reforms, but the workers would not go back until the conditions had been met.

On the last day of May the government decided to attack; the troops gathered outside the main gate and the loudspeakers called on the prisoners to surrender before it was too late. Ciszek heard more confessions and said Mass every morning to large crowds who flocked to communion. Suddenly on June 1, at 1:30 A.M., the army broke through the north gate. The prisoners snapped together, grabbed bricks, clubs, whatever weapons they had, and marched to confront the troops. The commander had drawn a line the prisoners were not to cross and placed his machine gunners to enforce it. Then, when the two forces were but 20 yards apart, a Lithuanian named Yurgis, whose mind had been damaged by interrogations, rushed ahead and hit a gunner with a brick, until the commander himself shot him down and ordered his men to fire. The front line of prisoners were cut down. Ciszek hit the dirt and the machine gun bullets whistled over his head. He looked back to see the earth strewn with corpses as prisoners cursed and moaned and women screamed and troops poured through the openings in the barbed wire fences and clubbed the workers with their rifle butts. Prisoners who preferred death to capture went into the latrines and slashed their wrists and slit their throats. The strike was broken, the survivors returned to work.

One quiet evening soon after, when Ciszek had spent the day breaking rocks at the quarry, he sat alone and thought about his life. He thought of home, his sisters, serving Mass, and he began to tremble. Fearing a breakdown, he tried to snap out of it. He saw a bird feeding its two young in their nest, he thought then of his father feeding him when he came home late from a Boy Scout outing. His heart filled with joy. He thought of the men killed in the revolt, how their mothers and fathers had loved them. Tears welled up. Suddenly another prisoner slapped him on the back to remind him to eat his supper, which the prisoner had saved for him. Look, Ciszek said to his companion, see the birds caring for their young. Suddenly the mother bird took off and "poof!" it fell dead. His fellow prisoner, delighted, had killed it with a rock.

Ciszek exploded in rage at the prisoner and fell into a depression that lasted days. The following Sunday he went to an old flooded quarry and swam. Then he climbed the hill and looked out over the city and reflected on how God had watched over him all these years. His confidence returned, and he lay down to sleep "like a trusting child."

In April 1955, having served his sentence, Ciszek was released. Norilsk, for a while, became his parish; then harassed intermittently by he KGB, he was forced to move to Krasnopyarsk, then to Abakan. He worked as a lab assistant or as an auto mechanic, all the while finding souls who needed him as a priest. Finally, he tried for the first time to contact his sisters, who sent him clothing and tried unsuccessfully to visit him. At least now America knew that he lived.

Then one day a policeman came and drove him to a meeting where, without explanation, he was told to pay his debts and pack his bags. Without explanation again, a KGB agent took him to Moscow, to dinner and the theater. He toured the city, walked by the graves of old Communists, including Americans, buried by the Kremlin walls. And there was the slab over Stalin's resting place. Inside Lenin's tomb he mounted the 14 steps to view the body, dressed in dark clothes and illuminated in a soft light. He said a prayer, "He was a man, after all." The next morning, at the airport, his head spinning, Ciszek met an American official from the consulate who called him "Father" and had him sign a paper restoring his American citizenship. Suddenly he understood. He wanted to sing. His ticket was for first class. But this short, round-faced, white-haired man had little sense of the world he was about to enter. As the plane took off and swung in a big circle, Ciszek turned to the window and saw the spires of the Kremlin in the distance. Slowly, carefully, he made the sign of the cross over the land he was leaving behind.

Freedom Breaks Loose

The year after Ciszek returned to America, Father General Janssens, who had been sick and not actively directing the Society for some time, died; but it was clear that, since so many leading Jesuits were *periti* (expert advisers who accompanied the delegates), the General Congregation to elect his successor could not meet until the Vatican II Council had completed its work. By the time it closed in December 1965, its 3,000 participants, including 480 *periti* from all over the world, plus 80 non-Catholic observers, had considered 9,300 proposals to its various commissions and produced 70 documents, reduced to 20 texts sent to the pope for approval. At the end there were 16 documents. Those which most involved the Jesuits were the Dogmatic Constitution on the Church (*Lumen Gentium*); on Divine Revelation (*Dei Verbum*), on the Sacred Liturgy (*Sacrosanctum Concilium*); on the Church in the Modern World (*Gaudium et Spes*); and the Declaration on Religious Freedom (*Dignitatis Humanae*).

Among the "new" ideas—rather reformulations of old truths— were the realization that the church is not just the hierarchy, clergy, and religious, but the whole People of God; the church's mission is not just the celebration of the sacraments, but the struggle for peace and justice in the world; the church includes all Christians, not just Catholics, and all religions can be a means of salvation; and the dignity of the human person is the foundation of religious liberty for all. The implications of these ideas, once unleashed, were monumental. For some the shock of change was too much; for others the feeling of liberation inspired a new depth of commitment to their vocations; for still others the liberation freed them from what they considered the constraints of the religious life—they left the Society and married.

There was a popular poster in the 1960s following the assassination of John F. Kennedy and the death of Pope John XXIII, who died after the first session of the Council. It showed the two men, from behind, holding hands and walking into the sunlight, as if together in heaven. The older John had said that the Council had been called not to condemn errors but to present doctrines in new forms that reflect modern thought. The younger John had called the new generation to service, to "Ask not what America will do for you, but what together we can do for the freedom of man."

For those who lived or marched through them, the American 1960s were an age of exhilarating freedom and matchless pain. Inspirational leadership came from John and Robert Kennedy and Martin Luther King, Jr., then came the traumatic assassinations of all three. In civil rights and racial justice, there was progress in voting rights, then the murders of civil rights workers and riots in Washington, Rochester, Newark and Detroit. Key books and films forced readers to rethink basic social relationships: Jane Jacobs's *Death and Life of Great American Cities* depicted so-called urban renewal as a destructive force; Joseph Heller's *Catch 22* and Stanley Kubrick's *Dr. Strangelove* revealed the insanity of the warlike mind; Betty Friedan's *The Feminine Mystique* said there is much more to being a woman than running a home. Michael Harrington, though furious at the dryness of his Jesuit philosophy courses at Holy Cross, found inspiration in the spirituality of Dorothy Day and the Catholic Worker movement, which helped press him to write *The Other America*, the exposé of the plight of the poor in the richest nation on earth.

On the level of religious consciousness, based on principles inspired by Vatican II, theologian Bernard Cooke, S.J., could explain to scholastics on retreat that the resurrection of Jesus and the empty tomb did not mean that the corpse of Jesus was resuscitated, got up, and walked around Palestine for 40 days before ascending to the Father, but that Jesus entered a new life in a new dimension, from which he made appearances to give courage to his disciples. For Robert Drinan, S.J., the document on the church in the world freed him to be elected congressman from Massachusetts and to oppose the Vietnam

War; for Daniel Berrigan, S.J., it meant destroying draft records and going to jail. Other Jesuits would court or accept arrest in the course of demonstrating for civil rights or against abortion.

For every priest for whom the Mass is not just a focus of private prayer but the high point of his public identity, 1967, the year the altar turned to face the people, reshaped the relationship between priest and congregation. In 1965–66 at Woodstock, the scholastics, led by the recently ordained fourth-year fathers and with the knowledge of the rector, had anticipated the Council's liturgical reforms and taken the form of the Mass into their own hands. Not just at Woodstock but in the other four theologates throughout the country, men were replacing the single community Mass with small-group sessions, writing their own experimental Eucharistic Prayers, splitting the Mass in parts, and inviting members of the small-group liturgies to improvise prayers and contribute to dialogue homilies, in homes, woods, and on beaches.

The Generation Gap Widens

When Pope Paul VI addressed the 31st General Congregation, the highest governing body of the Society of Jesus, in May 1965 it seemed to some of the delegates, representing 33,000 members, that, as they had gathered both to elect a new general and update their procedures in the light of Vatican II, perhaps because he had been educated by Jesuits from grammar school through the Gregorian University, the pope was preoccupied with the Society's past glories.

He was conscious of the Society's official devotion to his office, and he had a "new" mission for them, the "obstruction" of the spread of atheism. As Lacouture described the Society's situation that day: "The great Jesuit adventure of the twentieth century, necessitated in part by the Company's spinelessness throughout the nineteenth, found specific expression in the great *aggiornamento*, the opening up, the bringing up to date, of the Catholic Church proclaimed during the Second Vatican Council of 1962–1965."

Many of the discussions raised issues that would have to remain unresolved: Was there a "crisis" in obedience? Is operating parishes in accord with the institute? If not, how to justify the 1,200 Jesuit parishes throughout the world? Should certain laypersons bond themselves more formally to the Society? Under what circumstances should the general resign? For the first time the Society passed a decree on Jesuit dedication to the creative arts. This decree was partly the fruit of the efforts of the multitalented musicologist C. J. McNaspy, who had surreptitiously moved a piano into his office-room at *America,* and who had a special apostolate to encourage every young priest or scholastic who could sketch a face, sing or play a clear note, or write a good sentence. It also signified that the Society in the United States was attracting a new breed of men who put more emphasis on individual expression. Traditionally the artistic temperament had not thrived in the regimented macho-bachelor culture of the seminaries. The congregation would also elect a man determined to nurture the creative spirit.

The meeting quickly elected Pedro Arrupe, age 57, a Basque, educated first in five years of medical school in Madrid, then philosophy in Belgium, followed by theology both in Holland and at St. Mary's College in Kansas and tertianship in Cleveland. He spoke eight languages and had spent most of his Jesuit life in Japan. During World War II he was imprisoned and interrogated by the Japanese authorities for teaching ideas that did not conform with the official militarism of the state.

Was it an accident that the congregation had chosen a man not only from Ignatius's home territory, but who also bore an uncanny resemblance to the founder? He was, as Lacouture describes him and as all who met him would agree, short, slender, with high cheekbones, a high bony forehead and sloping bald skull, an eagle's-beak nose, and deep-set eyes. He was, like Ciszek, simple, humble, approachable. He also radiated joy. At a roof party during the congregation, Arrupe delivered two tenor solos, one in Basque, the other in Japanese.

In 1972 Pedro Arrupe addressed the newly formed Jesuit Institute of the Arts at Frascati, Italy. In a text written in his own hand, building his remarks around Browning's Fra Lippo Lippi, he revealed the extraordinary vision of the man who had been chosen to lead. The aim of Jesuit art—whether theater, poetry, or architecture—is not merely didactic or moralistic, but cultural, to form man in his fullness; it is also an apostolate to the Jesuit's fellow artist, not only to bring the artist to God, but to bring art to Christ. "From the bird, or a flower, or the marks on a fish in the river," he said, "we can lift our souls to God."

If Ciszek's most formative experience spread over 20 years, perhaps Arrupe's happened in that one day in 1945 when America dropped the first atomic bomb on Hiroshima, where, on the edge of town, Arrupe was novice master. Those who knew the 30-year-old Arrupe at the time describe him as abstracted, a former medical student who never read the newspapers, who had his head in the clouds. All that changed on August 6, at 8:15 A.M., when "a blinding light, like a flash of magnesium," and a "formidable explosion similar to the blast of a hurricane" blew their doors, windows, and walls into smithereens. Former medical student Arrupe turned the Jesuit house into a makeshift hospital and sent his 35 young men out to scrounge for food and medical supplies, as 150 wounded people with broken bones, huge burns and radiation blisters to be lanced, glass and wooden splinters embedded in eyes and chests, poured in. The suffering bodies writhed like snakes in their cots, yet without at word of complaint. The explosion was a moment, he said in 1970, that has no relation with time. "It belongs to motionless eternity." He went on:

> Sad eternity. A constant presence of that human tragedy. Human? No, inhuman, not merely because it spelt indiscriminate destruction of tens of thousands of lives, but also because it continues to torment humanity as an omen of the possible self-destruction of man, man who glorifies in himself. . . . Now yet another explosion is breeding in the womb of time, as millions die from hunger and sub-human existence. More than half the human family is under-nourished. Day by day the condition of the marginal sections of the peoples of the underdeveloped nations grows more unbearable. And who is responsible for this state of affairs? I do not think that a "sin" of this kind can be attributed to a few persons only. Rather a sizeable part of the human family is at fault.

The two formative experiences in Japan—his imprisonment and the bombing—do a lot to explain how a conservative religious Jesuit could transform a conservative organization into one radically dedicated to the service of the weak and the poor. When Paul VI called for a somewhat vague opposition to atheism, Arrupe identified the battle against atheism with "the battle against poverty, since poverty was one of the reasons that the working classes have abandoned the Church." He moved quickly to consolidate his leadership by traveling so widely that it might be said that within a few years every Jesuit in the world had met or had had an opportunity to meet the general.

Perhaps since the days of the founder, never had a general been so loved.

And hated. Change frightens men who thought that in joining the Society of Jesus they had stepped into a timeless warp, as if entering the cloister and closing the doors could save them from the stress of history. In the guerrilla warfare of inside Jesuit politics, especially in an atmosphere where open community discussions to air differences are not yet the norm, a prime tactic is the letter to Rome. This tactic can work, especially if the recipient of the letter is the kind of person who can be influenced by unproven allegations and who will protect the anonymity of the accusers. On December 3, at the end of the 31st General Congregation, Paul VI lamented in an address to the assembly, "Certain rumors have reached our ears concerning your Society, that have caused us great pain." Without being told, Arrupe knew that a group of Jesuits at a conference in Spain, who already saw him as unfaithful to the tradition, had written to the pope. This early tension between devotion and opposition was just the beginning to a public life as wonderful and as sad as any Jesuit—any human—story.

In America this uneasiness about the Society in flux showed itself in the generation gap. Fortunately the anxiety coincided with improved communications within the Society through the means of a variety of scholarly and popular media. In 1956 a new English translation from the original text of St. Ignatius's short autobiography, principally the story of his conversion, was published, and another in 1974. In 1974 George E. Ganss, S.J, director of the Institute for Jesuit Sources at St. Louis University, published a new edition of the constitutions of the Society with an introduction and commentary. In August 1971 the national office began the *National Jesuit News*, a monthly paper mailed to every member. The editor was Tom Curran, S.J., already editor of the New England *SJNews*, known for its willingness to cover a controversy and its lively several pages of letters. In 1969 Ganss's institute, through the American Assistancy Seminar on Jesuit Spirituality, began a series of original pamphlets, some on heated topics. Appropriately, the first two were "A Profile of the Contemporary Jesuit," by John Sheets, S.J., and "Authentic Spiritual Exercises of St. Ignatius," in which Ganss himself supported the movement to return direction of the Spiritual Exercises to the form Ignatius had used— one-on-one listening and dialogue between the director and the exercitant, rather than the preached retreat of the retreat houses where the director virtually lectured or preached to 20 men at once three or four times a day. This "new" insight had begun in the early 1960s when Jesuits who had made tertianship in England, Canada, and France brought the method back to America. It was a profound experience for middle-aged Jesuits in their 40s, as if they were making the Exercises for the first time.

Sheets's essay puts the challenges to Jesuits in the context of those confronting other contemporary men. Faced with change, "Many older people find themselves bewildered. They see all they stood for challenged and called into question. They see the call for open-mindedness and dialogue as an insidious threat to principles they have always held. They feel like strangers in the very house they have built, foreigners in a strange land they themselves settled."

In "The Trouble with the Younger Men" in *Woodstock Letters* (Winter 1965), the writer lists the complaints heard about his generation. They don't know how to have a good time, they are "soft," not "rugged," oversensitive and emotional. They are less willing to "rough it," to endure policies that seem pointless to them. To relieve their tensions they want movies, tobacco, trips, tranquilizers, psychiatrists, and spiritual fathers who will go along with their inclinations, whereas the earlier generation would let off steam by long walks and throwing rocks in the river. Nor do they sing the old songs. The scholastics answer these criticisms with, "They cannot act like adults if they are not treated like adults." A regent, age 30, teaching 25 hours a week, moderating three activities, and attending every school evening event, knows that his contemporaries are sitting on the stock exchange, trying cases in court, leading a company of marines, struggling through medical school or raising a fourth child. Finally, the younger men have seen houses where potentially productive men of all ages have stopped reading periodicals and professional journals, who teach the same material every year, who have ceased to grow. Will the young men of the 1960s end up like this?

The "New" Jesuits Speak

On Thursday, July 17, 1968, page 1 of the *New York Times* carried a story which both rocked the Society of Jesus and prompted observers to ask what in the world was happening to the American church.

Prominent Jesuit Resigns to Marry

Edward J. Sponga, S.J., age 50, having kept a part of his life secret for years, without attempting to formally separate himself from the Society where he had served as president of Scranton University, rector of Woodstock College, and now provincial of the Maryland Province, had married Mary-Ellen Florence Diamond Barrett, a 33-year old registered nurse, a divorced woman with three children, in Lansdowne, Pennsylvania. On July 18th the *Times* published an interview with Sponga in his new home. "I'm not out to prove any theory," he said. "This is a personal decision." He had met his new wife about ten years before when she had come to him for counseling. During the interview, her previous husband arrived to visit his children, who ran to him joyously yelling, "Daddy? Daddy? Daddy?"

To the *Times* correspondent, it seems, the children did not know whether they had lost their real father when they acquired a new one.

The *Times* added that during 1966–67, 501 diocesan priests and 210 members of religious orders had left the priesthood, and 310 were known to have married.

To many younger Jesuits, Sponga's departure was a blow because he had been perceived as an agent of change and thus as a sign of hope. To those who resisted the changes his leaving proved that his ideas were wrong.

In 1969 George Riemer, a 49-year-old writer, nervously made his way onto the campus of St. Stanislaus, in Florissant, Missouri, the novitiate of the Missouri Province. He had made the same journey 29 years before, at the age of 20, to join the Society. He left seven years later; now he was returning to write a book to be called *The New Jesuits*, a study, through 11 interviews of Jesuits from all over the country, of the Society at a critical, perhaps perilous, stage of its collective life. In the cemetery he found the grave of the *secundi*, the second-year man who introduced the new men (*primi*) to the rules. He recalled the various ways they had of breaking the rule of silence without saying a word: by a half-suppressed smile, by facial expressions, by deep sighs, by eye contact, by the way one walked, wore one's cassock, or hitched one's cincture.

He recalled the rules—*noli tangere* (no one shall touch another), *numquam duo* (no two should be alone together), and the ban on "particular friendships"—prescribed not only to inhibit homosexuality but to enforce an aloneness that gave superiors more exclusive control. And he remembered his special fondness for one of the men in his year and how he wanted to touch him, put his arm around him. And how he invited him for an afternoon walk, and helped him on with his sweater, and how they climbed up a rocky ravine and had to touch one another to help each other climb, and how they rested in a warm meadow and listened to the "buzzy sounds of bees and flies." And went home.

The 11 to be interviewed were strong individuals who had staked out objectives for themselves and were convinced that they had resolved the "hyphenated priest" syndrome—how to be a political activist, drama professor, bioethicist, militant black man, and loyal Jesuit at the same time. A few were established stars in their fields, others were in the "young men to watch" category.

Walter Ong was interviewed at Saint Louis University at the age of 57, about a dozen years before his influential book, *Orality and Literacy: The Technologizing of the Word* (1988), would appear. But the discussion, with his distinction between the Greek and Hebrew learning systems, anticipates the later development of his ideas. His early life, as he recalls it elsewhere, at Rockhurst College from 1929 to 1933 nurtured his genius. The college then was new and small—fewer than 200 students. A PhD was rare on the faculty. The philosophy courses, with the traditional Jesuit competitiveness, were "male ceremonial combat" —all very interesting, but not in touch with the world. The campus newspaper, however, the *Rockhurst Sentinel,* reached into bigger issues, won awards, and produced several respected journalists. Ong, when he was only 16, traveling in Europe as a Boy Scout for a 1939 Jamboree, wrote a series of articles for the *Kansas City Journal* on the scouts' adventures.

Ong was known for his research on Peter Ramus, a contemporary of St. Ignatius, whom he saw as a bridge between the Middle Ages and the modern world. His dissertation on Ramus, over 1,700 pages, was the longest ever handed in at Harvard. He did not know that at the time, but this experience as a basic newspaperman would prepare him, as a media philosopher as well as an English professor, to contradict his old mentor, Marshall McLuhan, to whom he dedicated his Ramus books, and who proclaimed the death of print. Ong told Riemer:

They are mistaken. Television and radio will help print. When print was invented, did it destroy writing? Just the opposite, and print is here to stay. Like writing is. New media do not cancel out the old. They build on them, reinforcing them—and this is what most people miss—radically changing their mode of existence and operation. But in their changed form the old media are stronger than ever.

The troubles in the Society, in the church, and in the civic order, said Ong, come from the same thing. Human society is going through a "reorientation process because of the technologizing of life." Because of technology we are overwhelmed with awareness, we know where all human groups are all over the world. Knowing more history than ever before, man is torn by the feelings of unity and diversity in the human family. This is the same insight, says Ong, that we learned from Teilhard de Chardin. On the level of Jesuit community life, Ong observed, the meanings of "I" and "we" have somewhat changed. In the past the structures may have held the community together; now we must talk about community, talk self-consciously of what it means to be together. But the older men find it hard to adapt to this other-directedness. Earlier Jesuits would not have consented to this interview, opening one's life for others to read in a book.

Ong's colleague, John Padberg, S.J., born in St. Louis in 1926, was the 14th Padberg since 1886 to attend St. Louis University. When Riemer met him he was academic vice president and had a doctorate from Harvard in intellectual history. The biggest challenge facing the Jesuits, he said, was to remain relevant. To serve the Church we must push it forward, be loyal gadflies, not "passively obey or react to an order or wish." Jesuits should be prophets and critics. He agrees with Dan Berrigan that too many Jesuits in a school or community just go along and never raise questions about its behavior. The Society faces two temptations: the "Supportive Back Brace Temptation," retreating into the old rules for support; and the "Gentleman's Club Temptation," becoming simply an organization of very high-minded secular humanists. But if we are to truly imitate the life of Jesus Christ, it won't be enough to merely support one another as comrades, it must be a relationship of friendship in the fullest sense of that word.

John Walsh, at one time a protégé of Mme. Maria Ouspenskaya, a proponent of the Stanislavski "method" acting style, was a graduate of the Yale Drama School and for 13 years a drama professor and director at Marquette. When interviewed, he was teaching dance to the scholastics at Florissant and at St. Louis. Now that the priest faces the people at the altar, every movement, every gesture, means much more than it did before. "We simply cannot love anymore," he tells Riemer. "Well, this is what Christ means. He taught us what compassion was, what love was, and he gives us a reason for loving one another." If Jesuits know this, says Riemer, they have failed to communicate it. The Jesuits, Walsh replies, have been late on Vietnam, race, and poverty; but now they have an opportunity to resacralize the world through the fine arts, through communication.

John Culkin, age 41, friend and disciple of Marshall McLuhan who had played a role in bringing McLuhan to Fordham as a distinguished professor, was impatient with the Jesuits' failure to seize the opportunity of using the electronic media with the same energy that the original Jesuits had used the stage and the printing press. According to McLuhan, the straight line for centuries had unconsciously been the hidden metaphor, the measure and model. "There's trouble now," says Culkin, "because the electronic media have broken print's grip on everything. Radio, the telephone, and TV have broken the printed line as a basic experience metaphor." Just as the God of Newtonian physics, "the clock-winder in the sky," is dead, says Culkin, "The personal God discovered through inner awareness and through other people is liable to be in for some very good innings in the future."

Recently ordained George Shoup, S.J., 33, holding a doctorate in cell biology and the Georgetown Kennedy Foundation's first Medical Ethics Scholar, is, when interviewed, a student at Yale Medical School. At the moment he is one of perhaps a dozen Jesuits in the country in medicine or psychiatry. Their numbers will grow. He starts talking in a long streak, pouring out a string of hard cases, some immediate, some speculative in 1969, less speculative in 2006. Who's going to live and who's going to die? What kind of human being should we let scientists make in their laboratories? Should two people with muscular dystrophy be allowed to reproduce when they will inevitably produce a crippled child? He would prefer they did not, but would not want the law to stop them. When we can clone humans, will we make *slaves*, or *fighting men* to wage our wars?

It used to be that our moral system was frozen, locked up in the natural law, based on the specific functions of bodily organs, and we imagined the body as a collage of superimposed images taken from philosophy, theology, and biology. "But Vatican II and Teilhard de Chardin opened things up and gave us a new understanding of Christ's human nature; and the psyche sciences gave us a new understanding of man's human nature."

Shoup can't see any excuse for abortion. If it's a human ovum fertilized by human sperm, it's human. You can imagine hardship cases that might justify it, but you can't build law on hardship cases. He does not think, however, the State should outlaw abortion. People should be thoroughly educated to make a responsible judgment, but "we should not try to legislate morality."

At the end of the interview, Riemer changes the topic and asks, "How did you feel when Father Sponga left the Society?"

"Enormously depressed. We lost a great leader. I felt very much like I felt when Jack Kennedy was assassinated."

Riemer edited together discussions with four younger men—Paul Weber, age 32, a "middle of the road" Wisconsin Jesuit whose peers imagined he was being groomed to be a superior; Ted Cunningham, 42, a militant black convert to Catholicism, teaching black culture at Creighton, and an assistant to the president; Bart Rousseve, 29, black, from New Orleans, studying theology at Boston Theological Institute; and Ken Feit, 30, a counterculture scholastic living in ghetto poverty and agitating for various reforms. For a while in those years, small groups of Jesuits would move into poor black neighborhoods to be witnesses to some solidarity with the poor and offer them some services. Weber participated in one of those projects; but from Cunningham's point of view they were not worthwhile experiments. There's a lot of talk about "thinking white" and "thinking black." Rousseve answers that a Jesuit should just "think human." On violence, Cunningham supports "responsible violence," one in which no one is killed, but, in order to "bring the oppressor to the bargaining table," he can send a few department stores up in flames. Rousseve does not believe in violence ever. In 1968 he was in Lincoln Park in Chicago during the protests at the Democratic National Convention. When the rioting broke out he stood on the sidewalk and wept bitterly wanting to do something, but he couldn't.

R. James Arenz, S.J., 45, is a priest-engineer at Loyola University, Los Angeles. After Oregon State University he went into aeronautical engineering and worked at Douglas Aircraft for five years before rediscovering his faith and joining the Society in 1950. The California novitiate was his first experience with a Catholic school. Riemer presses him on being part of the technology industry when it seems that technology is responsible for or has failed to solve so many human problems. Most bluntly he asks how a priest can conduct research that will be used to make weapons of war? Lenz replies that though his work is funded by the military, his results have a variety of human uses, including several "immediate benefits to man."

Arenz accepts the term, hyphenated-priest, but he does not accept the distinction between one's material and spiritual welfare, since Catholicism is devoted to the total welfare of man. People will look at him, he hopes, and see how he unifies these two goals. This is, after all, he says, "the implication of Teilhard de Chardin's *omega* point— that the physical universe in an important component in the evolvement of all creation toward ultimate fulfillment."

When Riemer sat down with Dan Berrigan in 1969, the 48-year-old Berrigan was a chaplain and teacher at Cornell University. He and his brother Phil, a Josephite priest, and seven other Catholic activists in May 1968 had raided the draft board office in Catonsville, Maryland, walked out with 380 A-1 files into the parking lot, dumped them into trash baskets, burned them with homemade napalm, and waited around for the police. He was tried and sentenced to three years in federal prison for destruction of government property and was ordered to begin his sentence on April 9, 1970.

The youngest of six sons of a socialist farmer-labor leader, whom Phil described as tyrannical, and a devout, patient mother, Dan joined the Jesuits in 1939 when he was 18. In France for tertianship in 1953 he met worker-priests and took from them a vision of what he thought the church should be. Teaching at Brooklyn Prep in 1954 he organized boys to work among impoverished Brooklyn Puerto Ricans. In 1957 his poetry collection, *Time without Number,* won the Lamont Prize, the first of a string of both poetry and nonfiction books on peace and religious and political issues. While teaching theology at LeMoyne in the early 1960s he developed a following among students dedicated to pacifism, civil rights, and peace. One, David Miller, was the first to burn his draft card.

Berrigan returned from a second trip to France, during which he spent time behind the Iron Curtain, all the more determined to oppose the Vietnam War. He helped found Clergy and Laymen Concerned about Vietnam—thus crossing swords with Francis Cardinal Spellman, who had been an early supporter of the American intervention and who was vicar for the armed forces. A young man whom Berrigan had influenced, Roger LaPorte, set fire to himself publicly in New York, in imitation of Vietnamese Buddhist monks who had immolated themselves in protest. Although Berrigan did not know him well, he spoke sympathetically of him at his memorial. Furious, Spellman demanded action from the Jesuit provincial, who, with mixed feelings, exiled Berrigan to Latin America for four months. *Commonweal* called the forced trip "a shame and a scandal, a disgustingly blind totalitarian act, a travesty on Vatican II."

In 1967 Berrigan accepted the Cornell position, in which he directed an ecumenical team of chaplains. In February 1968, with historian Howard Zinn of Boston University, he flew to Hanoi to participate in the release of three captured American fliers. Hanoi had permitted visits from several American journalists so that they might see with their own eyes the consequences of the American bombing strategy. Berrigan had opposed the war without seeing it up close. Now he returned home more angry than ever. His decision to raid the Catonsville draft board flowed naturally from what he had seen.

Riemer pushed him on the ambivalent relationship between Berrigan and the Jesuit order. Berrigan himself had talked to Arrupe on his trip to Europe and sensed in Arrupe's reluctance to publicly oppose the war a deeper resistance to change. Jesuit attachment to its "real estate," he said, limited its moral witness. "I love the Society very much," he said, "but I've had to look at it in a very real way since all this broke over me. I think we're going to die rather than change."

After the interview Berrigan, rather than report for jail, "went underground," for about four months, popping up here and there to give interviews to print journalists and on TV, until captured by the FBI on Block Island. During his 20 months in Danbury, Connecticut, federal prison, he taught a Great Books course and wrote two books, *The Trial of the Catonsville Nine* and *No Bars to Manhood*. Pedro Arrupe, who had said at a press conference that if the defense of freedom meant incarceration, a Jesuit had to take that risk, visited him in his cell.

The friendship between Berrigan and his admirers has long fueled their shared passion for justice. Dave Toolan, his friend and once his religious superior, told Berrigan's biographer: "He is a terribly sensitive and prickly person. He is also incredibly vulnerable. The first thing he needs after he goes out and pulls one of these actions is for you to go up to him and tell him you love him. He has this permanent feeling of being an outsider, of not belonging, in exile. He needs to be constantly welcomed back into the fold; told 'you're forgiven, come.'"

By 2006, of the 11 men interviewed by Riemer, Walter Ong had died at 90 in 2003, John Walsh had died in 2005, Gerald Lentz, 77, was at Loyola Marymount, and John Padberg was still at Saint Louis University, as director of the Institute of Jesuit Sources. And Dan Berrigan's friends were celebrating his 85th birthday at a big party in New York. All the others interviewed had left the Society.

Why Did So Many Leave?

Between 1958 and 1975, the number of American Jesuits peaked at 8,338 in 1960. Then, especially among novices and scholastics, it plummeted steadily, reaching its lowest point in 1972 (1970 was 7,055), with novices increasing slightly up to 1975. The number of priests rose until 1968, then steadily declined. On average, 34 percent of the novices who entered between 1958 and 1975 left within the two-year novitiate. In 1958 there were 2,431 scholastics preparing for the priesthood, when they would take over the classrooms and parishes and mission stations depending on their labor. By 1975 only 744, or 31 percent, remained. Since these were all young men who lived closely together, sometimes in groups of over 200, the emotional toll on the group could be devastating. Sometimes groups of friends would come up with a bottle of scotch and toast their departing brother late on his last night. More often he would disappear without a word.

There is no single explanation for the exodus. To some eyes the Society's failure to change quickly enough drove them out. To others, the changes themselves deprived the men of the spiritual structures that protected a religious vocation. Without the rules, the silence, the prayers that somehow ordered Ciszek's day even in a Siberian prison, these men said, "This is not the Society that I joined," and they slipped away. The most obvious change was geographical. Between 1965's 31st and the 32nd General Congregation in 1975, just about every novitiate, juniorate, philosophate, and theologate moved from a country or suburban milieu into a major city and near or onto a university campus—all demanding shifts in academic programs and lifestyle.

In each move the turmoil that marked the larger institutions like Shrub Oak and Woodstock was repeated across the country. In 1940, when *Theological Studies* was founded, there were six Jesuit theological faculties, including Cardinal Mundelein in Chicago, which Jesuits staffed for the diocese of Chicago. And many of them housed the philosophy program as well. By 1960 they were reduced to five, all determined to move to a place where theological education would be more modern, diversified, ecumenical, urban, and pastoral.

The Chicago Province Bellarmine School of Theology, established at West Baden, Indiana, in 1939, moved first to North Aurora, Illinois, in 1964, 40 miles west of Chicago. Within five years the students were getting restless. The decision was to move into a cluster of Protestant divinity schools in the Hyde Park neighborhood of the University of Chicago, on the grounds that this would be more stimulating theologically than the campus of Loyola University. The Missouri program, which had started at St. Louis University in 1899 and moved from St. Louis to St. Mary's, Kansas, in 1931, moved back to St. Louis in 1967. In California, the University of San Francisco invited Alma College (est. 1939) to join them, with the hope of making USF a major theological presence in the West; but Alma preferred the Graduate Theological Union (GTU), a consortium of divinity schools associated with the University of California at Berkeley. In New England, Weston (est. 1922) moved to Cambridge, Massachusetts, as a cooperating neighbor of Harvard Divinity School in 1969.

Woodstock had been debating its move since 1964. Yale, Fordham, Columbia, and, briefly, Georgetown all made bids, anxious to attract the faculty, which included John Courtney Murray, who himself favored Yale; Gustav Weigel, Walter Burghardt, Joseph Fitzmyer, and Avery Dulles. In 1970 Woodstock set itself up on Morningside Heights, on New York's upper West Side, home of Columbia University and Union Theological Seminary; and, for living space, it rented a series of apartments in the neighborhood. This was a truly radical departure from the norm. Jesuits in formation had in recent history lived under the same roof, accustomed to seeing just about everyone every day, including the faculty, spiritual fathers, and the rector. They prayed, dined, studied, and recreated together. Now young Jesuits had what every New Yorker to some degree cherishes—anonymity.

It was not long, however, before, due to falling numbers, six theology schools was too many. Alma and Saint Louis closed, and one more had to go. During the deliberations the provincials seem to have established the formation role as more important than the intellectual, and the formation directors and several of the provincials, all of whom visited all the schools, had reservations about the Woodstock lifestyle.

Hearing that the vote was going against them, Woodstock's rector, president, dean, and board chairman reminded Arrupe that he himself had encouraged Woodstock to face the challenges of New York, but Arrupe accepted the committee's decision, and it closed after its two years in the Big Apple. The Chicago experiment closed soon due to low enrollment, leaving one big ecumenical Jesuit theology school on each coast. As at Woodstock, they lived in small communities, though some in family homes rather than apartment complexes. They shared professors and classrooms with ministers and rabbis, with laymen and women, and religious women from all over the world. They shared liturgies with different faiths and by both osmosis, debate, and friendly contact were influenced by feminist theology, leading perhaps most to believe that women too should be priests.

Some New York Jesuits could not help but attribute the decision to close Woodstock to anti-New York prejudices harbored by fellow Jesuits from the hinterlands and frontier not lucky enough to have grown up in the center of the world. They focused their negative thoughts on the intellectual Catholic journalist, Garry Wills, himself a former Jesuit, trained as a classicist, who retained his affection for the Society and sent his son to Holy Cross. Wills had written an article on the new Woodstock for the trendy *New York* magazine. Reread today, the essay, though very negative in its analysis, is not so much an attack as an elegy for a dying apostolic experiment which he saw as an academic failure when academic excellence should have been its raison d'être. Wills began his research by visiting the former Maryland campus, which had been sold to the government's Jobs Corps, and picked up the story in New York when two men about to be ordained interrupted the ordination Mass to refuse the greeting of peace to New York's Terence Cardinal Cooke, also the military vicar, over his support for the Vietnam War.

Then for several days Wills toured the West Side residences, interviewed the men, tried to get a sense of how they actually spent their time, and concluded that Woodstock New York was a flop. Yes, there were successes, particularly the groups who read theology with Avery Dulles; but most men, concluded Wills, spent only a few hours a day studying theology. He ended with the observation that the two men most responsible for the move—consecutive rectors Sponga and Felix Cardegna—left. And other men he had met in his visit were on their way out.

The Woodstock episode and accounts of the new novice masters who discarded old practices are used as evidence by those who argue that the Society tumbled into crisis because it changed. Others answer that to keep young men in the woods, limit their social contact to young males like themselves, punish them for breaking rules with *culpas*, have them kneel in front of the group while others list their faults, make them whip themselves with cords and wear pointed chains digging into their thighs, forbid them to use one another's first names, limit their spiritual reading to pious medieval monk legends, and make obedience the center of all virtue is institutional suicide.

Robert Harvenak, S.J., a Chicago Province administrator and philosopher, attributes some of the exodus to the too-rapid expansion of the Society's works in the 1950s. Swept into the postwar boom, the Society entered an era of internal development and expansion with which it could not keep pace. It opened more high schools than it could staff. As the universities got bigger and bigger, men saw themselves destined for the educational ministry whether they wanted it or not. They felt trapped. They lost track of one another as individuals.

James J. Gill, S.J., a psychiatrist at Harvard, averred that the reasons why men left were often based on unresolved problems in their early lives that resurfaced with new challenges in the religious life. A man who left angry at superiors' bureaucratic foot dragging had in childhood resented his parents' failures to respond to his complaints. Some who had come from warm and happy families left because they could not find the same affection in the Jesuit community. Perhaps marriage would fulfill their yearning. At the same time, as Jesuits, they may have failed to work hard at developing friendships. While preaching love they had devoted all their time to their work and religious duties. Now could they learn to love?

The Birth Control Crisis

For a Catholic priest between the 1940s and early 1960s, the most common source of continuing moral education was the "Notes on Moral

Theology" section in *Theological Studies*, written during most of that time by the combined efforts of Jesuits John C. Ford and Gerald A. Kelly. They would read the articles on ethics in North American and European periodicals, and summarize and critique their content, for the most part following the case study method, in a way that could aid fellow priests in the confessional. In this way and in their books— *Contemporary Moral Theology* and Kelly's *Modern Youth and Chastity*, a popular pamphlet for students—considering moral theology as a science, they guided the priest faced on the other side of the confessional booth screen with thieves who did not know how to make restitution of stolen goods without revealing their identity, an adolescent with the habit of masturbation, the alcoholic who lapses and pours himself a drink, or the married woman whose husband approaches her wearing a condom. How vigorously must she resist? Ford's most prophetic contribution to moral theology may well have been his "The Morality of Obliteration Bombing" (*TS* 5, 1944), in which he argued, a year before Hiroshima, that the mass bombing of cities was "an immoral attack on the rights of the innocent." Today an average of four times a year requests from all over the world come in to reprint and translate that article.

Kelly, from the Missouri Province and a professor at St. Mary's, and Ford, from New England and a teacher at Weston who was also at Catholic University from 1958 to 1966, at a time when Catholic morality was preoccupied with sexuality, consistently supported what they saw as the church's unalterable condemnation of contraception. The official teaching was based on Pius XI's encyclical, *Casti Connubii* (On Christian Marriage), which condemned contraception and established procreation and mutual help of spouses as the primary and secondary ends of the sacrament.

And while the condemnation of artificial birth control was described as absolute, some Catholic theologians welcomed what was described in the 1930s as the "rhythm method," during which Catholic couples, by calculating the woman's cycle, could avoid pregnancy by avoiding intercourse on those days when the woman could conceive. In one of Fr. Daniel Lord's pamphlets, his alter ego, Father Hall, tells the "Bradley twins" that here, by devising rhythm, "Divine Providence entered the whole situation." On the other hand, some were wary of what Ford called the "birth control attitude of mind," which seemed like a license to enjoy material possessions while avoiding the responsibilities of parenthood. Thus Ford opposed publicizing rhythm, lest lay people make the decision to practice it on their own without seeking permission and advice from their confessors. Another argument concerned the "duty to procreate." If Catholic couples were obliged to have children, how many? In 1952 Kelly proposed that four or five would fulfill the duty, depending on the population trends. By 1963, when there was more public discussion of the population "bomb," Kelly reduced it to three or four.

Gradually, however, European theologians influenced by German Redemptorist moralist Bernard Haring, author of the *Law of Christ* (1954), and younger American clergy influenced by the new theology were evolving another emphasis in moral theology, away from focusing on individual acts and more on one's fundamental orientation, one's pattern of behavior responsive to God's love and oriented toward the service of other persons.

In the United States one of the central breakthroughs during these years, one with the greatest import for moral theology, due to both John Courtney Murray and the Canadian Jesuit philosopher and theologian Bernard Lonergan, was the concept of "historical consciousness." It held the idea that our understanding of a doctrine is influenced by the language and images of the era in which it was conceived, and therefore must be reinterpreted in the language of later generations. Father Lonergan, in the words of historian John T. McGreevy,

> described the trajectory of modern Catholicism as that of an institution moving from a classical worldview to one possessed of a "historical consciousness." The classicist worldview understood human nature as "always the same" and applied universal principles to "concrete singularity." Lonergan urged Catholics to begin with the human subject, not an abstract human nature, to use history to scrutinize "how the patterns of living, the institutions, the common meanings of one's place and time differ from those of another."

This insight helped Murray formulate how the church could move from a medieval concept of church-state relations to a modern one. And it helped the moral theologians and the majority of the birth control commission appointed by John XXIII explain how contraception could in some circumstances be justified. In short, the experience of so many faithful Catholic couples who used contraception convinced the moralists that this enhanced their love and strengthened their marriages.

In the final months of the Council and while meeting with the ongoing birth control commission, Ford traveled several times to Rome to lobby the pope personally for a statement in *Gaudium et Spes* reaffirming the evils of contraception. He mistakenly brought the legal scholar John T. Noonan, author of the history, *Contraception* (1965), into the meetings of the commission, having misread his book, which actually makes the argument for change. In his meetings with Paul VI and a group of cardinals, Ford acknowledged that the natural law argument was unconvincing but made the "slippery slope" case, that to give in on this issue would weaken the whole fabric of moral teaching and, above all, papal authority. The Council fathers declined to speak on contraception prior to the decision of the study commission, and wrote a footnote which Richard McCormick, S.J., Ford and Kelly's successor at *Theological Studies*, interpreted as an opening to change.

In 1968, following the publication of *Humanae Vitae*, the papal encyclical that condemned the use of any contraception, *America* (August 17), in a long editorial, clearly identified itself with the theologians and large number of lay Catholics well educated in philosophy and theology who presently "find themselves unable to assent fully to the encyclical's absolute rejection of artificial birth regulation."

District of Columbia

In the diocese of Washington, D.C., 39 priests who publicly supported the consciences of their parishioners who used contraception were disciplined, suspended from the ministry by Patrick Cardinal O'Boyle, whose adviser on moral theology was none other than John C. Ford.

One of those disciplined was Fr. Horace McKenna, S.J., a parish priest at St. Aloysius Church on Eye St., an inner-city parish just a stone's throw from the Capitol. The parish was attached to Gonzaga High School, one of the Jesuit preps that had decided not to abandon its crime-ridden neighborhood and flee to the suburbs. Born into a large middle-class family on New York's Upper West Side in 1899, Horace had joined the Society at St. Andrew-on-Hudson, and after ordination had succeeded John LaFarge in the predominately populated black parish at Ridge, Maryland. LaFarge, said Horace, "taught me zeal and love for my neighbor under all circumstances—yet a patient and wise love and not a foolish love; a love that is accompanied with spiritual training and practical economic exercise and the labors of daily life." A brave, spiritual, and witty man, McKenna made service of the black poor the center of his life. The previous summer he had tapped a young priest at Georgetown to help him escort a bus load of his inner-city children for an outing at Senator Robert Kennedy's swimming pool. Now he had to offend his friend the cardinal, who had consistently supported his work. When O'Boyle personally asked McKenna, by what authority do you contradict your bishop? McKenna answered, "Forty years in the confessional."

Meanwhile, another group of Jesuits at Georgetown who were teachers, not parish priests, drew up a calm and respectful statement on conscience, composed primarily by theologian William C. McFadden, S.J., to the cardinal expressing their "solidarity with our brother priests who are being disciplined for holding a position on conscience which we can scarcely distinguish from the teaching of several European hierarchies and which seems firmly grounded in the teaching of Vatican II and the tradition of theologians." A group of nine scholastics followed up with a letter to the provincial, expressing "fraternal unity" with the Jesuit signers: "Our priestly vocations are sustained in large part by witness of the lives of those older than ourselves in the Society." The cardinal told the provincial he wanted the signers to meet with Father Ford, perhaps with the hope that he could win them over. The discussion, which convened in the atmosphere of being a reprimand, was both frank and civil. At one stage, when asked why he as author of a courageous and controversial article on obliteration bombing could not show sympathy for dissenting priests, Ford replied that those promoting contraception were often the same people who believed that Joseph was the father of Jesus and that the bones of Jesus were still in Palestine. It was a reply consistent with his conviction that the church's teaching authority was at stake. Yet at the conclusion of the session, he said, to the surprise of some, "We don't seem to be that far apart." Tragically, the dispute between the cardinal and his diocesan priests continued for three years; by the time it was resolved, in favor of the priests, many had already left the priesthood.

A New Moral Theology Evolves

As Ford's influence waned, Richard A. McCormick, along with his non-Jesuit colleague Charles R. Curran, who had played the leading role in the *Humanae Vitae* debate, assumed the leadership among American moral theologians. McCormick was a strong personality, humble but not modest, conscious of his status and sharp tongued, but generous and thoughtful, respectful of tradition and the church. As author of the "Notes" from 1965 to 1984, McCormick both respected what was valid in the Thomistic tradition and moved it in new directions. As Curran described his friend's method in *Theological Studies* after his death in 2000, he saw the future theology as "open to the world and the church; adult, through its stress on responsibility; realistic; Catholic and catholic; and inspired by the teachings of Jesus." As the son of a nationally prominent doctor, a president of the American Medical Association, from Toledo, Ohio, McCormick was naturally drawn to medical issues and served several years at the Kennedy Institute at Georgetown, where he dealt with bioethical problems in genetics, artificial reproduction, artificial nutrition, and hydration. Though he did not develop a personal systematic approach, he was a proportionalist, which attempts to strike a middle ground between scholastic natural law and consequentialism or utilitarianism. This system requires one to consider all the circumstances of an act—the actor's intention, all foreseeable consequences, and the proportion between values and disvalues involved—before its rightness or wrongness can be decided. Besides the "Notes," he wrote six books and, with Curran, co-edited eleven volumes of *Readings in Moral Theology*, and he wrote regularly for *America* and other magazines.

Widely respected within the church, bishops would send him drafts of their statements before they were published for his evaluation; and he would tell them frankly if he foresaw an obligation to criticize them if they appeared. He was conscious of the freedom theologians needed to do their work; and as what he considered the Vatican "chill factor" settled over theologians in the 1980s. His leadership and encouragement fortified the younger men and women. After 1986, during his final active years as the John A. O'Brien Professor of Christian Ethics at the University Notre Dame, when he suffered from cancer, he turned his faculty residence into a bunkhouse for family and friends who joined him for football weekends.

Francis Canavan, S.J., the conservative Fordham political science professor, expert on Edmund Burke, popular with the bright students who wanted to go into law, and former associate editor of *America,* was mad. He was angry at Fordham president Leo McLaughlin, S.J., whose determination to make Fordham great was, in Canavan's opinion, destroying the university and all it was supposed to stand for. And he told the world this in the ironically titled article, "To Make a University Great," in *America* (July 15, 1967).

For evidence, Canavan quoted widely from the student paper, *The Ram,* ridiculing the students who want girls and liquor in their rooms, plus contraceptive information. He quotes one columnist: "Are students going to allow the university to decide matters of personal conscience for them? If anyone, then perhaps if we're bad they'll go to hell for us, too—if there is a hell." Canavan's argument, in which he surely spoke for many Jesuits in similar situations across the country, was the "slippery slope" logic: remove some of the restrictions long termed fundamental to Jesuit education, and the whole edifice will come crashing down. To the presidents who were engineering radical changes in all 28 colleges and universities in the early 1960s, this was a necessary revolution. To strong pockets of resisters, it was a "sellout."

Depending on whom one asks, "Leo," who when he was dean was much loved for his warm personality and lively imagination, either saved or ruined Fordham. With a gambler's bravado, he appointed laymen, including non-Catholics, as vice presidents; hired high-profile scholars like Marshall McLuhan and Margaret Mead; planned a deliberately-ethnic-balanced liberal arts college for Lincoln Center; started a three-three program with Fordham Prep; and founded, with Elizabeth Sewell as dean, the experimental Ben Salem College where no courses except Urdu were required and all decisions were made by consensus.

Most contentious was the decision to separately incorporate the Jesuit community from the university in order to qualify for the state aid available to nonsectarian institutions. A consultant, Walter Gellhorn, had recommended that crucifixes in the classroom could be seen as obstacles to receiving government funding. To McLaughlin's critics this symbolized his betrayal of Jesuit values. But, in the words of Tim Healy, S.J., McLaughlin's vice president and future director of the New York Public Library and president of Georgetown, Leo had been "dragging Fordham kicking and screaming into the twentieth century." But by the end of 1968 he had lost control of the finances and was replaced by Boston College's Father Michael Walsh. McLaughlin went to teach communications at a black college in the South. He left the Society and married. Later, after his wife died and he himself suffered from strokes, he returned to the Jesuit infirmary at Fordham for his final years.

How did the movement toward giving academic excellence, as measured by secular standards, priority, of which the Fordham case is but a dramatic example, begin? The watershed year, according to one historian, Paul A. Fitzgerald, S.J., was 1964, when "the presidents won tacit permission of the provincials to expand their colleges and universities with very little reference to 'higher superiors': they had also designed a revised constitution that guaranteed the freedom they coveted. Having slipped their Roman moorings, these Jesuit institutions glided smoothly into the mainstream of American academic life and discovered that their vessels were seaworthy."

The vessels were given more wind to their sails when Arrupe addressed the Jesuit Educational Association (JEA) in Loyola University, Chicago, in 1966. Two sentences stood out: "I encourage you to devote yourselves unquestioningly and unreservedly to the life of scholarship." Then he added, "There is harmony and high compatibility in the role of priest and teacher." The phrase was an indirect reference to a new problem. The younger men were losing interest in working at Jesuit universities.

Some leaned toward retreat work or the social apostolate. Some found the big universities with their isolated bachelor lifestyle in some of the big communities housing over a hundred men, many of whom valued their privacy over showing hospitality to lay faculty and other guests, cold and impersonal. The younger men were accustomed to shared prayer, sometimes in the context of an informal apartment liturgy with men and women friends. Some had other apostolic priorities. Since there were 820,000 Catholics on secular campuses and only 390,000 on Catholic campuses, should not Jesuits staff Newman clubs or seek faculty appointments at secular universities? And since there was no Catholic equivalent of Harvard or Yale, should not Jesuits pick one or two of their 28 colleges and make them university centers, move teams of the best scholars to the "best" institutions, and really compete with secular rivals? On the other hand, as Michael Walsh told a 1964 conference at Woodstock, large numbers did not matter. One or two good *scholarly* Jesuits in each department and a few good Jesuit administrators were enough to establish Jesuit identity.

In 1967 two connected events precipitated the situation Father Canavan found scandalous at Fordham and which threw the whole concept of Jesuit identity in question. First, in response to Vatican II's document on "The Church in the Modern World," the leading Catholic universities decided they would compete for excellence on the same terms as secular schools. In July a meeting of 26 presidents and other intellectuals at Notre Dame's villa house in Land O'Lakes, Wisconsin, issued a manifesto, "The Nature of the Contemporary Catholic University." It begins:

> The Catholic University today must be a university in the full modern sense of the word, with a strong commitment to and concern for academic excellence. To perform its teaching and research functions effectively the Catholic university must have a true autonomy and academic freedom in the face of authority of whatever kinds, lay or clerical, external to the academic community itself. To say this is simply to assert that institutional autonomy and academic freedom are essential conditions of life and growth and indeed of survival for Catholic universities as for all universities.

The second paragraph affirms that at the same time, it must be a "community of scholars, in which Catholicism is perceptively present and effectively operative." Finding the formulas to make paragraph 2 agree with paragraph 1 was the central challenge for the rest of the 20th century.

Second, in 1966 Paul C. Reinert, S.J., president of St. Louis University, was named president of the JEA, and he began to propose basic changes in the university structure: giving lay faculty a full voice, thus allowing them to vote on the appointment of Jesuit faculty; and establishing the universities as public trusts by creating lay-dominated boards of trustees and the separate incorporation of Jesuit communities. On June 23, 1967, the newly constituted board of laymen and Jesuits of Saint Louis University, the first separately incorporated Jesuit institution and now independent of Roman and provincial supervision, met for the first time. By 1972, 20 of the 28 Jesuit communities had gone through separate incorporation, though with some variations in the formulas at different schools. In some places the rector of the Jesuit community was a member of the board. In others a second all-Jesuit board retained certain powers. The major immediate effect was that provincials could no longer appoint a president or even assign a new Jesuit to a school. The young father had to go get his doctorate and send his resume around the country hoping for a call-back like any other candidate. With the new emphasis on excellence, the 28-year-old new layman PhD from Brandeis with several scholarly articles on his resumé, more loyal to the political science or chemistry profession than to Ignatian ideals, had the hiring edge on the 40-year-old Jesuit whose long course of studies and pastoral work delayed his degree.

This meant that the Jesuits would have to find a dozen ways of asserting their collective identity. In time they did this by occasionally "hiring for mission," selecting faculty of other religions or no religion who could learn to share, through workshops and seminars, Jesuit goals. They also did so by their "values" and Catholic studies academic programs; an aggressive campus ministry and rich liturgical life; moral leadership, often by emphasizing social justice, or volunteer work with the poor in Latin America; using the talents, especially in theology, of the former priests on the faculty; and opening up the Jesuit community for frequent socializing with the lay faculty, as the once isolated Jesuit "clubhouse" became a campus social and intellectual hub.

If the watershed year for the college presidents was 1964, when they attained the freedom to expand without being overseen by Rome, perhaps the most important step in this process was the establishment of the U.S. Jesuit Conference in 1972. This, for the first time, linked the provinces horizontally to one another without going through Rome. It gave the green light to cooperation, combining houses of formation. And now a man from the New York Province might, during his career, work in Kansas City, New Orleans, and San Francisco rather than spend 40 years in Brooklyn or the Bronx. It also stuck an element of instability into the lives of men who used to be "assigned" by superiors to a place. One might give up a tenured slot in one city to take one in another and be denied tenure there, and then suffer the anxiety of all the unemployed laymen in one's own generation.

A Variety of Jesuit Campuses Try to Deal with the Revolution

Across the country, with Fordham as only one example, the struggle to modernize played itself out in various ways. To some degree the political and social turmoil into which some campuses were thrown was a by-product of the national "golden age," when the opportunity for federal funds had changed the character of higher education in several ways. The availability of research grants transformed schools into "research institutions," those whose primary purpose is to generate new knowledge, to the point where teaching suffered. Graduate students taught the introductory courses and undergraduates seldom met the "star" professors. As universities expanded into knowledge factories, the spirit of a learning community withered.

As the Vietnam War escalated, the bombing of Hanoi, the use of napalm, the defoliation of the landscape, the atrocities at MyLai, and above all the invasion of Cambodia and the shooting of student demonstrators at Kent State called the war's morality into question. Universities with government contracts and who welcomed CIA and military recruiters on campus became the targets of student protests. For many faculty, the overall goal of teaching shifted from preparing the younger generation to contribute to society to opposing the structures that oppressed the minority population, the black, and the poor. On many campuses, this called for some rigorous self-examination of their governance structures, their core curriculums, and diversity, or lack thereof, in their admissions policies.

These tensions were particularly painful on Jesuit campuses because, with some exceptions, they did not have strong records of faculty research; faculty governance structures were not well developed; rector-presidents had a lot of authority and were not accustomed to strong dissent from the faculty, student leaders, or student or faculty publications; in crises, Jesuit presidents who had been selected by provincials or all-Jesuit boards might or might not have the rare combination of personality traits required.

Boston College

When Michael P. Walsh, S.J., assumed the presidency of Boston College in 1958, he was determined to bring the university into the mainstream without weakening its commitment to the church; but he was concerned by what was considered an excessive philosophy and theology requirement, taught by Jesuits who were intellectually below par, with the result that the better students were alienated by the instruction. So he appointed a committee of his allies to recommend a change, which reduced the combined requirement to nine courses. Then he pushed faculty to do more research, instituted an honors program, and argued that student values are more influenced by the environment of the campus than by class instruction. To celebrate B.C.'s centennial in 1963, he awarded an honorary degree to Harvard president Nathan Pusey, whose university a half-century before had declined to recognize the B.C. degree.

Walsh was widely regarded as a master politician. Physically he was soft-spoken, not-tall man, with sharp eyes, and a cigarette often clutched between his fingers. In conversation he would concentrate intently on his guest and speak in a confidential tone that convinced the listener that yes, he understood. He structured a faculty council and university planning committee that increased participation in governance without sacrificing his own executive power, and he engineered lay dominance of the trustees while reserving positions of influence for key Jesuits. By 1968, however, he was worn out and in poor health and stepped aside. Within a year, however, as a member of Fordham's board when McLaughlin had to be replaced, Walsh said, "I'll sacrifice myself" and took his place. At Fordham he quickly stabilized its finances. But in the fall of 1969 the Students for a Democratic Society (SDS), protesting the presence of ROTC on campus, attacked the administration building, broke into the president's office while Walsh was working there, and occupied the building until the campus security guards were called to expel them. In the spring, a student government-led group peacefully seized the same building and occupied it to protest the denial of tenure to a popular English professor. Following the invasion of Cambodia and the shootings at Kent State, someone set fire to the student center, and the campus was thrown into turmoil, which Walsh, never losing his cool, resolved by establishing a faculty-student-administrative council with advisory powers.

Walsh's B.C. successor, W. Seavey Joyce, S.J., lacked fund-raising experience and Walsh's political skills. Two consecutive large tuition hikes led to a student strike that temporarily closed down the campus. His own emotion of "genuine terror" when a "mob" of students marched on his residence led him to doubt his own abilities as a leader. When he had to use the police to clear a building in 1971, he and the board agreed he should resign.

Holy Cross

Forty-five minutes to the west at Worcester, Raymond J. Swords, S.J., in 1960 took the reins of B.C.'s sister—though to some considered a bitter rival—the College of the Holy Cross. Seeing that the Jesuit faculty, then 100 men, was bound to diminish, he moved to establish statutes to share governance, principally the educational policy committee, made up of the president, academic dean, and five elected faculty members, not to advise the administration but be the central committee of the faculty and report to the faculty. As at B.C., students complained that the theology and philosophy courses were the worst; so Swords removed five Jesuit teachers and appointed John E. Brooks, S.J., the theology chairman, who hired two non-Catholic laymen to teach Scripture. A Jesuit critic brought in John C. Ford to fight the hiring by appealing to Rome. But Brooks was determined to separate the teaching of theology as an academic discipline from promoting the faith. And he prevailed.

Swords sought to retire in 1968, but kept on to face perhaps the most emotionally disturbing crisis in the college's history. Ironically the college, which enrolled the Healy boys before the Civil War, in 1965, had a black enrollment of only about 12. In 1967 Arrupe addressed a letter on racism, written with the help of Lou Twomey, specifically to American Jesuits, reminding them that their record on this issue was weak, because they had been alienated from the poor, and were too quick to accept stereotypes and prevailing attitudes without questioning them. With energetic recruitment, scholarships, black studies courses, and setting aside a black corridor in the Healy residence hall, by 1969 blacks numbered 68.

Meanwhile, Holy Cross drew up procedures and appointed committees to anticipate whatever protests could disrupt student life over the Vietnam War. Father Swords declared himself against the war, and students and faculty joined for a Mass for Peace on the steps of Dinand Library to coincide with the Vietnam Moratorium Day on October 15. A majority of the students and faculty voted for a policy of "open campus," meaning that business firms and government agencies had a right to recruit on campus. But a new group, the Revolutionary Students Union (RSU), announced they would block the appearance of representatives from General Electric on December 10. When the recruiters arrived at the Hogan Center, the crowd of demonstrators, arms linked, prevented students from getting access to the visitors. The recruiters were forced to leave. The staff of the dean of men's office scanned the crowd and made a list of 16 who seemed most responsible for the violation. The judicial board determined that these 16 were "highly visible" in their participation and recommended suspension.

Of those 16 brought before the judicial board, 12 were white and four were black. The Black Student Union cried racism. It seems that of the 59 students engaged in the demonstration, 54 were white and five were black. Thus the dean of men had singled out 24 percent of the whites for discipline, but 80 percent of the blacks. BSU spokesman Theodore V. (Ted) Wells, '72, called the decision the product of "warped minds," and at the press conference the next day all the BSU members discarded their student ID cards and dramatically left the campus. If the suspension was enforced, they said, Holy Cross would go back to being an "all white" campus.

The dean, John Brooks, canceled classes so the students could talk it through. The trustees, who happened to be meeting at the time, got involved. Swords recruited a Worcester youth counselor, John F. Scott, as an intermediary. Scott recommended amnesty, and Swords accepted the recommendation. As Swords saw it, the majority of the community had originally supported the sanction, but changed when they perceived an injustice to the blacks. After managing more antiwar demonstrations in the spring, Swords was finally allowed to retire and Brooks was chosen to succeed him. At graduation, Swords told the assembly that their response "revealed the depth of your feeling and the authenticity of your concerns. From this point on, there is no turning back, no copping out." To a standing ovation, he called on them to "fight for life, for peace, for justice."

Seattle

On the other side of the country, Seattle University was driving its car into a dark tunnel. In the long history of the university, the years

1965–70 might appear as a passing embarrassment, interpreted as one of those endurance tests which, if they don't kill you, make you stronger; but it is more illuminating as a case study in presidencies, where the men selected may have been of talent, but their particular talents did not match the peculiar challenges of those years.

Jack Fitterer, S.J., began his presidency riding high. Enrollment was 4,200, the Business School was accredited, the new residence hall was almost finished, and Arrupe visited the campus in April 1966 and said: "The Catholic university will fulfill its mission only if there is rapport and understanding and mutual trust between the religious educator and the lay men and women who share his teaching apostolate." Unfortunately, Fitterer did not win the respect of the faculty, some of whom dismissed him as "Smiling Jack"—most likely because the smiling surface did not correspond to his policies. He also made the mistake, common to inexperienced presidents who wish to exert control, of unnecessarily antagonizing the student newspaper, in a decade where free expression, even on a Catholic campus, was seen as sacred as the sacraments. When the *Spectator* criticized two well-connected student officers for what it considered the misuse of a university credit card, Fitterer used his authority to suppress any further reports on the incident. To launch his "Decade of Distinction" and make Seattle a "Catholic Brandeis," the president hiked tuition 40 percent and enrollment plunged by 500 students; and a few months later he hiked it again. Determined to push ahead with his ambitious building plans, including a new physical education complex, he borrowed heavily. The operational debt hit $1 million, and there was no system to monitor costs and control budgets.

In 1967 a young, black education professor, one of only two African Americans on the faculty, Ronald Rousseve, who had been given a warning the previous year when he published a piece on "humanistic experiential humanism" in the *Spectator*, offered another on premarital sex and birth control. Fitterer ordered it stopped. The Faculty Senate tried to intervene, the students rallied, and the American Association of University Professors called for an investigation. Rousseve was convinced to resign. Two days later the other black faculty member resigned. One week later Martin Luther King, Jr., was assassinated, his death casting a cloud over Seattle's conflict. In May, ten English professors, two-thirds of the department, resigned, one accusing the administration of running a "pastoral ghetto" as he left.

Enrollment was down to 3,500 students, 100 of whom were black; Fitterer pressed ahead with several commitments on racial justice: an urban affairs institute, a black history course, and an office of minority affairs. He added the other reforms now common across the country: laymen on the board of trustees, separate incorporation, a charter of student rights. But the Vietnam War was moving what had been one of the most conservative student bodies in the country to the left. In February 1969 someone set fire to the ROTC building. When the Seattle archbishop endorsed bombing Hanoi, students and faculty walked out on graduation. In October 1969, to make matters worse, Fitterer killed two articles by faculty in the *SU Magazine* for an issue planned on the theme of dissent. Both pieces made their way to the *Spectator.* One spelled out the university's financial mess and said Fitterer's administration was "killing imagination and initiative and ultimately the institution itself." The controversy fed into the already planned October 15 Vietnam Moratorium. In fear, the administration canceled classes and the Mass of the Holy Spirit. The debt went up, enrollment went down, and Fitterer went out. Seattle's historian liked the metaphor of an out-of-control driver at the wheel of a car, who "never took his foot off the pedal."

Somehow Seattle reached as far as the Gonzaga theology department to appoint Fr. Kenneth Baker, known as a champion of orthodoxy, as president. Knowing that confronting protestors would be part of his job, he declared his willingness to talk. Confronting the deficit, he cut the $1.4 million operating deficit by half and began drafting bylaws for the lay board of trustees. But the racial climate was not at peace. An unknown person set off a bomb, shattering windows throughout the campus. The minority affairs director charged that Baker was slow on affirmative action hiring, and the urban affairs director said the campus was "permeated with racism." Baker's cost-cutting faculty cutback included dropping Rabbi Jacobowitz, whose course required students to wear yarmulkes and live for a week like Orthodox Jews. Since this saved only $1,000, some saw this as a religious more than financial pulling back, especially since Baker also wanted to change the name to Seattle "Jesuit" University.

The week in March when Baker welcomed Senator Barry Goldwater to speak on campus, intruders set fire to Xavier Hall and fled campus as security guards, newly hired by Baker, pulled their guns and fired at them. When student activists threatened to occupy the president's office if he didn't get rid of ROTC, Baker replied that he'd have them jailed. To complicate an already tense agenda, the chair of sociology passed up hiring a black candidate in favor of a young white honors student who had just graduated from Seattle in 1969. Just then the *Spectator* published a memorandum in which the sociology chair said there was no need for her department or the university to achieve racial balance. Confronted with 150 protesters demanding that the black candidate be hired and ROTC expelled, Baker would not yield. Next, he banned all unauthorized demonstrations. Enraged, another 150 marched on his office, several broke in, and, though no blows landed, a table, lamp and shelves of books hit the floor. Retreating off campus, the group picked up another 100 and marched back chanting, "Shut it down."

At a press conference, Baker blew his top. He had been held "captive" by six students who would be suspended. He would not tolerate this "return to the jungle," and promised a "head-on collision" with those who tried to make the school "serve black political needs." He challenged the news media to "turn their guns" on these "fascists." He suspended five students accused of invading his office, but the disciplinary board reinstated them: one was the victim of misidentification and the other evidence was too confusing to support convictions.

Enrollment kept sliding, the debt was still $1 million, and Baker almost doubled tuition. In September Baker made a mysterious trip to Rome to "see some people." When he returned he asserted his unlimited authority to expel students. Enrollment continued to go down. In October the new Oregon provincial, Father Kenneth J. Galbraith, called together the top administrators of Seattle and Gonzaga to discuss which school should be closed. It was agreed to give Seattle a little more time. In subsequent meetings, the regents, a group of lay financial advisers, wanted the Catholic dimension played down and Christian humanism stressed. This made sense in a state where the Catholic population was not high. It was agreed that Fitterer, who had stayed on as provost, should be replaced. On November 1, 1970, Baker wrote an appreciative and respectful farewell. As one of Baker's original Jesuit supporters put it, "He would have been a great president —forty years ago." Baker became editor of the conservative magazine, *Homiletic and Pastoral Review* and Fitterer left the Society and the Catholic Church, married, and became an Episcopalian minister in California.

During the next five years, the next president, Louis Gaffney, S.J., "like a paramedic at the scene of an automobile accident," says the house historian, "worked swiftly to stabilize the university and bind its wounds." He also led the faculty to willingly accept sacrifices to cut the budget and restore stability, and he started an experimental six-year continuum prep school and college with an emphasis on social justice and interdisciplinary studies, later named for Matteo Ricci. His successor, Edmund Ryan, S.J., a creative and hard-working president, suffered a physical collapse in his first year. His successor, William J. Sullivan, S.J., trained in France and Germany and at Yale, who had been dean of the School of Divinity at St. Louis University and Seattle's first provost, took over and stayed for 20 prosperous years. Today's visitor finds the campus one of the most beautiful Jesuit schools in the country, with no sign of its troubled '60s past.

The Society of Jesus as a whole, however was about to face the second great crisis of its life. Arrupe had unleashed a creative energy that modernized the men who had declined to leave. A backlash was inevitable.

15

Into the 21st Century

"The Sterner Way"

On March 7, 1975, on the last day of the 32nd General Congregation, which had been meeting for 96 days, Pedro Arrupe and his four newly elected general assistants left the meeting hall at the Jesuit headquarters to meet with Pope Paul VI in his offices on the other side of St. Peter's Square. It had been a rough three months. Several times during the meetings the pope, either directly or through intermediaries, had bluntly asked the assembled Jesuits if they realized what they were doing. Even more than during the 31st Congregation eight years before, Pope Paul had been upset by wild reports that "came to his ears" that the Society, supposedly especially devoted to himself, was being overtaken by radicals and Marxists and, most threatening of all, had plans to restructure the relationships among its members in a way that would alter—and weaken—its relationship to him.

Nevertheless, Arrupe and his lieutenants did their best to conclude the meetings on a civil note. They received the copy of the pope's address, which Arrupe would read to the delegates, and a gift from the pope to the Society in a large dark-green velvet and brass-bound antique case, which they carried ceremoniously back to the meeting hall. It was a 17th-century crucifix once owned by the great Jesuit theologian and cardinal, St. Robert Bellarmine. Paul VI was sending them a message. Bellarmine was a loyal defender of the Holy See. But, John Padberg points out, both the pope and the Jesuits knew that Bellarmine did not hesitate to tell the truth to authority when it was called for. For example, in his political philosophy Bellarmine granted the indirect, rather than direct temporal power of the papacy at a time when popes claimed God-given authority over emperors and kings.

To complete the unfinished business of the previous meeting and to deal with the alleged abuses that had accompanied the changes of the 1960s, Arrupe had called the congregation four years before, allowing time for full participation in the preparations, thus involving almost all 30,000 members in the process. After years of community meetings and elections, 236 delegates headed for Rome to sift through over a thousand *postulata*, or proposals, which might lead to either legislation or policy statements. Of the 36 delegates from the United States, New York had the largest number with six, most provinces had three. In the delegates' backgrounds, philosophy, theology, and history dominated; but others specialized in science, canon law, literature, and other fields. Among all the delegates the median age was 49, among the Americans, 51. The oldest of all was Paolo Dezza, age 73, who had been the confessor of both Pius XII and Paul VI, as well as an adviser to Arrupe. He was also blind.

As the deliberations unfolded, the delegates evaluated the quality of community life, which they felt had become more personal, more prayerful, and open in recent years; they tightened poverty and simplicity in living style by limiting the surplus which a community could maintain; and they scrutinized each apostolate as they asked how and where their limited resources should be directed. Behind the scenes, however, another situation threatened to undermine the deliberations and thwart the will of the great majority of the Society's members and leadership.

Rather than deal openly with their fellow Jesuits, a minority opposing all change, often with the cooperation of bishops and cardinals, made end-runs to the Vatican, even resorting to anonymous letters, to attack their fellow Jesuits. Arrupe, in a blunt address, described these men as those who "see themselves as not part of it (the Society), but rather judge it from outside . . . and pass judgment, even publicly and in harsh language and with bitterness, on what others do." These men had denounced the 31st General Congregation as a "deviation." If these back-door attacks were to continue, "it would render the government of the Society impossible." These men still included the group in Spain who said the Society had lost its roots, but numbered some Americans as well. Arrupe knew that whenever he would meet with the pope, another Jesuit who had the pope's ear might have gotten to him already.

The two hot issues with the potential to wreck rapport between the Society and the pope were "grades" and justice. The grades issue was pertinent to Americans raised in a society where at least theoretically one is not trapped in a social class. In the 16th century Ignatius had built his "company" around a small group of talented men with university training, at a time when many priests were simply illiterate. As the Society expanded, more quickly than foreseen, it began to distinguish between three "grades" of membership: the well-educated professed fathers, from whose ranks the leadership would be drawn; the "spiritual coadjutors," that is, priests who would help but not lead; and "temporal coadjutors," lay brothers who would not be ordained but would skillfully do all the other work—cooking, carpentry, construction—and maintain the large communities.

What may have worked for the 16th century did not, in the opinion of many North Americans and others, work for the 20th. The distinguishing mark of the professed father was that, after he pronounced his final vows of poverty, chastity, and obedience at the end of tertianship, he swore an additional loyalty to the pope in the "fourth" vow. It appeared scandalous to some that those with the vocations to the brotherhood but who were not called to the priesthood, would, through any terminology, be considered less "Jesuit" than the professed father. The strong desire of the congregation was to obliterate what they saw as an anachronistic distinction. For Americans it was a special affront in view of the urban democratic milieu from which so many had emerged. And it seemed incongruous to work the rhetoric of human rights, equality, and justice into Society documents while this archaic judicial distinction remained.

It is important here to understand, first, that, from the beginning, the fourth vow of obedience to the pope was with regard to mission. It called for a prompt willingness to take on a special task, such as going as a missionary to the New World. It was not a vow of "orthodoxy" to embrace all the pope's opinions, no matter what they were. Furthermore, the congregation did not seek to get rid of the vow but to extend it, apply it to all members, since all the members already shared in all the apostolic ventures of the Society.

Unfortunately, however, for reasons not entirely clear, the pope opposed any change in what he considered the fundamental rule of the order, which included, in his view, the fourth vow. He also feared the Society would cease to be a "priestly" order, since brothers are lay persons.

On Monday, December 16, 1974, Arrupe informed the plenary session of a letter, dated December 3, from Cardinal Villot, the papal secretary of state, according to which "The Supreme Pontiff . . . desires to let you know that such a change in the light of more careful examination seems to present grave difficulties which would impede the approval necessary on the part of the Holy See." Accustomed as they were to ambiguity in Roman documents, after prolonged consideration the delegates decided to interpret the letter as a warning about difficulties rather than a direct order not to discuss the topic. As deliberations continued, it became clear that the Society overwhelmingly wanted this change. In a straw ballot on January 22 they voted 228 to 8 to extend the vow to all members. The pope was not happy. He had personally told Arrupe he opposed the change; but Arrupe understood that legally he was not the master of the congregation and believed it best for the pope to learn what the congregation really thought. In the end there was no legislation extending the fourth vow. In practice, however, the fourth vow has been given to many men who were denied it years ago, and just about everyone who takes final vows takes four.

Decree 4, on the relationship between faith and justice, is the statement for which this congregation will be most remembered. It was not formally a juridical decree, but, says Padberg, "a message of guidance and inspiration to Jesuits everywhere." A year before, in an address to the alumni of Jesuit schools in Valencia, Spain, Arrupe had delivered a foretaste of its tone when he warned his listeners that "to be drugged by the comforts of privilege is to become contributors to injustice as silent beneficiaries of the fruits of injustice." Some walked out. This was not what they had come to hear. The impetus for the decree came especially from India and Latin America, and its antecedents are clearly in the Vatican II's Schema 13 and liberation theology. The congregation states: "There is no genuine conversion to the love of God without conversion to a love of neighbor and, therefore, to the demands of justice. Since evangelization is proclamation of that faith which is made operative in love of others, the promotion of justice is indispensable to it."

On the frontlines of the American high schools and colleges this meant changes in curriculum and the introduction of service projects to educate "men and women for others" in ministry to the poor. With his usual frankness Arrupe had warned his brothers that if they followed the spirit of this decree some of them would be killed, that benefactors, friends, and relatives would "accuse us of Marxism or subversion, and will withdraw their friendship from us." Did they really want to "enter on the sterner way of the cross?" Within a few years he would endure his own "crucifixion," and a few years after that a whole community of Jesuit scholars in Latin America would be slaughtered in the night.

Arrupe's "Crucifixion"

For the next five years Arrupe went about his work implementing the decrees, work complicated by the death in 1978 of Paul VI and the election of John Paul I, who in his five weeks' reign had called a meeting of Jesuit leaders and died the day before he was to address them. Then came the election of John Paul II, who, in the judgment of ex-Jesuit journalist Peter Hebblethwaite, was very wary of Marxism because of his experience in Poland and was cold and hostile to Arrupe. Arrupe continued to press the justice issues raised by Decree 4. In 1979 he attended the conference of Latin American bishops in Puebla, Mexico, and left all the more determined to hear "the cry of the suffering poor."

In the United States in 1980, still in the wake of Vatican II, there were fires to put out on the left and right. Rome ordered Massachusetts congressman Father Robert Drinan not to run for reelection; ostensibly this was because priests were not to hold elective office, but Drinan had also been criticized because he did not oppose the legalization of abortion. New England Jesuit Father William Callahan, a women's rights advocate, was ordered to return from the Quixote Center, which he had founded in Washington, to Boston and to be silent on the issue of women's ordination. On less weighty matters, Jesuit superiors reined in conservatives as well. In San Francisco, Father Cornelius Buckley, a faculty member at the St. Ignatius Institute, an ultraconservative school pocketed within the University of San Francisco, was ordered by his provincial to stop writing his column for the *National Catholic Register*. In his column he had frequently attacked the Jesuit School of Theology, falsely accusing its faculty and students of using jelly rolls for communion at "bizarre" liturgies. He also opposed their sunbathing nude on the roof.

But Arrupe had two major items on his agenda. The first led to a new work; the second concerned himself. In his travels he had been shocked by the sight of thousands of refugees, beginning with the boat people after the Vietnam War, wandering homeless through the world. He remembered that Ignatius and his first companions, within a year of arriving in Rome in 1537, were confronted with thousands of people driven out of their small towns into Rome by poverty, famine, disease, and cold. Ignatius and his friends gathered the victims into the large house a rich man had given them and begged food and firewood to keep them fed and warm. Within a year they had cared for 3,000 refugees out of a total population of 40,000. In 1980 Arrupe sent a cable to 20 major superiors asking them what they could do about what he saw as a modern version of the 16th-century crisis. This was the beginning of the Jesuit Refugee Service. By 2005, through social services, pastoral care, basic companionship, education, recruiting volunteers, and advocacy, it had touched the lives of over half a million people in 50 countries—including Kenya, the Sudan, Uganda, Ethiopia, Rwanda, the Congo, Liberia, Indonesia, Thailand, India, and throughout Europe and South and North America.

Finally, Arrupe, now 72, had made up his mind to resign. He was still vigorous, but he wanted to pass on the leadership before his powers faded. John Paul II, however, would not allow it. He told Arrupe himself that he did not want to have to get used to a "new person"; Hebblethwaite, however, speculated in the *National Catholic Reporter* (May 23, 1980) that the pope was not ready to face what might happen at another general congregation. In May 1981 John Paul II survived an assassin's bullet in St. Peter's Square. A few months later Arrupe unburdened himself to a small group of Jesuits. We are neither as powerful nor as good as some say, he said. We are ordinary people, not geniuses. The Society's strength, he said, was not in its intellectuality but in its "well-trained mediocrity," the "gift of ourselves." This may be his "swan song," he said. His strength was failing.

On August 7, getting off his plane at the Rome airport, he was struck down by a cerebral thrombosis. Barely able to speak, from his sickbed he met with his staff and appointed New York's Father Vincent O'Keefe, a theologian and former president of Fordham, the vicar general to run the Society until the new congregation could elect a successor. But John Paul II had other plans. For some time, perhaps a year, he had been listening to some of the voices, including those in Spain, still bitter about the "democratizing" of the Society under Arrupe, and he had planned what has been described as a brutal coup.

On October 6 Secretary of State Cardinal Casaroli arrived at noon to speak with Arrupe. Lacouture, in his history, asks whether the Holy Office knew that Arrupe could not speak and was no longer, according to the constitutions, the official head of the Society. Nevertheless, Casaroli required O'Keefe to leave the infirmary while he saw the sick man alone. The cardinal read Arrupe the letter from the pope, then called in O'Keefe because he couldn't understand Arrupe's attempts to speak. Arrupe signaled for O'Keefe to lead the cardinal to another room, where he would meet with Father Dezza. When O'Keefe returned, Arrupe was weeping.

John Paul II had canceled the congregation, removed O'Keefe as vicar general, and imposed Dezza as his "personal delegate" to run the Society in his name. An Indian Jesuit, a former general assistant to Arrupe, described it in *America* as Arrupe's crucifixion, and Karl Rahner said he failed to see "the finger of God" in what the pope had done. According to some reports, the pope had originally decided to appoint a member of another religious order to run the Jesuits, but the progressive Jesuit cardinal Carlo Martini of Milan talked him out of it.

As it turned out, the pope had been both misinformed and had miscalculated. Having been told that an estimated one-third of the Jesuits might leave, he pressed ahead, as if that purge would "cure" the Society of its alleged ills. The provincials were called to Rome and instructed to reexamine their men on their religious life, apostolates, fidelity to doctrine, and formation. Rather than rebel, the troops basically rolled with the punch, the provincials sent in their reports, and within 18 months were free to call the 33rd General Congregation, which chose on the first ballot a Dutch linguist who had worked most of his career in Lebanon, Peter Hans Kolvenbach, 55, rector of the Oriental Institute in Rome. He was a moderate, less charismatic, but perhaps better organized administrator than Arrupe, but very much at one with him on his dedication to social justice.

Arrupe's prediction that many would die if the church and the Society were serious about committing their lives to the poor came too true. By 1980 more than 800 priests and nuns in the secular clergy and various orders in Latin America had been killed, including three American nuns and an American church worker raped and killed in El Salvador in 1980, a Jesuit friend of Archbishop Romero, and Romero himself on March 24. In 1989, in the middle of the night, at the San Salvador University of Central America, U.S.-trained Salvadoran

Army troops invaded the Jesuit residence, dragged six priests, their housekeeper, and her daughter into the courtyard and blew their brains out with their rifles. Symbolically—and foolishly—the assassins saw themselves as thus defeating the Jesuits' ideas.

The effect among North American Jesuits was to reinforce their spiritual union with Latin America. As 17th-century Jesuits volunteered for the missions when they heard of the death of Isaac Jogues, contemporary Jesuits sought to continue the martyrs' work. If they couldn't go to Latin America, at least they could teach liberation theology at home and, by annual liturgies on their "feast day," they celebrated what the Salvadoran martyrs died for. At a memorial mass for the martyrs at the Church of St. Ignatius Loyola, New York, on November 22, 1989, Father Joseph O'Hare, president of Fordham, said, "Their critics will charge, if they had not 'meddled in politics,' their lives would not have been threatened. But such a criticism misunderstands the nature of any university, and most certainly the nature of a Catholic university. No university can isolate itself from the agonies of the society in which it lives."

Arrupe lived on in the Jesuit infirmary until 1991; as he approached the end, O'Keefe recalls, his face, his whole physical appearance, came to resemble that of Ignatius—whose death mask, kept in the archives, is familiar to all—to a remarkable degree.

"Ruined for Life"

The decrees of the 1995 34th General Congregation directed young Jesuits to have more direct contact with the poor, encouraged mature friendships and collaboration with other Jesuits and with women and men who are not Jesuits, and emphasized the equal status of the brothers. The main breakthrough in Jesuit-women relationships was coeducation—from Marquette's medical department in 1907 to the colleges in the 1960s and 1970s. This was accompanied by a steady increase in women faculty. In some Jesuit colleges and universities by 2006, women students outnumbered men by 60 to 40 percent. In the ten years following decrees 13 and 14 on cooperation with women and the laity, the percentage of women in administrative positions in Jesuit schools increased from 28 to 38 percent. Jesuits moved from the closed social life of a male environment to a new level of cooperation and friendship with women. Decree 14 is part formal reflection on the progress, part confession—"We have been part of a civil and ecclesial tradition that has offended against women"—and a call for practical solidarity with women invited to share in the Jesuit ministry.

The decrees also called for what they called "inculturation," breaking out of the cultural mindset in which each Jesuit has been raised. "Inculturation" builds on the missionary tradition of Matteo Ricci; it "points to the *mutuality* between the Gospel and the culture it engages." It is a "buried seed which draws its nourishment from the earth around it." In short, Jesuits root themselves in the culture they serve.

But Decree 13, "Cooperation with the Laity in Mission," speaks to what on the surface is the Society's biggest problem: its decline in numbers—through death, departures, and the decline in vocations. How can Jesuit works continue without Jesuits? But American Jesuits had been working closely with laypersons for years before the 34th General Congregation.

In 1955 Jesuits in Alaska decided to close their mission at Holy Cross, on the Yukon River, and refocus their efforts on a new high school in Copper Valley, 187 miles from Anchorage and 250 miles from Fairbanks, where Francis J. Gleeson, S.J., was bishop. The "parish" pastor, Jack Buchanan, S.J., responsible for 17 native American villages, wanted a school that would prepare the young people, including many orphans, to deal with the encroaching white culture. James "Jake" Spils, S.J., an experienced mission builder, was to direct construction. With little money, they begged equipment and inspired help from military bases, Gonzaga University engineering students, townspeople, and local religious women led by Sister George Edmond Babin, S.S.A., who recruited women from Regis College in Weston, Massachusetts, and opened the school in 1956, though it wouldn't be finished until 1962. Word spread that building a school for poor Alaskan natives was an exciting thing to do. Within a few years the Copper Valley school staff consisted of two Jesuit priests, two scholastics, a brother, six or seven sisters, and about 20 lay volunteers.

Living conditions were miserable—all the staff crammed into one unfinished building with butcher paper separating the "rooms," the outhouse across the creek out back, eating, cooking, sleeping, teaching, recreating in the same general space, but teaching courses like those in a prep school in the other 48 states. The winters were cold and dark, but they were too tied up in their work to notice. They had to hunt their food, kill caribou, rabbits, and an occasional moose or hope that a benefactor would deliver roadkill—a moose hit by a truck—for dinner. Eskimos brought them salmon. The mission was unorganized, caribou carcasses hung everywhere in the winter. There was no radio or TV.

But the volunteers were having the time of their lives. At the Copper Center Roadhouse they never had to pay for a burger or a beer because the local people knew they were volunteers. Above all they got to know the nuns and the priests as human beings, with faults like anyone else but real persons—something that as Catholics they had never seen before. They said of Fr. Spils that he had dirty fingernails on his hard-working hands, that he loved his bourbon and his pinochle, but that he was holy, he convinced them that God loved them. And Bishop Gleason made apple pie himself when the girls were coming and he was dressed like a bum. And he was great.

The volunteers developed a spirituality, but it was on their own terms. They would take a long walk along the river and look at the birds and contemplate what was happening; but the main thing was the experience of community, everyone believing in the school and sacrificing everything to make it work. If one knew anything of Ignatian spirituality, he or she could sense that this was it: using things of this world to serve God.

The program spread as volunteers began to staff schools in villages throughout Alaska—villages with only a hundred people, with no electricity, running water, or bathrooms, and only one church. These volunteers, more than the others, were adopted by Eskimo or Indian families and immersed in the local culture. Jesuits themselves had to get used to working with female volunteers; some became good friends, some left the Society to marry them.

It was 1958 before the Jesuits at Gonzaga realized they should organize the administration of its growing program. In 1959 those who had worked at Copper Valley organized as the Lay Apostolic Mission Boards (LAMB) and began to require letters of recommendation and screening. As mission volunteering became more popular, problems multiplied. Volunteers arrived unannounced, some were not psychologically ready and were asked to leave, others came and went home early. When Jack Morris, S.J., first worked at Copper Valley in 1957 as a young scholastic, he was, by his own admission, a bit of a stiff.

Conservative, he was scandalized at older Jesuits who, in his judgment, were not keeping all the rules. But soon the spirit of the place—the generosity, fun, and hard work—overtook him and made him a warmer human being. In 1963 he returned to Alaska to teach high school in Fairbanks and got a new sense of the volunteers' needs and problems. In 1964 Bishop Gleeson put him in charge of the program; he planned orientations, commissioned the volunteers in a ceremony, gave each a cross, and visited everyone during the year. Mary Webber, his assistant, borrowing an idea from the Peace Corps which had been established in 1961, suggested the name "Jesuit Volunteer Corps," plus the motto, "Older than the Peace Corps, twice as tough, and ten times more rewarding." Jack's metaphor for the experience was the "frontier," where the white and native cultures met and forced the volunteers to question old certainties.

Bill Davis, S.J., whose work with the Latin American missions had influenced his political ideas, took over the JVC in 1970 and expanded its operations into the cities of the Northwest. Within two years the number of volunteers increased from 100 to 230, and Davis assigned many to work with the poor even if the jobs had no Jesuit or church connection. With his assistant, Dennis Duffel, they developed essential "values," like community, simplicity, and social justice, plus celebrating community liturgies. A term emerged to describe the transformation the volunteers experienced: "ruined for life."

Throughout the 1970s, with its first full-time director, Larry Gooley, S.J., the JVC spread rapidly throughout the country as various provinces opened their own versions, modeled on the Oregon plan. In the urban milieu the volunteers, with no authority immediately in charge of the small communities, had to learn to shop, cook, clean, and get along with strangers—some neat, some sloppy; some mature, some not; some religious, some indifferent. Often the women outnumbered the men, feminism became an issue, romantic and sexual relationships increased tension. The JVC enlisted "support persons," nearby Jesuits or other adults experienced in ministry who would visit the communities. But as the work projects became more far-flung, fewer volunteers had any contact with Jesuits. Eventually the five regions agreed on five volunteer gatherings during the year: orientation, a fall workshop focused on community, a winter reorientation on social justice, a spring silent individually directed retreat, and a final reflection.

In the 1980s the various regions replaced Jesuit directors with women and even non-Catholics. The feeling was that what made the JVC Jesuit was not the number of Jesuits involved but its spirituality and mission; laypersons, trained, are as capable as Jesuits in being contemplatives in action, finding God in all things. The number of volunteers peaked at 450 around the turn of the century, declining partly because its success has inspired many similar movements. At its 50th anniversary in 2006, over 300 volunteers, over half from Jesuit institutions, were working in 54 places in the United States and eight other countries.

From Tacna to Chicago

In 1985 when Jeff Theilman graduated from Boston College, where he had been student president, after a summer which included a week sailing in the Virgin Islands, a job in the Massachusetts State House, and waiting tables in Faneuil Hall Marketplace in Boston, he flew in October into Tacna, Peru, a 30-block town on the Chilean border.

He was an "international" Jesuit volunteer, a logical extension of what had begun in Alaska, to Latin America. Weak in Spanish, not very good at sports, and not trained to teach anything, he had come as one of three volunteers to teach and coach basketball in one of the American-sponsored Jesuit high schools spread across Latin America. It was called Cristo Rey, inspired by the Spanish Jesuit, St. Miguel Pro, who was executed by a firing squad, simply for being a priest, during the Mexican Revolution in 1927. Captured while secretly, often in disguise, ministering to Mexican Catholics, his last words were, "Viva Cristo Rey!"—Long live Christ the King.

From the beginning things did not go well. Jeff's students, out of control, threw rocks at one another, called him obscene names, mocked him in public, and urinated on the classroom walls. At home his parents were splitting and his girlfriend postponed her promised visit. Meanwhile, he was both traumatized and transformed by the poverty he witnessed—from the corpse of a poor, fly-covered baby who died at birth, to the aimless street children of the Indians who migrated from the countryside into the city shantytowns and slums.

Where he didn't seem to click with the middle-class high school boys, he did with the shoe-shine boys and thieves. In a story that took almost four years to unfold, Jeff decided that what these boys needed was a center, not just a school, but a place where they could learn trades, get a decent meal, learn to read and write, and where their mothers, many of whom were single mothers with many children, could work with sewing machines—rather than work in a brothel. He endured depression, alienation from his girlfriend, the poverty of living in a family hut, cynical rich men who considered him naive. But, with the support of his Jesuit friend and mentor John Foley, he begged the land, raised the money through gifts from and trips to the States, and built the Cristo Rey Center for the Working Child before returning to Boston College Law School in 1989 and writing a book about his experiences, *Volunteer with the Poor in Peru.*

When Bradley M. Schaeffer, S.J., was named Chicago Province provincial in 1991, he saw it as an opportunity to act on one of his dreams: a new Jesuit high school for the Hispanic poor. Of the two parishes Cardinal Joseph Bernardin offered him, he took St. Procopius in the Pilsen-Little neighborhood; it was more crowded with young families, with more poor, and it had a school building. A year-long study showed a drop-out rate in the two local high schools of 55 and 73 percent, only a quarter of the parents having finished high school, an average household income of $22,500, and the presence of drugs and gangs. His committee came up with a bold new way to finance the project. The students would pay most of the tuition by working one day a week at a local business. The company hires four students (one works two days), the equivalent of one full-time person, and pays the salary to the Cristo Rey Corporation. With modular scheduling, the student, in four 80-minute classes, takes courses from 8 A.M. to 3 P.M., participates in a mandatory activity from 3 P.M. to 5, and does two more hours of supervised study each night. The school year is 11 months long. The parents, if they can, pay $1,500, the diocese adds $300 per student. September is devoted to orientation for the workplace, how to dress, arrive on time, and interact and form teams with fellow workers. They learn corporate organization, office technology, and conflict management. Meanwhile, the Chicago businessmen, many grateful for their own Jesuit educations, welcomed the experiment.

In 1995 Schaeffer called John Foley home from Peru, where he had worked for 35 years, to help run Cristo Rey. The following year the Cristo Rey Jesuit High School opened in the former elementary school with 100 students in grades 10 and 11. The next year Jeff Theilman, now a Connecticut lawyer moving into the insurance business, visited his old friend Foley in Chicago. They walked along Lake Michigan and Foley showed Jeff the boys and girls he was helping. Then he asked Jeff, "What are you doing for the Kingdom?"

By the summer of 2006 Jeff was Vice President for New Initiatives for Cristo Rey. The Cassin Educational Initiative Foundation and the Bill and Melinda Gates Foundation have given substantial support. Eleven schools, only a few of them Jesuit sponsored, in nine major metropolitan areas teach 2,300 students. The goal is 12,000 by 2012.

In January 2001 American Jesuits shared a moment of pride when John Paul II named Avery Dulles the first American Jesuit cardinal. With characteristic humility, Dulles, 82, author of 21 books, including *Models of the Church* (1974) and *Models of Revelation* (1983), interpreted the honor as a tribute to all American theologians and to the Society of Jesus. Son of Secretary of State John Foster Dulles, a prominent Presbyterian, Dulles's conversion to Catholicism was a gradual, rational process aided by reading Plato, hiring a Catholic tutor, and using his intuitive observations of nature. He survived naval service in World War II and an attack of polio, and entered the Society in 1946. In theology he never considered himself a major figure but a synthesizer who read de Lubac, Maritain, Rahner, and others and became the servant of their truths. Living simply in the Fordham Jesuit community, he has continued to write and lecture, unafraid of controversy, focusing on the basics: Christ and traditional Christian sources.

Four Controversies

The first years of the 21st century brought their own set of controversies and criticisms of the Society. Some echoed accusations of unorthodoxy that had appeared in two books in the 1980s—one by a professor at St. Louis, the other by a former priest based on alleged but undocumented "inside" Vatican sources. Other problems emerged from a long-simmering scandal in clerical culture. It began when New Orleans writer Jason Berry, in the *National Catholic Reporter*, broke the story of clergy sexual abuse of minors in Louisiana in the 1990s. It peaked in February 2004 when the National Board of Review, established by the U.S. bishops, reported that in the previous half-century nearly 4,400 priests (4 percent of all priests) had abused more than 10,600 minors. The report did not distinguish between diocesan priests and members of religious orders; with a few exceptions, the sensational press accounts did not focus on Jesuits, and it could be argued that because of the long, 13-year, course of training, most problems were dealt with before ordination. Nevertheless, even when they were not publicized, Jesuits gradually learned of this or that fellow Jesuit who had been credibly accused and removed from public ministry. Or experienced Jesuits began to remember incidents years ago when a student told them that Father so-and-so had "made a move." Now everyone was required to submit to workshops on how to avoid even the appearance of impropriety.

Meanwhile, occasional memoirs by Jesuit alumni would interrupt their praise of Jesuit mentors with an episode of remembered abuse. Joseph Califano, graduate of Brooklyn Prep and Holy Cross, who served in the Kennedy and Johnson administrations, had his bad experience on a high school retreat and his crisis of faith in his senior year. But he read the passage in Avery Dulles's conversion story, *A Testimonial to Grace,* and was inspired by Dulles's words, "I came into the church like one of those tired swimmers who closes his eyes as he jumps into the roaring sea. The waters of faith, I have found, are marvelously buoyant." The crisis passed.

Conservative Catholic magazines argued that tolerance of homosexuality in the priesthood, including a high proportion of homosexuals in the Society of Jesus, was itself a source of scandal. A new sociological study of the Society, *Passionate Uncertainty,* by Peter McDonough and Eugene Bianchi, himself a former Jesuit, based on a survey plus interviews with 200 present and 200 former Jesuits and 100 lay coworkers, found that the Jesuits who have remained are highly satisfied with their work and their leadership, although many are critical of the bishops and of the pope. In a community the authors describe as "gaying and graying," the younger Jesuits have a sense of living with their grandfathers who revel in nostalgia; the gays among them seek community by networking with one another, and those who are "straight" can feel alienated if a critical mass of a community is gay.

Jesuit watcher Garry Wills, reviewing the book for the *New York Review of Books,* says that outsiders became aware of the gay subculture when the *Kansas City Star* (January 30, 2000) reported that dozens of Jesuits were suffering and dying from AIDS.

The Society's institutional response to the situation, prompted by the report that the Vatican congregation was going to issue a proclamation banning all homosexuals from the priesthood, was to reaffirm a standing policy. If it is clear that God has called a gay man to the priesthood, celibacy, and the Society of Jesus, he should be accepted. The New York provincial, Gerald Chojnacki, in a letter to his province quoted in the *New York Times* (September 30, 2005), said he had participated in the funerals of "very fine and distinguished Jesuits who were gay"; and *America* repeatedly affirmed that good priests could be both gay and chaste.

The third 21st-century Jesuit controversy recalled the *America* battle of 1954 when Jesuit protests to Rome over Robert C. Hartnett's stand against McCarthyism forced him out of the editor's chair. In May 2005, shortly after Cardinal Joseph Ratzinger, head of the Congregation for the Doctrine of the Faith (CDF), was elected as Pope Benedict XVI, Fr. Thomas Reese, a political scientist, author of two books on power in the church, and a respected TV commentator during the election, was removed as *America* editor. The CDF, prodded by some American cardinals, began investigating *America* in 2000. Its alleged offense was not that it was heretical but that it printed articles on both sides of controversial issues—including "Dominus Deus," the congregation's document on Christ as the unique savior; same-sex marriage; stem-cell research; and reception of communion by political candidates who support legal abortion—when the Vatican authorities wanted all the articles to agree with magisterial teachings, even those not declared infallible.

At one point the Vatican attempted to impose a board of censors; but Cardinal Dulles wrote to Rome in *America*'s defense, and the editors made an effort to include conservative voices, including an article by an Opus Dei priest opposed to ordaining gays. But an essay by a leading Democratic congressman explaining how a practicing Catholic politician could support abortion rights renewed the battle. Reese was told to resign. *Commonweal* wrote: "If the moderate views expressed in *America,* views widely shared by the vast majority of lay Catholics, are judged suspect by the CDF, how is the average Catholic to assess his or her own relationship to the church?" (May 21, 2005).

The fourth controversy rose over the papal letter on higher education, *Ex Corde Ecclesiae* (1990)—"from the heart of the church"—a sort of belated response to the "Land O'Lakes" statement. Along with an exhortation on the goals of Christian scholarship, it includes, in its American application, a requirement for a *mandatum*, or formal approval from the local bishop for every Catholic theologian who would teach at a Catholic college or university. Through negotiations, articles, and resolutions, the university presidents, seeing this as an intrusive violation of the American understanding of academic freedom, resisted, dragging their feet. At the bishops' invitation, a senior Jesuit delegate traveled around the country for dialogue with individual bishops. As a result, for the most part, bishops have seen the universities as important diocesan assets and have preferred not to interfere with their internal workings.

For the Cardinal Newman Society, however, that was not enough. Led by a 1990 Fordham graduate, with 20,000 members who contribute a total of nearly $1 million in a year, the society sees the universities as having abandoned the faith, and the Newman Society has assumed the role of Christ casting the moneychangers from the temple. Specifically, it calls upon its members and church authorities to deny "Catholic" status to schools that permit the performance of *The Vagina Monologues* on campus, honor public figures who are "pro-choice," allow "pro-choice" or gay and lesbian student societies on campus, or house moral theologians who approved removing the feeding tube from Terry Schiavo. But they focus primarily on sexual issues, abortion and euthanasia, with little or no concern for other life issues like the death penalty, nuclear arms, or preemptive war.

For the presidents, the Cardinal Newman Society is an irritant, but a minor one. Their main concern is to have a really good university, determined by many criteria, including those used by *U.S. News & World Report* in its annual rankings. The best national universities usually include Georgetown, Boston College, Saint Louis, Fordham, Marquette, Loyola Chicago, and San Francisco. Holy Cross is the one Jesuit school in the top 50 liberal arts colleges both because it requires research and good teaching and because it is the only pure Jesuit liberal arts college, without a tacked-on Master's program in something. Eighteen others make mention among the best universities offering

Master's degrees (in 2004). Among the graduate schools, Georgetown and Boston College rate as top business schools; Boston College as a school of education; and Georgetown, Boston College, Fordham, Loyola California, Loyola Chicago, Saint Louis, and Santa Clara for its law schools. Third-tier law includes Creighton, Gonzaga, Loyola New Orleans, and Marquette. For the best medical school, Georgetown was on the list in 2006.

But excellence wears many faces. Every year or so, a Jesuit school's basketball team will burst into national news; graduates win Fulbright scholarships; alumni are elected to Congress or star in movies and Broadway shows. Or the school struggles to attract 500 students to its freshman class if it is to meet its budget and survive. Collectively, in 2005, 215,398 students enrolled in American Jesuit colleges and universities, taught by 19,272 faculty, 337 of whom were Jesuits. There are about 1,673,446 living alumni. The 49 schools in the Jesuit Secondary School Association (JSEA) educate approximately 44,000 young men and women a year. Fifteen of the schools are coeducational and 21 percent of the students are minorities. Of the 3,000 faculty, nearly 200 are Jesuits. Jesuits also sponsor a growing number of Nativity Schools and middle schools directed at minority students in poor neighborhoods.

Nativity schools, middle schools serving the sixth to eighth grade, which got their start in 1971 in the Nativity Parish on New York's lower East Side, are deliberately small, neighborhood based, and directed toward the inner-city poor. They serve the families of their students by assuming the role of a second family; so the student-faculty relationships are personal rather than institutional. Since 1991 there has been an explosion in the spread of these schools, which now number over 50 and have been consolidated with the work of other religious orders and called the NativityMiguel Network of Schools.

In short, the Society of Jesus is taking on more work rather than cutting back; and they are sharing the burden with laypersons and other religious orders who share their goals.

Finally, Another Cross-Country Tour

The year 2006 was the 450th anniversary of the death of St. Ignatius and the 500th anniversary of the births of St. Francis Xavier and

Blessed Peter Faber—a good year to repeat the midcentury Margaret Bourke White tour for *Life* magazine of Jesuit works in America and Honduras. But today *Life* has been replaced by the TV documentary. Imagine a traveling camera crew dropping in on communities that might offer clues to where the Society is headed.

If they were to see everyone, they could shoot 3,079 faces, including 2,620 priests, 201 scholastics, and 176 brothers; that's 175 fewer than the previous year. The United States has roughly 15 percent of the 19,565 Jesuits in the world.

To put those numbers into perspective, 40 novices entered in 2005. Their average age was 28.7 years, including several in their 40s; of those who entered, 33 to 35 percent, based on past records, may continue on to ordination. If the entrance, retention, and death rates remain the same, there might be 2,000 Jesuits in the United States in 2020 and 1,100 in 2050. The American Jesuits of the future may stabilize at about 1,000 to 1,200 men.

In 2006, the median Jesuit age was 67.6 years; the average was 64.7. But as several recent studies of the priesthood have shown, the men in their 60s and 70s are most dedicated to its reforms because they experienced both the pre-and post-Vatican II church, while recent seminarians look back to the cultic priesthood, the Latin Mass, and ornate and prolonged liturgies—bows, incense, and bells—for their spirituality. In these matters the Society of Jesus has room for all; and as its governance becomes more democratic, the administrators will work these differences out.

Today the largest communities naturally are those of the largest universities, where membership ranges from 50 to 100. Boston College, with 104 members in 2006, will represent the largest American Jesuit complex when it completes its merger with the Weston School of Theology in Cambridge. This move will have accomplished in an exceptional way what had been recommended by various Jesuit committees in the 1930s and 1960s but was disregarded: that the Society should concentrate its resources in one or two places in order to achieve the greater good in competition with secular institutions.

But across the country the size of the community varies according to what each group has to do. Out of 218 communities, 82 had one to five members in 2006. At the high end, 19 had 30 or more.

A fairly representative community would be Saint Peter's in Jersey City with 23 members, of whom 15 work in the college. The others, insofar as health allows, work in other apostolates. All the wages they earn from salary, saying parish Masses, or writing articles go directly to the community. As a general rule, Jesuits work until they drop.

In a typical house the men make their own breakfast and lunch, though some may serve soup, salad, and sandwiches. They rise before 7:00 A.M., pray then or later according to each one's practice, teach three or four courses a semester, go to committee meetings and moderate student activities, counsel people who seek them out, and say Masses at convents and prisons.

For exercise some play golf or take long walks. The number of long-distance runners has shrunk in recent years. At most colleges, faculty hired within the last 30 years know they must do research and publish articles and apply for grants and sabbaticals. Community mass is at 5:15 P.M., followed by about 30 minutes of recreation with a before-dinner cocktail or soda. Today almost no one smokes, and those who do drink, drink less than years ago. In many houses this "preprandial" time, followed by dinner, is the only time when everyone can be together and talk.

Conversation among the seniors gravitates to ailments and old stories repeated again; but any group of Jesuits is a mini-encyclopedia in itself, and one can throw out a question, rather than look it up, and usually count on an answer. Every house has an extensive reference library and a broad collection of magazines and newspapers which the men devour. They talk sports, tease one another, and entertain guests and international visitors. They talk politics, with an effort, not always successful, to avoid blow-ups. Democrats tend to be in the majority; but all are antiabortion and a few have drifted away from the Democratic line. Most opposed the Iraq war. After dinner, years ago they would gather to watch the network TV evening news; since now the news is broadcast during dinnertime, those who are not going out return to the TVs in their rooms. Though the modern residences grant each his own small bathroom, in the older large communities the room has a sink, but the men must walk down the hall to the common bathroom with its booths for toilets and showers. Some retire as early as 10 P.M., others work until midnight—or fall asleep in their chairs. They drive one another to and from the hospital and show up for wakes and funerals of alumni, students, and one another.

Some Clues to the Future

Colleges take part of their identity from where they are. Regis University, almost as if it was a frontier outpost, is the only Jesuit university between Rockhurst in Kansas City and the three in California. Its origins go back to the Jesuit College of the Sacred Heart in Las Vegas, Nevada (1878); but when Denver looked like richer territory, the Jesuits moved there, keeping the same name, in 1888 and changed its name to Regis College in 1921.

In 1971 Regis was entering its own modern era, with an all-time high enrollment of 1,269 students and a growing number of women. Racial integration was moving slowly; there were just 14 black students. The following year the new president, David M. Clarke, S.J., began a program of expansion, particularly in adult education, including an MBA degree, and establishing off-campus sites, including in Las Vegas where the school had begun.

As he ended his tenure in 1990, Clarke proposed that university status would make Regis the only Catholic university between Omaha and the Pacific Ocean, protect the institution's position as a leader in adult learning in Colorado, and attract faculty and grants. The search for a new president combined self-examination and a listing of the values the new administration should promote. The Jesuit tradition ranked high, though, as is true in other institutions, some participants were more committed to the term "Jesuit" than to the word "Catholic." But a recurring theme was the desire for innovative and flexible programming.

In 1992 the board chose Michael Sheeran, S.J., a political scientist who had been at Regis as a teacher and administrator since 1975, as president. Before the end of his first year, before his own inauguration, Sheeran brought Regis its special "moment in history" by engineering a brief meeting on campus between Pope John Paul II and President Bill Clinton on August 12, 1993. Each arrived in his own helicopter and greeted the crowds. They came together in the president's dining room in Carroll Hall, strolled across campus to hold a joint press conference, and then flew away. Then Sheeran returned to his work, tailoring modern education to the needs of the students. Central to this was the School of Professional Studies (SPS), a combining of the career programs, and its entry in the growing field of distance education. By the end of the century, SPS had become one of the largest online degree programs among United States colleges and universities, and by 2003 Regis had the largest online, adult-oriented program among Jesuit schools in the world. There were trade-offs. Innovative ways had to be found to make online education genuine Jesuit education, when Jesuit education has traditionally been a highly personal, face-to-face encounter. Meanwhile, the Denver Jesuits turned Regis High School into a two-division school—one for boys, the other for girls—and opened Arrupe Jesuit High School, modeled on Cristo Rey.

To the north, the University of Detroit, founded in 1877, struggled with the economic ups and downs of its city, in its "imperative," in the words of its dean in 1928, "to train young men and women in the mysteries of commerce and industry." As it entered its second 100 years, the urban university was dealing with a set of problems that raised questions about its future: the city's Catholic population was moving to the suburbs; its black ghettos had exploded in the 1967 riots; the auto industry declined, crime rose, and the quality of urban life went down; the state's public universities improved and drew the better students. Detroit University's austerity program in the early 1970s, including cutting faculty, prompted faculty unionization in 1976, and a threatened strike was averted in March 1977. In the 1980s Detroit University, Mercy College, run by the Sisters of Mercy, and Marygrove College, facing similar problems, including enrollment decline, discussed merger. Two years of discussions and mission statements led to the consolidation of Detroit and Mercy into the University of Detroit-Mercy, with Sister Maureen Fay, O.P., as the first non-Jesuit—and woman—president of a Jesuit university.

In the heartland, Rockhurst had also become a university, and—following Detroit-Mercy and Georgetown, which named a layman, John J. DeGioia, president in 2001—in 2006 was the third Jesuit university to name a non-Jesuit as president: Father Thomas B. Curran, a member of the Oblates of St. Francis de Sales. Rockhurst's outgoing president, having served as both provincial of the Missouri Province and having enhanced Rockhurst's campus and reputation, took a leave of absence from the Society of Jesus and then quickly returned.

When Hurricane Katrina headed toward Loyola University New Orleans on Saturday, August 26, 2005, students had already arrived on campus, ready for Monday's first class. Sunday morning at 10:30 a string of Loyola cars and vans filled with faculty, staff, and 140 students joined the terrified exodus on route I-10 toward Baton Rouge, Lafayette, and as far west as Houston. Many Jesuits, including those from the prep, took refuge at Grand Coteau, outside Lafayette, the old novitiate where their religious lives had begun. Lay faculty found homes with friends and relatives in Dallas, Chicago, Atlanta, indeed spreading their families all over America. With email and phone service down in New Orleans, it was days and weeks before enough communications links could be patched together to let one another know they were alive and sheltered. Houston University Law School accommodated 320 Loyola students and one Jesuit law professor. Led by Charlie Currie, S.J., AJCU president, the 27 other Jesuit colleges and universities immediately welcomed 1,241 Loyola refugees as first-semester students. Some offered free housing, food, and financial aid. The two largest groups were Loyola Chicago, which took 252, and Saint Louis, which took 130. But in every school both the hosts and visitors got a new sense of what it meant to be "men and women for others," and the institutions, some of which historically have not rushed to cooperate, got a new feeling for what makes them one.

Jesuit High School was flooded on the first floor, but Spring Hill and Loyola escaped major damage. Loyola paid the faculty full first-semester salaries; but by summer 2006 it was clear to the administration that, in anticipation of a fall 2006 enrollment drop, the university would have to reorganize and cut some departments and faculty.

Eight months after the disaster, law professor Bill Quigley, editor of Lou Twomey's *Blueprint for Social Justice*, in the spirit of its founder published a memoir of his five days and four nights as a volunteer in the hospital where his wife was a nurse, with 2,000 people, no electricity, no running water, a small amount of bottled water, and no food. As eight feet of water surrounded the building, helicopters fluttered overhead, touched down, and took away the babies without telling the mothers where. The dead lay in the corridors and floated outside the door. By spring 2006, there was no public hospital in the city, corpses were still being found in houses, and old people were living in their cars. Katrina had killed 1,282 residents and 987 were still missing. Nearly 300,000, mostly the poor, had not returned. Nevertheless, says Quigley, "For every campaign of injustice and ugliness, there are people struggling despite the odds to create opportunities for justice and beauty" (*Blueprint*, Fall 2005–Spring 2006).

In 1962 the New York Province took responsibility for a mission in

Nigeria, and by 2005, with over 80 native Nigerian members, the great majority scholastics, Nigeria was cut loose as a province on its own. About a half dozen American Jesuits remained to work. In 1995 they broke ground for Loyola Jesuit College (LJC), situated deliberately in the new capital Abuja, where, it was hoped, its central location would make it equally accessible to the whole country. When it opened in 1996, 400 boys and girls took the entrance exam and 101 enrolled; in 2005, 120 were accepted out of 2,300. Its students now place at the top in the national examinations. LJC was already a success story—in a nation where corruption and inefficiency had made success a stranger to all but the corrupt. On December 10, 2005, a DC-9, carrying 127 passengers crashed and burned at the Port Harcourt airport in Nigeria, killing over 107. Sixty of the dead were LJC students on the way home for Christmas. Only one student survived. In one crash Loyola had lost one-tenth of its student body.

Mourning the loss, Peter Schineller, S.J., its president, called attention to Nigeria's notorious airline safety record, inadequate communications, lack of ambulances, bad roads on which the ambulances must drive, and no water at the airport to douse the flames. In a letter to *The (Nigeria) Guardian* the parent of a boy who had taken another plane wrote bluntly that the skies were not safe, the one hour of domestic flights is "an hour of subdued terror characterized by a deafening muteness that ends only when the plane lands." "Nigeria is a country peopled by the under-privileged and ruled principally by underprivileged who have become privileged through corruption. LJC is the exact opposite, it is an institution where those who are intellectually and materially privileged are groomed to be sensitive to the underprivileged through the prism of morality, service, and humanity."

Coming to Rest

Let us imagine that the film crew dropping in on Denver, Detroit, Kansas City, New Orleans, and Abuja comes to rest on the Massachusetts coast above Cape Cod. If the Jesuits have a number of country or seaside villas—like New York's Cornwall on Hudson, St. Joseph's Chelsea in Atlantic City, Wisconsin's lakeside Waupaca, Oregon's Hayden Lake, or New Orleans' cabin at Waveland on the Gulf Coast which

Katrina blew away—it is because benefactors and superiors, knowing that religious men must occasionally rest as well as work until they drop, have left something in their wills or bought some nice house that also serves as a retreat house and conference center. One of the more beautiful is Boston College's big stone and wood house on Cohasset Harbor, designed in 1880 by H. H. Richardson for Dr. John H. Bryant, the yachtsman, and bought in 1932 by Boston College.

One day in July 2006 the guests included a young priest doctoral student from New Orleans, who was the host; a priest who had worked 35 years in the same school; a moral theologian specializing in medical ethics; three more graduate students—an Indonesian philosopher, a Romanian social worker, and a Korean sociologist; two men who had served in Baghdad; and two who had recently been to a meeting in Rome where Fr. General Kolvenbach announced that he had the pope's permission to resign and had called a congregation to elect his successor. Kolvenbach gave two reasons. Though he appears vigorous and quick, he was getting old—he would be 80 when the congregation would meet. And he wanted new blood, with new creativity, to chart the future.

What will the future look like? Every Jesuit knows the story of Ignatius telling a confidante that if the whole Society were to be abolished it would take him only ten minutes of prayer to accept the loss. He was illustrating the need for "indifference," emotional detachment from created things to allow greater freedom to serve God. If the Society lasts, the stories in this chapter—JVC, Cristo Rey, lay presidents of Jesuit universities and high schools, the company of international students, and the commitment to faith and justice—point where the Society is headed. In planning for the 35th General Congregation, the American assistancy gave priority to "people suffering from structurally entrenched poverty"—refugees, inner-city populations, and the 800 million people in the world who go to bed hungry.

Let us give the last word to Ignatius, mediated through Karl Rahner, who died in 1984 but who in 1979 composed a letter to a modern Jesuit, as if he were Ignatius reflecting on the Society's history and speaking to it today. "One thing remains certain," he says. "It is possible for men to know God." The Jesuit's role, through the Exercises and his worldview, is to help people find God in "everything," especially in love of neighbor. Will there be enough Jesuits to do this? "There will always be men who on seeing the Crucified and Risen Jesus, pass by all the idols of this world and dare to give themselves unconditionally to the incomprehensibility of God, seen as love and mercy. How many they are numerically and in proportion to mankind as a whole is ultimately of no importance, if the Church alone as the sacrament of salvation for the whole world remains present in it."

Notes and Sources

Abbreviations

AC   James Hennessey, *American Catholics*

ACS&S   Charles Morris, *American Catholic, Saints and Sinners*

ACE   Jay P. Dolan, *American Catholic Experience*

CAF   John T. McCreevy, *Catholicism and American Freedom*

HSJ   William Bangert, *History of the Society of Jesus*

RAS   author's *Fordham: A History and Memoir*, observation, or interviews

TFJ   John O'Malley, *The First Jesuits*

WL   *Woodstock Letters*

Notes to the Prologue

There are dozens of books on the Society of Jesus which survey the Society's history. For the purposes of this study, the most important are William V. Bangert, S.J.'s encyclopedic *A History of the Society of Jesus* (hereafter HSJ), though its treatment of the modern era is brief, and John O'Malley, S.J.'s more recent and beautifully written, *The First Jesuits* (hereafter TFJ). There are also several books on the Society's early years and biographies of the first saints by James Brodrick, S.J., which have been enormously influential in the formation of the current generation of Jesuits. Two major recent biographies of St. Ignatius Loyola are Jose Ignacio Tellechea Idigoras's *Ignatius Loyola, the Pilgrim Saint* and William Meissner, S.J.'s *Ignatius of Loyola: The Psychology of a Saint*. George Ganss, S.J.'s edited *Ignatius of Loyola: The Spiritual Exercises and Selected Works* contains an excellent summary of his life, his autobiography, and his basic writings, in addition to an analysis of Jesuit spirituality. An indispensable treasure of American Jesuit history is *Woodstock Letters* (hereafter WL), a periodical published from Woodstock College, the first American Jesuit seminary, in Maryland, from 1872 until Woodstock moved to New York in 1970. Intended as a bond of union among American Jesuits, similar to the *Relations*, it published firsthand reports from various houses, obituaries, letters from military chaplains and missionaries—the raw material of history. The story of the Society's first attempt to establish itself in Florida and the Southern states, along with the story of Pedro Martinez, is from Michael Kenny, S.J.'s the *Romance of the Floridas: The Finding and the Founding;* the Martinez account is also in a pamphlet, *Pedro Martinez, S.J., Martyr of Florida.* On Jesuits and Jews, see James Bernauer, S.J., "The Holocaust and the Search for Forgiveness," *Studies in the Spirituality of Jesuits,* 36/2 Summer 2004. For women Jesuits, see Lisa Fullam, "Juana, S.J.: The Past (and Future?) Status of Women in the Society of Jesus," *Studies in the Spirituality of Jesuits,* 31/5 November 1999.

Notes to Chapter I

Most of the chapter is based on HSJ, TFJ, Jonathan Wright's *God's Soldiers,* plus Frederick Coppleston, S.J.'s *History of Philosophy.* The quote calling these decades "the most glorious" is from Peter Masten Dunne, S.J., *Pioneer Jesuits in Northern Mexico.*

Notes to Chapter 2

The standard source for Andrew White and the founding of the Maryland colony is the Thomas Hughes *History of the Society of Jesus in North America, Colonial and Federal,* vol. 1. The most recent is John D. Krugler, *English and Catholic, The Lords Baltimore in the Seventeenth Century.* Robert Emmett Curran, S.J.'s edited *American Jesuit Spirituality, The Maryland Tradition, 1634–1900,* includes documents through the 18th century. Curran's *The Maryland Jesuits, 1634–1833,* with Gerald P. Fogarty, S.J., and Joseph T. Durkin, S.J., is a short history of the early years of the Maryland Province. James Hennesey, S.J.'s *American Catholics: A History of the Roman Catholic Community in the United States* and Jay P. Dolan's *The American Catholic Experience: A History from Colonial Times to the Present* (hereafter ACE), coming from different perspectives, put the Society's work in the context of early American history. Rory T. Conley's *The Truth in Charity: A History of the Archdiocese of Washington* is an illustrated general survey. The description of the Maryland countryside is from the author's (hereafter RAS) travels.

Notes to Chapter 3

A popular biography of Isaac Jogues which had a strong impact on young Catholics in the 1940s is Francis Talbot, S.J., *Saint among Savages.* The major source from which all historians on the era draw is Reuben Gold Thwaites's edition of *The Jesuit Relations and Allied Documents: Travels and Explorations of the Jesuit Missionaries in New France, 1610–1791* (73 vols.). The *Relations* were long letters, detailed reports on their missionary efforts, sent to religious superiors in France and then often widely circulated to publicize the Society's work in New France. Though it usually took a year for the *Relations* to get to readers, they had enormous influence in building enthusiasm for the missions among both Jesuits and lay readers. For the most part, the descriptions here of the captivity and sufferings of Jogues and other martyrs are based on accounts in the more accessible one-volume edition edited by Edna Kenton. The narrative, methods, and evaluation of the French missionaries come from Francis Parkman, *The Jesuits in North America in the Seventeenth Century,* and James Axtell, *The Invasion Within: The Conquest of Cultures in Colonial North America,* and his *After Columbus: Essays in the Ethnohistory of Colonial North America.* Also helpful are J. H. Kennedy, *Jesuit and Savage in New France,* James T. Moore, S.J., *Indian and Jesuit: A Seventeenth-Century Encounter,* and ACE. The preeminent historian on Eusebio Kino is Herbert Eugene Bolton, who edited and translated *Kino's Historical Memoir of Pimeria Alta, 1683–1710,* 2 vols., and wrote *Rim of Christendom, A Biography of Eusebio Francisco Kino,* plus a condensed version in *The Padre on Horseback.* My main source on Marquette is Joseph P. Donnelly, S.J., *Jacques Marquette, S.J., 1636–1675;* Raphael N. Hamilton, S.J., in *Marquette's Explorations: Narratives Reexamined,* weighs the evidence on the validity or invalidity of certain documents. Margaret and Stephen Bunson, *Faith in the Wilderness: The Story of the Catholic Indian Missions,* is a comprehensive survey. For the accomplishments of Fr. Buechel I rely on Ross Alexander Enochs, *The Jesuit Mission to the Lakota Sioux* and material by Raymond Bucko, S.J., sent by Michael Steltenkamp, S.J.

Notes to Chapter 4

The background of the restoration of the Society is in HSJ, ACE, and AC. Annabelle M. Melville's *John Carroll of Baltimore, Founder of the American Catholic Hierarchy* is the source on Carroll's later thinking about the Society's strengths and weaknesses. Anthony Kohlmann's story is from Francis X. Curran, S.J., *The Return of the Jesuits.* The Adams-Jefferson correspondence is in Lester J. Cappon, ed., *The Adams-Jefferson Letters: The Complete Correspondence between Thomas Jefferson and Abigail and John Adams,* 2 vols.

Notes to Chapter 5

The description of the Ratio and the characteristics of Jesuit education and a typical early Jesuit community at Fordham is drawn partly from TFJ and RAS. Robert Ignatius Burns, S.J., in *The Jesuits and the Indian Wars of the Northwest,* and Wilfred P. Schoenberg, S.J., in *Paths to the Northwest: A Jesuit History of the Oregon Province,* give sweeping narratives of various Jesuit enterprises in the Northwest, with considerable attention to Peter de Smet. John J. Killoran, S.J., in *"Come, Blackrobe": De Smet and the Indian Tragedy,* emphasizes the failure of U.S. Indian policy. John Upton Terrell, *Black Robe: The Life of Pierre-Jean DeSmet,*

Explorer and Pioneer, is good popular biography, but without documentation. For the story of the Italian influence, see Gerald McKevitt, S.J., "Northwest Indian Evangelization by European Jesuits," *Catholic Historical Review,* 91, October 2005. The basic essay on the selling of Jesuit slaves is Robert Emmett Curran, S.J., "Splendid Poverty: Jesuit Slaveholding in Maryland, 1805–1838," *Catholics in the Old South: Essays on Church and Culture* and in *The Bicentennial History of Georgetown,* vol. 1. Edward F. Beckett, S.J., adds information and interpretation to Curran in "Listening to Our History: Inculturation and Jesuit Slaveholding," *Studies in the Spirituality of Jesuits,* 28/5 November 1996. Cyprian Davis, S./S.B. adds context in "Black Catholics in Nineteenth-Century America," *U.S. Catholic Historian,* 5, 1, 1966. For the piety of Fathers Weninger and Wigel, see John McGreevy, *Catholicism and American Freedom: A History* (hereafter CAF). For John Bapst see *Woodstock Letters,* 16, 17, 18 20, 33, and Donald F. Crosby, S.J., "Jesuits Go Home: The Anti-Jesuit Movement in the United States, 1830–1869, *WL,* 97, 1968. The letters of John Bapst on the establishment of Saint Peter's College in Jersey City are in Richard J. Cronin, S.J., *The Jesuits and the Beginning of Saint Peter's College.*

Notes to Chapter 6

The story of Robert Gould Shaw's college experience is longer in RAS. That book is based on the war letters and commentary in *Blue-Eyed Child of Fortune: The Civil War Letters of Colonel Robert Gould Shaw,* edited by Russel Duncan, and on Shaw's earlier letters published in *Robert Gould Shaw, Letters,* in the New York Public Library. The adventures of Peter Tissot and Michael Nash are also in RAS, and based on WL, Tissot in vols. 14, 19, 43, and 45, Nash in vols. 14 through 19. The broader analysis of the Catholic Church during the war is from *CAF,* including the story of Archbishop John B. Purcell in Cincinnati. David R. Dunigan, S.J., describes the Civil War lifestyle at Boston College in *A History of Boston College.* The mood on the Georgetown campus, plus most of the Georgetown history and Patrick Healy, S.J., biography is based on R. Emmet Curran's *Bicentennial History of Georgetown.* The St. Louis and part of the Cincinnati accounts are from Gilbert J. Garraghan, S.J., *The Jesuits of the Middle United States,* vol. 3, while the Santa Clara scenes are in Gerald McKevitt, *The University of Santa Clara, A History, 1851–1977. A Frenchman, a Chaplain, a Rebel: The War Letters of Pere Louis-Hippolyte, S.J.,* translated and edited by Cornelius M. Buckley, S.J., presents the Jesuit chaplaincy from the Southern point of view. The "Tartuffian" characterization of Bixio is Buckley's. The considerations of Patrick Healy's motivations and feelings, based on letters in the Archives of the Maryland Province of the Society of Jesus, the quotations from those letters, along with the description of his later life and the attitudes of his family, draws on James O'Toole, *Passing for White: Race, Religion, and the Healy Family, 1820–1930.*

Notes to Chapter 7

Most of the history of early Woodstock College is based on Edmund Granville Ryan, S.J.'s "An Academic History of Woodstock College in Maryland (1869–1944): The First Jesuit Seminary in America," his unpublished doctoral dissertation for the Catholic University of America, Washington, D.C., 1964. My copy is borrowed from the Woodstock Collection in the Georgetown University Library. I have also gone back to his sources in *WL*, as indicated in the text. The descriptions of the buildings, grounds, countryside, and course of studies are also based on my experience. I was the editor of *WL* from 1966 to 1967. The fullest account of the German Jesuit experience in New York and the Midwest is Francis X. Curran's *The Return of the Jesuits.* Gilbert J. Garraghan, S.J., *The Jesuits of the Middle United States,* vol. 3, treats the establishments of each of the colleges, particularly in chap. 40, "The Colleges." I rely on him when histories of the individual institutions are not available. James Brady's *The First Hundred Years: Canisius College, 1870–1970* is helpful. Cleveland's St. Ignatius College changed its name to John Carroll University. See Donald P. Gavin, *John Carroll University: A Century of Service.* My summary of the intellectual and church-state currents of the end of the century is a combination of ACE, CAF, ACS&S, and AC. Cardinal Mazzella appears in Ryan, the other histories, and WL. Joseph P. Conroy, S.J.'s *Arnold Damen, S.J.* is a hagiographic biography that includes several legends he might believe. Several long letters between Damen and his superiors which I have quoted are included in the Chicago section of Garraghan.

Notes to Chapter 8

The main source for this chapter is Kathleen A. Mahoney, *Catholic Higher Education in Protestant America: The Jesuits and Harvard in the Age of the University.* The summary of the two young Jesuits' imaginary trip is based on Garraghan, vol. 3, chaps 37, 38, and 40. A much shorter version of the Boston College–Harvard controversy is in Charles F. Donovan, S.J., David R. Dunigan, S.J., and Paul Fitzgerald, S.J., *History of Boston College from the Beginnings to 1990.* The analysis of the quality of Jesuit intellectual life is partly from Marianne Gallagher, "The Jesuits at Boston College in the Late 19th Century," Master of Theology thesis, director John W. O'Malley, S.J., Weston School of Theology, 2003. The quote from modernist William Laurence Sullivan is in R. Scott Appleby, *"Church and Age Unite!"* For an evaluation of Anthony J. Mass, S.J., and

Walter Drum, S.J., see Gerald P. Fogarty, S.J., *American Catholic Biblical Scholarship: A History from the Early Republic to Vatican II*. An admiring biography of Father Drum is Joseph Gorayeb, S.J., *The Life and Letters of Walter Drum, S.J.* This includes the description of his teaching at Woodstock.

Notes to Chapter 9

Along with the bound volumes of *America*, the fiftieth anniversary special issue, April 11, 1959, contains a wealth of historical reflections by the editors. Especially, for this chapter, see the lead article by Thurston N. Davis, S.J., "What Is *America?*" and John LaFarge's "Views of a Country Pastor." I also have my recollections from several years as a scholastic summer editor and socio-literary columnist in the late 1960s. I have used John LaFarge's autobiography, *The Manner Is Ordinary*, mainly for his early priesthood years; but, since LaFarge is often not very forthcoming, for the years of controversy, including early *America* years, the development of his ideas on race, and the encyclical, the best source is David W. Southern, *John LaFarge and the Limits of Catholic Interracialism 1911–1963*. Peter McDonough covers much of the same territory in *Men Astutely Trained* but with a slightly different analysis. McDonough's history, which also develops the interaction of Fathers LaFarge, Lord, Walsh, Maher, and Dunne, and the West Baden meetings, is very useful. The story of LaFarge's disappointment with Fordham's reluctance to integrate the college is also in RAS. Daniel Lord's *Played by Ear* is not so much an autobiography as a collection of his reflections. Thomas F. Gavin, S.J.'s biography of Lord, *Champion of Youth* is reverential and admiring, but critical in acknowledging both the hostility Lord encountered within the Society and Lord's shortcomings as an administrator at the end of his career. George Dunne, S.J.'s memoir, *King's Pawn*, is widely considered one of the best books by an American Jesuit. The story of Dunne's encounter at St. Louis U. is recounted in Dunne, Southern, McDonough, and most recently in Paul J. Shore, "The Message and the Messenger: The Untold Story of Father Claude Heithaus and the Integration of Saint Louis University," in *Trying Times: Essays on Catholic Higher Education in the 20th Century*, edited by William M. Shea.

Notes to Chapter 10

The opening summary history of Jesuit chaplains relies on Gerard F. Giblin, S.J., *Jesuits as Chaplains in the Armed Forces, 1917–1960*. Fr. Herbert P. McNally's letters are from WL (71), while the anonymous account of the battle in Holland is in *WL* (74). From there on, the principal source is Donald Crosby, S.J., *Battlefield Chaplains: Catholic Priests in World War II*. I have, however, augmented Crosby's account of the *Franklin* with details from Joseph T. O'Callahan, S.J.'s *I Was Chaplain on the Franklin*. The commentary on the anti-Japanese attitudes of some chaplains is based on Crosby. In the section on Zacheus J. Maher, S.J., the opening picture of St. Andrew-on-Hudson is from the author's experience. The Mrs. Roosevelt story is a legend, but plausible. The text of Maher's "Memorial of the Informal Visitation of the American Assistancy" can be found in the files or house libraries of those American Jesuit houses that have preserved it.

Notes to Chapter 11

The outline of the postwar era leans on John Tracy Ellis's chapter, the "triumph" of Catholic culture, and takes material from *ACS&S*, with additional material on the labor schools from Peter McDonough's *Men Astutely Trained*. The story of Fr. Terence Shealy, S.J., is also in RAS. James T. Fisher, in "John M Corridan, S.J., and the Battle for the Soul of the Waterfront, 1948–1954," tells the Corridan story in *U.S. Catholic Historian* 16 (Fall 1998) and again in *Company*, Summer 2003. The additional material on Phil Carey, S.J., is from MacDonough and the author's recollections. The story of Cardinal Spellman's meeting with Corridan is in *ACS&S*. C. J. McNaspy's biography of Louis J. Twomey, S.J., *At Face Value*, is based largely on research by John Payne, S.J., with an introduction by Walker Percy and Afterword by David Boileau, plus some recollections by the author. Joseph Fichter, S.J., tells his own story, including a chapter on the suppression of *Southern Parish* research, in *One Man Research*, while Bentley Anderson, S.J., *Black, White, and Catholic: New Orleans Interracialism, 1947–1956*, supplies the context and narrative frame for Fichter's story. Edmund A. Walsh, S.J.'s story is in *A Catholic Cold War*, by Patrick McNamara, while the Iraq aspect of his career relies on Joseph F. MacDonnell, S.J., *Jesuits by the Tigris: Men for Others in Baghdad*. George H Dunne, S.J., tells his own story in *King's Pawn*. For Joseph R. McCarthy at Marquette and another analysis of the meeting between Edmund Walsh and McCarthy, see Thomas C. Reeves, *The Life and Times of Joe McCarthy*. The most thorough study of the relationship between McCarthy and Catholicism and the specifics of the internal Jesuit battle over McCarthy is Donald F. Crosby, S.J., *God, Church, and Flag*.

Notes to Chapter 12

The account of the Shadowbrook fire is based on a series of articles by F. X. Shea, S.J., in the *SJNews*, the monthly newspaper of the New England Province, December 1973 to June 1974, and on my interviews with two of the survivors, Joseph Appleyard, S.J., and John J. Higgins, S.J. The introductory overview of American higher education after World War II is based first on Richard Freeland's *Academia's Golden Age,* then on William P. Leahy, S.J., *Adapting to America,* and Paul A. Fitzgerald, *The Governance of Jesuit Colleges in the United States, 1920–1970.* The particular role of Loyola Chicago University is from Lester F. Goodchild, "The Turning Point in American Jesuit Higher Education: The Standardization Controversy between the Jesuits and the North Central Association, 1915–1940," *History of Higher Education Annual* 6 (1986). The Report of the Commission on Higher Studies of the American Assistancy of the Society of Jesus, 1931–1932, also known as the Macelwane Report, is an unpublished manuscript available only in some Jesuit archives. I was able to study it through the cooperation of the Association of Jesuit Colleges and Universities, Washington, D.C., and the archives of Boston College. The best commentary on the report is William M. Shea, "Jesuits and Scholarship," in *Trying Times: Essays on Catholic Higher Education in the 20th Century.* The story of Fordham's loss of accreditation and the history of Shrub Oak are in RAS. What Theologian Frank would have learned at Fordham from Fathers Donceel and Ewing is based on my conversations with those men. The information on Loyola Marymount in the 1950s draws on Michael E. Engh, S.J., "History of Loyola Marymount University," in the LMU Faculty Handbook. Father Burchard Villager, S.J.'s contribution to Santa Clara and St. Joseph's is in David R. Contosa, *Saint Joseph's, Philadelphia's Jesuit University 150 Years.* Gerald McKevitt, S.J.'s *The University of Santa Clara* is also the source for that material and for the first part of the paragraphs on Bernard Hubbard, S.J. The story about Douglas MacArthur and Hubbard's illness is based on A. D. Spearman, S.J.'s obituary of Hubbard in *WL.* George Dunne's experience with Hubbard is in Dunne's *King's Pawn.* Alan Ziajka's *Legacy and Promise* recounts the University of San Francisco's "golden age," and the earthquake and aftermath. The Catalbo story is based on both Gerald McKevitt, S.J.'s "'The Jump That Saved the Rocky Mountain Mission': Jesuit Recruitment and the Pacific Northwest," in *The Pacific Historical Review,* and Walt Crowley's *Seattle University.* Wilfred P. Schoenberg, S.J.'s *Gonzaga University* provides the context for the story of Bing Crosby's relationship with Gonzaga, including his participation in building the library, while Gary Giddins's *Bing Crosby: A Pocketful of Dreams, The Early Years* gives the details of Crosby's student life. William J. Sullivan, S.J.'s introduction is in Walt Crowley's *Seattle University.*

Notes to Chapter 13

The statistics on the number of Jesuits come from the Jesuit Curia in Rome. Samuel K. Wilson, S.J.'s quote is from Lester Goodchild's PhD dissertation for the University of Chicago in 1986, "The Mission of the Catholic University in the Midwest, 1842–1980." With other sources, I rely on Jean Lacouture's *Jesu-*

its: A Multibiography for both the historical context of the 1940s and 1950s, his interpretation of the Society's situation, and for some information on the life of Teilhard de Chardin and the role of Karl Rahner. Among other articles on Teilhard, see Thomas M. King, S.J., "A Holy Man and Lover of the World," *America*, March 28, 2005; Joe Orso, "Pierre Teilhard deChardin, S.J.: A Visionary's Influence Still Felt Today," *Company*, Winter, 2005; and the *America* editorial, March 28, 2005. The condition of biblical scholarship, again, relies on Gerald Fogarty, S.J., *American Catholic Biblical Scholarship: A History from the Early Republic to Vatican II*. The quotes from Vatican II documents come from Walter M. Abbott, S.J., *The Documents of Vatican II* (1966), a marvelous feat of publishing, appearing right after the Council with commentaries from scholars involved in their composition. The survey of the relationship between French and American intellectualism is guided by John T. McGreevy's *CAF*. The Gannon-Maritain story is in RAS. Both Teilhard and Rahner are profiled in my *Dante to Dead Man Walking*, and I have repeated some of those ideas. More recent articles on Rahner include James Bacik, "Is Rahner Obsolete?" *Commonweal*, January 28, 2005; Leo O'Donovan, "Losing Oneself and Finding God," *America*, November 8, 2004; as well as the chapter in Ronald Modras, *Ignatian Humanism*. John Deedy's chapters on Leonard Feeney and John Courtney Murray in *Seven American Catholics* are ideal personal portraits of those men. I lived on-and-off with Murray and Walter Burghardt at Woodstock and made my ordination retreat under Murray. Recent appreciations of Murray include Robert W. McElroy, "He Hold These Truths," *America*, February 7, 2005, and Gregory A. Kalsheur, "American Catholics and the State," *America*, August 29, 2004. For the most thorough analysis of Murray's social thought and the step-by-step reasoning that brought him to his conclusions, see J. Leon Hooper, S.J., *The Ethics of Discourse: The Social Philosophy of John Courtney Murray*. Since Murray died before he could update "The Dangers of the Vows" in the spirit of Vatican II for publication, David J. Casey, S.J., reconstructed the talk from two of Murray's personal copies, one with Murray's own handwritten emendations, together with a number of slightly varying mimeographed copies.

Notes to Chapter 14

The story of Walter Ciszek is based on Walter J. Ciszek, S.J., with Daniel L. Flaherty, S.J., *With God in Russia*, and the same authors' *He Leadeth Me*, plus George M. Anderson's "Jesuits in Jail: Ignatius to the Present," *Studies in the Spirituality of Jesuits*, September 1995. The general summary of the Vatican Council II draws on Richard P. McBrien, ed., *Encyclopedia of Catholicism*, and the summary of the 1960s uses James T. Patterson's *Grand Expectations, The*

United States, 1945–1974. The descriptions of Woodstock College in the 1960s come from the author's experience. For the histories of the General Congregations, see John W. Padberg, S.J., *Together as a Companionship: A History of the Thirty-First, Thirty-Second, and Thirty-Third General Congregations of the Society of Jesus.* For a good biographical note on Pedro Arrupe and a collection of his speeches, see Pedro Arrupe, S.J., *A Planet to Heal.* Arrupe's personal account of Hiroshima is in *The Catholic Worker,* August–September 2005, and in *Pedro Arrupe: Essential Writings,* edited by Kevin Burke, S.J. The material on the background of the congregation concerning Pope Paul VI is in Manfred Barthel, *The Jesuits;* Lacouture, *Jesuits: A Multibiography;* and Peter Hebblethwaite, *Paul VI: The First Modern Pope.* On the generation gap, "The Trouble with the Younger Men" in WL was by this author. The profiles of the men in the 11 interviews in George Riemer's *The New Jesuits* were supplemented by information from an interview with Walter Ong, S.J., by Robert J. Imbs, S.J., in 1977, transcribed by Wilburn Stancil of Rockhurst University; and Murray Polner and Jim O'Grady, *Disarmed and Dangerous: The Radical Lives and Times of Daniel and Philip Berrigan.* The statistics and analysis of men leaving the Society come from Joseph M. Becker, S.J., "Changes in the U.S. Jesuit Membership, 1958–1975: A Symposium," *Studies in the Spirituality of Jesuits,* January and March 1977. The comments by Robert F. Harvenek, S.J., and James J. Gill, S.J., are in the symposium. The history of the moves of the seminaries and the changes in formation are based on Becker's *The Re-Formed Jesuits.* The numbers of Jesuits at ten-year intervals are from the Curia in Rome and from the Jesuit Conference in Washington, D.C. Garry Wills's article on Woodstock in *New York* is republished as a chapter in *Bare Ruined Choirs.* The roles of John Ford, S.J., and Gerald Kelly, S.J., in the contraception debate are in both Leslie Woodcock Tentler's *Catholics and Contraception* and CAF. Charles E. Curran summarizes Richard A. McCormick's career in "Notes on Richard A. McCormick," *Theological Studies* 61 (2000). Additional details on McCormick's personality are from his friend Philip C. Rule, S.J., and the author's experience. The story of the Jesuit response to Cardinal Boyle's disciplining of the Washington priests comes from John S. Monagan's *Horace, Priest of the Poor,* his biography of Horace McKenna, and from documents in the author's possession, and the author's participation. The events at Fordham during the leadership of Leo McLaughlin are in the author's history of Fordham. The background of the move toward separate incorporation is in Alice Gallin, O.S.U., *Negotiating Modernity,* and Paul A. Fitzgerald, *The Governance of Jesuit Colleges in the United States, 1920–1970.* The events at Boston College come from Richard M. Freeland, *Academia's Golden Age,* and at Holy Cross from Anthony J. Kuzniewski, S.J., *Thy Honored Name.* For Seattle, see Walt Crowley, *Seattle University: A Century of Jesuit Education.*

Notes to Chapter 15

Most of the account of the 32nd General Congregation draws on John W. Pad-berg's "The Society True to Itself: A Brief History of the 32nd General Congregation of the Society of Jesus," in *Studies*, May–September 1983. The background information concerning the meetings with Paul VI draws on Peter Hebblethwaite's *Paul VI* and Lacouture's *Jesuits*. Lacouture also gives an account of Arrupe's removal. Vincent O'Keefe, S.J., also gave an account in the Jesuit newsletter *News and Features*, May 2005. David Gibson's *The Rule of Benedict* has up-to-date scholarship on both John Paul II's treatment of Arrupe, the killing of the El Salvador Jesuits, and on the removal of Fr. Thomas Reese from *America*. Simon Hendry's doctoral dissertation, "Ruined for Life," is both a history of the Jesuit Volunteer Corps' founding and an analysis of its spirituality. Jeff Theilman's *Volunteer with the Poor in Peru*, cowritten with this author, recounts his Peru experience. He followed up in correspondence with this author. George Kearney's writings, including his unfinished history of Cristo Rey and his summary for *Partners* magazine, were most helpful. A summary of Avery Dulles's career is this author's "His Father's Son, *Fordham* magazine, Fall 1998. See also Mike Forde, "Fordham Jesuit First U.S. Theologian Made Cardinal," *The Ram*, Fordham University, January 25, 2001. For negative books and articles on the Society, including accusations of homosexuality, see James Hitchcock, *The Pope and the Jesuits*; Malachi Martin, *The Jesuits*; Paul Shaughnessy, S.J., "The Gay Priest Problem," *Catholic World Report*, November 2000, and "Are the Jesuits Catholic?" *Weekly Standard*, May 3, 2002. For a Cardinal Newman Society article, see Patrick J. Reilly, "How Catholic Is Georgetown University?" *Catholic World Report*, April 2006. The statistics on the Society in America come by courtesy of Thomas Gaunt, S.J., Jesuit Conference in Washington, D.C. Those on higher education are from Fr. Charles L. Currie, S.J., and his staff at the Association of Jesuit Colleges and Universities; on secondary education, from the JSEA Web site. On Regis, see Ronald S. Brockway, *Regis: Beyond the Crest*; on Detroit-Mercy, see Herman J. Muller, S.J., *Legacy of Excellence*, plus a talk on UDM's mission by John M. Staudenmaier, S.J. Larry Lorenz describes the reaction of the New Orleans Province to Hurricane Katrina in *Conversations* magazine, Spring 2006. *Everybody's Challenge*, published by the JRS in Rome, contains the Essential Documents of the Jesuit Refugee Service, 1980–2000. Peter Schineller, S.J.'s article on the plane crash in Nigeria is in *America*, May 8, 2006. Karl Rahner's "Ignatius of Loyola Speaks to a Modern Jesuit" is in his book, *Ignatius of Loyola* (1979). Fr. William Byron, S.J.'s writings contributed to the summary of what the Jesuit future might hold.

Select Bibliography

Abbott, S.J., Walter, ed. *The Documents of Vatican II*. New York: Guild Press, America Press, Association Press.

Anderson, S.J., Bentley. *Black, White, and Catholic: New Orleans Interracialism, 1947–1956*. Nashville: Vanderbilt University Press, 2005.

Appleby, R. Scott. *"Church and Age Unite!"* Notre Dame: University of Notre Dame Press, 1992.

Arrupe, Pedro, S.J. *A Planet to Heal*. Rome: International Center for Jesuit Education, 1977.

Axtell, James. *The Invasion Within: The Conquest of Cultures in Colonial North America*. New York: Oxford University Press, 1985.

———. *After Columbus: Essays in the Ethnohistory of Colonial North America*. New York: Oxford University Press, 1990.

Bangert, S.J., William V. *A History of the Society of Jesus*. St. Louis: Institute of Jesuit Sources, 1972.

Barthel, Manfred, translated and adapted by Mark Howson. *The Jesuits: History and Legend of the Society of Jesus*. New York: William Morrow, 1982.

Becker, S.J., Joseph M. *The Re-Formed Jesuits*. Vol. I: *A History of Changes in Jesuit Formation during the Decade 1965–1975*. San Francisco: Ignatius Press, 1992.

———. "Changes in U.S. Jesuit Membership, 1958–1975: A Symposium." *Studies in the Spirituality of Jesuits*, January and March 1977.

Beckett, S.J., Edward F. "Listening to Our History: Inculturation and Jesuit Slaveholding." *Studies in the Spirituality of Jesuits* 28/5 (November 1996).

Bolton, Herbert Eugene. *Rim of Christendom: A Biography of Eusebio Francisco Kino, Pacific Coast Pioneer*. New York: Macmillan, 1936.

———. *The Padre on Horseback*. Chicago: Loyola University Press, 1963.

———. ed. and trans. *Kino's Historical Memoir of Pimeria Alta, 1683–1711*. 2 vols. Cleveland: Arthur Clark, 1919.

Brady, Charles A. *The First Hundred Years: Canisius College, 1870–1970*. Buffalo: Canisius College, 1969.

Brockway, Ronald S. *Regis, Beyond the Crest*. Denver: Regis University, 2003.

Bunson, Margaret and Stephen. *Faith in the Wilderness: The Story of the Catholic Indian Missions*. Huntington, Indiana: Our Sunday Visitor Publishing Division, 2000.

Burghardt, S.J., Walter. "A Half Century of Theological Studies: Retrospect and Prospect." *Theological Studies* 50 (1989).

Burns, S.J., Robert Ignatius. *The Jesuits and the Indian Wars of the Northwest.* New Haven: Yale University Press, 1966.

Califano, Jr., Joseph A. *Inside: A Public and Private Life.* New York: Public Affairs, 2004.

Capizzi, Joseph E. "For What Shall We Repent? Reflections on the American Bishops, Their Teaching, and Slavery in the United States, 1839–1866," *Theological Studies* 65 (2004).

Cappon, Lester J., ed. *The Adams-Jefferson Letters: The Complete Correspondence between Thomas Jefferson and Abigail and John Adams.* 2 vols. Chapel Hill: University of North Carolina Press, 1959.

Ciszek, S.J., Walter J., with Daniel L. Flaherty, S.J. *With God in Russia.* New York: McGraw-Hill, 1964.

———. *He Leadeth Me.* Garden City, NY: Doubleday, 1973.

Conley, Rory T. *The Truth in Charity: A History of the Archdiocese of Washington.* Strasbourg, France: Editions duSigne, 2000.

Conroy, S.J. Joseph P. *Arnold Damen, S.J.: A Chapter in the Making of Chicago.* New York: Benziger Brothers, 1930.

Contosta, David R. *Saint Joseph's: Philadelphia's Jesuit University, 150 Years.* Philadelphia: Saint Joseph's University Press, 2000.

Coppleston, S.J., Frederick. *A History of Philosophy.* Garden City, NY: Doubleday, 1962 (1952).

Cronin, S.J., Richard J. *The Jesuits and the Beginning of Saint Peter's College.* Jersey City, NJ: Saint Peter's College, Peacock Press.

Crosby, S.J., Donald F. *God, Church, and Flag: Senator Joseph R. McCarthy and the Catholic Church, 1950–1957.* Chapel Hill: University of North Carolina Press, 1978.

———. *Battlefield Chaplains: Catholic Priests in World War II.* Lawrence: University of Kansas Press, 1994.

———. "Jesuits Go Home: The Anti-Jesuit Movement in the United States, 1830–1860." *Woodstock Letters* 97 (1968).

Crowley, Walt. *William J Sullivan, S.J.: A Celebration of Seattle University's Renaissance during 20 Years under its 20th President.* Seattle: Seattle University, 1996.

———. *Seattle University, a Century of Jesuit Education.* Seattle: Seattle University, 1991.

Curran, Charles E., ed. *Moral Theology: Challenges for the Future, Essays in Honor of Richard A. McCormick, S.J.* New York: Paulist Press, 1990.

———. "Notes on Richard A. McCormick." *Theological Studies* 61 (2000).

Curran, S.J., Francis X. *The Return of the Jesuits.* Chicago: Loyola University Press, 1966.

Curran, S.J., Robert Emmett, ed. *American Jesuit Spirituality: The Maryland Tra-dition, 1634–1900.* New York: Paulist Press, 1988.

———. *The Bicentennial History of Georgetown.* Vol. 1: *From Academy to University.* Washington, D.C.: Georgetown University Press, 1993.

———. " 'Splendid Poverty': Jesuit Slaveholding in Maryland, 1805–1838." In *Catholics in the Old South: Essays on Church and Culture.* Macon, GA: Mercer University Press, 1983.

———, Gerald P. Fogarty, S.J., and Joseph T. Durkin, S.J. *The Maryland Jesuits, 1634–1833.* Baltimore: Maryland Province of the Society of Jesus, 1976.

Davis, O.S.B., Cyprian. "Black Catholics in 19th Century America." *U.S. Catholic Historian* 5 (1966).

Decrees of General Congregation 34. Rome: Curia of the Superior General, 1995.

Deedy, John. *Seven American Catholics.* Chicago: Thomas More Press, 1978.

Dolan, Jay P. *The American Catholic Experience: A History from Colonial Times to the Present.* New York: Doubleday, 1985.

Donnelly, S.J., Joseph P. *Jacques Marquette, S.J., 1636–1675.* Chicago: Loyola University Press, 1968.

Donovan, S.J., Charles F., David R. Dunigan, S.J., and Paul A. Fitzgerald, S.J. *History of Boston College from the Beginnings to 1990.* Chestnut Hill, MA: University Press of Boston College, 1990.

Dunigan, S.J., David R. *A History of Boston College.* Milwaukee: Bruce, 1947.

Dunne, S.J., George H. *King's Pawn.* Chicago: Loyola University Press, 1990.

Dunne, S.J., Peter Masten. *Pioneer Jesuits in Northern Mexico.* Los Angeles: University of California Press, 1944.

Ellis, John Tracy. *American Catholicism.* Chicago: University of Chicago Press, 1969.

———. *Perspectives in American Catholicism.* Baltimore· Helicon, 1963.

———. "American Catholics and the Intellectual Life." *Thought,* Autumn 1955.

Engh, S.J., Michael E. "History of Loyola Marymount University." From the LMU Faculty Handbook. Unpublished ms.

Enochs, Ross Alexander. *The Jesuit Mission to the Lakota Sioux.* Kansas City: Sheed and Ward, 1996.

Everybody's Challenge: Essential Documents of Jesuit Refugee Service, 1980–2000. Rome: Jesuit Refugee Service, 2000.

Faherty, S.J., William B. *Better the Dream, Saint Louis: University and Community, 1818–1968.* St. Louis, MO: Saint Louis University Press, 1968.

———. *Men to Remember: Jesuit Teachers at Saint Louis University, 1829–1979.* St. Louis, MO: Saint Louis University Press, 1997.

Farley, S.J., Michael A. "Farewell from the Editor's Desk." *Theological Studies* 66 (December 2005), 735–738.

Fichter, Joseph H. *One-Man Research: Reminiscences of a Catholic Sociologist.* New York: John Wiley and Sons, 1973.

Fisher, James T. "John M. Corridan, S.J., and the Battle for the Soul of the Waterfront, 1948–1954." *U.S. Catholic Historian* 16 (Fall 1998).

Fitzgerald, S.J., Paul A. *The Governance of Jesuit Colleges in the United States, 1920–1970.* Notre Dame, IN: University of Notre Dame Press, 1984.

Fogarty, S.J., Gerald F. *American Catholic Biblical Scholarship: A History from the Early Republic to Vatican II.* San Francisco: Harper and Row, 1989.

Foley, S.J., Albert S. *Bishop Healy: Beloved Outcaste.* New York: Farrar, Straus and Young, 1954.

———. "Adventures in Black Catholic History: Research and Writing," *U.S. Catholic Historian* 5 (1981).

Freeland, Richard M. *Academia's Golden Age.* New York: Oxford University Press, 1992.

Gache, S.J., Pere Louis-Hippolyte. *A Frenchman, a Chaplain, a Rebel: The War Letters of Pere Louis-Hippolyte Gache, S.J.* Trans. Cornelius M. Buckley, S.J. Chicago: Loyola University Press, 1981.

Gallagher, Marianne. "The Jesuits at Boston College in the 19th Century." Master of Theology thesis. Weston School of Theology, 2003.

Gallin, Alice, O.S.U. *Negotiating Identity.* Notre Dame, IN: University of Notre Dame Press, 2000.

Ganss, S.J., George, ed. *Ignatius of Loyola: The Spiritual Exercises and Selected Works.* New York: Paulist Press, 1991.

———. *The Jesuit Educational Tradition and Saint Louis University.* St. Louis, MO: Saint Louis University Press, 1969.

Garraghan, S.J., Gilbert J. *The Jesuits of the Middle United States.* 3 vols. New York: America Press, 1938.

Gavin, Donald P. *John Carroll University: A Century of Service.* Kent, OH: Kent State University Press, 1985.

Gavin, S.J., Thomas F. *Champion of Youth: A Dynamic Story of a Dynamic Man, Daniel A. . Lord, S.J.* Boston: St. Paul, 1977.

Giblin, S.J., Gerard F. *Jesuits as Chaplains in the Armed Forces, 1917–1960.* Woodstock, Maryland: Woodstock College Press, 1961.

Gibson, David. *The Rule of Benedict.* New York: HarperCollins, 2006.

Giddins, Gary. *Bing Crosby: A Pocketful of Dreams. The Early Years, 1903–1940.* New York: Little, Brown, 2001.

Gleason, Philip. *Contending with Modernity: Catholic Higher Education in the Twentieth Century.* New York: Oxford University Press, 1995.

———. *Keeping the Faith: American Catholicism Past and Present.* Notre Dame, IN: University of Notre Dame Press, 1987.

———. "The First Century of Jesuit Education in America: An Overview." Unpublished paper given at the American Catholic Historical Association, March 1976.

Goodchild, Lester Francis. "The Mission of the Catholic University in the Midwest, 1842–1980: A Comparative Case Study of the Effects of Strategic Policy Decisions upon the Mission of the University of Notre Dame, Loyola University of Chicago, and DePaul University." PhD dissertation, Department of Education, University of Chicago, 1986.

———. "The Turning Point in American Jesuit Higher Education: The Standardization Controversy between Jesuits and the North Central Association, 1915–1940." *History of Higher Education Annual* 6 (1986), 81–116.

Gorayeb, S.J., Joseph. *The Life and Letters of Walter Drum, S.J.* New York: America Press, 1928.

Greer, Allan. *Mohawk Saint: Catherine Tekakwitha and the Jesuits.* New York: Oxford University Press, 2005.

Halsey, William M. *The Survival of American Innocence: Catholics, in an Era of Disillusionment, 1920–1940.* Notre Dame, IN: University of Notre Dame Press, 1980.

Hamilton, S.J., Raphael N. *Marquette's Explorations: The Narratives Reexamined.* Madison: University of Wisconsin Press, 1970.

Harrington, Michael. *Fragments of a Century.* New York: Simon and Schuster, 1972.

Hebblethwaite, Peter. *Paul VI: The First Modern Pope.* New York: Paulist Press, 1992.

Hendry, S.J., Simon. "'Ruined for Life': The Spirituality of the Jesuit Volunteer Corps." PhD dissertation, Graduate Theological Union, Berkeley, California, 2002.

Hennesey, S.J. *American Catholics: A History of the Roman Catholic Community in the United States.* New York: Oxford University Press, 1981.

Himes, O.F.M., Kenneth R., ed. *Modern Catholic Social Teaching: Commentaries and Interpretations.* Washington, D.C.: Georgetown University Press, 2004.

Hitchcock, James. *The Pope and the Jesuits.* New York: National Committee of Catholic Laymen, 1984.

Hooper, S.J., J. Leon. *The Ethics of Discourse: The Social Philosophy of John Courtney Murray.* Washington, D.C.: Georgetown University Press, 1986.

Hughes, Thomas. *History of the Society of Jesus in North America,* vol. 1: *Colonial and Federal.* New York: Longmans, Green, 1907.

Idigoras, S.J., Jose Ignacio Telechea. *Ignatius of Loyola: The Pilgrim Saint.* Trans. Michael Buckley, S.J. Chicago: Loyola University Press, 1944.

Kearney, George. "Risk and Reward." *Partners,* magazine of the Jesuit Chicago Province.

Kennedy, J. H. *Jesuit and Savage in New France.* New Haven: Yale University Press, 1950.

Kenny, S.J., Michael. *The Romance of the Floridas: The Finding and the Founding.* New York: AMS Press, 1934 (1970).

———. *Pedro Martinez, S.J., Martyr of Florida, 1566.* Pamphlet.

Killoran, S.J., John J. *"Come, Blackrobe": DeSmet and the Indian Tragedy.* St. Louis: Institute of Jesuit Sources, 2003.

Krugler, John D. *English and Catholic: The Lords Baltimore in the Seventeenth Century.* Baltimore: Johns Hopkins University Press, 2004.

Kuzniewski, S.J., Anthony J. *Thy Honored Name: A History of the College of the Holy Cross, 1843–1994.* Washington, D.C.: Catholic University of America Press, 1999.

Lacouture, Jean. *Jesuits: A Multibiography.* Trans. Jeremy Legatt. Washington, D.C.: Counterpoint, 1995.

LaFarge, S.J., John. *The Manner Is Ordinary.* New York: Harcourt, Brace, 1954.

———, and Margaret Bourke-White. *A Report on the American Jesuits.* New York: Farrar, Straus and Cudahy, 1956.

Laveille, S.J., E. *The Life of Father De Smet, S.J.* Trans. Marian Lindsay. Chicago: Loyola University Press (1915), 1981.

Leahy, S.J., William P. *Adapting to America: Catholics, Jesuits, and Higher Education in the Twentieth Century.* Washington, D.C.: Georgetown University Press, 1991.

Leonard, S.J., William J. *Where Thousands Fell.* Kansas City: Sheed and Ward, 1995.

Lord, S.J., Daniel A. *Played by Ear.* Chicago: Loyola University Press, 1956.

MacDonnell, S.J., Joseph F. *Jesuits by the Tigris: Men for Others in Baghdad.* Boston: Jesuit Mission Press, 1994.

———. *If These Stones Could Speak: The Phenomenal Growth of Fairfield University's Campus.* Fairfield: Fairfield University, 1996.

Macdougall, S.J., Angus L. *Brebeuf: A Giant in Huronia.* Midland, Ontario: Martyrs' Shrine, 1970.

———. *Jogues: "This Living Martyr."* Midland, Ontario: Martyrs' Shrine, 1971.

———, ed. *Martyrs of New France.* Midland, Ontario: Martyrs' Shrine, 1972.

Maher, S.J., Zacheus. "Memoriale of the Informal Visitation of the American Assistancy." Unpublished ms., 1943.

Mahoney, Kathleen A. *Catholic Higher Education in Protestant America: The Jesuits and Harvard in the Age of the University.* Baltimore: Johns Hopkins University Press, 2003.

Martin, Malachi. *The Jesuits: The Society of Jesus and the Betrayal of the Roman Catholic Church.* New York: Simon and Schuster, 1987.

Maynard, Theodore. *The Story of American Catholicism.* New York: Macmillan, 1942.

McCoog, S.J., Thomas N., ed. *The Murcurian Project: Forming Jesuit Culture, 1573–1580*. St. Louis, MO: Institute of Jesuit Sources, 2004.

McCormick, S.J., Richard A. *The Critical Calling: Reflections on Moral Dilemmas since Vatican II*. Washington, D.C.: Georgetown University Press, 1989.

McDonough, Peter. *Men Astutely Trained: A History of the Jesuits in the American Century*. New York: Free Press, 1992.

———, and Eugene C. Bianchi. *Passionate Uncertainty: Inside the American Jesuits*. Berkeley: University of California Press, 2004.

McGreevy, John T. *Catholicism and American Freedom: A History*. New York: W. W. Norton, 2003.

McGucken, S.J., William J. *The Jesuits and Education*. New York: Bruce, 1932.

McKevitt, S.J., Gerald. *The University of Santa Clara: A History, 1851–1977*. Stanford, CA: Stanford University Press, 1979.

———. "Northwest Indian Evangelization by European Jesuits." *Catholic Historical Review* 91 (October 2005), 688–713.

———. "Jesuit Higher Education in the United States." *Mid-America, An Historical Review* 73 (October 1991).

———. " 'The Jump That Saved the Rocky Mountain Mission': Jesuit Recruitment and the Pacific Northwest." *Pacific Historical Review* 55 (August 1986).

McNamara, Patrick. *A Catholic Cold War: Edmund A. Walsh, S.J., and the Politics of American Anticommunism*. New York: Fordham University Press, 2005.

McNaspy, S.J., C. J. *At Face Value: A Biography of Father Louis J. Twomey, S.J.* New Orleans: Institute of Human Relations, Loyola University of the South, 1978.

Meissner, S.J., William. *Ignatius of Loyola: The Psychology of A Saint*. New Haven: Yale University Press, 1992.

Melville, Annabelle M. *John Carroll of Baltimore, Founder of the American Catholic Hierarchy*. New York: Charles Scribner's Sons, 1955.

Modras, Ronald. *Ignatian Humanism*. Chicago: Loyola Press, 2004.

Moore, S.J., James T. *Indian and Jesuit: A Seventeenth-Century Encounter*. Chicago: Loyola University Press, 1982.

Morris, Charles R. *American Catholic: The Saints and Sinners Who Built America's Most Powerful Church*. New York: Random House, 1997.

Muller, S.J., Herman J. *Advancing the U of D Legacy: University of Detroit, 1978 to 1990*. Detroit: University of Detroit-Mercy Press, 2003.

Murray, S.J., John Courtney. *We Hold These Truths*. New York: Sheed and Ward, 1960.

———. "The Danger of the Vows." *Woodstock Letters* 96 (Fall 1967).

Naughton, Jim. *Catholics in Crisis*. Reading, MA.: Addison-Wesley, 1996.

O'Callahan, S.J., Joseph. *I Was Chaplain on the Franklin*. New York: Macmillan, 1956.

Odozor, C.S.Sp., Paulinus. *Richard McCormick and the Renewal of Moral Theology*. Notre Dame, IN: University of Notre Dame Press, 1995.

O'Malley, S.J., John W. *The First Jesuits*. Cambridge, MA: Harvard University Press, 1993.

O'Toole, James. *Passing for White: Race, Religion, and the Healy Family, 1820–1930*. Boston: University of Massachusetts Press, 2002.

Padberg, S.J., John W. *Together as a Companionship: A History of the 31st, 32nd, and 33rd General Congregations of the Society of Jesus*. St. Louis, MO: Institute of Jesuit Sources, 1994.

———. "The Society True to Itself: A Brief History of the 32nd General Congregation of the Society of Jesus," December 2, 1974–March 7, 1975. *Studies in the Spirituality of Jesuits*, May–September 1983.

Parkman, Francis. *The Jesuits in North America in the Seventeenth Century*. Williamstown, MA: Corner House Publishers, 1970 (1895).

Patterson, James T. *Grand Expectations*. New York: Oxford University Press, 1996.

Polner, Murray, and Jim O'Grady. *Disarmed and Dangerous*. New York: Basic Books, 1997.

Reeves, Thomas C. *The Life and Times of Joe McCarthy*. New York: Stein and Day, 1992.

Riemer, George. *The New Jesuits*. Boston: Little, Brown, 1971.

Rollings, Willard Hughes. *Unaffected by the Gospel*. Albuquerque: University of New Mexico Press, 2004.

Ryan, S.J., Edmund Granville. "An Academic History of Woodstock College in Maryland (1869–1944): The First Jesuit Seminary in North America." PhD dissertation, Catholic University of America, Washington, D.C., 1964.

Schoenberg, S.J., Wilfred P. *Paths to the Northwest: A Jesuit History of the Oregon Province*. Chicago: Loyola University Press, 1982.

———. *Gonzaga University, Seventy-Five Years, 1887–1962*. Spokane: Gonzaga University, 1963.

Shea, S.J., F. X. "The Shadowbrook Fire." *SJNEews*, December 1973–June 1974.

Shea, William M., ed. *Trying Times: Essays on Catholic Higher Education in the 20th Century*. Tampa: Scholars Press, University of South Florida, 1999.

———. "Jesuits and Scholarship: A Reading of the Macelwane Report." In *Trying Times: Essays on Catholic Higher Education in the 20th Century*. Tampa: Scholars Press, University of South Florida, 1999.

Southern, David W. *John LaFarge and the Limits of Catholic Interracialism, 1911–1963*. Baton Rouge: Louisiana State University Press, 1996.

Spearman, S.J., A. D. "Father Bernard R. Hubbard (1888–1962)." *Woodstock Letters* 94 (Fall 1965).

Stansell, S.J., Harold L. *Regis: On the Crest of the West*. Denver: Regis Educational Corporation, 1977.

Talbot, S.J., Francis. *Saint among Savages: The Life of Isaac Jogues.* New York: Harper and Brothers, 1935.

Tentler, Leslie Woodcock. *Catholics and Contraception: An American History.* Ithaca, NY: Cornell University Press, 2004.

Terrell, John Upton. *Black Robe: The Life of Pierre-Jean DeSmet, Missionary, Explorer and Pioneer.* New York: Doubleday, 1964.

Theilman, Jeff, and Raymond A. Schroth, S.J. *Volunteer with the Poor in Peru.* New York: Paulist Press, 1991.

Thwaites, Reuben Gold, ed. *The Jesuit Relations and Allied Documents: Travels and Explorations of the Jesuit Missionaries in New France, 1610–1791.* 73 vols. Cleveland: Burrows Brothers, 1898.

———. Selected and edited by Edna Kenton. 1 vol. New York: Vanguard Press, 1954.

Wills, Garry. *Bare Ruined Choirs.* Garden City, NY: Doubleday, 1972.

Wright, Jonathan. *God's Soldiers.* New York: Doubleday, 2004.

Zeyen, S.J., Thomas E. *Jesuit Generals: A Glimpse into a Forgotten Corner.* Scranton, PA: Scranton University Press, 2004.

Ziajka, Alan. *Legacy and Promise: 150 Years of Jesuit Education at the University of San Francisco.* San Francisco: University of San Francisco Press, 2005.

Index

Adams, Henry, 119
Adams, John, 57
Al Hikma University, 163–164
Altham, John, S.J., 22
America, xi, 115, 274
American Council on Education (ACE), 180
Aquaviva, Claudius, S.J., 15, 16, 17
Arenz, R. James, S.J., 235
Arrupe, Pedro, 227, 261–266
Association of American Universities (AAU), 179
Association of Catholic Trade Unionists (ACTU), 148
Association of Jesuit Colleges and Universities (AJCU), 281
Auriesville, New York, xii
Axtell, James, 40–41
Azevedo, Ignatius, S.J., 15

Babin, Sr. George Edmond, S.S.A., 267
Baghdad College, 163–164
Baker, Kenneth, S.J., 256
Bangert, William, S.J., 49, 58
Bapst, John, S.J., 73–76
Barnes, Francis, 108
Barrett, Alfred, S.J., 202
Barzun, Jacques, 86
Beckx, Peter, S.J., 88, 93, 98
Behrens, Henry, S.J., 93
Bellarmine School of Theology, 239
Bellarmine, St. Cardinal Robert, S.J., 18
Benedict XIV, 70
Berrigan, Daniel, S.J., 226, 236, 237
Berry, Jason, 273
Birth control crisis, 241–247
Bishops' Plan for Social Reconstruction, 123
Bixio, Joseph, S.J., 82
Blakely, Paul L., S.J., 120

Blueprint for Social Justice, 281
Bobadilla, Nicholas, S.J., 7
Boileau, David, 160
Bolton, Herbert Eugene, 44
Boniface VIII, 210
Borgia, St. Francis, S.J., 19
Boscovich, Roger Joseph, S.J., 50
Boston College, 58, 76, 80, 86, 110
Bourke-White, Margaret, 174, 175
Bradstreet, John, S.J., 136
Brebeuf, St. Jean de, S.J., 28, 29, 31, 36, 37
Brogan, Denis, 203
Brooks, John E., S.J., 253
Brosnahan, Timothy, S.J., 107
Brown, Leo, S.J., 155
Brownson, Orestes, 80, 85
Buchanan, Jack, S.J., 267
Buckley, Cornelius, S.J., 263
Buechel, Eugene, S.J., 69
Buffalo German Mission, 90–93
Burghardt, Walter, S.J., 212, 213
Burns, Robert Ignatius, S.J., 66
Burrowes, Alexander J., S.J., 180
Burton, John F. X., S.J., xi

Callahan, Daniel, 214
Callahan, William, S.J., 263
Calvert, Cecil, Lord Baltimore, 21, 22, 24
Campbell, Thomas, S.J., 116, 202
Campion High School, 59
Campion, St. Edmund, S.J., 18
Canavan, Francis, S.J., 247
Canisius College, 62, 90
Cannon, Thomas, B., S.J., 132
Cardinal Newman Society, 275
Cardoner River, 7
Carey, Phil, S.J., 148
Carroll, Charles, 51–52
Carroll, John, S.J., 51–55, 71
Carroll, William, S.J., 170, 172

Carvalho e Mello, Sebastian Jose de
    (Pombal), 50
Casassa, Charles, S.J., 186
Cataldo, Giuseppe, S.J., 67, 192, 193
Catholic Biblical Association, 204
Catholic Biblical Quarterly, 204
Catholic Federation for the Promotion of
    Better Race Relations, 121
Catholic Interracial Council of New York,
    121
Catholic Theological Society of America,
    213
Catholic University of America, 90
Cavanaugh, Paul W., S.J., 133
Chabanel, Noel, S.J., 28
Chelsea Villa, 282
Chicago Fire, 98
Chinese rites, 19
Chronicle, 121
Church in the Modern World, 207, 224,
    249
Ciszek, Walter, S.J., 217–224
Clarke, David M., 279
Clement XIV, 50
Cohasset Villa, 283
College of the Sacred Heart, 92
Comey, Denis, S.J., 175
Commission on Financing Higher Educa-
    tion, 178
Commonweal, xi, 214, 274
Congar, Yves, O.F.M., 214
Congregation of Mary (CM) (Sodality),
    125
Cooke, Terence, Cardinal, 240
Conant, James B., 177
Connell, Francis J., C.SS.R., 213
Connolly, Michael N., S.J., 173
Constitutions of the Society of Jesus, xii,
    4, 10, 20
Cooke, Bernard, S.J., 225
Cooper, Harold L., S.J., 159
Copley, Thomas, S.J., 25
Corcoran, Francis, S.J., 171
Corkery, Frank, S.J., 195
Cornwall on Hudson, xii
Corridan, John, S.J., 148–154
Creedon, John B., 161
Creighton, Edward and John, 104
Creighton University, 62
Cristo Rey schools, 270–272

Crosby, Bing, 147, 194–195
Crosby, Donald, S.J., 135, 141, 158
Culhane, Eugene, S.J., 217
Culkin, John, S.J., 234
Cummings, William, S.J., 133
Cunningham, Ted, S.J., 235
Curran, Charles R., 246
Curran, Thomas B., Oblates, 280
Curran, Tom, S.J., 229
Currie, Charles, S.J., 281
Cushing, Richard J. Archbishop, 210

Damen, Arnold, S.J., 96–101
Daniel, Antoine, S.J., 28
Daniel, Constance, 121
Davis, Thurston N., S.J., xii, 116, 217
Deasy, James J., S.J., 137, 138
Declaration on Religious Freedom, 224
DeGioia, John J., 280
Delaney, John, 123
deLubac, Henri, S.J., 214
Departures from the Society, statistics on,
    238
DeSmet, Peter, S.J., 63–69, 81
Detroit-Mercy, University of, 62, 280
Detroit University, 104
DeVoto, Bernard, 67
Dezza, Paolo, S.J., 260, 265
Divino Afflante Spiritu, 204
Dogmatic Constitution on the Church, 224
Dolan, Jay, 55
Dominus ac Redemptor, 50
Donceel, Joseph, S.J., 185
Drinan, Robert, S.J., 225, 263
Droley, Francis, 122
Drum, Walter, S.J., 100, 116
Dubourg, William, Bishop, 61
Dulles, Avery, S.J., Cardinal, 272
Dunne, George, S.J., 126–130, 131, 166

Eliot, Charles W., 105, 106
Ellard, Gerald, S.J., 202
Ellis, John Tracy, 147, 203
England, John, Bishop, 70
Enlightenment, 49
Ewing, J. Franklin, S.J., 185
Ex Corde Ecclesiae, 275

Fairfield University, 63, 195
Favre, Pierre, S.J., 7

Fay, Sr. Maureen, O.P., 280
Federated Colored Catholics (FCC), 121
Feeley, Raymond, S.J., 174
Feeney, Leonard, S.J., 209–211
Feit, Ken, S.J., 235
Fenton, Joseph, 213
Fenwick, Benedict, S.J., 52, 117
Fenwick, George, S.J., 84
Fichter, Joseph H., S.J., 157–159
Fitterer, Jack, S.J., 255
Fitzgerald, Paul A., S.J., 248
Fitzmyer, Joseph, S.J., 204
Ford, John, S.J., 242–245
Fordham University, 25, 60, 62, 77, 102, 108
Franklin, Benjamin, 52
Freeland, Richard M., 176
Frese, Joseph R., S.J., xi
Frieden, John, S.J., 191
Fruyts, John, S.J., 98

Gache, Louis-Hippolyte, 82, 83
Gaffney, Louis, S.J., 258
Gallicanism, 18
Gannon, Robert I., S.J., 205
Gannon, Thomas, S.J., 109, 115
Ganss, George E., S.J., 229
Garnier, Charles, S.J., 28
Garraghan, Gilbert J., 202
General Congregations: 31st, 226, 260; 32nd, 259; 33rd, 265; 34th, 266; 35th, 283
Georgetown University, 52, 62, 72, 80, 122, 130; School of Foreign Service, 160
Gervase, Thomas, S.J., 22
Gibbons, James, Cardinal, 94
Gill, James J., S.J., 241
Gilmore, Bishop, 92
Gilmore, James A., S.J., 133
Gleason, Philip, 61
Gleeson, Francis J., S.J., 267, 269
Glennon, John, Archbishop, 128
Gonzaga University, 62, 102, 147, 192, 267
Gooley, Larry, S.J., 269
Goupil, St. Rene, S.J., xii, 28
Graham, Robert, S.J., 217
Grassi, John Anthony, S.J., 53
Gumbel, Richard, 159

Hartnett, Robert, S.J., xi, 165–169, 217
Harvenak, Robert, S.J., 241

Hayden Lake Villa, 282
Healy, Patrick, S.J., 84; family of, 84; at Georgetown, 84–85
Healy, Tim, S.J., 247
Hebblethwaite, Peter, 263
Hecker, Isaac, 85
Heithaus, Claude, S.J., 128–130
Hiroshima, 141, 210, 227
Hogan, Aloysius, S.J., 184
Holloran, Patrick, S.J., 128
Holy Cross College, 62, 80
Holy Trinity Church, 83
Homosexuals, 274
Hubbard, Bernard, S.J., 175, 188–190
Hughes, John, Archbishop, 80, 91
Hughes, Thomas A., S.J., 202
Humanae Vitae, 244
Humani Generis Unitas, 124
Hurricane Katrina, 280

Ignatius Loyola, xii, 4–13, 264
Inculturation, 18, 267
Inquisition, 6
Institute for Jesuit Sources, 229
Institute for Social Science (ISS), 128
Interracial Justice, 123
Interracial Review, 121
Ireland, John, Bishop, 94

Jansenism, 49
Janssens, Jan Baptiste, S.J., 167, 158
Jefferson, Thomas, 57
Jesuit colleges and universities, enrollment, 276
Jesuit Educational Association (JEA), 182, 248
Jesuit Refugee Service, 264
Jogues, St. Isaac, S.J., xii, 28–35
John XXIII, 243
John Carroll University, 62
Jolliet, Louis, 38
Joset, Joseph, S.J., 64
Joyce, W. Seavey, S.J., 252
Juana of Spain, 12

Keane, John J., Bishop, 90, 95
Kelly, Gerald A., S.J., 242
Kelly, Tom, S.J., 171
Kino, Eusebio, S.J., 42–46
Knights of Labor, 94

Kohlmann, Anthony, S.J., 52–54, 61, 117
Kolvenbach, Peter-Hans, S.J., xii, 265

Lacouture, Jean, 201, 226
LaFarge, John, S.J., 90, 118–124, 147, 174
Lalande, Jean de, S.J., 28
Lallement, Gabriel, S.J., 28, 36
Land O'Lakes manifesto, 249
Laynez, Diego, S.J., 7, 132
Ledochowski, Wlodimir, S.J., 123, 141, 150
Legouais, Thomas, S.J., 91
LeMoyne College, 63, 122, 195
Leo XIII, 109
Leonard, William, S.J., 141
Linehan, Daniel, S.J., 174
Lippmann, Walter, 204
Lord, Daniel, S.J., 124, 131, 148
Loyola College, Baltimore, 62, 93
Loyola Institute of Human Relations, 154
Loyola Jesuit College, Nigeria, 282
Loyola Marymount University, 186
Loyola Seminary, Shrub Oak, 184
Loyola University, Chicago, 62, 179–181
Loyola University, New Orleans, xii, 4–
    13; Law School, 157; Music School, 156
Lubianka, 217
Lynch, William F., S.J., 203

Maas, Anthony J., S.J., 111, 117
Maher, Zacheus, S.J., 125, 126, 129, 141–
    145
Manresa Retreat House, Staten Island, 149
Manresa, Spain, 5
Maritan, Jacques, 205
Markoe, John, S.J., 128
Markoe, William, S.J., 121, 128
Marquette, Jacques, S.J., 37–40
Marquette University, 62, 104, 130, 166
Martinez, Pedro, S.J., 4, 13–14
Martin Garcia, Luis, S.J., 109, 115
Maynard, Theodore, 202
Mazzella, Camillus, S.J., 88, 89, 95
McBrian, Richard, 208
McCarthy, Joseph R., 164–169
McCormick, Richard, S.J., 244, 246
McCormick, William J., 152
McElroy, John, S.J., 70, 100, 132
McFadden, William C., S.J., 245
McGreevy, John T., 79, 243
McKenna, Horace, S.J., 120, 244–246

McKenzie, John L., S.J., 204
McKenzie, Roderick, S.J., 203
McLaughlin, Leo, S.J., 247
McMahon, John, S.J., 167
McNally, Herbert, S.J., 133
McNaspy, C. J., S.J., 156, 159, 227
McSherry, William, S.J., 72, 73
Meany, Stephen J. S.J., 132
Menendez de Aviles, Don Pedro, 3
Meyer, Rudolph, S.J., 109
Mobberly, Joseph, S.J., 71
Modras, Ronald, 209
Montserrat, 5
Moore, Lyle, 193
Moriarty, Frederick J., S.J., 204
Morris, Charles, 93, 165
Morrissey, James P., S.J., 187
Mulcahy, Stephen, S.J., 170, 172
Mulledy, Thomas, S.J., 72, 73
Muollo, Henry, S.J., 173
Murphy, William Stack, 81
Murray, John Courtney, S.J., 201, 202, 204,
    205, 211, 243

Nadal, Jerome, S.J., 13
Nash, Michael, S.J., 78, 86
National Catholic Reporter, 264, 273
National Federation of Catholic College
    Students (NFCCS), 158
National Jesuit News, 229
Negro slavery, 26, 27
New York Literary Institution, 53
Nobili, Giovanni, S.J., 81
Nobili, Robert de, S.J., 18
Noonan, John T., 244
North Central Association of Colleges
    and Secondary Schools (NCA), 179

O'Boyle, Patrick, Cardinal, 244
O'Callaghan, Joseph, S.J., 133, 139–140
O'Connor, James, Bishop, 104
O'Gorman, John, xii
O'Hare, Joseph, S.J., 266
O'Keefe, Vincent, S.J., 264, 265
Old St. Joseph's Church, Philadelphia, 26,
    83, 118
Oliver, Hudson J., 121
O'Malley, Austin, S.J., 108
O'Malley, John, S.J., 60
On Christian Marriage, 242

Ong, Walter, S.J., 232, 233
On the Sacred Liturgy, 224
O'Toole, James M., 84
Ottaviani, Alfredo, Cardinal, 213

Padberg, John, S.J., 233, 262
Paraguay *reductions,* 15
Paresce, Angelo, S.J., 88
Parkman, Francis, 41
Parsons, Wilfred, S.J., 148, 202
Pascendi Dominici Gregis, 109
Paul III, 10
Paul V, 19
Paul VI, 226, 259, 263
Percy, Walker, 154
Perron, James, S.J., 91
Perry, Henry, S.J., 173
Pius VI, 58
Pius X, 109
Pius XI, 123, 242
Pius XII, 122, 124, 199, 204
Poe, Edgar Allan, 61
Point, Nicholas, 82
Post, John, S.J., 172
Purcell, John B., Archbishop, 81

Quadragesimo Anno, 123
Quigley, Bill, 281

Rahner, Hugo, S.J., 12
Rahner, Karl, S.J., 16, 201, 208–209, 265, 283
Ram, The (Fordham school paper), 247
Rappuglioso, Filippo, S.J., 68
Ratio Studiorum, 10, 17, 22, 60, 110
Reese, Thomas, S.J., 274
Regimini militantis Ecclesiae, 10
Regis University, 62, 279
Reinert, Paul, S.J., 249
Report of the Commission on Higher Studies of the American Assistancy of the Society of Jesus, 1931–32 (Macelwane Report), 179, 181–184
Rerum Novarum, 94, 123, 149
Rey Anthony, S.J., 132
Ricci, Lorenzo, S.J., 59
Ricci, Matteo, S.J., 18, 19, 42, 43
Richards, Havens, S.J., 106
Riemer, George, 231
Rigge, Joseph and William, 104

Rockhurst University, 62, 232, 280
Rodriguez, Simon, S.J., 7
Rogel, Juan, S.J., 13
Roothaan, Joannes, S.J., 59, 64, 65, 72, 73
Roser, Isabel, 11
Rousseve, Bart, S.J., 235
Rousseve, Ronald, 255

Sabetti, Aloysius, S.J., 89
Saeta, Francis Xavier, S.J., 45
St. Andrew-on-Hudson, 83, 219
St. Charles College, 82
St. Clement's Island, 21
St. Francis Xavier (high school), New York, 102
St. Ignatius Church (Charles County, Md.), 21, 118
St. Ignatius College (John Carroll), in Cleveland, 62, 92
St. Ignatius College (San Francisco, University of), 187
St. Ignatius Loyola Church, N.Y.C., 215
St. Inigoes (Maryland), 21, 102
St. Joseph's University (Philadelphia), 62, 80
St. Louis University, 62, 103, 122, 128
St. Mary's City (Maryland), 21
St. Mary's College, Kansas, 155, 239
St. Peter's College (Jersey City), 62, 122, 277
St. Xavier College (Cincinnati), 103
Salmeron, Francisco, S.J., 7
Sanchez, Pedro, S.J., 42
San Francisco earthquake, 191
Santa Clara University, 62, 82, 122
Satolli Francesco, Archbishop, 95
Schaeffer, Bradley M., S.J., 271–272
Schoenberg, Wilfred P., S.J., 193
Schulberg, Bud, 148, 154
Seattle University, 62, 192
Sertium Laetitiae, 122, 123
Shadowbrook novitiate, 170–174
Shaw, Robert Gould, 77–78
Shea, F. X., S.J., 170
Shealy, Terence, S.J., 148
Sheeran, Michael, S.J., 279
Sheets, John, S.J., 229
Shoup, George, S.J., 234
Shuster, George N., 202
Sitting Bull, 66, 67

Smarius, Cornelius, S.J., 98
Sollicitudo Omnium Ecclesiarum, 58
Southern, David W., 120
Southwell, St. Robert, S.J., 18
Spellman, Francis, Cardinal, 153, 214, 237
Spils, James, S.J., 267
Spiritual Exercises, xii, 4, 6, 16, 24, 26, 84
Sponga, Edward, S.J., 231
Spring Hill College (Mobile, Ala.), 62, 82, 83
Stanley, David, S.J., 204
Suarez, Francisco, S.J., 17, 22
Sublimus Deus, 70
Sullivan, William J., S.J., 196, 258
Sullivan, William Laurence, 110
Summi Pontificatus, 124
Suppression of the Society of Jesus, xii, 49–51
Suver, Charles F., S.J., 132, 137
Swords, Raymond J., S.J., 253
Syllabus of Errors, 214

Talon, Jean, 38
Teilhard de Chardin, Pierre, S.J., 127, 185, 201, 206–208
Testem Benevolitiae, 95
Thebaud, Augustus, S.J., 70
Theilman, Jeff, 270–272
Theological Studies, 211, 242
"Theology of liberation," 212
Tierney, Richard, S.J., 183
Tierney, Richard Henry, S.J., 116
Timon, John, Bishop, 91
Tissot, Peter, S.J., 79–80, 86
Tocqueville, Alexis de, 58
Toolan, David, S., S.J., x, 237
Tribble, Arthur B., S.J., 171
Turner, Thomas Wyatt, 121
Twomey, Louis, S.J., 146, 154–157

Ultramontanism, 18
Unam Sanctam, 210
University of Central America, San Salvador, 265

Vagnozzi, Egidio, Archbishop, 214
Valignano, Alexander, S.J., 18, 20
Van Quickenborne, Charles, S.J., 61, 63
Villager, Burchard, S.J., 82
Villareal, Francisco, S.J., 13
Villot, Cardinal, 261
Vitellechi, Mutius, S.J., 15

Walsh, Edmund, S.J., 123, 160–163
Walsh, John, S.J., 233–234, 238
Walsh, Michael, S.J., 248, 251
Waupaca Villa, 282
Weber, Paul, S.J., 235
Weigel, Gustave, S.J., 212
Weninger, Francis X., S.J., 71, 91, 96
Wheeling College (later University), 196
White, Andrew, S.J., 21, 22, 25
White, Robert F., N.S.J., 172
Wills, Garry, 240, 241
Wilson, Francis B., S.J., 204
Wilson, Samuel K., S.J., 200
Woodstock College, xi, 76, 88, 96
Woodstock Letters, 89, 95, 99, 102, 104, 122, 133, 215, 230
Woodstock, New York, 240
Wright, Jonathan, 51
Wynne, John J., S.J., 116, 202

Xavier Labor School (New York City), 148
Xavier, St. Francis, S.J., 3, 7, 43, 108
Xavier University (Cincinnati), 62

Young, Walter, S.J., 171

Zook, George, 177

About the Author

Raymond A. Schroth, S.J., is Professor of Humanities at Saint Peter's College, as well as a Jesuit priest and journalist. He has been a professor and/or academic dean at five Jesuit colleges and universities. He is the author of six books, including *Fordham: A History and Memoir, Dante to Dead Man Walking: One Reader's Journey through the Christian Classics*, and *The American Journey of Eric Sevareid*. A former editor of *Commonweal*, he has also written more than 300 articles and reviews on politics, religion, and the media, which have appeared in such publications as the *Los Angeles Times*, the *Boston Globe, Newsday*, and the *Newark Star-Ledger*, and he is an award-winning media critic for the *National Catholic Reporter*, for which he writes a regular column on television.